Place and Nature

PLACE AND NATURE:
ESSAYS IN RUSSIAN ENVIRONMENTAL HISTORY

Edited by

David Moon, Nicholas B. Breyfogle, Alexandra Bekasova

Set in 11 point Adobe Garamond Pro

Cover Image: The small stone harbour in the Solovetskii rural locality, including the old building of the Solovetskii Biological Research Station and a replica of the ship used by Peter I on his 1694 visit to the islands (front cover) and part of the Solovetskii Maritime Museum (back cover). Photograph by Nicholas Breyfogle, Solovetskie Islands, 2013.

British Library Cataloguing in Publication Data
A catalogue record for this book is available from the British Library

ISBN   978-1-912186-16-7 (HB)

CONTENTS

CONTRIBUTORS

Alexandra Bekasova is Research Fellow at the Laboratory for Environmental and Technological History and Associate Professor at the National Research University Higher School of Economics (NRU HSE), St Petersburg, Russia. Her research focus is on the history of mobility, transportation and technology, and environmental history. Her publications include: 'From Common Rocks to Valuable Industrial Resources: Limestone in Nineteenth-Century Russia', *The Extractive Industries and Society* 7 (2020); with Evgenii Anisimov and Ekaterina Kalemeneva, 'Books that Link Worlds: Travel Guides, the Development of Transportation Infrastructure, and the Emergence of the Tourism Industry in Imperial Russia, Nineteenth–Early Twentieth Centuries', *Journal of Tourism History* 8 (2) (2016); with Julia Kulikova and Martin Emanuel, 'State Socialism and Sustainable Urban Mobility: Alternative Paths in St Petersburg since the 1880s', in Martin Emanuel, Frank Schipper and Ruth Oldenziel (eds), *A U-Turn to the Future: Sustainable Urban Mobility since 1850* (Berghahn Books, 2020).

Nicholas B. Breyfogle is Associate Professor of History at The Ohio State University, USA. He is the author of *Heretics and Colonizers: Forging Russia's Empire in the South Caucasus* (Cornell University Press, 2005) and editor or co-editor of *Eurasian Environments: Nature and Ecology in Imperial Russian and Soviet History* (University of Pittsburgh Press, 2018); *Nature at War: American Environments and World War II* (Cambridge University Press, 2020); and, with Mark Sokolsky, *Readings in Water History* (Cognella Academic Press, 2020), among other volumes. He is currently completing the book, *Baikal: the Great Lake and its People*. He is co-editor of the online magazine *Origins: Current Events in Historical Perspective,* origins.osu.edu.

Andy Bruno is Associate Professor of History and Environmental Studies at Northern Illinois University, USA, and an affiliated researcher with Tiumen State University, Russia. He is the author of *The Nature of Soviet Power: An Arctic Environmental History* (Cambridge University Press, 2016). The research for this chapter was supported by a grant from the Russian Science Foundation (Project No. 20-68-46044), 'Imaginary Anthropocene: Environmental Knowledge Production and Transfers in Siberia in the 20th and 21st Centuries'.

Robert Dale is Lecturer in Russian History at Newcastle University, UK. His research focuses on the late Stalinist period (1945–1953), particularly the reconstruction of urban space and communities, and urban flooding over longer periods. He is the author of *Demobilized Veterans in Late Stalinist Leningrad: Soldiers to Civilians* (Bloomsbury Academic, 2015).

Catherine Evtuhov is Professor of History at Columbia University, USA. She is the author of *Portrait of a Russian Province: Economy, Society, and Civilization in 19th-Century Nizhnii Novgorod* (University of Pittsburgh Press, 2011), among other works; and a recent recipient of grants from the Georgetown Environment Initiative and the Rachel Carson Center for Environment and Society.

Ekaterina Kalemeneva is Senior Lecturer at the Department of History, and Junior Researcher at the Laboratory for Environmental and Technological History, NRU HSE St Petersburg, Russia. Trained as a historian, she studies urbanisation in the Russian Arctic and Far North in the twentieth century and the role of scientists and architects in shaping of Soviet northern industrial towns in the 1960s. Her research interests include urban history, history of science and environmental history. Her publications include 'From New Socialist Cities to Thaw Experimentation in Arctic Townscapes: Leningrad Architects Attempt to Modernise the Soviet North', *Europe-Asia Studies* **73** (3) (2019).

Arkady Kalikhman, Doctor of Science (Physics), Professor at Irkutsk State University, Irkutsk, Russia. His latest book, co-authored with Tatiana Kalikhman, is *Iuzhnyi Baikal: Priroda i liudi* (Rossiiskaia Akademiia Nauk, Sibirskoe otdelenie, Institut Geografii, 2019).

Tatiana Kalikhman, Doctor of Science (Geography), Senior Research Fellow at the Institute of Geography of the Siberian Section of the Russian Academy of Sciences Irkutsk, Russia. Her latest book, co-authored with Arkady Kalikhman, is: *Iuzhnyi Baikal: Priroda i liudi* (Rossiiskaia Akademiia Nauk, Sibirskoe otdelenie, Institut Geografii, 2019).

Elena Kochetkova is Associate Professor and Researcher at Laboratory for Environmental and Technological History at NRU HSE St Petersburg, Russia. She is an author of several peer-reviewed articles on the history of the Soviet environment and technology, including 'Industry and Forests: Alternative Raw Materials in the Soviet Forestry Industry from the mid-1950s to the 1960s', *Environment and History* **24** (2018); and, with P. Pokidko, 'Soviet Industrial Production and Waste Dispersal: A Case Study of Pulp and Paper Plants on the Karelian Isthmus, 1940s–1980s', *Scandinavian Economic History* **67** (3) (2019); and is currently working on a monograph on the history of industrial forests in the late Soviet Union.

Alexei Kraikovski is based in the Laboratory for Environmental and Technological History, NRU HSE St Petersburg, Russia. He has been involved in major Russian and international research projects related to the environmental history of the Russian North for almost twenty years. His major expertise is focused on the problems of history and heritage related to the interaction between the Russian society and water environment in the sixteenth through eighteenth centuries. He is the author of numerous peer-reviewed publications.

Julia Lajus is Head of the Laboratory for Environmental and Technological History and Associate Professor at the Department of History, NRU HSE St Petersburg, Russia. In 2011–2015 she served as vice-president of the European Society of Environmental History. Her research focuses on the history of field sciences and environmental history of marine and polar areas. She has considerable experience in international projects and recently led the project 'Natural Resources in the History of Russia' funded by the Russian Science Foundation. Her recent publications include chapters in the books: *Competing Arctic Futures: Historical and Contemporary Perspectives* (Palgrave Macmillan, 2018) and *Eurasian Environments: Nature and Ecology in Imperial Russian and Soviet History* (Pittsburgh University Press, 2018).

David Moon is Professor of history at the University of York, UK, Honorary Professor at the School of Slavonic and East European Studies, University College London, and was Visiting Professor at Nazarbayev University, Nur-Sultan, Kazakhstan in 2018–20. His interests include Russian, Eurasian and transnational environmental history. His most recent books are: *The American Steppes: The Unexpected Russian Roots of Great Plains Agriculture, 1870s-1930s* (Cambridge University Press, 2020); *The Plough that Broke the Steppes: Agriculture and Environment on Russia's Grasslands, 1700-1914* (Oxford University Press, 2013); ed. with Peter Coates and Paul Warde, *Local Places, Global Processes: Histories of Environmental Change in Britain and Beyond* (Windgather Press, 2016). He was lead investigator on the Leverhulme Trust International Network 'Exploring Russia's Environmental History and Natural Resources' in 2013–16.

Alan Roe is Visiting Assistant Professor at West Virginia University, USA. He is the author of *Into Russian Nature: Tourism, Environmental Protection and National Parks in the Twentieth Century* (Oxford University Press, 2020). He has worked as a tour guide in the Altai Mountains in Siberia and on the Kamchatka Peninsula in the Russian Far East.

Bryce Stewart is Senior Lecturer in the Environment and Geography Department at the University of York, UK. As an ecologist he specialises in the management and conservation of fisheries in marine and freshwater environments. He is particularly well known for his research on Marine Protected Areas. Among other publications, he is the lead author of 'Marine Conservation Begins at Home: How a Local Community and Protection of a Small Bay Sent Waves of Change Around the UK and Beyond', *Frontiers in Marine Science* 7 (2020) and 'Making Brexit Work for the Environment and Livelihoods: Delivering a Stakeholder Informed Vision for Agriculture and Fisheries', *People and Nature* 1 (4) (2019).

Mark Sokolsky is an instructional designer at the Royal Military College of Canada in Kingston, Ontario. He is the author of several articles and book chapters on Russian colonisation and environmental change in the Russian Far East, including 'Between Predation and Protection: Forests and Forestry in Late Tsarist Primor'e', *Sibirica* 13 (2) (2014), and is co-editor, with Nicholas Breyfogle, of *Readings in Water History* (Cognella Academic Press, 2020).

ACKNOWLEDGEMENTS

This volume draws on the experiences of a series of field and research trips and scholarly workshops in northern and eastern Russia by members of an international team based at universities in the Russian Federation, the United Kingdom and the United States of America between 2013 and 2016. We visited the Solovetskie Islands (Solovki) in the White Sea in the summer of 2013, Lake Baikal in Eastern Siberia in the summer of 2015 and the Urals region in the summer of 2016. These visits combined explorations of the local environments and academic workshops in those places. In addition, we held more conventional scholarly meetings in St Petersburg in 2013 (twice) and 2016.[1]

These activities received generous funding from the Leverhulme Trust for an International Network entitled 'Exploring Russia's Environmental History and Natural Resources'.[2] We acknowledge further support – financial, logistical, and otherwise – from the Georgetown Environment Initiative,[3] The Ohio State University, and the European University at St Petersburg and the National Research University Higher School of Economics (NRU HSE) Campus in St Petersburg, both in Russia. A debt of gratitude is due to Victoria Beale, who served as Leverhulme Network Facilitator, and worked tirelessly to organise the network's activities. We were fortunate to have members of our team with the expertise and experience to arrange our visits to Solovki and the Urals, which were coordinated by Julia Lajus, Alexei Kraikovski and Catherine Evtuhov. We are grateful to the staff members of the Solovetskii Maritime Museum and especially to Svetlana Rapenkova, the museum's administrator. In the Urals region, our thanks are due to Ekaterina Shestakova of the Faculty of Social Sciences and Humanities, the NRU HSE Campus in Perm', as well as to Galina Iankovskaia, the head of the Division for Multidisciplinary Historical Research, Perm' State University, who gave us a deeper insight into the history of the places we visited. We should thank also Julia Zaparii of the Federal State Autonomous Educational Institution of Higher Education, Boris N. Yeltsin Ural Federal University, who helped to organise the workshop in Ekaterinburg. Many thanks to Elena Krasikova, research assistant from the Laboratory of

---

1. A slightly different group visited Chernobyl' in 2016, although the issues explored differed from those discussed in this volume.

2. For the network website, see University of York, 'Exploring Russia's History and Natural Resources'.

3. Georgetown University, 'Georgetown Environment Initiative'.

Environmental and Technological History, NRU HSE St Petersburg, who helped us to organise our trips to Solovki and the Urals. Dylan Harris of Lupine Travel organised our trip to Lake Baikal. In Irkutsk, we benefitted greatly from the help of Arkady Kalikhman, Professor at Irkutsk State University, and Tatiana Kalikhman, Senior Research Fellow at the Institute of Geography of the Siberian Branch of the Russian Academy of Sciences (Irkutsk). In Ulan-Ude, we were generously assisted by Nikolai Tsyrempilov, who was then Head of the History Department at Buriat State University and Senior Research Fellow at the Institute for Mongolian, Buddhist and Tibetan Studies of the Russian Academy of Sciences (he is currently Associate Professor in the School of Sciences and Humanities at Nazarbayev University, Nur-Sultan, Kazakhstan). We express our thanks to Mikhail Evgen'evich Ovdin, director of the nature reserve (*zapovednik*) that includes Barguzin, for permitting our visit, and Aleksandr Afanas'evich Ananin, scientific director of the Barguzin *Zapovednik*, who was our host at Davsha and guide through the Barguzin forests.

The editors would also like to thank Sarah Siff for her work in editing the contributions to this volume by our Russian colleagues, Chase McDaries and Angela Brintlinger for their translation and Mark Sokolsky for his hard work and patience in preparing the volume for publication. This publication has been made possible, in part, through support from the Center for Slavic and East European Studies at The Ohio State University through funding from the International and Foreign Language Education division of the US Department of Education. We thank Oxford University Press for permission to publish the chapter by Alan Roe, which appeared in slightly modified form in his monograph *Into Russian Nature: Tourism, Environmental Protection, and National Parks in the Twentieth Century* (2020), and the journals *Origins: Current Events in Historical Perspective*, *The Ecologist* and *Arcadia* for permission to republish the four photographic essays in Part 2, 'Being There'.

The book would not be possible without the many efforts and support of The White Horse Press. Thanks are due to Andrew Johnson, who carefully drew the maps to our specifications and, especially, to Sarah Johnson for her commitment to the book throughout the period of its gestation.

BIBLIOGRAPHY

Georgetown University. 2020. 'Georgetown Environment Initiative'. https://environment.georgetown.edu/.

University of York. 2016. 'Exploring Russia's History and Natural Resources'. http://www.york.ac.uk/history/research/majorprojects/russiasenvironmentalhistory/.

LIST OF FIGURES, MAPS AND TABLES

Figures

Introduction

Chapter 4

Chapter 6

Chapter 7

Chapter 8

Maps

Tables

Chapter 11

ABBREVIATIONS

Universities, Institutes and Scientific Organisations

AN – Academy of Sciences
AN SSSR – Academy of Sciences of the USSR
DVO RAN – Far Eastern Branch of the Russian Academy of Sciences
ICES – International Council for the Exploration of the Sea
INMERO – Institute for Frozen Earth Science
IRGO – Imperial Russian Geographic Society
OIAK – Society for the Study of the Amur Region (Amur Society)
RAN – Russian Academy of Sciences
RGO – Russian Geographical Society
SO RAN – Siberian Branch of the Russian Academy of Sciences

Ministries, Institutions and Organisations

Angarstroi – Angara Construction Administration (Soviet Union)
BAM – Baikal-Amur Mainline (Railway)
CPSU – Communist Party of the Soviet Union
Gosplan – State Planning Commission (Soviet Union)
Gosstroi – State Construction Administration (Soviet Union)
Gulag – Main Administration of Camps (Soviet-era prison camp system)
GUZZ – Main Administration of Agriculture and Land Management (Imperial Russia)
IUCN – International Union for the Conservation of Nature
KEPS – Commission for the Exploration of Natural Productive Forces (Imperial Russia and Soviet Union)
Komsomol – Communist Party Youth League (Soviet Union)
Soiuzgiproleskhoz – All-Union Landscape Research-Design Institute (Soviet Union)
Soiuzpushnina – State Fur Company (Soviet Union)
SOPS – Council on the Exploration of Productive Forces (successor to KEPS) (Soviet Union)
Sovnarkom – Council of People's Commissars (Soviet Union)
UNESCO – United Nations Educational, Scientific and Cultural Organization
VOLO – Vladivostok Society for Amateur Hunters
VOOP – All-Russian Society for Nature Protection

VSNKh – Supreme Council of National Economy (Soviet Union)
UNEP – United Nations Environment Programme
USAID – United States Agency for International Development

Geographical and Technical Terms

ASSR – Autonomous Soviet Socialist Republic
BEZ – Buffer Ecological Zone
CEZ – Central Ecological Zone
EZAI – Ecological Zone of Atmospheric Influence
GES – Hydroelectric Station
MPI – Maximum Permissible Impact
PA – Protected Area
RSFSR – Russian Soviet Federative Socialist Republic
SSR – Soviet Socialist Republic
TerSKOP – Territorial Complex Scheme for Nature Protection
TOI DVO RAN – The Pacific Oceanological Institute of DVO RAN
USSR/SSSR – Union of Soviet Socialist Republics

ARCHIVAL AND BIBLIOGRAPHIC ABBREVIATIONS

Archives and Collections

ARAN – Archive of the Russian Academy of Sciences
AVNP – Archive of the Vodlozero National Park
GAAO – State Archive of Arkhangel'sk Oblast'
GAMO – State Archive of Murmansk Oblast'
GAPK – State Archive of Primorskii Krai
GARF – State Archive of the Russian Federation
GARB – State Archive of the Republic of Buriatiia
GARO – State Archive of Rostov Oblast'
NARK – National Archive of the Republic of Karelia
PSZ – Complete Collection of the Laws of the Russian Empire
RGAE – Russian State Archive of the Economy
RGASPI – Russian State Archive of Social and Political History
RGA VMF – Russian State Naval Archive
RGIA – Russian State Historical Archive
RGIA DV – Russian State Historical Archive of the Far East
SPb II RAN – Archive of the St Petersburg Institute of History of the Russian
    Academy of Sciences
TsGAIPD–SPb – Central State Archive of Historical-Political Documents for
    St Petersburg
TsGA-SPb – Central State Archive of St Petersburg

Archival and Bibliographic Abbreviations

d. – delo (file)
f. – fond (collection)
ob. – oborot (reverse)
op. – opis' (inventory)
l., ll. – list, listy (page, pages)
No/no. – number
p. – page(s)
T. – tom (volume)

1.

PLACE AND NATURE: AN INTRODUCTION

David Moon, Nicholas B. Breyfogle, Alexandra Bekasova and Julia Lajus

This book offers new perspectives on the environmental history of the lands that have come under Russian and Soviet rule by paying attention to 'place' and 'nature' in the intersection between humans and the environments that surround them.[1] Through a series of carefully selected, linked case studies, the book highlights the importance of local environments and the specificities of individual places in understanding the human-environment nexus. This focus is accentuated by the fact that the authors have travelled extensively in the places they write about. They have first-hand experience of the specificities of local natural systems, and have gained a sense of how these places look, sound, taste, feel and smell. They have met, talked to, interviewed and in other ways engaged with members of the local populations, including the specialists in a variety of disciplines who study these places and ecosystems and the people who manage and administer them. In this way, our collective research also makes an important methodological intervention to the research and practice of environmental and perhaps also other fields of history: that to write robust history, historians need to embed themselves in the places and environments they study. In this way, our work underscores that 'place' and 'nature' are both topics of study and theoretical models and methodological approaches for scholarship.[2]

---

1. For recent historiographical analyses of Russian environmental history, see Breyfogle, 'Toward an Environmental History of Tsarist Russia and the Soviet Union'; Lajus, 'Russian Environmental History'. On the representation, or misrepresentation, of Russian and Soviet environmental history in global environmental histories, see Moon, 'The Curious Case of the Marginalization or Distortion of Russian and Soviet Environmental History in Global Environmental Histories'. On climate history, see Bruno, 'Climate History of Russia and the Soviet Union'.

2. For an application of such an approach in another part of the world, see Coates, Moon and Warde (eds), *Local Places, Global Processes*.

Place and Nature: An Introduction

The essays primarily consider the period from the early nineteenth to the early twenty-first centuries and, where appropriate, delve back further in time. They investigate continuity and change across multiple political systems: from the rise of modern Russia under the tsars, through the Soviet era and into the first decades of the post-Soviet Russian Federation. These centuries saw Russian imperial expansion into the far reaches of Eurasia, greater human mobility as a result of developments in transportation infrastructure, more intensive exploitation of natural resources with the onset of industrialisation, which gathered pace in Soviet times, and a growing sense among some scientists, political figures and members of the wider public of a need to protect and conserve 'nature'.[3] The geographical focus of the book is more distinctive and serves to complement and enhance the scope of existing works on the environmental history of this part of the world. The chapter studies are located in two important, diverse and, in the context of environmental history, relatively under-researched regions: 1) the Northwest and the European North of Russia, extending from St Petersburg through Karelia to the White Sea and Kola Peninsula; and 2) Siberia and the Pacific Far East.[4]

Place and Nature

The importance of 'place' and 'nature' in human and environmental history is a central analytical theme and methodological approach of our research on Russia and the Soviet Union. In our book, we are interested in how human engagement and input transforms the wider, undifferentiated 'spaces' of the natural world into culturally meaningful and technologically-differentiated 'places'. Here we build on the foundational work of Yi-Fu Tuan on the differences between 'space' and 'place'. As he argues, 'space' is more abstract than 'place': 'What begins as undifferentiated space becomes place as we get to know it better and endow it with value'. For Tuan, 'Place is security, space is freedom ... and places are centres of felt value where biological needs, such as those for food, water, rest and procreation, are satisfied'. In an earlier book, he analysed the concept of 'Topophilia' – or love of place – which he summarised as the 'affective bond between people and place or setting', which is 'vivid and concrete as personal

---

3. See Oldfield, Lajus and Shaw, 'Conceptualizing and Utilizing the Natural Environment', pp. 1–15; Breyfogle (ed.), *Eurasian Environments*. For global comparisons, see McNeill, *Something New Under the Sun* and McNeill and Engelke, *The Great Acceleration*.

4. On Russian environmental history, see the bibliography that the Leverhulme Project team developed: Moon (ed.), 'Russian Environmental History'.

David Moon, Nicholas B. Breyfogle, Alexandra Bekasova and Julia Lajus

experience'.[5] In a fashion, what Tuan describes is what we have tried to do in our explorations and research: focussing in on particular places, getting to know them better through personal experience and differentiating them from the wider, and more abstract, spaces that surround them. We learned how the 'places' we visited and studied had acquired meanings over time, how they shifted from 'spaces' to 'places' as their inhabitants used them to provide sustenance and shelter and endowed them with spiritual significance.[6]

The term 'nature', also central to our book, has a long history during which its meanings have been slippery and ambiguous. In some definitions, humans are distinct from, indeed somehow above, nature or the natural world. In this sense, 'nature' is either a resource to be controlled and used without concern by humans for their purposes or has been degraded by human activities and deemed worthy of protection or conservation to mitigate human influence. Just as prevalent have been meanings of nature that encompass human bodies.[7] A solution to this dilemma, that mirrors the distinction between 'space' and 'place', has been proposed by environmental historians Sverker Sörlin and Paul Warde with their concept of 'environing': under human influence, 'nature' transforms (in an ongoing process) into 'environment'.[8] Thus, the chapters here explore how abstract 'spaces' acquired meanings and became 'places'; whilst in a similar process, 'nature' became (and continues to become) the 'environment'.

As environmental historians, we are first of all studying places that are known for their particular natural value: reserves where 'wilderness' or rare biological species are protected; places and regions whose natural beauty took on cultural importance through centuries of admiration and appropriation, such as Lake Baikal or Solovki, and where that cultural and natural importance is considered threatened by human economic activities. We are also interested in studying in detail the shared process, across multiple locations, of the transformation of 'natural' places into 'unnatural' exploited landscapes and the long-lasting legacy that such a transformation produces. When we arrived at these different places, we brought with us concepts, myths, predispositions

5. Tuan, *Space and Place*, pp. 3–4, 6; Tuan, *Topophilia*, p. 4.
6. A great deal has been written about 'place', 'space' and 'history'. See Casey, 'Boundary, Place, and Event in the Spatiality of History'; Casey, *Getting Back into Place*; Gandy, *The Fabric of Space*; Adams, Hoelscher and Till (eds), *Textures of Place*.
7. For recent discussions, see Ducarme and Couvet, 'What Does "Nature" Mean?'; Warde, 'The Environment', pp. 32–46; LeCain, *The Matter of History*.
8. This concept is discussed by Kraikovski and Lajus in this volume.

and prejudices that we obtained through scholarship and previous experiences of field visits.

After 'the new spatial turn' it is no longer possible to continue 'taking space for granted'.[9] Although the materiality of landscape, environment and heritage is real, space and place are constructed during the human encounter with them and re-constructed by analysis and writing. Through practices of writing we inevitably come to the well-established understanding of the existence of contact zones between the outside observer or writer and his/her objects of study.[10] With such a notion of a contact zone, one of the most productive aspects of our methodological approach – namely that we not only see the places with our own eyes but also communicate with local experts – turns out to be a bit less straightforward. Local experts mediate between outside researchers and the environment-cultural heritage nexus. They also actively form our visual perceptions through field excursions and our writing through narratives they produced. For instance, at the Barguzin *Zapovednik* at Lake Baikal, we found ourselves in the decayed Davsha settlement of an almost abandoned natural reserve. The memory of the *zapovednik*'s heyday was mostly locked in a small museum, surrounded by smog and the smell of forest fires that were rapidly engulfing the forests and mountains around us.[11] But the narrative that was repeatedly told us was one about wilderness and wild bears that might be looking at us from beyond each tree.[12] Confronted with the evidence of changing atmospheric and lake conditions, it was often difficult to sustain this narrative that was built to serve the gaze of outsiders.

Thus, the most obvious question we needed to ask ourselves was: does the wilderness and even nature itself exist? For more than twenty years, environmental historians have underscored that wilderness is a social construct, that, in the well-known words of William Cronon, there is 'trouble with wilderness' and we are 'getting back to the wrong nature'.[13] Scholars, such as Sörlin and Warde, have also argued that nature no longer exists. 'Nature' came to an end after being gradually transformed by technologies invented by people. In its place, humans have created 'environment' and the process of 'environing' is

---

9. Baron, 'New Spatial Histories of Twentieth Century Russia and the Soviet Union', p. 381.

10. Pratt, *Imperial Eyes*; Bravo and Sörlin, 'Narrative and Practice – an Introduction'.

11. On the fires, see the essay by Bryce Stewart in this volume

12. See the essay by David Moon in this volume for the stories about bears.

13. Cronon, 'The Trouble with Wilderness', pp. 7–28.

David Moon, Nicholas B. Breyfogle, Alexandra Bekasova and Julia Lajus

going on rapidly and, in some ways, irretrievably.[14] However, when we arrive at a place that we expect still to be 'wild', we all-too-often forget this theoretical knowledge. We are so much touched by stunning landscapes and tales of local guides who, consciously or not, produce the narratives that we as scholars try to avoid. This clash of personal experience with theory, which we cannot help but undergo during field research, makes place-based environmental history a difficult endeavour, although a very transformative one.

Through our several years of place-based research, we have experienced the 'multiplicities of nature': how controversy around one place and even one object arises because experts produce multiple versions of the place-object.[15] When we study 'place' and 'nature', we see simultaneously many layers that history formed there. How should we deal with that kind of multiplicity? Do we consider the place or landscape as a kaleidoscope or palimpsest or do we conceptualise it as a conglomerate bearing scars?[16] How can we discern between an environmental legacy that humans consider valuable and has become a recognised, celebrated cultural 'heritage' and a legacy that humans perceive as a burden – such as a pollution – that should be overcome and eradicated? How can we organise our personal and group 'assignment of meaning to place' through reading, mapping, observation, learning of names and contacts with local knowledge and memories?[17] The editors hope that the chapters in this book may contribute further to such discussions.

Environmental historians are well placed to analyse these concepts and to locate them in specific places over time due to the multi- and interdisciplinarity that lies at the heart of 'environmental history'. Our team of authors includes scholars who trained specifically as environmental historians, and others who came to this branch of history from other branches, such as social history, cultural history and the history of science, or from other disciplines including the natural sciences. In these chapters we have brought our areas of disciplinary expertise and combined them with personal engagement with these places.

'Place-based environmental history' has been a developing field in recent years, based on a recognition that meaningful environmental histories are difficult to write solely from conventional research in documentary and other types of evidence, and can only be enhanced by personal experiences of the places we study and encounters with peoples who live and work there, learning from their

14.   Sörlin and Warde, 'Making the Environment Historical – An Introduction'.
15.   See Jørgensen, 'Environmentalists on Both Sides', 51–68, p. 53.
16.   Storm, *Post-Industrial Landscape Scars*.
17.   Bassin, Ely and Stockdale (eds), *Space, Place, and Power in Modern Russia*, p. 16.

'local' and 'expert' knowledge. There are different approaches to such studies. A few years ago, a team of British-based environmental historians researched the histories of a series of places in collaboration with the organisations responsible for managing them, including a private water company, the state forestry administration and nature conservation organisations, and in dialogue with local inhabitants. The findings of this team both reinforced and challenged their understandings of their places and their trajectories in space and time.[18] A group of scholars in the environmental humanities travelled to the Island of Lundy in the Bristol Channel, between Southwest England and South Wales, and found that the visit 'encouraged us to reflect on questions of boundedness and connectedness; identity and belonging; isolation and community; and how disciplinary habits both frame and unsettle our responses to a new place. This might be characterised as an exercise in provocative dislocation.'[19] A more specific list of reasons for 'place-based research' have been advanced by Heather D. Green: '1) it provides insights not accessible otherwise; 2) it allows us to build relationships over time; 3) it offers opportunities to collaborate with locals; and 4) it provides an ongoing connection to our sites of study'.[20]

A specialist in the Soviet and post-Soviet space who has made exploration a central part of her research is Kate Brown. She has emphasised the limits of text-based research and of prioritising the temporal over the spatial. Reflecting on her approach, she has written:

> My adventures have often gone catastrophically wrong. I rarely find what I am seeking. I get lost, make mistakes, pursue foolish assumptions, and commit culturally insensitive blunders. In the course of these hapless misadventures I have relied on the kindness of strangers ... to show me the road, and to tell me their stories. ... The premise of this book is that travelling can be a form of negotiation, an unravelling of certainties and convictions and a reassembling of the past, aided by strangers who generously open their doors to reveal histories that are in play, contingent, and subjective.[21]

Brown's work guided our own explorations into place and nature in Russia's environmental history.

---

18.   Coates, Moon and Warde (eds), *Local Places, Global Processes*.

19.   Howkins et al., 'An Excursion in the Environmental Humanities'.

20.   Green, 'Problems of Place'. For illuminating and thought-provoking reflections on place-based research in environmental history by graduate students and early career scholars who identify as women, trans and non-binary, see *Environmental History Now*, 'Problems of Place'.

21.   Brown, *Dispatches from Dystopia*, pp.1–2.

David Moon, Nicholas B. Breyfogle, Alexandra Bekasova and Julia Lajus

Water Histories

The majority of the chapters here focus on water history and the 'human-water' relationship: the importance of aquatic environments in local cultures; the exploitation of marine, lacustrine and riverine resources; and efforts to protect these environments and resources. The essays explore the centrality of floods and water-control to the 'making' of St Petersburg; the special significance of White Sea islands for monastic life in the North; industrialisation and nature protection efforts at Lake Baikal; and water exploitation and pollution in Karelia.[22]

Water lies at the very core of the human experience and aquatic history intersects with myriad facets of human history: as a means of transportation, a home for other species (both threatening and nourishing to human health), a core part of religious practice and portal to spiritual worlds, a source of energy, the fount of food, a boundary or border and a source of leisure and beauty. Water has been fought over, served as a weapon of war and is at the core of myriad diplomatic treaties. For most of human history, migratory communities stayed close to water sources where they found access not only to the life-sustaining liquid but food as other species made their homes at water holes and rivers. When water supplies dwindled or because dangerous, humans moved on to another source. Water and new practices of its manipulation – especially irrigation and storage – were at the foundation of the revolution of human agricultural settlement, including the growth of towns and more intricate state and social structures, beginning at the outset of the Neolithic era.[23]

Human-water history is also the history of hydraulic engineering. Humans have redirected and impounded water for irrigated agriculture, flood control and to facilitate transportation.[24] After two centuries of redesign and reconstruction, for example, the Rhine River today looks fundamentally different from in 1815: straightened, canalised, deepened and reduced from multiple branches to one.[25] Humans have dried wetlands to separate dry land from wet,

---

22. For an introduction to water history, see Breyfogle and Sokolsky (eds), 'Introduction to Water History'; Tvedt, *Water and Society*. Examples of water histories of tsarist Russia and the Soviet Union include: Peterson, *Pipe Dreams*; Breyfogle (ed.), *Eurasian Environments*; Teichmann, *Macht der Unordnung*; Obertreis, *Imperial Desert Dreams*; Jones, *Empire of Extinction*; Sokolsky, 'Taming Tiger Country'; Demuth, *Floating Coast*; Chu, *The Life of Permafrost*; Breyfogle and Brown, *Hydraulic Societies*.

23. Mithen, *Thirst*; Breyfogle and Sokolsky (eds), 'Introduction to Water History'.

24. Peterson, *Pipe Dreams*; Resiner, *Cadillac Desert*; Morgan, *Running Out?*; Zhang, *The River, the Plain, and the State*; Pietz, *The Yellow River*.

25. Cioc, *Rhine*; Blackburn, *Conquest of Nature*.

create fields for agriculture and protect cities, from the English Fens to the Netherlands and the Spanish draining of Tenochtitlan to make Mexico City.[26] The shift to steam-powered machines – tools that combined fossil fuel energy with the power of water in its gas form – allowed the pumping of impressive quantities of groundwater to the surface from aquifers.[27] Water has offered humans a source of energy, beginning with the water wheel and expanding exponentially with the development of hydroelectricity.[28] And humans have built elaborate systems of pipes, taps, reservoirs and purification systems to bring potable water to urban areas and dispose of their waste – often creating tensions between communities up- and downstream.[29]

Floods (more water than humans desire in a given place at a given time for their needs) and droughts (too little) are common in the human experience of the hydrosphere. Some floods are part of annual cycles as rain falls or snows melt in the spring. These floods bring with them silt and other nutrients that renew the fertility of the soil, flushing away dangerous salts in the process – along the Nile River, for instance, the floods are welcome and the lifeblood of the region. Other floods are periodic, based on shifts in ocean and atmospheric temperatures, and some are human-induced tools of war. The ability to mitigate floods or respond to flood disasters offered legitimacy to political leaders. Flood and drought prevention efforts and hydraulic engineering often benefitted certain social and ethnic groups above others, prompting demands for environmental justice.[30]

Oceans, lakes and rivers have offered humans indispensable sources of food for tens of thousands of years, especially with fish, aquatic mammals and various types of aquatic vegetation. Humans have generally kept close to shore, fishing inland rivers and lakes, and have been wary of heading off onto the open ocean. However, in more recent decades, changes in fishing technologies – internal combustion boat engines, new types of nets and refrigeration – and scientific understandings of fish migration patterns have fundamentally

---

26. Candiani, *Dreaming of Dry Land*; TeBrake, 'Taming the Waterwolf'; Ash, *Draining of the Fens*.

27. Opie, Miller and Archer, *Ogallala*; Cathcart, *Water Dreamers*; Jones, *Desert Kingdom*.

28. Reynolds, *Stronger than a Hundred Men*; White, *The Organic Machine*; Sneddon, *Concrete Revolution*; D'Souza, *Drowned and Dammed*.

29. Melosi, *The Sanitary City*

30. Muscolino, *The Ecology of War in China*; Davis, *Late Victorian Holocausts*; Zhang, *The River, the Plain, and the State*; Courtney, *The Nature of Disaster in China*; Steinberg, *Acts of God*.

David Moon, Nicholas B. Breyfogle, Alexandra Bekasova and Julia Lajus

transformed fishing activities, taking fishers far from home. The result has been unsustainable levels of fish extraction and struggles over who should have access to specific fishing sites.[31]

The dual processes of urbanisation and industrialisation – combined with the unprecedented global population growth of the last century – produced both quantitative and qualitative transformations in water pollution and toxicity. Water has long been home to bacteria, viruses, and other water-based micro-organisms that can cause dangerous diseases in humans (even well before humans realised it). Beginning in the nineteenth century, as urban populations grew, so too did the spread of water-borne disease, as towns struggled to deal with human and animal waste. The revolution in public health and urban water purification infrastructures that resulted produced a foundational change in the safety of water, public health and longevity of urban dwellers.[32]

However, beginning in the nineteenth and especially in the twentieth century, the human manufacture of new chemicals, pharmaceuticals, fertilisers and pesticides fundamentally changed the scale and types of water pollution and toxicity. Water quality came under new assaults from the chemical, fossil-fuel and biological wastes of industrialisation and the rise of factory farming and chemical fertilisers. As we see in several chapters here, the acceleration of water pollution and toxicity generated a human reaction. The result has been an evolving water protection movement that has struggled to balance economic demands with effects on water and the multiple species that rely on it. Evolving scientific theories – such as 'dilution is the solution to pollution' and 'maximal assimilative capacity' – have permitted shifting levels of pollution. Looming over these water-quality debates has been the shadow of social and ethnic diversity and the sacrifice of certain communities for the benefits of others. For instance, what were considered acceptable levels of dumping for logging and mining interests around Lake Superior were deadly threats to the native Anishinaabe.[33]

---

31. Bogue, *Fishing the Great Lakes*; Fagan, *Fishing*; Demuth, *Floating Coast*; Jones, *Empire of Extinction*; White, *The Organic Machine*; Sokolsky, 'Taming Tiger Country'; Josephson, 'The Ocean's Hot Dog'.

32. Broich, *London*; Blackford, *Columbus, Ohio,* pp. 49–115; Melosi, *The Sanitary City.*

33. Langston, *Sustaining Lake Superior*; McNeill, *Something New Under the Sun*, Ch. 5; Cioc, *The Rhine*; McGucken, *Lake Erie Rehabilitated.*

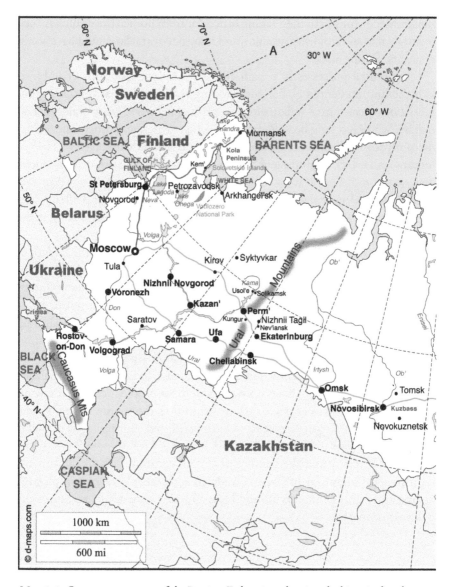

Map 1.1. Contemporary map of the Russian Federation, showing the historical and current Trans-Siberian Railway and various other railway lines traversing Russia, the locations of nature reserves discussed in the book (in green) and other locations of the chapters in this book. Source: Created by Andrew Johnson at The White Horse Press using d-maps.com: © d-maps https://www.d-maps.com/carte.php?num_car=15058&lang=en. Additional data from CC-BY-SA OpenStreetMap and contributors https://en.wikipedia.org/wiki/ Trans-Siberian_Railway#/media/File:Transsib_international.svg.

David Moon, Nicholas B. Breyfogle, Alexandra Bekasova and Julia Lajus

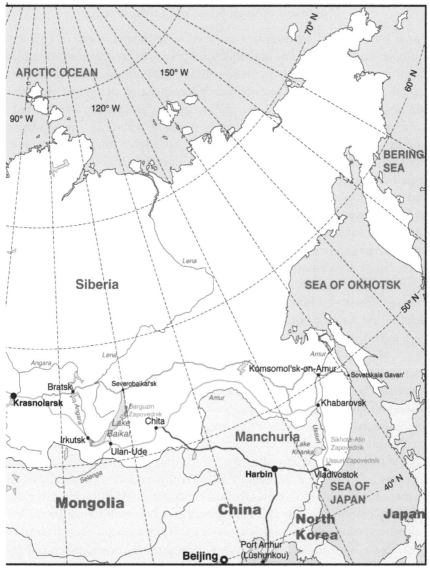

All place names are current. ——— St Petersburg – Moscow Railway
Historical names are ——— St Petersburg – Murmansk Railway
explained in the book. ——— Trans-Siberian (route changed over time)
——— Circum-Baikal Railway
⌐ Rivers ⌐ Nature reserves ——— Chinese Eastern Railway
——— Baikal-Amur Mainline (BAM)

Cities and towns

● **> 1 million people**
● 100,000 – 1 million
• < 100,000 people

Place and Nature: An Introduction

Movement through Space and Environment

Space, mobility and environment are underlying themes in several chapters. Complex and diverse forms of mobility are persistent processes across human history, patterned not only by socio-cultural and political contexts, but also spatial, environmental and technological phenomena. Since its rapid expansion in the seventeenth century, Russia's politics, society and culture have exerted a profound influence on human movement throughout Eurasia. The circulation of people, information and things across this huge space transformed populations, restructured collective and individual identities and created enduring legacies.[34] As migrants, pilgrims, travellers and tourists moved, they encountered various environments, which required different understandings of 'nature' and different techniques and cultures to engage with the natural world. Thus, Orthodox monks moved north to Solovki in the White Sea, encountering new environments and different spiritual cultures; tourists travelled around Siberia; settlers moved, voluntarily and not, to the Kola Peninsula in the North and to Siberia and the Far East; and perhaps most symbolically, in the early eighteenth century, Russia established a new capital city, St Petersburg, on a marshy river delta in the extreme Northwest, where the inhabitants had to learn to deal with recurring floods.

Mobility history and environmental history are 'kindred fields', as Tom McCarthy has noted. 'When we think about movement and transportation in human history, environmental consequences seem inevitable ... People go places and take things with them – commodities and trade goods, as well as vermin, weeds, disease and, perhaps most important, the ideas in their heads ... Roads and railroad tracks are literally fixed to the land, ground that has been surveyed, cleared and often graded for that purpose. So are canals and ... rivers ...'[35] Among a set of future research opportunities, he pointed to the study of how mobility is connected to the natural world through energy and to an exploration of various mobility practices to better understand travellers' behaviour, perceptions and motivations. It was Wolfgang Schivelbusch's seminal book that pushed many historians to rethink interrelations between technological interventions and transformation of landscapes, production of space, mobility phenomena and crucial changes in travel practices.[36] Scholarship that focuses on the relationships between technologies of travel (including narra-

34. Siegelbaum and Moch, *Broad Is My Native Land*; Randolph and Avrutin (eds), *Russia in Motion*.

35. McCarthy, 'A Natural Intersection', p. 61

36. Schivelbusch, *The Railway Journey*. See also Kern, *The Culture of Time and Space*.

tives) and the production of perceptions and knowledge, with an emphasis on the role of science and technology as producers of landscapes, physical as well as imagined, is growing rapidly.[37] Emphasising the importance of the study of 'mobility's complex environmental significance on local, regional, national and global scales' in historical perspective, Jay Young, Ben B. Radley and Colin M. Coates remind us about the importance of path dependency when dealing with environmental transformations caused by the implementation of large transportation infrastructural projects. They stress that 'lines and networks transform the environment by their construction, and they also impose path dependencies … they can "lock" a society or community into certain patterns of movement and interaction with the environment, steering people and developments between connected places and those that are located "off the beaten path"'.[38]

Recently published scholarship on environmental history, mobility studies and technological history significantly broadens our understanding of nature and landscape from an essentialist fact to socially-constructed, and therefore changing, phenomena.[39] Reminding us that 'the transportation infrastructures of the modern era discovered, partially defined, and always changed the landscapes they transected', Thomas Zeller suggests approaching them as 'landscapes of transportation', which are understood as technological and socio-cultural construction. Arguing that 'it is not possible to separate the production of knowledge about landscape and transportation … from the level of their cultural meaning', he pointed out that 'most experiences of landscapes … were mediated technologically'.[40]

Nature Conservation and Protection

The words 'Russia' or 'Soviet Union' and 'environment' have tended to conjure up images of gargantuan schemes to conquer nature by ruthlessly exploiting resources, building large industrial cities from scratch that polluted their surroundings and inhabitants, damming rivers and destroying their ecosystems and ecological disasters too numerous to mention that were brought about by

---

37. For example, see Bravo and Sörlin (eds), *Narrating the Arctic*; White, *Railroaded*.

38. Young, Radley and Coates, 'Moving Natures in Canadian History', p. 13.

39. On the importance of studying the intersections of technological and environmental issues in historical perspective, see Stine and Tarr, 'At the Intersection of Histories', pp. 601–40. On methodological convergence of history of technology and environmental history, also see Williams, 'Nature out of Control'.

40. Zeller, *Driving Germany*, pp. 5–6.

Place and Nature: An Introduction

careless human actions directed at increasing economic output without regard for the environment.[41] Without denying these 'negative' environmental consequences of Russian and Soviet economic development, the authors here argue that this was only one part of the story. This book builds on existing research on nature protection by presenting innovative case studies of conservation for scientific research, recreation and tourism and the experiences of the scientists and tourists who learned to understand environments in new ways.

The origins of nature protection in this part of the world can be traced back to hunting parks for the tsars and aristocrats in the sixteenth and seventeenth centuries. This motive persisted. In his essay in this volume, Mark Sokolsky traces the origins of wildlife conservation in Russia's Far East in the late nineteenth century among societies of 'gentlemen' who wished to protect their hobby of hunting deer, elk, goats, and game birds. Another motive for nature protection was provided by the foundation of the Russian Navy at the end of the seventeenth century by Peter I (the Great, 1682–1725): preventing the population from felling tall trees suitable for shipbuilding. The state and elites continued to protect various natural resources for their exclusive use.[42]

Another motive to protect nature was aesthetic: over the nineteenth and twentieth centuries, Russia's writers and landscape painters came to appreciate and value their native landscapes. This period saw the development of tourism, as Russians with money and time began to explore the landscapes of their homeland, especially as railways and steam-powered riverboats eased transport problems in such a vast country.[43] It was not until the latter part of the twentieth century, however, that national parks were established in the Soviet Union and post-Soviet states solely for purposes of tourism, recreation and aesthetic appreciation of nature.[44] Russia's relatively late arrival to national parks distinguishes it from many other countries, such as Switzerland and the United States, where such motives were the initial reasons for setting aside large areas of land for protection.[45]

---

41. For a detailed analysis that emphasises the negative aspects, see Josephson et al., *An Environmental History of Russia*.

42. Dulov, *Geograficheskaia sreda i istoriia Rossii*, pp. 186–200; Weiner, *Models of Nature*, pp. 7–18.

43. Ely, *This Meager Nature*; Costlow, *Heart-Pine Russia*.

44. Roe, *Into Russian Nature*.

45. Kupper, *Creating Wilderness*; Gissibl, Höhler and Kupper (eds), *Civilizing Nature*; Howkins, Orsi and Fiege (eds), *National Parks beyond the Nation*; Wakild, *Revolutionary Parks*.

David Moon, Nicholas B. Breyfogle, Alexandra Bekasova and Julia Lajus

From the end of the nineteenth century and for much of the twentieth, however, the major motive in the Russian and Soviet states for protecting nature was scientific: the 'natural world' was considered worthy of protection as vital sites for scientific research, both pure and applied. This was the basis for the network of *zapovedniks*: strict, scientific nature reserves that date back to end of the nineteenth century. One of the pioneers was the soil scientist Vasilii Dokuchaev. In the wake of the drought, crop failure and famine of 1891–92, he was sponsored by the Russian government to research ways of making agriculture in the steppe region less susceptible to drought and more sustainable. He set aside three areas of land that he believed had not been altered by human activity. They were protected from all human endeavours except for scientific research. The protected areas were to serve as 'models of nature' and the results of research into their environments as baselines to test ways of using the land for agriculture that were sustainable, i.e. emulated or copied the 'natural' vegetation and processes that occurred independent of humans.[46] At the same time as Dokuchaev's work, a landowner in southern Ukraine, Friedrich Faltz-Fein, set aside an area of 'virgin', unploughed steppe for protection on his estate at Askania Nova. It is still there to this day and is a major site for research in steppe ecology.[47]

The idea of designating plots of land from which human activity was excluded for scientific research was influential. It was the basis for the network of *zapovedniks* that developed in late-Imperial Russia, the Soviet Union and the post-Soviet states. In the early twentieth century, Russian scientists set the goal of establishing *zapovedniks* in all the main types of environment in Russian, later Soviet, territory: tundra, forest, forest-steppe, steppe, desert, mountains and lakes. *Zapovedniks* were established also to protect certain species of fauna and flora. These reserves and the scientists who worked on them had mixed experiences in the Soviet Union. They struggled to justify protecting nature in a state that was committed to exploiting natural resources for the benefit of economic development. At various times, *zapovedniks* and their scientists came under attack, and reserves were reduced in size, or closed altogether; at other times, they were revived and the authorities recognised their value. The original scientific rationale of protecting sites of supposed 'virgin' nature was challenged by ecologists in the mid-twentieth century and superseded by more nuanced understandings of the interaction between the human and non-human

---

46. Moon, 'The Environmental History of the Russian Steppes', pp. 149–174.
47. Boreiko, *Askania-Nova*; Natsional'na akademiia agrarnikh nauk, 'Biosfernii zapovednik "Askaniia-Nova" imeni F.E. Fal'ts-Feina'.

worlds and reasons to protect certain sites. The chequered history of nature protection in the Soviet Union has been admirably researched and analysed by Feliks Shtil'mark and Douglas Weiner.[48]

It is important to remember that the *zapovedniks* are not national parks, intended for the preservation of national landscapes or for recreation, but sites for scientific research. When we visited the Barguzin reserve on Lake Baikal in 2016, we needed official authorisation from the director. (That said, 'eco-tourism' has recently become a growing important revenue stream for the scientific reserves since the collapse of the Soviet Union.) The International Union for the Conservation of Nature (IUCN) has devised a hierarchy of categories of protected areas. The Soviet and post-Soviet *zapovedniks* are in Category 1a: Strict Nature Reserve. These are:

> Protected areas that are strictly set aside to protect biodiversity and also possibly geological/geomorphological features, where human visitation, use and impacts are strictly controlled and limited to ensure protection of the conservation values. Such protected areas can serve as indispensable reference areas for scientific research and monitoring.

National parks fall into the IUCN's second category and are defined as:

> Large natural or near natural areas set aside to protect large-scale ecological processes, along with the complement of species and ecosystems characteristic of the area, which also provide a foundation for environmentally and culturally compatible spiritual, scientific, educational, recreational and visitor opportunities.[49]

Both these types of protected areas feature in this book, for example Nicholas Breyfogle's analysis of the establishment of the Barguzin *Zapovednik* in 1916 and Alan Roe's detailed discussion of the origins of the Vodlozero National Park in Karelia that was formally established in 1991. Issues of nature protection and conservation, and our experiences of exploring and researching the history of protected sites, constitute a major theme of this book.

The Northwest and the European North of Russia

Several contributions to this book deal with interrelations between humans and the environment in the Northwest and the European North of Russia, which

---

48. Feliks Shtil'mark, *History of the Russian Zapovedniks*; Weiner, *A Little Corner of Freedom*; Weiner, *Models of Nature*.

49. IUCN, 'Protected Area Categories'.

David Moon, Nicholas B. Breyfogle, Alexandra Bekasova and Julia Lajus

is often represented as a region of lakes, rivers and forests, not easy to inhabit because of rather harsh climate and poor soil. It also served as a 'window to the West' with its access to the Baltic, the White and the Barents Seas and boundaries with Nordic countries. The area of the European (or historically 'the Russian') North is usually considered to stretch from the border with Scandinavia to the Northern Urals and is conceptualised as being a part of the 'Old North' of Northern Europe.[50] The frontier movement in the North was mostly finished by the end of the sixteenth century (in contrast to colonisation of the southern and eastern parts of the Russian Empire, which continued as late as the twentieth century). The early, slow and relatively peaceful penetration into the northern areas of peasant and monastic settlement might be one reason that the North is often missing in most of histories of Russian colonisation.[51]

Fish and marine mammals were crucial natural resources here, and access to them was the major driving force for colonisation.[52] The fur hunt was also significant in the early period, albeit less than in Siberia.[53] Later, with first signs of industrialisation, northern forests and minerals became more important pull factors for migration and settlement in the North. In the eighteenth century, the colonisation of the North gained the distinctive features of a colonial-type policy, with the application of the Dutch model of large trade monopolies for marine resources.[54] However, the geopolitical role of the region diminished because of the foundation of a new capital on the Baltic Sea.

Movement towards the sea, which Russians began in the fourteenth century, was coupled with the foundation of St Petersburg in the beginning of the eighteenth century: a seaport, metropolis and the new capital, situated on islands in the Neva River delta, at the eastern end of the Gulf of Finland, surrounded by rivers, streams and canals. Peter I used the creation of this new city as an instrument to transform Russia into an important naval and commercial power. Being developed as 'a space of modernities', it was a highly contested one.[55] It was designed as a port city of a new type for Russia: for ocean-going

---

50. Keskitalo (ed.), *The Politics of Arctic Resources*.

51. Shaw, 'The Settlement of European Russia during the Romanov Period (1613–1917)'; Lajus, 'Colonization of the Russian North'.

52. Lajus, Kraikovski and Yurchenko, 'Sea Fisheries in the Russian North c. 1400–1850'; Kraikovski, '"The Sea on One Side, Trouble on the Other"'.

53. Martin, 'Russian Expansion in the Far North'. On the Siberian fur economy, see the chapter by Breyfogle in this volume.

54. Kraikovski, 'Profits from under the Water', pp. 34–49.

55. Anisimov, *Iunyi grad*; Shaw, 'St. Petersburg and Geographies of Modernity', pp. 6–29.

ships and oriented towards the water of the Neva River and through it to the Baltic Sea.

The city's aquatic environment setting was a great advantage, facilitating its quick rise, economic growth and architectural development.[56] The river itself and the vast water network that connected the rapidly growing new capital with areas in the Russian hinterland both facilitated and hindered the development of the city's complex supply system based on interrelated water and land transportation.[57] Floods were a regular and remarkable feature of city life and one of the most demanding characteristics of the Neva River.[58] Changing, sprawling and dealing with contradictory challenges, the city of St Petersburg (renamed three times: to Petrograd in 1914, to Leningrad in 1924 and then back to St Petersburg in 1991) was an experimental urban laboratory of planning visions, urban management practices and resilience. The city's transformation into an industrial metropolis and important transportation hub required the continuous mobilisation of enormous quantities of multiple resources.[59] They were needed not only to establish this grandiose city in a peripheral and inaccessible region with a hostile environment, but also to provide material and food supplies. The creation and maintenance of a vast infrastructure network of water and land communications transformed the spatial configuration of European Russia.

With the construction of the railway from St Petersburg (then Petrograd) to the new port of Murmansk near the Barents Sea coast during World War One, the European North became better connected with the city and the railway itself became formative for the economy of Karelia and the Kola peninsula.[60] In the 1920s, the Soviet government substituted the Canadian technological model of modernisation of the North for the late-nineteenth century, unsuccessful state policy of coastal colonisation according to the Norwegian model.[61] From being a 'frozen frontier' and then a resource 'backyard' of the country, the region gradually gained a military imagery as a symbolic 'façade' of the empire.[62] Finally, the Soviet industrial and military colonisation, which began

56. Kraikovski and Lajus, 'The Neva as a Metropolitan River of Russia', pp. 339–64; Kraikovski and Lajus, 'Living on the River over the Year', pp. 235–52; Kraikovski and Lajus, 'The Metropolitan Bay', pp. 1–12.

57. Jones, *Bread upon the Waters*.

58. Dills, 'Cracks in the Granite', pp. 479–96.

59. Bater, 'Between Old and New'; Idem, *St. Petersburg*; Ruble, *Leningrad*.

60. Baron, *Soviet Karelia*; Bruno, *The Nature of Soviet Power*.

61. Lajus, 'In Search for Instructive Models', pp. 110–36.

62. Eklund et al., 'Imageries and Historical Change in the European Russian Arctic', pp. 200–220.

David Moon, Nicholas B. Breyfogle, Alexandra Bekasova and Julia Lajus

in the 1930s, turned the region into the most populated and polluted parts of the Arctic.[63]

Siberia and the Pacific Far East

The second and third sections of the book explore place and nature across the remarkable expanses of Siberia, from the Ural Mountains in the west to the Lake Baikal watershed and the Pacific shores of the Russian Far East. The word 'Siberia' often conjures up images of vast frozen tundra and the horrors of exile and the Gulags. Yet, as the chapters in this book make clear, the massive Siberian region of the Russian Federation is more physically beautiful, ecologically diverse and bountiful in human society and culture than these two pervasive images allow. Siberia was and is a crucial component of Russia – economically, culturally, strategically and socially – constituting more than three-quarters of Russia's landmass, although only a small percentage of the total population, and forty per cent of the land in Asia.

Located at the meeting of Russia, China, Korea, Mongolia, Japan and the United States, Siberia is of tremendous geopolitical importance, embroiling Russia in myriad entanglements (and friendships) in the Asia-Pacific zone.[64] The region is home to an extraordinary human diversity with a remarkable history and matchless ethno-cultural amalgam.[65] It is a region enormously well-endowed with natural resources, including furs, salt, lumber, fish and sea mammals, oil and gas, water and hydroelectricity and a vast range of essential minerals and metals (such as iron, copper, nickel, diamonds and gold).[66] Through the region's vast expanses, forests, permafrost and wetlands, Siberia also boasts multiple climatic zones, natural wonders and large numbers of endemic and endangered species.

The beginning of Russian expansion into Siberia and the Russian Far East (and on into the North Pacific and Alaska) is traditionally dated to 1582, with the invasion of the Cossack Ermak Timofeevich into the Siberian Khanate.[67] Navigating the region's many rivers and drawn on by the extraordinary wealth in furs that Siberia offered, Russian hunters, trappers and explorers

---

63. Bruno, *The Nature of Soviet Power*.

64. Rieber, *Struggle for the Eurasian Borderlands*; Schimmelpenninck van der oye, *Toward the Rising Sun*; Stephan, *Russian Far East*; Linkhoeva, *Revolution Goes East*.

65. Forsyth, *History of the Peoples of Siberia*; Vitebsky, *Reindeer People*.

66. Demuth, *Floating Coast*; Jones, *Empire of Extinction*; Tichotsky, *Russian Diamond Colony*; Josephson, *Conquest of the Russian Arctic*; Wood (ed.), *Siberia*.

67. Sunderland, 'Ermak Timofeevich'.

raced across the region, arriving at the Pacific Ocean in 1639. The imposition of Russian political authority over the succeeding decades came with violence towards the native peoples and the expansion of the Orthodox Church, with forts, churches and monasteries as beachheads of colonial expansion. The story of Russian Siberia is filled with tales of business empires built and lost, from the Stroganovs and the Demidovs to the Russian America Company, and harrowing tales of exploration and discovery.[68] Siberia was a land of dreams and hopes, where even the shallow, shoal-covered Amur River could be envisioned as a Russian Mississippi.[69]

Russians came to dominate the region through multiple means: economic expansion and resource extraction; exploration, cartography and the development of scientific knowledge; and the construction of transportation, communication, energy, industrial and urban infrastructure and technologies of control.[70] The Russian presence also came with increasing waves of human migration: fur traders, missionaries, religious non-conformists, political prisoners and criminals, peasant migrants in search of land and freedoms and the vast movement of Soviet-era workers to populate new economic centres and sensitive border regions.[71] The movement across space and place – through new and ever-changing ecological zones – brought Russians into contact with a wide range of new environments and peoples, transforming all involved in the encounters. The native Siberian population was savaged by the new arrivals and found their communities and cultures shattered by conversion efforts, competition for land use, disease and multiple waves of civilising missions, especially Soviet efforts to bring socialist modernity.[72]

Chapter Summaries

The book opens with a rich and thought-provoking essay by Alexei Kraikovski and Julia Lajus that explores the Solovetskie islands – or Solovki – in the White Sea in the European North of Russia. Together, the two authors have

---

68. Lincoln, *Conquest of a Continent*; Lantzeff and Pierce, *Eastward to Empire*.

69. Bassin, *Imperial Visions*.

70. Kivelson, *Cartographies of Tsardom*; Josephson, *New Atlantis Revisited*; Jones, *Empire of Extinction*; Josephson, *Industrialized Nature*; Hill and Gaddy, *The Siberian Curse*.

71. Shulman, *Stalinism on the Frontier of Empire*; Breyfogle, Sunderland and Schrader (eds), *Peopling the Russian Periphery*; Treadgold, *The Great Siberian Migration*.

72. Znamenski, *Shamanism and Christianity*; Chakars, *The Socialist Way of Life in Siberia*; Demuth, *Floating Coast*; Grant, *In the Soviet House of Culture*.

David Moon, Nicholas B. Breyfogle, Alexandra Bekasova and Julia Lajus

long experience studying the islands, which they have encountered from the perspectives of scientists, historians and the tourism industry. This gives them the unparalleled ability to analyse the natural-scientific and historical-cultural story of the islands. They emphasise the importance of distinguishing between 'nature' and the 'environment'. They describe the interactions with the 'nature' of Solovki by settlers and visitors through both religious and scientific practices. The gradual 'environing' of the islands through human activities can be seen from the development of the monastic economy through the terrible Gulag times to today. It is these social practices that have turned 'spaces' of Solovki into the 'places' that take centre stage in the essays that comprise this book.

Andy Bruno takes us to another place not too far away from Solovki: Lake Imandra, above the Arctic Circle on the Kola Peninsula. He presents a biography of the lake, going back deep into geological time to explain its origins and in historical time to chart its interaction with its human neighbours. For many centuries, these were indigenous Sami people, but centuries later, during the Soviet period, newer arrivals caused the lake's pollution as a consequence of mining and industrial development. Locating the local concerns of this lake in Russia's European North in the global context of accelerating human impact on the environment, Bruno indicates the value of focussing on specific places to explore the implications of the onset of the Anthropocene.

Alan Roe's essay links a place – a vast area of old-growth forest straddling the border of Karelia and Arkhangel'sk Oblast' – and a person, Ukrainian-born Oleg Cherviakov. Following a life-changing visit in the late 1980s, Cherviakov campaigned tirelessly to protect an area of this forest from the Soviet timber industry that was relentlessly felling trees across northern Russia. For Cherviakov, protecting the forest had cultural and spiritual meaning, and he believed promoting tourism could make it economically viable. Based on his personal acquaintance with both the place and the person, Alan Roe charts the establishment of the Vodlozero National Park in the difficult years around the collapse of the Soviet Union in 1991.

The final chapter of the book's first section takes us from rural environments to an urban one: St Petersburg. Once the capital city of Imperial Russia and, as Leningrad, the second city of the Soviet Union, its identity and experiences have been shaped by its founder's choice to locate his new city in the low-lying delta of the Neva River, where successive generations of inhabitants have transformed this marshy space into a place they call home. Robert Dale offers a watery perspective on the city's landscape by comparing the great floods of 1824 and 1924 and how the city's government and inhabitants responded.

Place and Nature: An Introduction

Once seemingly powerless in the face of periodic surges of water from the Gulf of Finland, the city entered a new phase in its environmental history in 2011 with the completion of a 25-kilometre dam to protect it.

Spotlighting our theme of personal engagement with place and nature, the book's second section presents a series of concise 'postcards' or photo essays, in which the authors relate their experiences of particular places. Solovki's environment and long history are brought sharply into focus by Nicholas Breyfogle's description of his visit to these remarkable islands. Catherine Evtuhov narrates her travels around the Ural Mountains – traditionally the boundary between 'European' and 'Asian' Russia – to explore the local industry, mining and transport infrastructure, which she and her colleagues observed through the lens of the region's burgeoning industrial-heritage tourism business. 'Lake Baikal in peril' was the reaction of Australian marine biologist Bryce Stewart to his encounter with 'one of the world's greatest aquatic wonders' in the heart of Siberia. He learned that the lake's unique ecosystem is threatened by plans to dam one of the rivers flowing into it, warming waters in the lake, and forest fires that shrouded it in smoke whilst he and his fellow explorers were there. One of these, historian David Moon, uses a tale they were told by the Barguzin *Zapovednik* scientific director about starving bears resorting to eating each other during a desperately hungry winter to ponder the environmental history of this remote region from an ursine perspective.

The photo essays have brought us a long way from the European North of Russia to Siberia, and the essays that comprise the book's third part explore the places, spaces and environments of this immense region. Mobility is the theme of the opening essay by Alexandra Bekasova and Ekaterina Kalemeneva. They analyse how places along the route of the Trans-Siberian Railway were presented in guidebooks as 'landscapes of transportation' to the growing numbers of tourists who made the journey in the final decades of Imperial Russia. Whilst the railway was represented as a symbol of prestige, progress and power, the territories through which it ran – with their dense forests, mountains, rivers and lakes only lightly brushed by human habitation – were described as 'wild'. The railway made distant areas and landscapes, like Lake Baikal, accessible for larger numbers of business travellers, settlers and tourists. Along with rail services and modern conveniences offered on board express trains, the impressive views and panoramas from the railway around Lake Baikal also evolved into commodities that could be demanded and purchased.

The next chapter presents an invaluable local perspective on Lake Baikal by Arkady and Tatiana Kalikhman. The Kalikhmans are scholars based in Ir-

David Moon, Nicholas B. Breyfogle, Alexandra Bekasova and Julia Lajus

kutsk, the largest city near the lake, and draw on their experience of more than four decades' active involvement in campaigns and programmes to study and protect the lake's environment. They offer a survey of the encounters between Baikal and the human populations who have lived around it, assigned spiritual significance to its waters, exploited its resources, studied it and posed serious challenges to its ecosystems. They conclude their essay with a guarded optimism for the future. Their essay nicely sets the scene for the following two essays, which offer detailed case studies in Baikal's contested environmental history.

The start of strict scientific protection of one part of the lake, its shores and its flora and fauna came in 1916 with the establishment of the Barguzin *Zapovednik* on its remote, northeastern side. In keeping with the theme of this volume, Nicholas Breyfogle, a regular traveller to Baikal, presented an earlier version of his essay at a seminar held in the *zapovednik's* meeting house in Davsha, only a few metres from the lake's waters (see Figure 12.1). His chapter explores the origins of Russia's first state-sponsored *zapovednik*, which began as an effort to protect rapidly disappearing sable from localised extinction and led to decades of ecosystem-based nature protection and scientific study. Breyfogle focuses especially on the interplay of human decision-making and non-human causation in the development of the nature reserve.

The tension between conservation and exploitation of the waters and other resources of Lake Baikal in the period from the 1950s to the 1970s is analysed by Elena Kochetkova. Her essay reveals the tensions between different types of Soviet institutions. Industrial ministries and Gosstroi (the central State Committee for Construction) wanted the lake's resources to serve the cause of Siberian industrial development. To this end, pulp and paper mills were built on its shores and one of its feeder rivers. Concerned about pollution of its pristine waters, and unconvinced by the technologies employed, scientists in the East Siberian Branch of the Academy of Sciences spoke out, inaugurating the 'struggles for Baikal' that other local scientists, such as the Kalikhmans, joined in. The Baikal Pulp and Paper Mill finally closed in 2013, but it would be premature to conclude that this was the end of Baikal's encounter with the people who live around it.

Our journey from the islands, lakes, forests of the European North, and the largest city in northwestern Russia, across the Ural Mountains, along the Trans-Siberian Railway to Lake Baikal is completed by Mark Sokolsky. His essay analyses nature conservation in the province of Primor'e, on Russia's Pacific coast. After the Russian Empire acquired the territory from Qing China in 1858–60, Russian settlers encountered unfamiliar fauna, including spotted deer, wild goats, leopards and the iconic Amur tiger. Sokolsky considers how the notion of conserving this distinctive fauna developed initially not from the scientific reasons that lay behind the 'struggle for Baikal', but from concerns among the region's settler elites to protect the game they hunted for sport from poachers. Only later, Sokolsky demonstrates, did the cause of nature conservation in this far-eastern region acquire the broader motives, in particular scientific, that lay behind the network of *zapovedniks* established in Russian and Soviet lands. His essay thus completes our travels through the diverse spaces and landscapes that have come under Russian rule, and illustrates how the evolution of ideas of conserving nature in this particular place were part of a wider Russian, Eurasian and global story.

Being There

Travel writer Kapka Kassabova has recently written that 'history is written above all by those who weren't there'. Her book on the border zone between Bulgaria, Turkey and Greece is an eloquent example of how travel writers can bring to life places and the histories of people who have lived in them.[73] This book is written by environmental historians who were there and who have sought to bring to life these places, environments and the experiences of their inhabitants. We could not have produced this book and its insights if we had not also hiked and biked through them, sailed across them, rowed around them, swum in them, got covered in mud, been swarmed by mosquitos and other insects and been observed by bears, who kept silent and made sure we could not see them. On other occasions, we hid ourselves so that we could observe rare and endangered species, like the nerpa, the endemic freshwater seals living on Baikal's Ushkan'i Islands. Whilst we were there, we also met people who have devoted their lives to studying their places and environments, managing them, guiding visitors and campaigning to protect them from harm. They generously shared their time and knowledge with us. To get to our places, we flew in airplanes, travelled in trains, rode in buses and sailed across seas and lakes on ferries and multiple other boats. On one memorable occasion, we nearly did not get there (to Cape Khoboi on Ol'khon Island in Lake Baikal). The driver of one of our four-wheel-drive utility vehicles, an otherwise invincible Soviet-designed UAZ-452, omitted to engage the second axle and we got stuck in the sand. Digging it out taught us important lessons – ones we appreciated all the more after we were on our way.

---

73. Kassabova, *Border*, p. xviii.

David Moon, Nicholas B. Breyfogle, Alexandra Bekasova and Julia Lajus

Figure 1.1: The photos show members of the research team exploring the forests and waters of the Solovetskie Islands and Lake Baikal in the summers of 2013 and 2015.

Group photo outside the Davsha meeting house in the Barguzin Zapovednik.
Back row, L-R: Arkady Kalikhman, Elena Kochetkova, Andy Bruno, Tatiana Kalikhman, Nicholas Breyfogle, David Moon, Catherine Evtuhov, Bryce Stewart, Boris Gasparov, Alexandra Bekasova, Julia Lajus.
Front row, L-R: Aleksandr Ananin, Ekaterina Kalemeneva, Hazel Long, Mark Sokolsky, Alan Roe.

BIBLIOGRAPHY

Adams, Paul C., Steven D. Hoelscher and Karen E. Till (eds). 2011. *Textures of Place: Exploring Humanist Geographies*. Minneapolis: University of Minnesota Press.

Ash, Eric. 2017. *The Draining of the Fens: Projectors, Popular Politics, and State Building in Early Modern England*. Baltimore: Johns Hopkins University Press.

Anisimov, Evgeniy. 2003 *Iunyi grad. Peterburg vremen Petra Velikogo*. St Petersburg: Dm. Bulanin.

Baron, Nick. 2007. 'New Spatial Histories of Twentieth Century Russia and the Soviet Union: Surveying the Landscape'. *Jahrbücher für Geschichte Osteuropas* 55 (3): 374–400.

Baron, Nick. 2007. *Soviet Karelia: Politics, Planning and Terror in Stalin's Russia, 1920–1939*. London: Routledge.

Bassin, Mark. 1999. *Imperial Visions: Nationalist Imagination and Geographical Expansion in the Russian Far East, 1840–1865*. New York: Cambridge University Press.

Bassin, Mark, Christopher Ely and Melissa K. Stockdale (eds). 2010. *Space, Place, and Power in Modern Russia: Essays in the New Spatial History*. Dekalb, IL: Northern Illinois University Press.

Bater, James H. 1986. 'Between Old and New: St. Petersburg in the Late Imperial Era'. In Michael Hamm (ed.), *The City in Late Imperial Russia*, pp. 43–78. Bloomington: Indiana University Press.

Bater, James H. 1976. *St. Petersburg: Industrialization and Change*. Montreal: McGill-Queen's University Press.

Blackburn, David. 2007. *The Conquest of Nature: Water, Landscape, and the Making of Modern Germany*. New York: W.W. Norton & Company.

Blackford, Mansel G. 2016. *Columbus, Ohio: Two Centuries of Business and Environmental Change*. Columbus: Trillium and Ohio State University Press.

Bogue, Margaret Beattie. 2000. *Fishing the Great Lakes: An Environmental History, 1783–1933*. Madison, WI: University of Wisconsin Press.

Boreiko, Vladimir Evgen'evich. 1994. *Askania-Nova: Tiazhkie versty istorii (1826–1993)*. Kiev: Kievskii ekologo-kul'turnyi tsentr.

Bravo, Michael and Sverker Sörlin. 2002. 'Narrative and Practice – an Introduction'. In Michael Bravo and Sverker Sörlin (eds), *Narrating the Arctic: A Cultural History of Nordic Scientific Practices*, pp. 3–32. Canton, MA: Science History Publications.

Bravo, Michael and Sverker Sörlin (eds). 2002. *Narrating the Arctic: A Cultural History of Nordic Scientific Practices*. Canton, MA: Science History Publications.

Breyfogle, Nicholas. 2018. 'Toward an Environmental History of Tsarist Russia and the Soviet Union'. In Breyfogle (ed.), *Eurasian Environments: Nature and Ecology in Imperial Russian and Soviet History*, pp. 3–19. Pittsburgh: University of Pittsburgh Press.

David Moon, Nicholas B. Breyfogle, Alexandra Bekasova and Julia Lajus

Breyfogle, Nicholas (ed.). 2018. *Eurasian Environments: Nature and Ecology in Imperial Russian and Soviet History*. Pittsburgh: University of Pittsburgh Press.

Breyfogle, Nicholas and Mark Sokolsky. 2020. 'Introduction to Water History'. In Nicholas Breyfogle and Mark Sokolsky (eds), *Readings in Water History*, pp. v–x. San Diego: Cognella Academic Publishing.

Breyfogle, Nicholas and Philip Brown (eds). 2021. *Hydraulic Societies: Water, Power, and Control in Greater Eurasia History*. Corvallis, OR: Oregon State University Press.

Breyfogle, Nicholas, Abby Schrader and Willard Sunderland (eds). 2007. *Peopling the Russian Periphery: Borderland Colonization in Eurasian History*. New York: Routledge.

Broich, John. 2013. *London: Water and the Making of the Modern City*. Pittsburgh: University of Pittsburgh Press.

Brown, Kate. 2015. *Dispatches from Dystopia: Histories of Places Not Yet Forgotten*. Chicago: University of Chicago Press.

Bruno, Andy. 2016. *The Nature of Soviet Power: An Arctic Environmental History*. New York: Cambridge University Press.

Bruno, Andy. 2018. 'Climate History of Russia and the Soviet Union'. *WIREs Climate Change* 9:e534. https://doi.org/10.1002/wcc.534.

Candiani, Vera. 2014. *Dreaming of Dry Land: Environmental Transformation in Colonial Mexico City*. Stanford: Stanford University Press.

Casey, Edward S. 2007. 'Boundary, Place, and Event in the Spatiality of History'. *Rethinking History* 11 (4): 507–512.

Casey, Edward S. 1993. *Getting Back into Place: Toward a Renewed Understanding of the Place-World*. Bloomington: Indiana.

Cathcart, Michael. 2010. *The Water Dreamers: The Remarkable History of Our Dry Continent*. Melbourne: The Text Publishing Company.

Chakars, Melissa. 2014. *The Socialist Way of Life in Siberia: Transformation in Buryatia*. Budapest: Central European University Press.

Chu, Pey-Yi. 2020. *The Life of Permafrost: A History of Frozen Earth in Russian and Soviet Science*. Toronto: University of Toronto Press.

Cioc, Mark. 2006. *The Rhine: An Eco-Biography, 1815–2000*. Seattle: University of Washington Press.

Coates, Peter, David Moon and Paul Warde (eds). 2016. *Local Places, Global Processes: Histories of Environmental Change in Britain and Beyond*. Oxford: Oxbow Books/ Windgather Press.

Costlow, Jane. 2012. *Heart-Pine Russia: Walking and Writing the Nineteenth-Century Forest*. Ithaca, NY: Cornell University Press.

Courtney, Chris. 2018. *The Nature of Disaster in China: The 1931 Yangzi River Flood*. New York: Cambridge University Press.

Place and Nature: An Introduction

Cronon, William. 1996. 'The Trouble with Wilderness: Or, Getting Back to the Wrong Nature'. *Environmental History* **1** (1): 7–28.

Davis, Mike. 2017. *Late Victorian Holocausts: El Niño Famines and the Making of the Third World*. New York: Verso.

Demuth, Bathsheba. 2019. *Floating Coast: An Environmental History of the Bering Strait*. New York: W.W. Norton & Company.

Dills, Randall. 2014. 'Cracks in the Granite: Paternal Care, the Imperial Façade, and the Limits of Authority in the 1824 St. Petersburg Flood'. *Journal of Urban History* **40** (3): 479–96.

D'Souza, Rohan. 2006. *Drowned and Dammed: Colonial Capitalism and Flood Control in Eastern India*. New Delhi: Oxford University Press.

Ducarme, Frédéric and Denis Couvet. 2020. 'What Does "Nature" Mean?' *Palgrave Communications* **6** (14). https://doi.org/10.1057/s41599-020-0390-y.

Dulov, A.V. 1983. *Geograficheskaia sreda i istoriia Rossii: konets XV–seredina XIX v.* Moscow: Nauka.

Eklund N., J. Lajus, V. Borovoy, E. Kalemeneva, D.L. Lajus, D. Stogova, A. Vlakhov and U. Wråkberg. 2019. 'Imageries and Historical Change in the European Russian Arctic'. In E. Carina H. Keskitalo (ed.), *The Politics of Arctic Resources. Change and Continuity in the 'Old North' of Northern Europe*, pp. 200–220. New York: Routledge.

Ely, Christopher. 2002. *This Meager Nature: Landscape and National Identity in Imperial Russia*. DeKalb: Northern Illinois University Press.

Environmental History Now. 2020. 'Problems of Place'. https://envhistnow.com/category/problemsofplace/.

Fagan, Brian M. 2017. *Fishing: How the Sea Fed Civilization*. New Haven: Yale University Press.

Forsyth, James. 1992. *A History of the Peoples of Siberia: Russia's North Asian Colony, 1581–1990*. New York: Cambridge University Press.

Gandy, Mathew. 2014. *The Fabric of Space: Water, Modernity, and the Urban Imagination*. Cambridge, MA: MIT Press.

Gissibl, Bernhard, Sabine Höhler and Patrick Kupper (eds). 2012. *Civilizing Nature: National Parks in Global Historical Perspective*. New York: Berghahn Books.

Grant, Bruce. 1995. *In the Soviet House of Culture: A Century of Perestroikas*. Princeton, NJ: Princeton University Press.

Green, Heather D. 2019. 'Problems of Place: The Importance of Place in Research'. *Environmental History Now*. 7 March. https://envhistnow.com/2019/03/07/the-importance-of-place-in-research/.

Hill, Fiona and Clifford G. Gaddy. 2003. *The Siberian Curse: How Communist Planners Left Russia out in the Cold*. Washington, DC: Brookings Institution Press.

Howkins, Adrian, Marianna Dudley, Peter Coates, Tamsin Badcoe, Sage Brice, Andy Flack, Daniel Haines, Paul Merchant, Laurence Publicover, Richard Stone and Alice Would. 2019. 'An Excursion in the Environmental Humanities: Some Thoughts on Fieldwork, Collaboration, and Disciplinary Identity Following a Day Trip to the Island of Lundy'. *Green Letters: Studies in Ecocriticism* **23** (1): 39–53.

Howkins, Adrian, Jared Orsi and Mark Fiege (eds). 2016. *National Parks beyond the Nation: Global Perspectives on 'America's Best Idea'*. Norman, OK: University of Oklahoma Press.

IUCN. 2020. 'Protected Area Categories'. https://www.iucn.org/theme/protected-areas/about/protected-area-categories.

Jones, Robert E. 2013. *Bread upon the Waters: The St. Petersburg Grain Trade and the Russian Economy, 1703–1811*. Pittsburgh: University of Pittsburgh Press.

Jones, Ryan Tucker. 2014. *Empire of Extinction: Russians and the North Pacific's Strange Beasts of the Sea, 1741–1867*. New York: Oxford University Press.

Jones, Toby Craig. 2010. *Desert Kingdom: How Oil and Water Forged Modern Saudi Arabia*. Cambridge, MA: Harvard University Press.

Jørgensen, Dolly. 2013. 'Environmentalists on Both Sides: Enactments in the California Rigs-to-Reefs Debate'. In Dolly Jørgensen, Finn Arne Jørgensen and Sara Pritchard (eds), *New Natures: Joining Environmental History with Science and Technology Studies*, pp. 51–68. Pittsburgh: University of Pittsburgh Press.

Josephson, Paul. 2008. 'The Ocean's Hot Dog: The Development of the Fish Stick'. *Technology and Culture* **49** (1): 41–61.

Josephson, Paul. 2014. *The Conquest of the Russian Arctic*. Cambridge, MA: Harvard University Press.

Josephson, Paul. 1997. *New Atlantis Revisited: Akademgorodok, the Siberian City of Science*. Princeton, NJ: Princeton University Press.

Josephson, Paul. 2002. *Industrialized Nature: Brute Force Technology and the Transformation of the Natural World*. Washington, DC: Island Press.

Josephson, Paul, Nicolai Dronin, Ruben Mnatsakanian, Aleh Cherp, Dmitry Efremenko and Vladislav Larin. 2013. *An Environmental History of Russia*. New York: Cambridge University Press.

Kassabova, Kapka. 2017. *Border: A Journey to the Edge of Europe*. London: Granta.

Kern, Stephen. 1983. *The Culture of Time and Space, 1880–1918*. Cambridge, MA: Harvard University Press.

Keskitalo, E. Carina H. (ed.). 2019. *The Politics of Arctic Resources: Change and Continuity in the 'Old North' of Northern Europe*. London and New York: Routledge.

Kivelson, Valerie A. 2006. *Cartographies of Tsardom: The Land and its Meanings in Seventeenth-Century Russia*. Ithaca, NY: Cornell University Press.

Kraikovski, Alexei. 2015. '"The Sea on One Side, Trouble on the Other": Russian Marine Resource Use before Peter the Great'. *Slavonic and East European Review* **93** (1): 39–65.

Kraikovski, Alexei. 2019. 'Profits from under the Water: The International Blubber Market, Russian Monopolistic Companies and the Idea of Whaling Development in the Eighteenth Century'. *International Journal of Maritime History* **31** (1): 34–49.

Kraikovski, Alexei and Julia Lajus. 2010. 'The Neva as a Metropolitan River of Russia: Environment, Economy and Culture'. In Terje Tvedt and Richard Coopey (eds), *A History of Water*. Series II, Vol. 2, *Rivers and Society: From Early Civilizations to Modern Times*, pp. 339–64. London: I.B. Tauris.

Kraikovski, Alexei and Julia Lajus. 2017. 'Living on the River over the Year: The Significance of the Neva to Imperial St. Petersburg'. In Martin Knoll, Uwe Lubken and Dieter Schott (eds), *Rivers Lost, Rivers Regained: Rethinking City-River Relations*, pp. 235–252. Pittsburgh: Pittsburgh University Press.

Kraikovski, Alexei and Julia Lajus. 2019. 'The Metropolitan Bay: Spatial Imaginary of Imperial St. Petersburg and Maritime Heritage of the Gulf of Finland'. *Humanities* **8** (1): 1–12.

Kupper, Patrick. 2014. *Creating Wilderness: A Transnational History of the Swiss National Park*. New York: Berghahn Books.

Lajus, Julia. 2011. 'Colonization of the Russian North: A Frozen Frontier'. In Christina Folke-Ax, Niels Brimnes, Niklas Thode Jensen and Karen Oslund (eds), *Cultivating the Colony: Colonial States and their Environmental Legacies*, pp. 164–190. Athens, OH: Ohio University Press.

Lajus, Julia. 2018. 'Russian Environmental History: A Historiographical Overview'. In S. Ravi Rajan and Lise Sedrez (eds), *The Great Convergence: Environmental Histories of BRICS*, pp. 245–73. Oxford: Oxford University Press.

Lajus, Julia. 2013. 'In Search for Instructive Models: The Russian State at a Crossroads to Conquering the North'. In Dolly Jørgensen and Sverker Sörlin (eds), *Northscapes: History, Technology, and the Making of Northern Environments*, pp. 110–136. Vancouver: University of British Columbia Press.

Lajus, Julia, Alexei Kraikovski and Alexei Yurchenko. 2009. 'Sea Fisheries in the Russian North c. 1400–1850'. In David J Starkey, Jon Th. Thor and Ingo Heidbrink (eds), *A History of the North Atlantic Fisheries*. Vol. 1, *From Early Times to the Mid-Nineteenth Century*, 41–64. Bremerhaven: Deutsches Schiffahrtsmuseum.

Langston, Nancy. 2017. *Sustaining Lake Superior: An Extraordinary Lake in a Changing World*. New Haven: Yale University Press.

Lantzeff, George V. and Richard A. Pierce. 1973. *Eastward to Empire: Exploration and Conquest on the Russian Open Frontier to 1750*. Montreal: McGill-Queen's University Press.

David Moon, Nicholas B. Breyfogle, Alexandra Bekasova and Julia Lajus

LeCain, Timothy J. 2017. *The Matter of History: How Things Create The Past*. New York: Cambridge University Press.

Lincoln, W. Bruce. 2007. *The Conquest of a Continent: Siberia and the Russians*. Ithaca, NY: Cornell University Press.

Linkhoeva, Tatiana. 2020. *Revolution Goes East: Imperial Japan and Soviet Communism*. Ithaca, NY: Cornell University Press.

Martin, Janet. 1988. 'Russian Expansion in the Far North. X to mid-XVI Century'. In Michael Rywkin (ed.), *Russian Colonial Expansion to 1917*, pp. 23-44. London: Mansell Publishing Ltd.

McCarthy, Tom. 2009. 'A Natural Intersection: A Survey of Historical Work on Mobility and the Environment'. In Gijs Mom, Gordon Pirie and Laurent Tissot (eds), *Mobility in History: The State of the Art in the History of Transport, Traffic and Mobility*. Neuchatel: Editions Alphil–Presses universitaires suisses.

McGucken, William. 2000. *Lake Erie Rehabilitated: Controlling Cultural Eutrophication, 1960s–1990s*. Akron, OH: University of Akron Press.

McNeill, J.R. 2000. *Something New Under the Sun: An Environmental History of the Twentieth-Century World*. New York: W.W. Norton & Company.

McNeill, J.R. and Peter Engelke. 2014. *The Great Acceleration: An Environmental History of the Anthropocene since 1945*. Cambridge, MA: The Belknap Press of Harvard University Press.

Melosi, Martin. 2008. *The Sanitary City: Environmental Services in Urban America from Colonial Times to the Present*. Pittsburgh: University of Pittsburgh Press.

Mithen, Steven. 2012. *Thirst: Water and Power in the Ancient World*. Cambridge, MA: Harvard University Press.

Moon, David. 2017. 'The Curious Case of the Marginalization or Distortion of Russian and Soviet Environmental History in Global Environmental Histories'. *International Review of Environmental History* **3** (2): 31–50.

Moon, David. 2013. *The Plough that Broke the Steppes: Agriculture and Environment on Russia's Grasslands, 1700–1914*. Oxford: Oxford University Press.

Moon, David. 2005. 'The Environmental History of the Russian Steppes: Vasilii Dokuchaev and the Harvest Failure of 1891'. *Transactions of the Royal Historical Society* **15**: 149–174.

Moon, David (ed.). 2016. 'Russian Environmental History'. *Zotero.org*. https://www.zotero.org/groups/271874/russian_environmental_history/items/6UVBWWNA/library.

Morgan, Ruth. 2015. *Running Out? Water in Western Australia*. Crawley: University of Western Australia Publishing.

Muscolino, Micah S. 2014. *The Ecology of War in China: Henan Province, the Yellow River, and Beyond, 1938–1950*. New York: Cambridge University Press.

Natsional'na akademiia agrarnikh nauk. 2020. 'Biosfernii zapovednik "Askaniia-Nova" imeni F.E. Fal'ts-Feina'. http://askania-nova-zapovidnik.gov.ua/

Obertreis, Julia. 2017. *Imperial Desert Dreams: Cotton Growing and Irrigation in Central Asia, 1860–1991.* Göttingen: V&R Unipress.

Oldfield, Jonathan, Julia Lajus and Denis J.B. Shaw. 2015. 'Conceptualizing and Utilizing the Natural Environment: Critical Reflections from Imperial and Soviet Russia'. *Slavonic and East European Review* **93** (1): 1–15.

Opie, John, Char Miller and Kenna Lang Archer. 2018. *Ogallala: Water for a Dry Land.* Lincoln: University of Nebraska Press.

Peterson, Maya. 2019. *Pipe Dreams: Water and Empire in Central Asia's Aral Sea Basin.* New York: Cambridge University Press.

Pietz, David. 2015. *The Yellow River: The Problem of Water in Modern China.* Cambridge, MA: Harvard University Press.

Pratt, Mary Louise. 1992. *Imperial Eyes: Travel Writing and Transculturation.* New York: Routledge.

Randolph, John and Eugene M. Avrutin (eds). 2012. *Russia in Motion: Cultures of Human Mobility since 1850.* Urbana, IL: University of Illinois Press.

Resiner, Marc. 1993. *Cadillac Desert: The American West and Its Disappearing Water.* New York: Penguin Books.

Reynolds, Terry S. 1983. *Stronger than a Hundred Men: A History of the Vertical Water Wheel.* Baltimore: Johns Hopkins University Press.

Rieber, Alfred J. 2014. *The Struggle for the Eurasian Borderlands: From the Rise of Early Modern Empires to the End of the First World War.* New York: Cambridge University Press.

Roe, Alan. 2020. *Into Russian Nature: Tourism, Environmental Protection, and National Parks in the Twentieth Century.* Oxford: Oxford University Press.

Ruble, Blair A. 1998. *Leningrad: Shaping a Soviet City.* Berkeley: University of California Press.

Schimmelpenninck van der oye, David. 2001. *Toward the Rising Sun: Russian Ideologies of Empire and the Path to War with Japan.* DeKalb, IL: Northern Illinois University Press.

Schivelbusch, Wolfgang. 1987. *The Railway Journey: The Industrialization of Time and Space in the Nineteenth Century.* Foreword by A. Trachenberg. Berkeley and Los Angeles: University of California Press.

Shaw, Denis J.B. 2003. 'St. Petersburg and Geographies of Modernity'. In Anthony Cross (ed.), *St Petersburg, 1703–1825*, pp. 6–29. Basingstoke: Palgrave Macmillan.

Shaw, Denis J.B. 'The Settlement of European Russia during the Romanov Period (1613–1917)'. *Soviet Geography* **30** (3): 207–28.

Shtilmark, Feliks. 2003. *History of the Russian Zapovedniks, 1895–1995*. Translated by G.H. Harper. Edinburgh: Russian Nature Press.

Shulman, Elena. 2008. *Stalinism on the Frontier of Empire: Women and State Formation in the Soviet Far East*. New York: Cambridge University Press.

Siegelbaum, Lewis H. and Leslie P. Moch. 2014. *Broad Is My Native Land: Repertoires and Regimes of Migration in Russia's Twentieth Century*. Ithaca, NY: Cornell University Press.

Sneddon, Christopher. 2015. *Concrete Revolution: Large Dams, Cold War Geopolitics, and the US Bureau of Reclamation*. Chicago: University of Chicago Press.

Sokolsky, Mark. 2016. 'Taming Tiger Country: Colonization and Environment in the Russian Far East, 1860–1940'. PhD diss., Ohio State University.

Steinberg, Ted. 2006. *Acts of God: The Unnatural History of Natural Disaster in America*. New York: Oxford University Press.

Stephan, John J. 1994. *The Russian Far East: A History*. Stanford: Stanford University Press.

Stine, Jeffrey K. and Joel A. Tarr. 1998. 'At the Intersection of Histories: Technology and the Environment'. *Technology and Culture* 39 (4): 601–640.

Storm, Anna. 2014. *Post-Industrial Landscape Scars*. New York: Palgrave Macmillan.

Sunderland, Willard. 2012. 'Ermak Timofeevich (1530s/40s–1585)'. In Stephen M. Norris and Willard Sunderland (eds), *Russia's People of Empire: Life Stories from Eurasia, 1500 to the Present*, pp. 16–25. Bloomington, IN: Indiana University Press.

Sörlin, Sverker and Paul Warde. 2009. 'Making the Environment Historical – An Introduction'. In Sverker Sörlin and Paul Warde (eds), *Nature's End: History and the Environment*, pp. 1–19. Basingstoke: Palgrave Macmillan.

TeBrake, William H. 2002. 'Taming the Waterwolf: Hydraulic Engineering and Water Management in the Netherlands during the Middle Ages'. *Technology and Culture* 43 (3): 475–499.

Teichmann, Christian. 2016. *Macht der Unordnung: Stalins Herrschaft in Zentralasien 1920–1950*. Hamburg: Hamburger Edition.

Tichotsky, John. 2000. *Russia's Diamond Colony: The Republic of Sakha*. Amsterdam: Harwood Academic.

Treadgold, Donald W. 1957. *The Great Siberian Migration: Government and Peasant in Resettlement from Emancipation to the First World War*. Princeton: Princeton University Press.

Tuan, Yi-Fu. 1977. *Space and Place: The Perspective of Experience*. Minneapolis: University of Minnesota Press.

Tuan, Yi-Fu. 1974. *Topophilia: A Study of Environmental Perception, Attitudes, and Values*. Englewood Cliffs, NJ: Prentice-Hall.

Tvedt, Terje. 2016. *Water and Society: Changing Perceptions of Societal and Historical Development.* New York: I.B. Tauris.

Vitebsky, Piers. 2005. *The Reindeer People: Living with Animals and Spirits in Siberia.* Boston: Houghton Mifflin.

Wakild, Emily. 2011. *Revolutionary Parks: Conservation, Social Justice, and Mexico's National Parks, 1910–1940.* Tucson: University of Arizona Press.

Warde, Paul. 2016. 'The Environment'. In Peter Coates, David Moon and Paul Warde (eds), *Local Places, Global Processes: Histories of Environmental Change in Britain and Beyond,* pp. 32–46. Oxford: Windgather Books.

Weiner, Douglas R. 1988. *Models of Nature: Ecology, Conservation and Cultural Revolution in Soviet Russia.* Bloomington: Indiana University Press.

Weiner, Douglas R. 1999. *A Little Corner of Freedom: Russian Nature Protection from Stalin to Gorbachev.* Berkeley: University of California Press.

White, Richard. 1995. *The Organic Machine: The Remaking of the Columbia River.* New York: Hill and Wang.

White, Richard. 2012. *Railroaded: The Transcontinentals and the Making of Modern America.* New York: W.W. Norton & Company.

Williams, Rosalind. 2000. 'Nature out of Control: Cultural Origins and Environmental Implications of Large Technical Systems'. In Miriam R. Levin (ed.), *Cultures of Control,* pp. 41–68. Amsterdam: Hardwood Academic.

Wood, Alan (ed.). 1987. *Siberia: Problems and Prospects for Regional Development.* Beckenham: Croom Helm.

Young, Jay, Ben B. Radley and Colin M. Coates. 2016. 'Moving Natures in Canadian History: An Introduction'. In Jay Young, Ben B. Radley and Colin M. Coates (eds), *Moving Natures: Mobility and the Environment in Canadian History,* pp. 1–22. Calgary: University of Calgary Press, 2016.

Zeller, Thomas. 2007. *Driving Germany: The Landscape of the German Autobahn, 1930–1970.* New York: Berghahn Books.

Znamenski, Andrei A. 1999. *Shamanism and Christianity: Native Encounters with Russian Orthodox Missions in Siberia and Alaska, 1820–1917.* Westport, CT: Greenwood Press.

Zhang, Ling. 2016. *The River, the Plain, and the State: An Environmental Drama in Northern Song China, 1048–1128.* New York: Cambridge University Press.

PART I.

THE NORTHWEST AND THE EUROPEAN
NORTH OF RUSSIA

2.

'THE SPACE OF BLUE AND GOLD': THE NATURE AND ENVIRONMENT OF SOLOVKI IN HISTORY AND HERITAGE

Alexei Kraikovski and Julia Lajus

The Solovetskie Islands, more commonly known as Solovki, are often described as 'the space of blue and gold' in guidebooks and other popular literature. The poet Sergei Esenin first described them this way as he travelled through the Russian North in 1917, characterising Solovki's combined natural features as a powerful, eternal force governing the behaviour of its human inhabitants.[1] This image provides a starting point for an environmental analysis of these 'most remarkable islands', which, in spite of being remote and small, occupy a significant place in Russian history.[2] Globally, Solovki is known as a place of cultural heritage, with the remarkable architecture of its medieval monastery, monuments connected with wars and other historical events across many centuries and sites of memory from the first Soviet concentration camp, known under the acronym SLON.[3] The uniqueness of this heritage is recognised for its intrinsic connection with the 'natural' world. The diverse human-built environment forms 'cultural landscapes' – of small monastic premises, roads, canals, dams, marine quays – that transition into the landscapes of the remote parts of the islands that look closer to their pre-human state and are surrounded by seascapes.[4]

---

1. See Zakharov, Savchenko and Drozdkov, *Letopis' zhizni i tvorchestva S. A. Esenina*, p. 46; Esenin, 'Nebo li takoe beloe'.

2. Robson, *Solovki*.

3. SLON is an acronym from the Russian words for 'Solovetskii [Labour] Camp of Special Designation'. *Slon* is also the Russian word for elephant.

4. Vedenin and Kuleshova, 'Kulturnyi landshaft kak ob"ekt kulturnogo i prirodnogo naslediia'.

'The Space of Blue and Gold'

Memories of the place and politics of Solovki's history are widely discussed and contested.[5] Most authors emphasise the uniqueness of the place not only because of its cultural and historical contexts, but also because of its natural features.[6] This chapter analyses the place of nature in the long-term history of Solovki and the transformation of the islands' 'nature' into 'environment'. Our analysis utilises Sverker Sörlin and Paul Warde's conceptualisation of the difference between nature and environment. They define environment as a product of the process of 'environing' – the transformation of nature under human activities.[7] They argue, 'Nature needs no humans, but there is an environment only where humans live and where humans have entered into a self-conscious relationship with their surroundings.'[8] This chapter responds to Sörlin and Warde's call to avoid conflating environment and nature in historical narratives.

In the case of Solovki, nature existed, and exists, side by side with humans. Monks perceived it in its spiritual connections with religious practices; scientists considered it as a set of objects for scientific observations and experiments; and museum professionals, touristic guides and visitors saw it as an ideal for imagination and conservation. In all these interactions with nature, humans perceived it ahistorically as eternal. However, when 'nature' is established as historical, it becomes 'environment'.[9] In the process of environing that began at Solovki many centuries ago with the monastic practices of nature transformation, then continued during the whole history of the human presence on the archipelago, a very distinct environment was created. It has two strongly contrasting parts. On one hand are cultural landscapes where nature has been environed under careful, spiritually rich governance and has long been considered invaluable heritage. On the other hand is an environment of the ordinary, everyday life of a small, poor northern settlement where people for decades have struggled for their wellbeing. Visitors who come to Solovki witness both, prizing the first and trying to avoid or close their eyes to the second. Many visitors also want

---

5.   See Bogumił and Voronina, 'Islands of One Archipelago'; Shtorn and Buteiko, 'Bor'ba za ogranichennoe prostranstvo pamiati na Solovkakh'.

6.   Sobolev, *Priroda Solovetskikh ostrovov.* The best-known general books remain Skopin, *Na Solovetskikh ostrovakh* and Skopin, *Solovki.* See also Kolosova, *Prirodno-geografich-eskii analiz istoricheskikh territorii.*

7.   Sörlin and Warde, 'Making the Environment Historical – An Introduction'; for further development of this methodology, see Sörlin and Wormbs, 'Environing Technologies: A Theory of Making Environment'.

8.   Ibid., pp. 2–3.

9.   Ibid., p. 3.

Alexei Kraikovski and Julia Lajus

to overcome both kinds of environments. They search for a 'real nature' – for a wilderness which they sincerely believe exists.[10]

This chapter is divided into three parts. First, it considers the monastic experience of nature and its environing effects. It then discusses pilgrim and tourist perceptions of religious and managerial monastic practices of nature and environment at Solovki in order to explore the construction of the iconic image of the islands. Finally, the paper briefly analyses the history of scientific research on Solovki and discusses scientific encounters with nature as a part of its environmental heritage. The overall aim of the chapter is to analyse the entangled vision of Solovki during almost six centuries of its history. It was a dynamic narrative of multifaceted interaction between changeable human societies and fragile northern nature that was transforming into environment during these centuries, giving rise to a profound cultural myth.

The Solovetskie Islands, an archipelago of six large and more than a hundred small islands, are situated in the White Sea about fifty kilometres from the mainland and 165 kilometres south of the Arctic Circle. The archipelago's diverse landscapes include marshy plains, impressive rock formations, extensive boreal forests and abundant fresh water in numerous lakes. Its climate is milder than that in the interior of the Russian North due to the influence of the sea. There are no big predators or snakes on the islands, making it more comfortable for early settlers and even creating a myth that some large predators, such as wolves, were expelled from the island by the saints who founded the monastery. In general, the number of mammal species on the islands is only a quarter of that on the mainland nearby. Conversely, the number of bird species is very high, including rare and threatened species. The aquatic life on and around the islands is also quite rich. It includes commercial species of fish, especially the White Sea herring (with its local population named Solovki herring), navaga, plaice and cod, five species of freshwater fish and marine mammals, including beluga whales and two species of seals.[11]

Orthodox monks reached the islands seeking to establish the ideal Christian life, and in 1438 they founded the monastery.[12] In 1478, the Novgorod republic, which had supervised the monastery, became a part of the Muscovite

---

10. For methodological discussions on the constructive character of wilderness, see Cronon, 'The Trouble with the Wilderness'; Adelson et al. (eds), *Environment*, pp. 280–310.

11. Sobolev, *Priroda Solovetskikh ostrovov*.

12. The process of expansion of the monasteries to the frontier areas of Russia is known as the monastic colonisation of the Russian North. See Fennell, *A History of the Russian Church to 1488*, pp. 207–09.

state, and the new sovereign offered even better support to the Solovki monks.[13] The monastery received numerous economic and taxation privileges and developed a sophisticated infrastructure, including a transportation network and industrial facilities controlled by the monks on the islands and in the large coastal areas. In the seventeenth century, the church dominated the regional salt market and governed the rich fishing grounds along the coasts of the White Sea and its rivers.[14] Across many centuries, the monastery remained one of the most powerful, rich and artistically impressive spiritual, administrative, economic and cultural centres of the Russian North. After the secularisation of church lands in 1764, when state authorities confiscated monastic possessions in most of Russia, the archipelago itself with all its resources remained in the monastery's possession. This lasted until 1920, when the new Soviet government dissolved the monastic brotherhood. Valuable church belongings were confiscated, and the monastery building was destroyed in a terrible fire. In 1923, the Soviet government established on the islands the Gulag camp that existed until 1939, with the transformation from a camp to a prison. Then the Soviet navy assumed control over the islands and in 1944 founded a settlement near the abandoned monastery premises.

In 1967, the monastery architectural remains became the core of the Solovetskii State Historical-Architectural Museum-Reserve, at first a branch of the Arkhangel'sk Museum of Local Lore. In 1974, it became independent and the word 'natural' was added to its name. Many backpackers, after looking at the semi-ruined architecture, then hiked off to spend time in nature. In October 1990, the monastery reopened and, after the collapse of the Soviet Union in 1991, all military activities were stopped at Solovki. A year later, UNESCO listed the site as a world cultural heritage object. Currently, about 900 residents live in the settlement whilst the monastery has a brotherhood of about ninety people of various statuses. The monastery is rapidly expanding, restoring its old premises not only on Bol'shoi Solovetskii Island but also, since 2000, on the island of Anzer, once established and now revived as a particularly spiritual place with landscapes less transformed by humans.

---

13.   For details, see Birnbaum, *Lord Novgorod the Great.*

14.   For details, see Ivanov, *Monastyri i monastyrskie krest'iane v XVI–XVII vekakh*; Savich, *Solovetskaia votchina XV–XVII v.*; Lajus et al., 'The Use of Historical Catch Data to Trace the Influence of Climate on Fish Populations'; Lajus et al., 'Sea Fisheries in the Russian North c. 1400–1850'; Kraikovski et al., 'Between Piety and Productivity'.

Alexei Kraikovski and Julia Lajus

Nature and Environment in Religious Space

Nature played a crucial role in the monastic community from the very beginning of Russian monastic life. The monastery could not have been built just anywhere. Indeed, the Orthodox hermits sought specific natural settings that could be conceptualised as a model of paradise on Earth. The location had to have special characteristics that made it suitable for an ideal Christian life. Monastic tradition offered narratives that explained the foundation of the monasteries through the direct intervention of supernatural power, indicating that a particular place was ordained to accommodate monks. For instance, the author of the Life of St. Zosima and St. Savvatii (Savvaty), two of the founders of the Solovetskii Monastery, describes an angel forcibly driving local fishermen from the islands by beating one of their wives, in order to reserve the blessed land exclusively for the monks. This episode became an important part of the local iconographic tradition, helping to substantiate the idea of the archipelago as a holy space.[15]

The concept of the holy space, as M. Dadykina has recently shown in the case of another monastery in the Russian North, is important for understanding the relationships between monks and island space, landscapes and waterscapes through their economic activities.[16] As monastic land possessions expanded across the islands, the monks had to build a sophisticated system of transportation to connect the different parts. Roads and water routes served as instruments of space management, transforming the archipelago into a unified holy space. All the different places of tamed nature/environment, in which monks organised everyday life and economic activity, were united into an undifferentiated, more abstract space, connected with both wild nature and divine holy space.[17] With no clear division between the spheres of natural, human and divine at this time, monks negotiated with nature through practices in which God and nature were united.[18] As a result, the landscape with its natural objects was subordinated to the 'religious space' created by the monastery.

The Solovetskii Monastery, however, is unique because the islands are surrounded by a sea, not a lake, more closely matching folklore references suggesting mythical islands always located 'in the sea, in the Ocean ...'. The

---

15. Mineeva, *Problemy kompleksnogo analiza drevnerusskogo agiograficheskogo teksta*, p. 147; Tutova et al., *Sokhranennye sviatyni Solovetskogo monastyria*, p. 52.

16. Dadykina, 'Upravliaia prostranstvom'.

17. Kivelson, *Cartographies of Tsardom*.

18. Arnold, *Negotiating the Landscape*, pp. 29–30.

topography of islands constitutes an important part of Russian Orthodox culture and cultural mythology. Islands are considered sacred spaces with both Edenic and infernal features, where mere humans undergo remarkable transformations alongside the surrounding nature.[19] Monasteries in Russia were quite often built on islands. One of the founders of Solovetskii Monastery, St. Savvatii, had been a monk at Valaam Monastery, located on an island in Lake Ladoga.[20] According to hagiography, he somehow learned about the existence of even more remote islands in the White Sea and reached them in order to find an isolated place for religious life. Not only had remoteness and isolation been important, but also, according to several examples of theophany in religious texts, it was a direct demand from God to a monk to create an abode amid untouched nature, signifying order and vision and fitting harmonically with the ascetic life of a hermit devoted to God.[21] The texts on Solovki emphasised the might of nature and the abundance of natural riches. The perception of Solovki as an earthly Eden in these texts was attributed to both groups of devotees: monks and pilgrims. God gave the islands to his hermits in order 'to show here on earth what would be granted to the righteous men there, at his Tsarsdom'.[22]

Thus the initial impetus of hermit life was to step out of history, with all its human deeds, and grow closer to God in the wilderness. The angel casting out the local fishermen was an attempt to veer away from the historical process of environing – a process that is, nonetheless, unavoidable to any human civilisation. To circumvent simple everyday environing, the monks transformed their practices of dealing with nature and its resources into a religiously bounded transformation (transfiguration): 'environing' of nature by its intentional 'improvement', making the landscape closer to ideal Edenic landscapes. The monks' arrival could be conceptualised as a reverse movement: from a historically defined 'environment' to a metaphysical space in which ahistorical 'nature' is embedded.

Transformation is the most important action for the islands' religious space and it is no coincidence that the main church of the Solovetskii Monastery is named the Cathedral of the Transfiguration, echoing the transfiguration of Christ in the Gospels. The conversion of a secular person into a monk is conceptualised as a profound transformation. All practices including dealing with nature became different afterward and these practices can only be understood

19. Maksimov, *Ostrovnye monastyri*; Gornitskaia and Larionova, *Mesto, kotorogo net....*

20. Parppei, *The Oldest One in Russia*, p. 19.

21. Popova, 'Semiotika sakralnogo prostranstva monastyrei Pomor'ia', p. 161.

22. Nemirovich-Danchenko, *Belomor'e i Solovki*, pp. 205–06.

properly in the context of monastic experience.[23] For Christians, especially monks, praying did not cease outside the church or other sanctuaries, but rather accompanied their entire engagement with 'nature' – and engagement that transformed it into 'environment'. The monks could not start any process, be it fishing, collecting timber or voyaging at sea, without consulting God and his saints. Among the saints the most important in the Russian Orthodox Church was St. Nicholas the Wonderworker, patron of travellers, especially at sea. Marine space was threatening and thus required more intensive praying, according to monastic and visitors' accounts.[24] Founders of the monastery who became saints themselves were considered of great assistance in people's encounters with the sea. In one of the earliest hagiographic documents, from before 1503, among 23 miracles they performed posthumously, nine were connected with natural perils at sea.[25]

Choosing the islands as an ultimate destination for developing monastic religious life, the first colonisers brought the Orthodox search for remote Edenic places face to face with the indigenous cultures of the Finno-Ugric and Sami peoples of the White Sea area, who considered islands parts of an alternative world and used them primarily as graveyards and sanctuaries. Monastic colonisation of the Russian North did not simply destroy the sacred world of indigenous cultures, but appropriated it and tried to fold it into the Orthodox cosmos.

The Solovetskii Monastery functioned on multiple levels in terms of nature and environment. The monastery appears to be a geographic point marking the spatial expansion of the Orthodox religious system to the distant North. It therefore manifested the area's unique character as a space having certain connections to supernatural forces, including God's protection for the local people. This perspective is described within the theoretical framework of the 'spatiality of religion'.[26] A second perspective, known as the 'contextuality of religion', considers how communities rework religious systems into local expression that makes the monastery an important element of the local culture.[27] Moreover, through this contextualisation, the monks' religious and economic practices became representations of 'Russianness' and 'Northern-

23. See the discussion of that idea in relation to the monastic water management in Kraikovski, Dadykina and Kalemeneva, 'The Water Management in the Russian Monasteries, 16th–18th cc.'; see also Arnold, *Negotiating the Landscape*, p. 7.

24. Kraikovski, '"The Sea on One Side, Trouble on the Other"', pp. 54–5.

25. Morozov, 'Morskie chudesa Solovetskikh sviatykh'.

26. Stump, *The Geography of Religion*, pp. 6–7.

27. Ibid.

ness'. This perspective is crucial when considering the history of interaction between newcomers, the local community and the cultural practices of visiting the islands. Finally, a third vision, namely the construction of social spaces, is useful to study the role of the monastery in shaping the social space beyond its immediate religious significance. This vision might be helpful today in considering heritage management and tourism in the context of the religious life of the monastic community.[28]

After the monastery was established, the community exerted multifaceted control over the area, including the technological management of the surrounding environment. In the sixteenth century, the monks transformed the environment of the islands through major infrastructural innovations and the acclimatisation of useful animals such as reindeer.[29] The hegumen Philip (Kolychev), who later became Metropolitan of Moscow and was canonised by the church as St. Philip, initiated the rebuilding of the monastic complex as a powerful fortress with the impressive Cathedral of the Transfiguration at the centre.[30] The hagiography of St. Philip described these projects as his personal concern as he 'dug up the big mountains, furrowed the valleys, directed the water from one lake to another, linked twenty lakes to a further fifty-two lakes, delivered a water supply to the monastery and … the convent, and constructed the mill for the brotherhood'.[31] Constructing the impressive network of canals required technical knowledge that Philip likely brought from Moscow, where he spent his childhood and would have observed the city's hydraulic engineering systems. The Russian capital adopted a number of technologies from Italy in the sixteenth century, including hydraulic expertise.[32]

Whilst building the infrastructure, the monks had always to keep in mind the specific features of the islands as a territory inseparable from the sea. Connection with and dependence on the sea formed a maritime cultural landscape that 'incorporates all behaviours, beliefs, activities, and physical

---

28. Ibid.

29. Fokina and Chernkova, '"Korabl' snegov" na Solovkakh', p. 147.

30. Brumfield, *Tradition and Innovation in the Sixteenth-Century Architecture of Solovetskii Transfiguration Monastery.*

31. Fedotov, *Sviatoi Filipp, Mitropolit moskovskii*, p. 164.

32. See Pod'iapolskii, 'Deiatelnost' italianskikh masterov na Rusi i v drugikh stranakh Evropy v kontse XV–nachale XVI veka'; see also, Shvidkovskii, *Russian Architecture and the West*, pp. 77–144.

and social constructs oriented socially and spatially towards maritimity'.[33] Maritimity – i.e. the combination of features informing the specific maritime character of the community – is especially visible through the lens of landscapes of mobility (inlets, dams, lighthouses, quays) through which most connections between the islands and mainland were maintained. One of the most visible examples is the stone dam at Muksalma that still serves as an exemplar of such a work among devotees of natural landscapes. Another example is 'Philip's fish cages' — stone receptacles that kept fish alive to be eaten later by the monks. At the same time, reindeer were imported and have thrived on the islands ever since. (At the very end of the nineteenth century about 300 reindeer lived on the islands).[34]

Thus, it is evident that, whilst prizing wild and sacred nature, the monks could not avoid 'environing' it. But they conceptualised this process through a religious worldview and their everyday practices. The example of Solovki serves to demonstrate the statement by Sörlin and Wormbs that 'invoking the environing turns the focus of environment not so much on the disturbance or destruction of it wrought by humans, but rather to a dynamic relationship with vast, sometimes threatening, but also resourceful surroundings that humans were meant to transform and could turn into an ever-changing product of their ingenuity and practice'.[35]

The monks developed and modernised the infrastructure over the centuries. Observers of the nineteenth and twentieth centuries, including pilgrims, created a model narrative basis for the Solovki myth, paying special attention to environmental control as an important characteristic of the holy space. Monks continued to transform nature on the island, both intentionally and otherwise. The best-known example was the creation of the Botanical Garden. Another instance was a transfer of lake whitefish (*riapushka*) from the Nikolskii fish hatchery in Novgorod region to Solovki, where its population grew rapidly.[36]

The writer and traveller Vasilii Nemirovich-Danchenko, who visited the archipelago in 1874, described the monks as some kind of 'experts on nature' who could implement technological control because they believed that the technical skills used were blessings of God rather than matters of education.[37] Mikhail

---

33. Caporaso, 'A Dynamic Processual Maritime Archaeological Landscape Formation Model', p. 7.

34. Fokina and Chernkova, '"Korabl' snegov" na Solovkakh'.

35. Sörlin and Wormbs, 'Environing Technologies'.

36. Alekseeva and Makhrov, 'O proiskhozhdenii riapushki na Solovetskikh ostrovakh'.

37. Nemirovich-Danchenko, *Belomor'e i Solovki*, pp. 289–90.

Prishvin, later a well-known writer, who in his younger years was interested in ethnography and travelled extensively in the Russian North, noted that when he mentioned to the monks that he came with a mission from the Russian Geographical Society to document the islands, the monks answered that they had no geography there at all. He explained that their 'geography' consisted of a unique combination of landscape management, economic activities and spiritual practices.[38] Therefore, the description of Solovki as a specific space where the monks obtained God's support in order to transform severe 'nature' into a controlled and well-organised 'environment' formed the background for tourist imaginings and descriptions of the archipelago.

Perceptions of Nature by Solovki Visitors

The monastery became a popular destination for visitors rather early. Before the 1917 revolution, most visits to Solovki were connected with pilgrimage. Pilgrims travelled to the spiritual centre on the White Sea area as early as the second half of the fifteenth century.[39] Thenceforth monastic authorities paid a lot of attention to the development of pilgrimage; the list of visitors includes some of the most prominent names among the Russian nobility, even ruling tsars. Two things in the history of visitations to Solovki are important from an environmental and spatial perspective in pre-modern and early modern times. First, pilgrimage practices made the development of transportation infrastructure a priority. Second, the visitors by themselves could become an important factor in the development of the archipelago as a heritage zone.

Isolated on the islands, the monastery needed to develop access to shipping to organise pilgrimage in a significant and 'industrial' way. This process is clearly seen in eighteenth-century shipping reports. For instance, in 1790, officials at the port of Arkhangel'sk recorded 52 vessels departing to Solovki, which was approximately seven per cent of the total outgoing domestic shipping at that harbour.[40] However, Arkhangel'sk was only one port for transportation to Solovki: the number of vessels that went to Solovki from the Karelian coast and the town of Onega was about four times higher; thus in 1777 only about one third of visitors came from Arkhangel'sk. The overall number of visitors grew from around 1,300 in the 1730s to more than 6,000 in the 1780s. In that

---

38.   Prishvin, *Za volshebnym kolobkom*.

39.   See Zhitenev, *Istoriia russkogo pravoslavnogo palomnichestva v X–XVII vekakh*, pp. 262–3.

40.   GAAO f. 1367, op. 2, d. 1223.

period, most pilgrims were men: only seven per cent were women in 1777.[41] In the second half of the eighteenth century, more than a thousand pilgrims could stay at the monastery at once.[42] In the early twentieth century, the annual number of pilgrims rose to about 20,000.[43]

The growing numbers of visitors were very profitable for the monastery and helped to sustain it after the secularisation of church property and the closing of the majority of monasteries in Russia in 1764. The most popular time to visit the islands was June, probably because peasant visitors wanted to return home by the harvest season. They may also have known that in the second half of the summer the winds were usually much stronger and thus sailing to and from Solovki could be quite risky.[44] Visitors most often chose to visit in late May and June for the feast day of the local saint, Philip, for Trinity Sunday (*Troitsa*), when Orthodox believers celebrated Pentecost, and for the feast day of Saints Peter and Paul. For the last feast day, the monastery usually organised a fair that attracted mostly local visitors.

Pilgrimage visits were organised by private ships according to domestic commercial shipping regulations, including petitions to the authorities for permission to leave a port with the pilgrims listed on the manifest.[45] Early eighteenth-century customs documents also demonstrate the system of taxing pilgrimage shipping, which was based on tithe payments and was overall the same as the taxation of commercial shipping. For instance, in 1710, Mikhailo Odinakii from Kholmogory delivered to Solovki 32 pilgrims who chartered his transportation boat (*izvoznyi karbas*) for 2 altyns (equal to 0.06 roubles) per person. In total, the skipper got 64 altyns (1 rouble 92 kopecks) and paid taxes of 6 altyns (18 kopecks).[46] In other words, the pilgrimage to Solovki made some contribution to the regional economy and infrastructure development. Only after the mid-nineteenth century did the monastery itself become an active participant in steamship development in the North to facilitate further increases

---

41. Bogdanova and Kopytova, 'Palomnichestvo v Solovetskii monastyr' vo vtoroi polovine XVIII veka', p. 55.

42. Ibid, p. 60.

43. Robson, 'Transforming Solovki', p. 49.

44. Robson, *Solovki*, p. 163.

45. For the general description of the shipping regulations see, Kraikovski, '"The Sea on One Side, Trouble on the Other"'; examples of petitions are kept for instance in: GAAO f. 1, op. 1, d. 3.

46. SPb II RAN f. 10, op. 3, d. 39, l. 2ob.

in the numbers of pilgrims.[47] Beginning in the 1880s, the recently organised Arkhangel'sk-Murman Steamship Company also operated trips to Solovki.[48]

The visits by Russian monarchs are especially demonstrative of the transformation of Solovki into a heritage zone. For instance, Peter I's visit to the archipelago in early June of 1694 was commemorated for his life narrowly being spared during a heavy storm. The second time Peter visited the monastery was in 1702, on his way with his army to Lake Ladoga and then to the Neva River, where St Petersburg was founded the following year. The tsar's visits were rather useful for the monastery, which managed to win new privileges. Moreover, the tsar's historic travels there made important contributions to the heritage of the archipelago.[49]

Thus, the Solovetskii Monastery occupied an important place in Russian travel literature.[50] Several things are important in these texts. Descriptions of the visits include conceptualisation of visitors' travel practices. In other words, the texts combine description of nature, analysis of the observers' intentions and the results of the observation. For instance, Petr Fedorov, a doctor who visited Solovki in the late 1880s, described his visit as an extremely hard and dangerous undertaking only possible for those who had a very strong personal intention to complete it. Indeed, he argued, from 15 to 25 per cent of pilgrims regularly died on the road. The pious trip itself took place in dirty conditions on board overcrowded barges with a high risk of disease. It was also expensive. As a result, Fedorov argued, the monastery received annually many fewer visitors than other big monasteries of the Russian North that were situated in more populated areas. However, Solovki pilgrims considered this trip a source of divine experience that could be had only there.[51]

Educated visitors were of course interested not only in the religious experience but also in the historic and artistic value of the monastery and the archipelago's unique landscapes. Pilgrims were religious visitors but also tourists in a more secular, material sense of the word. The ordinary pilgrims, whose main purpose was to attend church services, were also attentive to their

---

47. For a contemporary experience, see for instance Leikin, *Po Severu dikomu*, p. 148.

48. For a historical overview of the development of the Arkhangelsk-Murman Steamship Company see Owen, *Dilemmas of Russian Capitalism*, pp. 134–48.

49. See for details Bespiatykh, *Arkhangel'sk nakanune i v gody Severnoi voiny (1700–1721)*, pp. 157–62, 387–90.

50. See Pashkov, *Kareliia i Solovki glazami literatorov pushkinskoi epokhi*; Martynov, *Solovki v literature i folklore*.

51. Fedorov, *Solovki*, pp. 123–41.

surroundings. It was important for them that they were sailing to the island by a long voyage, placing their lives in the hands of God and the saints. During the voyage pilgrims could themselves re-experience the adventures of the saints, the founders of the monastery, which they knew about from the hagiographic literature. Thus, the religious experience for them began with nature, not just religious abstraction.

Visitors did not merely observe but also conceptualised the islands and the monastery in memoirs and other descriptions. Embedded in these texts is an image of Solovki as a part of the bigger concept of the Holy Land, the Russian Thebaid.[52] This image had been used for decades rather actively to describe and conceptualise the history of the colonisation of the extreme northern regions – transformation achieved through a combination of hard, pious work and Orthodox holiness to create a beneficial land blessed by God and settled with devoted Orthodox Christians living near numerous monasteries. This story eventually became part of the Solovki heritage and now serves as a basis for tourism.

The sea is perhaps the most important element shaping the tourist experience and touristic management practices. As Russia is a generally land-locked country, encounters with the sea hold special significance for Russian people. Most tourists, arriving by boat from the Karelian shore, encounter the sea before arriving at the monastery, which arises quite mysteriously in front of the boat after two hours' journey. A description of the marine voyage opens all the memoirs about travels to Solovki.[53]

Because the sea is so important for the overall image of Solovki, marine fauna became an attraction for its visitors. Fishing for cod and herring, or at least tasting them in a local cafe, is a significant experience of being near the sea. But the apotheosis of encountering marine fauna is whale watching. Since at least the nineteenth century, visitors have considered beluga whales a most worthy element of Solovki's wild nature. Nemirovich-Danchenko mentioned that a monk tried to show him a beluga whale from the shore, but he could see nothing and concluded that the whale watching on Solovki was only possible for the locals, who were used to the specific optics of the White Sea environment.[54] However, he observed whales from the steamship on the return from

52. The name referred to the desert area of central Egypt which became the cradle for monasticism in the first centuries of Christianity. See Muraviev, *Russkaia Fivaida na Severe*; Averianov, 'Severnaia Fivaida'; Ely, 'The Picturesque and the Holy'.

53. See, for a recent example, the Solovki photo essay by Nicholas Breyfogle in this volume.

54. Nemirovich-Danchenko, *Belomor'e i Solovki*, pp. 339–40.

Solovki and used this observation to begin a discussion of the link between the maritime character of the area with its intensive shipping and picturesque marine life and the recreational opportunities of the healthy climate and the possibility of swimming in the sea.[55]

Seagulls had a special meaning at Solovki, where their appearance was the first sign of spring. Gulls are the most common creatures to be met during the voyage to the islands, offering entertainment to the travellers. Most visitor accounts begin with notes about unbelievable numbers of the birds there and their protection by the monastery and pilgrims.[56] They even nested on the monastery grounds, where there were no dogs or other predators to disturb them. Bird hunting was forbidden at Solovki, as was the case at many other Russian monasteries.[57] People walked near or even over the nests, but the gulls were not afraid.[58] The more northerly Trifono-Pechengskii Monastery organised the conservation of eider duck nesting places on the islands in the Barents Sea, and the same is true about the Solovetskii Monastery, especially in its possessions in Onega Bay.[59]

In some texts, visitors draw clear distinctions between nature and environment. For instance, Mikhail Prishvin, at that time a young writer and traveller, wrote that the numerous wild birds and animals he had seen near the monastery or under monastic supervision all looked unreal, as if they were a specially designed show for visitors. Prishvin wanted to see wild nature, but apparently felt that the monks had substituted a well-organised, beautiful environment in place of wild nature.[60] He was upset to learn that idyllically constructed relationships with animals coexisted with cruel sealing and reindeer hunting that the monastery organised in more remote places.

However, Prishvin was disappointed with the religious practices on Solovki and turned to nature for the experience of holiness. He ended his travelogue with the following words: 'Solovki is really a Holy land, but ... but ... I believe in that only when I am feeding seagulls with pilgrims'.[61] Thus, he found quasi-religious experience in the unification of people and nature,

---

55. Ibid., p. 345.

56. See, for instance, Maksimov, 'Poezdka v Solovetskii monastyr'', p. 42, 56; Fausek, 'Na zoologicheskoi stantsii', p. 433- 4.

57. Kozhevnikov, 'Monastyri i okhrana prirody'.

58. Sluchevskii, *Poezdki po Severu Rossii v 1885–1886 godakh*, pp. 13- 4.

59. Goriashko, 'Attempts to Establish Eider Farms in the USSR, and Why These Failed'.

60. Prishvin, *Za volshebnym kolobkom*, pp. 88–91.

61. Ibid., p. 99.

Alexei Kraikovski and Julia Lajus

but was in reality dissatisfied with both – the people and the nature. Both had been distorted, driven far away from the ideal of a spiritually rich world that he tried but failed to find.

When Prishvin again travelled to Solovki in 1933 during the period of the Gulag, he mentioned the absence of gulls but wrote, 'I do not grieve about them too much, you know, I like wild birds, but monks understood too well the decorative meaning of seagulls. They preserved them, pilgrims fed them too much with their pies, and fat holy birds cried and pooped terribly'.[62] By this time, the decorative, artificial connections between partly tamed birds and religious monks and pilgrims lost its value along with the overall loss of holiness in Soviet Solovki. Nature was pushed further away, whilst environment moved closer. In general, during this terrible time, the perceptions of nature and environment were polarised. The human experience of environment was miserable, with endless everyday problems of coldness, lack of hygiene and so much more. Natural resources were heavily used (or, more correctly, misused) by ever-accelerating environing. It was quite symbolic that people who were imprisoned by the new Soviet power were forced to fell trees, destroying the unique landscapes of the islands that the tsars had so prized. Due to this destruction, no virgin wild forests remain at Solovki; what we see today is all new growth after there was no old-growth left to cut.

In order to escape all the brutality unleashed on the environment (for people and by people), prisoners sought instead a metaphysical nature in which they might find another reality where they could feel freedom and the presence of God. In their memoirs, they often mentioned that the closeness to nature helped them keep their hope and their sanity. Some remembered finding consolation and sanctuary in the wilderness, something completely unrelated to the human filth of the Gulag.[63] Imprisoned believers saw the forest as a church and used the concealment of groundcover for praying. The absence of large carnivorous animals gave additional metaphysical proof that the Solovki forests were peaceful, beginning from the times of the monastery's founders, who sent all dangerous animals away from the islands. On a different level, forces of nature, like the sea, wind or open sky could be perceived as infernal and elicited a feeling of godforsakenness among the prisoners.[64] They felt that reality on Solovki was deceptive and the after-world was proximate.[65] Such a

62. Prishvin, 'Beloe more', p.112.

63. Volkov, *Pogruzhenie vo t'mu*, p. 451.

64. Umniagin, 'Priroda i okruzhaiuschii mir v vospominaniiakh solovetskikh uznikov'.

65. Likhachev, *Vospominaniia*, p. 173.

perception of nature is tightly connected with the overall meaning of Solovki – both in the previous centuries and in the times of the labour camp – as place of trial and the possible elevation of man by overcoming evil.[66]

The archipelago certainly was not a destination for tourism between the 1920s and 1960s. However, in the early period of the Gulag, the islands were partly open for visitors, not only for officials and such luminaries as Maksim Gor'kii – invited with the express purpose of providing a positive image of the camp for the Soviet people – but also ordinary excursionists, including schoolchildren from local towns on the coast. After 1933, when the Solovki labour camp was dissolved and became a branch of a larger camp and then transformed into a prison, the islands were much more closed.

The situation would change only after 30 August 1960, when the Council of Ministers of the RSFSR issued a resolution 'On the further improvement of the protection of monuments in the RSFSR'. The document mentioned the archaeological sites of the Solovki archipelago among valuable monuments that had to be 'put in order and transformed into objects of museum demonstration'.[67] Subsequently, the past became one of the most important foci of cultural work as 'political elites attempted to establish new sites of national memory that could bind the country together'.[68] Therefore, the rapid development of local historical knowledge combined with observation and representation of the cultural heritage can be considered the 'local dimension' of this process.[69] Thus, beginning in the 1960s, tourists appeared on the archipelago in greater and greater numbers, and they began to envision Solovki anew.

The logistics of Soviet tourism – similar to the pre-revolutionary ones – were built on the sea transportation, and the very trip to Solovki was advertised as an entertaining cruise. In the 1980s, the network of touristic routes from coastal points to the islands was impressively wide. For instance, it included regular connections to Kandalaksha – a rather small settlement in the north-western corner of the White Sea – not to mention big centres like Arkhangel'sk and Murmansk.[70] 'Comfortable tourist ships' for recreational tourism in Arctic waters, including the Solovki archipelago, are mentioned in descriptions of the

---

66. Umniagin, *Obraz Solovkov v russkoi literature XX veka*, p. 27.

67. Council of Ministers of the RSFSR, 'O dal'neishem uluchshenii dela okhrany paniatnikov kul'tury v RSFSR'.

68. Donovan, '"How Well Do You Know Your Krai?"', pp. 464–83.

69. Ibid.

70. See Golubev, 'Belomorskie reisy Kanina', p. 14.

Alexei Kraikovski and Julia Lajus

new Soviet Arctic – a space that was technologically advanced and habitable for the builders of communism.[71]

Anti-communist Russian émigrés immediately and heavily criticised Soviet tourism to the Solovketskie Islands. For instance, in December 1966 the Russian émigré journal *Chasovoi* (issued in Belgium) published an article representing the Soviet tourism industry on Solovki as a perfect example of cynicism. What the Soviet authors described as a manifestation of patriotism by visiting a remarkable heritage site of national importance, one anti-Soviet journalist labelled as frivolous pastime on a site of national tragedy. Solovki, to his mind, was a place exclusively for praying, not for recreation.[72]

Soviet authorities attempted to offer a conception of the islands as suitable for tourists, but in the context of Soviet secularism, religious sites could not be popular destinations. Religion as such was to be separated from the everyday life of the Soviet commoner. It was represented in specialised museums and studied in research institutions as a phenomenon of the past.[73] The atheistic state had to offer Soviet tourists an acceptable interpretation of the region's religious heritage. The Soviet state thus asked tourists to see an icon as a masterpiece of art and a church as an architectural feat. Through this perspective, the monastic complexes were supposed to 'revive for travellers the glorious pages of the Russian past'.[74] In order to 'hide' religious meaning, this Soviet paradigm represented the Solovki Monastery to the public in a variety of ways, including as a fortress defending the Russian North from foreign invaders.[75] The Gulag legacy, certainly, was completely hidden. As a result, the natural wonders – as an attractive alternative to the religious past – necessarily occupied an important place in the image of the archipelago offered to its tourists. It is possible to conclude even that the search for wilderness was one of the prime attractions for tourists visiting Solovki at that time. Today, at least thirty per cent visit for that reason, according to sociological surveys.[76]

---

71. See for instance, Kiselev and Tulin, *Kniga o Murmanske*, p. 66.

72. See Bondarenko, 'Vershiny tsinizma', p. 21.

73. For instance, in the Museum of Religion and Atheism that was placed in Kazan' Cathedral in Leningrad, one of the few museums of that kind in the world. See for more detailed analysis Takahashi, 'Religion as an Object of Science in Atheistic Society', pp. 11–9.

74. Zeldina, *Po Sovetskoi Rossii*, p. 10.

75. See for instance, Frolov and Zakharchenko, *Solovetskie ostrova*.

76. Shtorn and Buteiko, 'Bor'ba za ogranichennoe prostranstvo pamiati na Solovkakh', p. 248.

The remains of the monastery and such cultural landscapes as roads and canals lent yet more appeal to a place with a long history of human interaction and struggle with nature.

Research and the Production of Heritage: Solovki Nature and Environment through the Lens of Knowledge

The first naturalists to visit Solovki arrived at the end of the eighteenth century. In June 1772, academician Ivan Lepekhin, member of an expedition organised by the Imperial Academy of Sciences, spent several days there. He produced a geographic description of the islands – including a map, which he received from a remarkable local inhabitant, Krestinin, who told Lepekhin that it had been drawn by one of the monks.[77] Lepekhin described in detail the relief, landscapes and vegetation of the islands, but mostly focused on the history of the monastery.[78] In 1789, Aleksandr Fomin also visited Solovki and included local knowledge in his descriptions of the White Sea.[79] For instance, according to a map held at the monastery, there were 177 lakes. However, not all them were counted because the person who had made the map was not allowed to miss church services and therefore could not travel too far away.[80] Fomin provided the names of trees, but complained that he did not know botany well enough to describe the islands' herbs. He noted the absence of snakes on the islands and the large number of seagulls.[81] He also mentioned the local herring as the best of the White Sea.[82]

However, systematic studies of nature on and around Solovki began only after the organisation of the Society of Naturalists at St Petersburg University in 1868.[83] The Society was especially focused on marine life. After several seasonal expeditions to Solovki and its surroundings, the group organised a permanent biological station there. It opened in 1881 and became the second marine biological station in the Russian Empire after the one in Sevastopol'. Nikolai Wagner, a professor at St Petersburg University, helmed the first station at the monastic household premises just opposite the main monastery, in cooperation

---

77. Lepekhin, *Puteshestvie akademika Ivana Lepekhina*, p. 45.

78. Ibid., pp. 43–82.

79. Fomin, *Opisanie Belogo moria s ego beregami i ostrovami voobsche*.

80. Ibid., p. 77. Now more than 550 lakes are described in the islands.

81. Ibid., p. 86.

82. Ibid., p. 90.

83. See Fokin, Smirnov, Laius, *Morskie biologicheskie stantsii Russkogo Severa (1881–1938)*.

with the monastery's officials. A sign on the building read, 'Biological Station of Solovetskii Coenoby'. At that time, it was located further north than any other biological station in the world.

The organisation of the station was a rare, positive example of science and religion coexisting in the Russian Empire. Professor Wagner maintained friendly relations with the head of the monastery, a well-educated person willing to support science.[84] According to one description, the monastery 'helped fill the needs of the Society. We had two boats at our disposal and three novices in our service. ... We were constantly visited by those who wanted to see the "sea monsters". They were monks and novices themselves, as well as pilgrims.'[85]

The good relationship between the monastery and the station did not last long, however. In 1899, a new head of the monastery complained to church authorities about the inappropriate behaviour of the naturalists at the station: they did not take part in church services, ate meat during Lent and 'spent their days on excursions, their nights observing their catch, and then slept to midday'.[86] The hegumen even went so far as to argue that the station had already completed all of the work it could do: 'no new discoveries have been made recently, and no new varieties of already known species have been found'.[87] These views betray a misunderstanding (or misrepresentation) of the station's goals: to develop the knowledge and infrastructure for zoologists to do significant research in the morphology and embryology of marine organisms, crucial to the development of the field of evolutionary biology. Moreover, the station became a foundational place for marine ecological research. St Petersburg zoologist Nikolai Knipovich began to study the distribution of marine organisms in connection with environmental factors in the Dolgaia Inlet of the Bol'shoi Solovetskii Island.[88] All these important studies continued long after the station was moved farther north, in 1899, and renamed the Murman Biological Station. The building of the former station still exists at Solovki, but acknowledgement of its important role in the development of marine science in Russia is now absent even at the museum.

---

84. Correspondence between the hegumen Melentii and prof. Wagner was recently published by Fokin, 'Biologicheskaia stantsiia Solovetskoi obiteli', pp. 81–9.

85. Unpublished memoirs by Mikhail N. Rimskii-Korsakov, cit. by Fokin, Smirnov and Laius, *Morskie biologicheskie stantsii Russkogo Severa (1881–1938)*, p. 18.

86. Deriugin, 'Murmanskaia biologicheskaia stantsiia. 1899–1905. Istoricheskii ocherk', p. 3.

87. Ibid.

88. Fokin, Smirnov, Laius, *Morskie biologicheskie stantsii Russkogo Severa (1881–1938)*.

'The Space of Blue and Gold'

During the period of the labour camp, when the nature of Solovki was primarily a resource to be exploited, it was also an object of scientific study. By 1923, several research organisations had been established in the camp. These included the 'Commission for the comprehensive scientific survey of nature of Solovetskie Islands' and *'Biosad'* (Biological Garden). In 1925, the commission was transformed into the Solovetskii Society for Local Lore, at first as a branch of Arkhangel'sk Society; but it soon became independent.[89] The society published a journal that was freely distributed in the USSR. In 1927, its members proposed to renew the biological station at Solovki, requesting support from Academy of Sciences and other central institutions.[90] However, changes in the Gulag regime and the transformation of the camp to a prison put an end to all these plans.

Professional scientists, who were numerous among Gulag prisoners, found it possible to conduct research and publish it in the society's journal.[91] Zoologists, botanists, meteorologists and many other specialists participated in this activity, which focused on the practical use of natural resources. In addition to a programme of breeding fur-bearing animals in cages, another sought to acclimatise non-native biological species including, successfully, the muskrat.[92] Mathematician and Orthodox philosopher Father Pavel Florenskii was involved in, among other activities, studies of marine algae intended to increase iodine production for medicine.[93] Thus, environing went on at full speed even during these terrible times.

A new page in the history of the Solovki was turned in the 1960s by mass tourism, which brought new approaches toward local nature. Tourists considered nature an integral part of the cultural heritage that made the islands remarkable and worth visiting. It is no wonder that, after 1974, the nature of the islands and surrounding seascapes became one of the main objects of attention for the 'Solovetskii State Historical-Architectural and Natural Museum-Reserve'. The use of the term 'museum-reserve' (*muzei-zapovednik*) for the cloistral complex and surrounding landscape deserves special discussion. Maria Kaulen, in her recent monograph, offers an impressive picture of the evolution of Soviet 'museumification' and protection of heritage objects, elaborating and coining

89. Goriashko, 'Biostantsiia osobogo naznacheniia'.

90. Zakhvatkin, 'K vosstanovleniiiu Solovetskoi biologicheskoi stantsii'.

91. Soshina, 'Muzei Solovetskogo obschestva kraevedenia (1925–1937)'.

92. Generozov, *Ondatra. Amerikanskaia vykhukhol' i ee akklimatizatsiia na Solovetskikh ostrovakh.*

93. Pyman, *Pavel Florensky.*

this concept. In the 1920s the authors of Soviet guidebooks had proposed new terms such as church-museum, manor-museum, monastery-museum and city-museum in order to describe their distinctive and multifaceted vision of heritage phenomena. These concepts were not yet theoretically developed, but were linked to the societal demand for the large-scale 'museumification' of objects associated with religion and the former nobility, which were considered undesirable in the new post-revolutionary reality, alongside a reinterpretation of their past meanings.[94] Predictably, churches, cathedrals and monasteries constituted a significant part of this reconceptualised heritage. These religious buildings eventually became a central issue for the monument conservation movement that was 'connected with aesthetic and patriotic education, propaganda toward the West ... and the development of Soviet and foreign tourism' and therefore a key to 'understanding the dominant ideal in late socialist society (1953–1985)'.[95]

Indeed, both terms 'museumification' and 'museum-reserve' became a part of Soviet museum practice only later, in late 1950s.[96] The concept of museum-reserve is rather dynamic, and recent literature has explored its shifting meaning among museum professionals in Russian and post-Soviet communities.[97] However, the museum-reserve may be seen as a Soviet (and rather successful) version of the global phenomenon of open-air museums. The evolution of the term from the bottom to the top of the Soviet social and professional hierarchy is quite remarkable. For museum professionals directly involved in the practical work on the lower level of heritage protection, this term is used to label the specific museum structure that preserves and represents complex systems such as buildings and landscapes. That is, both nature and the built environment were museumified, often inseparably. The very name museum-reserve indicated devotion to the representation and study of both types of the islands' treasures – architectural and natural.[98] For governmental bodies, by contrast, this term

---

94. Kaulen, *Muzeefikatsiia istoriko-kul'turnogo naslediia Rossii*, pp. 17–18.

95. Takahashi 'Church or Museum? The Role of State Museums in Conserving Church Buildings, 1965–1985', p. 503.

96. Kaulen, *Muzeefikatsiia istoriko-kul'turnogo naslediia Rossii*, p. 22.

97. See for instance, Kaulen et al. (eds), *Muzei-zapovedniki – muzei budushego*; Kepin, 'Definitsiia poniatiia "muzei-zapovednik"', pp. 80–7; Timofeeva, 'Muzei-zapovedniki v sfere kulturnogo turizma'.

98. For a detailed chronology of the museum's principal activities, see the archives of SGIAPMZ, Lopatin, M.V. et al., 'Materialy k istorii Solovetskogo gosudarstvennogo museia-zapovednika', pp. 4–23.

means a specific legal status that is granted by the authorities and guarantees some legal protection to all the parts of a museum complex.[99]

Therefore the granting of museum-reserve status to Solovki marked both the complexity of the museumified environment and the high level of state protection for its objects (both natural and human-made) recognised as valuable by the authorities. However, whilst being recognised as a valuable heritage site for all Soviet citizens, the management of the site was organised through regional authorities who could combine both cultural and natural heritage protection regardless of juridical legitimisation of such complex sites on a national level. Studies of nature and conservation were core parts of museum activities. In addition, the Arkhangel'sk authorities issued rules for tourist visits that banned all hunting, completely closed the island of Anzer, and undertook conservation measures for the eider duck.[100]

The archives of the Solovki museum show that nature was the most popular subject of both excursions and exhibitions in the 1970s and 1980s. Indeed, from 1976 to 1988, the museum organised fourteen exhibitions devoted to nature but only ten to the architectural monuments. Strong focus on the study and conservation of nature remained during 1980s and 1990s, when the ecological dimension of research became stronger at the museum, forming the basis for a regional committee on nature protection.[101] Not only museum researchers, but also biologists from Moscow, Leningrad/St Petersburg and Arkhangel'sk conducted field studies devoted to forests, birds, fish, marine ecology, algae and the behaviour of marine mammals, among other topics. Along with fundamental research, applied fisheries research flourished, including algae production.

In 1992, the Solovki ensemble was added to the UNESCO World Heritage List, but only as a cultural heritage site. In 1995, it was also included in the Russian State List of the Most Valuable Objects of Cultural Heritage of the Peoples of Russia. This act of recognition of the historical and cultural significance of the Solovetskie Islands had the consequence of disrupting the relationship between the cultural and natural heritage components because the latter did not receive any protection. The situation became even more complicated when the site was transferred to the direct control of the Ministry

---

99.   Kaulen, 'Muzei pod otkrytym nebom: mnogoobrazie modelei i problema vybora', pp. 13–14.

100. Kononov, 'Solovetskii zakaznik'.

101. SGIAPMZ archives: Martynov, 'Spravka of deiatel'nosti Solovetskogo gosudarstvennogo istoriko-kul'turnogo muzeia zapovednika za 30 let'.

of Culture in 1998. At that moment, the museum lost its status as a scientific institution and became instead solely an institution of culture. The same year, the museum made a failed attempt to apply for UNESCO protection for its natural heritage. A new application was presented at a 2005 UNESCO summit in Tokyo. This time, the reaction of UNESCO was positive, but the Russian side withdrew the application due to some internal disagreements. After a long period of conflict between the museum and rapidly growing monastery, in 2009 the museum was subordinated to the monastery when the head of the monastery also became head of the museum.[102]

Since 2012, several attempts have been made to find the proper juridical form for the Solovetskie Islands as a protected territory to address the new challenges of contemporary Russian reality. An initial proposal was to turn Solovki into a national park.[103] This form of regulation would suit the needs of the islands very well, as it proposes different zones of protection, with more-strict and less-strict preservation of natural objects and landscapes in comparison with nature reserves (*zapovedniks*), which have completely closed protection zones. Then there was discussion of the idea of establishing a *zakaznik* – a form of protected territory that, in contrast to a national park, includes only nature and excludes cultural heritage.[104] However, even such a regime of nature conservation was considered too strict by several actors. Not only the monastery, but also regional authorities and business interests intent on developing the use of natural resources on the islands and in surrounding waters (fisheries, alga production) strongly opposed this idea.[105]

During the past couple of decades, research and nature protection have almost completely disappeared. For instance, the Department of Nature at the museum had fifteen members in 1990 and only three in 2014.[106] The museum now has almost no capacity for research and ecological education. Moreover, a rich exhibition on nature, which included many topics on human-nature relationships and had been a central part of the museum since 1969, was re-

102. Spaso-Preobrazhenskii Solovetskii stavropigial'nyi muzhskoi monastyr', 'Namestnik i igumen Solovetskogo monastyria arkhimandrit Porfirii'. For a discusison of the efforts to include Lake Baikal on the UNESCO World Heritage List, see the chapter by Arkady and Tatiana Kalikhman in this volume.

103. Cherenkova, 'K voprosu o statuse prirodnykh kompleksov Solovkov'. On national parks and other protected territories, see also the Introduction to this volume and the chapters by Alan Roe and Nicholas Breyfogle.

104. *Cherenkova, Obosnovanie sozdaniia prirodnogo zakaznika 'Solovetskii arkhipelag'.*

105. See, for instance, Moskvoretskaia, 'Solovki: pamiatnik ili akvaferma?'.

106. Kononov, 'Solovetskii zakaznik'.

moved in 2009 from the Hegumen's Building due to growing demands of the monastery for space. So far, another location for the exhibit has not been found.

This decline in attention to nature has led to significant debates about the construction and modification of social and environmental spaces around the monastery. Indeed, both the natural and cultural heritage supported the growing tourist industry. As such, the unity of the islands and the buildings – human, nature and environment – provides jobs and incomes. Yet without proper management, environmental problems – such as lack of sewage system and proper waste management – became very severe on the main island.[107]

The natural heritage, however, is still important for tourism on the islands. Visitors 'consume' Solovki in a variety of ways: organised excursions with professional guides, voyages on private boats around the islands, paddling along numerous canals in rented boats or private kayaks and hiking or cycling through the forests and swamps along very poor roads. Nowadays, whale watching has become an inseparable part of the Solovki experience, and the whales themselves are described as part of the islands' aquatic heritage complex, alongside local fish cuisine and recreational boating. All these phenomena are listed in the guidebooks as 'musts' for the visitor. Moreover, Solovki was recently included on a list of the top thirty tourist destinations in the Russian Federation.[108] Contact with marine life, especially whales, represents the clearest experience of contact with wild nature –the sea has its own agency and its creatures appear and disappear without any human control. The tourists also show a strong interest in the ancient modes of taming nature: the construction of the walls, canals, modes of marine voyages and old boats, Phillip's fish cages and an early twentieth-century hydropower station that is awaiting reconstruction. The botanical garden is presented as a paradise created by religious commitment. In general, there is a lot of attention to the history of taming nature as a part of spiritual practice. In contrast, the Gulag experience is shown not only as a struggle with an evil political power, but as a struggle with severe nature. This theme is especially pronounced at Sekirnaia Mountain and Bol'shoi Zaiatskii Island.

The heritage of Solovki, in spite of having different layers from different historical periods, could not be considered as a palimpsest, a type of heritage where the next layer substitutes and hides the previous one.[109] On Solovki, all layers of natural and human heritage are alive and visible, and they are embedded

---

107. Nevmerzhitskaia, 'The Solovetsky Archipelago, Russia'.

108. See Golomolzin, *Rossiia. Putevoditel' Top-30*, p. 17.

109. Kinossian and Wråkberg, 'Palimpsests'.

Alexei Kraikovski and Julia Lajus

in what is often called the 'cultural landscape', a human-built world in which nature is strongly environed. Thus, as Anna Storm has already shown regarding other types of heritage in which nature is completely environed – such as former industrial sites – it is more productive to conceptualise such heritage as scars that are the reminder, the trace of the wound.[110]

Nature and Environment: The Lessons of History

By emphasising the complex, entangled history of nature and environment in a small but remarkable place in northern Russia, this chapter opens several historical lines of inquiry. First, our analysis of the space of the archipelago through the perspective of religious geography reveals numerous contesting visions of nature and environment at Solovki, all interacting with the monastery heritage complex. Approaching the monastery as an 'object' that manifests the Orthodox character of the local culture, we see the human-built environment as the exclusive achievement of a religious community driven by devotion and faith. Similarly, Soviet practices on Solovki demonstrate that the secular state could also use the instruments provided by this religious geography to develop consistent concepts and continuing narratives about the enviro-religious past. The cultural landscapes created by the long-term process of environing on Solovki are valuable not only to believers but to the general public as well – a fact that is confirmed by UNESCO supervision of the site. When representatives of the Orthodox Church and secular experts meet today to discuss the future of the Solovki archipelago – although they are not always able to find a common vision and often, unfortunately, are quite reluctant to compromise – both undoubtedly consider the monastery with the surrounding cultural landscapes a human-built environment of the highest value.[111] However, to organise their use and preservation in a way that would be suitable to both groups is a challenge. It is more difficult to divide these landscapes into particular zones dedicated to believers and to visitors than it is to divide the space inside a church – the compromise that is often used in large cathedrals not only in Russia but in other parts of Europe.

Another even deeper tension lies in local contextualisation of natural and religious spaces, imagining them as spaces of 'blue and gold'. Indeed, the monks and the secular inhabitants of the archipelago, as they built their lives around the monastery, all considered the nature of Solovki, along with its history and

110. Storm, *Post-Industrial Landscape Scars*.

111. See Arkhangel'skii, 'Tem Vremenem'.

culture, as indispensable parts of local life and experience. However, they did not share the same feeling of being 'local', a difference that is readily observable to outsiders. For people who live on the islands, environmental problems – the absence of a sewage system, degradation of forests and the limitation of access to natural resources – are the most important. By contrast, for 'experts of nature' the major concern is the conservation of particular landscapes and species that are considered most valuable and often conceptualised as part of eternal nature, of the wilderness. Different groups of actors who live between 'nature' and 'environment' construct narratives that suit their needs. For the monastery, since the earliest times, narratives of wild nature served as aspiration and justification for its transformation of the island's spaces through religious practices. Visitors supported different narratives of contact with both wilderness and cultural landscapes full of historical and spiritual meanings in order to increase the value of their experience.

Today, current misunderstandings and disagreements about nature protection and the uses of cultural and natural heritage as tourist attractions reflect a lack of understanding of the difference between 'nature' and 'environment' that we have analysed in this chapter across several historical periods. A better understanding of this difference would help different groups of actors to answer the following questions: What would they really like to preserve if wild nature did not exist anymore? How could the baseline, according to which the cultural landscape should and could be preserved, be set? Could we detach in our discourses and debates purely environmental problems (such as a lack of waste management) from the problems of nature conservation and protection? Is it possible to deal with them separately and, thus, probably, more effectively? We hope that a new approach – based on the ideas and methodology of nature, environment and environing that we borrowed from Sverker Sörlin and Paul Warde – might not only enrich our understanding of historical pasts of this singular island place but also make those pasts usable.

BIBLIOGRAPHY

Arkhiv Sankt-Peterburgskogo instituta istorii Rossiiskoi Akademii Nauk (SPb II RAN, Archive of the St Petersburg Institute of History of the Russian Academy of Sciences).

Adelson, G., J. Engell, B. Ranalli and K.P. Van Anglen (eds). 2008. *Environment: An Interdisciplinary Anthology*. New Haven and London: Yale University Press.

Alekseeva, Ia. and A. Makhrov. 2017. 'O proiskhozhdenii riapushki na Solovetskikh ostrovakh: arkhivnye dokumenty v issledovanii mikroevoliutsii'. *Priroda*. No. 7: 37–46.

Arkhangel'skii, Aleksandr. 2009. *Tem Vremenem. Televizor s chelovecheskim litsom.* Moscow: AST, Astrel.

Arnold, Ellen F. 2013. *Negotiating the Landscape: Environment and Monastic Identity in the Medieval Ardennes.* Philadelphia: University of Pennsylvania Press.

Averianov, K. 2016. 'Severnaia Fivaida: nasledie Sergiia Radonezhskogo'. In Ia.V. Leontiev and Ia.V. Sonina (eds), *Prepodobnyi Makarii Kaliazinskii – sviatoi zastupnik zemli Russkoi. Sbornik dokladov Vtorykh Makarievskikh kaliazinskikh chteniia,* pp. 16–34. Tver: SFK Ofis.

Bespiatykh, Iurii. 2010. *Arkhangel'sk nakanune i v gody Severnoi voiny (1700–1721).* St Petersburg: Blits.

Birnbaum, Henrik. 1981. *Lord Novgorod the Great: The Historical Background.* Bloomington: Slavica Publishers.

Bogdanova, A. and N. Kopytova. 2013. 'Palomnichestvo v Solovetskii monastyr' vo vtoroi polovine XVIII veka'. *Solovetskoe more. Istoriko-kul'turnyi al'manakh.* No. 12: 51–63.

Bogumił, Z. and T. Voronina. 2018. 'Islands of One Archipelago: Narratives about the Solovetskie Islands and the Memory of Soviet Repressions'. *Laboratorium* **10** (2): 104–21.

Bondarenko, B. 1966. 'Vershiny tsinizma'. *Chasovoi* 486 (12): 21.

Brumfield, W. 2003. 'Tradition and Innovation in the Sixteenth-Century Architecture of Solovetskii Transfiguration Monastery'. *The Russian Review* **62** (3): 333– 65.

Caporaso, A. 2017. 'A Dynamic Processual Maritime Archaeological Landscape Formation Model'. In A. Caporaso (ed.), *Formation Processes of Maritime Archaeological Landscapes,* pp. 7–29. Cham: Springer.

Cherenkova, N. 2004. 'K voprosu o statuse prirodnykh kompleksov Solovkov'. *Solovetskoe more. Istoriko-literaturnyi al'manakh.* No. 3: 217–25.

Cherenkova, Nadezhda. 2014. *Obosnovanie sozdaniia prirodnogo zakaznika 'Solovetskii arkhipelag'.* Moscow: Minpriroda RF.

Council of Ministers of the RSFSR. 1960. 'O dal'neishem uluchshenii dela okhrany paniatnikov kul'tury v RSFSR' Resolution No. 1327. 30 August. http://docs.cntd. ru/document/9012089.

Cronon, W. 1996. 'The Trouble with Wilderness: Or, Getting Back to the Wrong Nature'. *Environmental History* **1** (1): 7–28.

Dadykina, M. 2016. 'Upravliaia prostranstvom: organizatsiia Spaso-Prilutskim monastyriom vodnykh kommunikatsii i ikh struktura (XVI–XVII cc.)'. *Quaestio Rossica* **4** (3): 123–40.

Deriugin, K. 1906. 'Murmanskaia biologicheskaia stantsiia. 1899–1905. Istoricheskii ocherk'. *Trudy Imperatorskogo Sankt-Peterburgskogo Obschestva Estestvoispytatelei* 37 (4): 1–60.

Donovan, V. 2015. '"How Well Do You Know Your Krai?" The Kraevedenie Revival and Patriotic Politics in Late Khrushchev-Era Russia'. *Slavic Review* 74 (3): 464–83.

Ely, Christopher. 2003. 'The Picturesque and the Holy. Visions of Touristic Space in Russia, 1820-1850'. In J. Cracraft and D. Rowland (eds), *Architectures of Russian Identity: 1500 to the Present*, pp. 80–89. Ithaca: Cornell University Press.

Esenin, Sergei. 1995. 'Nebo li takoe beloe'. In S. Esenin, *Polnoe sobranie sochinenii v 7 tomakh.* Vol. 1, *Stikhotvoreniia*, pp. 164–5. Moscow: Golos, Nauka.

Fausek, V. 1889. 'Na zoologicheskoi stantsii: Iz poezdki na Beloe more'. *Vestnik Evropy* 3 (6): 433- 61.

Fedorov, Petr. 1889. *Solovki.* Kronshtadt: Kronshtadtskii Vestnik.

Fedotov, Georgii. 2000. *Sviatoi Filipp, Mitropolit moskovskii. Prilozhenie – Zhitie i podvigi Filippa, Mitropolita Moskovskogo i vseia Rusi.* Moscow: Martis.

Fennell, John. 2013. *A History of the Russian Church to 1488.* New York: Routledge.

Fokin, S. 2013. 'Biologicheskaia stantsiia Solovetskoi obiteli'. *Solovetskoe more. Istoriko-literaturnyi al'manakh.* No. 2: 75–89.

Fokin, Sergei, Aleksei Smirnov and Julia Laius. 2006. *Morskie biologicheskie stantsii Russkogo Severa (1881–1938).* Moscow: KMK Press.

Fokina, T. and N. Cherenkova. 2011. '"Korabl' snegov" na Solovkakh'. *Solovetskoe more. Istoriko-literaturnyi al'manakh.* No. 10: 147–58.

Fomin, Aleksandr. 1797. *Opisanie Belogo moria s ego beregami i ostrovami voobsche; takzhe chastnoe opisanie ostrovnoi kamennoi griady, k koei prinadlezhat Solovki, i topografiia Solovetskogo monastyria s ego ostrovami; s priobscheniem puteshestviia v 1789 godu v onyi monastyr', predstavlennoe v pis'makh.* St Petersburg: Imperatorskaia Akademiia Nauk.

Frolov, Aleksandr, and Aleksandr Zakharchenko. 1985. *Solovetskie ostrova: Solovetskii gosudarstvennyi istoriko-arkhitekturnyi i prirodnyi muzei-zapovednik.* Moscow: Sovetskaia Rossiia.

Generozov, Vladimir. 1927. *Ondatra. Amerikanskaia vykhukhol' i ee akklimatizatsiia na Solovetskikh ostrovakh.* Solovki: Biuro pechati USLON.

Golomolzin, Evgenii. 2014. *Rossiia. Putevoditel' Top-30. Eto nuzhno uvidet!* St Petersburg: Piter.

Golubev, V. 1982. 'Belomorskie reisy Kanina'. *Morskoi flot.* No. 1: 14.

Gornitskaia, Liubava and Marina Larionova. 2013. *Mesto, kotorogo net... Ostrova v russkoi literature.* Rostov na Donu: Izd. UiNTs RAN.

Goriashko, A. 2005. 'Biostantsiia osobogo naznacheniia'. *Biologiia, ezhenedel' noe prilozhenie k gazete 'Pervoe sentiabria'.* No. 16: 2–9.

Goriashko, A. 2017. 'Attempts to Establish Eider Farms in the USSR, and Why These Failed'. *Arcadia: Explorations in Environmental History.* No. 14. https://doi. org/10.5282/rcc/7897

Gosudarstvennyi arkhiv Arkhangel'skoi oblasti (GAAO, State Archive of the Arkhangel'sk Oblast').

Ivanov, Vladimir. 2007. *Monastyri i monastyrskie krestiane v XVI–XVII vekakh.* St Petersburg: Izdatel'stvo Olega Abyshko.

Kaulen, Maria. 2012. *Muzeefikatsiia istoriko-kul'turnogo naslediia Rossii.* Moscow: Eterna.

Kaulen, M. 2015. 'Muzei pod otkrytym nebom: mnogoobrazie modelei i problema vybora'. In M. Kaulen, G. Rudenko and I. Chuvilova (eds), *Muzei-zapovedniki – muzei buduschego,* pp. 11–34. Elabuga: ElTIK.

Kaulen, Maria, Gulzada Rudenko and Irina Chuvilova (eds). 2015. *Muzei-zapovedniki – muzei buduschego.* Elabuga: ElTIK.

Kepin, D. 2016. 'Definitsiia poniatiia "muzei-zapovednik"'. *Iskusstvo i kultura* 1 (21): 80–7.

Kinossian, Nadir and Urban Wråkberg. 2017. 'Palimpsests'. In J. Schimanski and S. F. Wolfe (eds), *Border Aesthetics: Concepts and Intersections,* pp. 90–110. New York and Oxford: Berghahn Books.

Kiselev, Aleksei and Mikhail Tulin. 1977. *Kniga o Murmanske.* Murmansk: Murmanskoe knizhnoe izdatel'stvo.

Kivelson, Valerie. 2006. *Cartographies of Tsardom: The Land and Its Meanings in Seventeenth-Century Russia.* Ithaca: Cornell University Press.

Kolosova, Galina. 1999. *Prirodno-geograficheskii analiz istoricheskikh territorii: Solovetskii arkhipelag.* Moscow: Institut Naslediia.

Kononov, P. 2014. 'Solovetskii zakaznik: ne speshit' i esche raz podumat'. *Pravda Severa* 105 (1): 8–9.

Kozhevnikov, G. 1913. 'Monastyri i okhrana prirody'. *Utro Rossii.* No. 278. http:// ecoethics.ru/g-a-kozhevnikov-monastyiri-i-ohrana-prir/.

Kraikovski, A. 2015. '"The Sea on One Side, Trouble on the Other": Russian Marine Resource Use before Peter the Great'. *The Slavonic and East European Review* 93 (1): 39–65.

Kraikovski A., M. Dadykina and E. Kalemeneva. 2018. 'The Water Management in the Russian Monasteries, 16th–18th cc.'. In F. Ammannati (ed.), *Gestione dell'acqua in Europa (XII-XVIII secc.)/Water Management in Europe (12th-18th centuries),* pp. 319–36. Prato: Istituto Datini.

Kraikovski, A., M. Dadykina, Z. Dmitrieva and J. Lajus. 2020. 'Between Piety and Productivity: Monastic Fisheries of the White and Barents Sea in the 16th–18th Centuries'. *Journal of the North Atlantic.* No. 42: 1–21.

Lajus, D., J. Lajus, Z. Dmitrieva, A. Kraikovski and D. Alexandrov. 2005. 'The Use of Historical Catch Data to Trace the Influence of Climate on Fish Populations: Examples from the White and Barents Sea Fisheries in the 17th and 18th centuries'. *ICES Journal of Marine Science* **62** (7): 1426–35.

Lajus, J., A. Kraikovski and A. Yurchenko. 2009. 'Sea Fisheries in the Russian North c. 1400–1850'. In D.J. Starkey, J.T. Thor and I. Heidbrinck (eds), *A History of the North Atlantic Fisheries,* Vol. 1, pp. 41–64. Bremerhaven: Deutsches Schiffahrtsmuseum.

Leikin, Nikolai. 2007. *Po Severu dikomu.* Arkhangel'sk: Barashkov Iu. A.

Lepekhin, Ivan. 1805. *Puteshestvie akademika Ivana Lepekhina.* St Petersburg: Imperatorskaia Akademiia nauk.

Likhachev, Dmitrii. 1995. *Vospominaniia.* St Petersburg: Logos.

Maksimov, S. 2010. 'Poezdka v Solovetskii monastyr''. In S. Iakovlev (ed.), *V Solovetskuiu obitel'. Putevye zametki i vospominaniia o Solovetskikh ostrovakh,* pp. 38–75. Arkhangel'sk: Pravda Severa.

Maksimov, S. 1989. 'Ostrovnye monastyri'. In S. Plekhanov (ed.), *Po Russkoi zemle,* pp. 264–89. Moscow: Sovetskaia Rossiia.

Martynov, Aleksandr (ed.). 2015. *Solovki v literature i folklore.* Arkhangel'sk: SAFU.

Mineeva, Sofia. 1999. *Problemy kompleksnogo analiza drevnerusskogo agiograficheskogo teksta: na primere Zhitiia prep. Zosimy i Savvatiia Solovetskikh.* Kurgan: KGU.

Morozov, S. 2005. 'Morskie chudesa Solovetskikh sviatykh'. *Solovetskoe more. Istoriko-literaturnyi al'manakh.* No. 4: 9–14.

Moskvoretskaia, Z. 2017. 'Solovki: pamiatnik ili akvaferma?'. *Russkaia ryba. Vchera, segodnia, zavtra.* 2 March. http://rusfishjournal.ru/publications/monument-or-akvaferma/

Muraviev, Andrei. 1855. *Russkaia Fivaida na Severe.* St Petersburg: III Otdelenie EIV Kantseliarii.

Nemirovich-Danchenko, Vasilii. 2013. *Belomor'e i Solovki.* Moscow: Ripol Klassik.

Nevmerzhitskaia, Julia. 2006. 'The Solovetsky Archipelago, Russia'. In G. Baldacchino (ed.), *Extreme Tourism: Lessons from the World's Cold Water Islands,* pp. 159–66. New York: Routledge.

Owen, Thomas. 2005. *Dilemmas of Russian Capitalism: Fedor Chizhov and Corporate Enterprise in the Railroad Age.* Cambridge, MA: Harvard University Press.

Parppei, Kati. 2011. *'The Oldest One in Russia': The Formation of the Historiographical Image of Valaam Monastery.* Leiden: Brill.

Alexei Kraikovski and Julia Lajus

Pashkov, Alexandr. 2000. *Kareliia i Solovki glazami literatorov pushkinskoi epokhi, v 2-kh tomakh.* Petrozavodsk: Petrozavodskii gosudarstvennyi universitet.

Pod"iapol'skii, Sergei. 1986. 'Deiatelnost' italianskikh masterov na Rusi i v drugikh stranakh Evropy v kontse XV–nachale XVI veka'. *Sovetskoe iskusstvoznanie.* No. 20: 62–91.

Popova, L. 2017. 'Semiotika sakral'nogo prostranstva monastyrei Pomor'ia'. *Vestnik slavianskikh kul'tur.* No. 44: 159–69.

Prishvin, Mikhail. 1908. *Za volshebnym kolobkom. Iz zapisok na Krainem Severe Rossii i Norvegii.* St Petersburg: Izdatel'stvo A.F. Devriena.

Prishvin, Mikhail. 2010. 'Beloe more'. In S. Iakovlev (ed.), *V Solovetskuiu obitel'. Putevye zametki i vospominaniia o Solovetskikh ostrovakh,* pp. 87–117. Arkhangel'sk: Pravda Severa.

Pyman, Avril. 2010. *Pavel Florensky: A Quiet Genius: The Tragic and Extraordinary Life of Russia's Unknown da Vinci.* New York: Continuum.

Robson, Roy R. 2004. *Solovki: The Story of Russia Told Through Its Most Remarkable Islands.* New Haven: Yale University Press.

Robson, Roy R. 2007. 'Transforming Solovki: Pilgrim Narratives, Modernization, and Late Imperial Monastic Life'. In Mark D. Steinberg and Heather J. Coleman (eds), *Sacred Stories: Religion and Spirituality in Modern Russia,* pp. 44–60. Bloomington: Indiana University Press.

Savich, Aleksandr. 1927. *Solovetskaia votchina XV–XVII v.: Opyt izucheniia khoziaistva i sotsialnykh otnoshenii na krainem severe v drevnei Rusi.* Perm': Permskii Gosudarstvennyi Universitet.

Shtorn, E. and D. Buteiko. 2016. 'Bor'ba za ogranichennoe prostranstvo pamiati na Solovkakh'. *Neprikosnovennyi zapas* 108 (4): 232–48.

Shvidkovsky, Dmitry. 2007. *Russian Architecture and the West.* New Haven: Yale University Press.

Skopin, Vladimir. 1991. *Na Solovetskikh ostrovakh.* Moscow: Iskusstvo.

Skopin, Vladimir. 1994. *Solovki: Istoriia, Arkhitektura, Priroda.* Moscow: Iskusstvo-Terra.

Sluchevskii, Konstantin. 2009. *Poezdki po Severu Rossii v 1885–1886 godakh.* Moscow: OGI.

Sobolev, Aleksandr. 2005. *Priroda Solovetskikh ostrovov.* Arkhangel'sk: SGIAPMZ.

Solovetskii gosudarstvennyi arckitekturnyi i prirodnyi muzei-zapovednik (SGIAPMZ, Solovetskii State Architectural and Natural Museum-Zapovednik).

Sörlin, S. and P. Warde. 2009. 'Making the Environment Historical – An Introduction'. In S. Sörlin, P. Warde (eds), *Nature's End: History and the Environment,* pp. 1–19. Basingstoke: Palgrave Macmillan.

Sörlin, S. and N. Wormbs. 2018. 'Environing Technologies: A Theory of Making Environment'. *History and Technology* **34** (2): 101–25.

Soshina, A. 2004. 'Muzei Solovetskogo obshchestva kraevedeniia (1925–1937)'. *Solovetskoe more. Istoriko-literaturnyi al'manakh.* No. 3: 130–42.

Spaso-Preobrazhenskii Solovetskii stavropigial'nyi muzhskoi monastyr' Russkoi pravoslavnoi tserkvi (Moskovskii Patriarkhat). 2009. 'Namestnik i igumen Solovetskogo monastyria arkhimandrit Porfirii'. 13 September. http://solovki-monastyr.ru/abba-page/namestnik/

Storm, Anna. 2014. *Post-Industrial Landscape Scars.* New York: Palgrave Macmillan.

Stump, Roger W. 2008. *The Geography of Religion: Faith, Place, and Space.* Plymouth: Rowman & Littlefield Publishers.

Takahashi, S. 2009. 'Church or Museum? The Role of State Museums in Conserving Church Buildings, 1965-1985'. *Journal of Church and State* **51** (3): 502–17.

Takahashi, S. 2012. 'Religion as an Object of Science in Atheistic Society: The Function of the Historical Museum of Religion and Atheism in Late Socialist Russia'. In T. Mochizuki and Sh. Naeda (eds), *India, Russia, China: Comparative Studies in Eurasian Culture and Society*, pp. 11–19. Sapporo: Slavic Research Center.

Timofeeva, L. 2015. 'Muzei-zapovedniki v sfere kul'turnogo turizma'. In M. Lisovskaia (ed.), *Muzei v mire kultury. Mir kultury v muzee (Trudy St. Peterburgskogo gosudarstvennogo instituta kul'tury, 212),* pp. 197–203. St Petersburg: SPb Institut Kul'tury.

Tutova, T.A, I.A. Bobrovnitskaia et al. 2001. *Sokhranennye sviatyni Solovetskogo monastyria: katalog vystavki.* Moscow: Belyi bereg.

Umniagin, V. 2016. 'Priroda i okruzhaiushchii mir v vospominaniiakh solovetskikh uznikov'. *Solovetskoe more. Istoriko-kulturnyi al'manakh.* No. 15: 89–94.

Umniagin, Viacheslav. 2018. *Obraz Solovkov v russkoi literature XX veka. (Na materialakh vospominanii solovetskikh uznikov i romannoi prozy 2000-kh gg.).* Kand. Diss. (Avtoreferat). Institut mirovoi literatury.

Vedenin, Iu. and M. Kuleshova. 2004. 'Kul'turnyi landshaft kak ob'ekt kul'turnogo i prirodnogo naslediia'. *Izvestiia RAN. Seriia Geograficheskaia.* No. 1: 7–14.

Volkov, Oleg, 1989. *Pogruzhenie vo t'mu.* Moscow: Molodaia gvardiia.

Zakharov, Aleksandr, Tatiana Savchenko and Vladimir Drozdkov. 2004. *Letopis' zhizni i tvorchestva S.A. Esenina: v piati tomakh.* Vol. 2, *1917–1920.* Moscow: IMLI RAN.

Zakhvatkin, A. 1927. 'K vosstanovleniiu Solovetskoi biologicheskoi stantsii'. *Karelo-Murmanskii krai.* No. 2: 37–40.

Zeldina, Galina. 1971. *Po Sovetskoi Rossii.* Moscow: Kniga.

Zhitenev, Sergei. 2007. *Istoriia russkogo pravoslavnogo palomnichestva v X–XVII vekakh.* Moscow: Indrik.

3.

POLLUTED PEARL OF THE NORTH:
LAKE IMANDRA IN THE ANTHROPOCENE

Andy Bruno

The glistening water, cool and clear, greeted geographer Garviil Rikhter upon his return to Lake Imandra on the Kola Peninsula in the middle of the 1920s. His crew crossed the bountiful body of water from a new railway station bearing the lake's name to the Monche Inlet on the western side. Only a postal office had existed there during his previous visit in 1914. A Sami hunter, coachman and guide named Kalina Arkhipov remembered a fourteen-year-old boy who had been to Imandra before, but seemed surprised to realise that the grown-up Rikhter was standing before him. According to Rikhter's account, Arkhipov offered his assistance to this itinerant group of Soviet scientists curious about the area's natural resources.

As an adolescent, Rikhter had explored the region as a tourist with his older brothers. The alluring romantic vision of well-known nature writer Mikhail Prishvin had attracted the family to the North. Late in life in the 1970s, Rikhter attributed his decision to concentrate much of his scholarship on the physical geography of the Far North to the nature he encountered during this youthful adventure. 'The astonishing beauty and simultaneous originality of the untouched nature of the Kola Peninsula made such a great and indelible impression on me that I "rooted" for the North, as sports fans would say, for my whole life, chose geography as my specialisation and spent most of my life studying it'. Rooting for the North and drawing inspirations from its supposedly 'untouched' environment, however, did not entail only studying it. Whilst developing enough of a conservationist eye to rue the pollution of the lake from municipal and industrial sources, Rikhter also facilitated the dramatic industrialisation of the Lake Imandra basin. He recalled with pride, 'I was a witness and participant in many explorations of the region, and before my eyes a distant and neglected borderland turned into an advanced industrial centre of the Far North, equal to no other from the other countries of the world', and modestly acknowledged his own role, 'I am also happy that I managed to make a contribution, however small, to the study and assimilation of this wonderful land, which I consider to be my second (scientific) homeland'.[1]

There is a lot going on in Rikhter's reminiscences: an evocation of wild Russian nature, an attachment to a location of scientific fieldwork, a depiction of development as enhancing a region, and a notion of heroism within the individuals who contributed to industrialisation. One thing that strikes me as especially significant given the concerns of this volume is the deep connection between a particular landscape and world-historical changes to the natural environment. Rikhter seems to want to tie the concrete and local to broad trajectories in the human experience of the twentieth century. Or, to state it another way, he wants to unite actions taken upon a specific place with humanity's entrance into the Anthropocene.

The concept of the Anthropocene has exploded onto the scene in the twenty-first century as a way to capture the scale and novelty of recent environmental change. Geologists, social scientists and humanists discuss and debate the notion that human beings are now a major geological agent on the earth. Our impacts are so great as to have triggered a new geologic epoch beginning around 1945 or sometime before (dating the Anthropocene is a matter of heated debate). The Anthropocene Working Group of the International Commission on Stratigraphy has proposed officially establishing the Anthropocene as a geological epoch, though the larger body continues to debate whether or not to accept this recommendation.[2]

Conceptual predecessors for the Anthropocene, including Vladimir Vernadskii's theory of the noosphere as a realm in which human reason shaped the earth's geology (as discussed by Alan Roe elsewhere in this volume), have appeared over the years, but none has attracted quite as much attention as this twenty-first century neologism. An allure of the Anthropocene framework for understanding changes to the planet is that it cuts straight to the enormity of global anthropogenic modifications without dwelling on the nuances or counter-currents of modern environmental history. However, it also raises contentious questions about human agency, root causes and local landscapes.

If the Anthropocene implies 'the age of man', does that mean that humans now must act as if they are in control? Critical appraisals of the Anthropocene idea note that this dangerous implication threatens to re-entrench an overconfidence about bending nature to human will that certainly predates discussions

---

1. Rikhter, 'Chest' otkrytiia', 7 Apr. 1977, p. 2. Also see Semenov-Tian-Shanskii, 'Pamiati Rikhtera', 30 Oct. 1980, p. 4; ARAN f. 544, op. 1, d. 362, ll. 1–9.

2. Subramanian, 'Anthropocene Now'.

of a new geological epoch and might have gotten us into this situation in the first place. As Timothy LeCain writes, 'in suggesting that humans were indeed powerful enough to cause such global ecological shifts, the Anthropocene concept also tends to encourage the hubristic modernist faith in the human ability to fix the resulting problems'.[3] In defence, Jeremy Davis counters that the Anthropocene 'is not an anthropocentric concept ...human societies exert a novel and distinctive degree of sway in the physical world, but other creatures still continue independently to exert their own powers'.[4] Another criticism of the Anthropocene idea is that by appealing to the collective responsibility of humanity, it masks the disproportional and far more consequential influence of the wealthy and elites. Some even suggest replacing the Anthropocene with the Capitalocene to better highlight capitalism as the root cause of environmental crisis.[5] Such critiques typically minimise any distinctiveness of communist countries through appeals to the distorting logic of competitive world systems.[6] Other commentators believe that the Anthropocene adequately accounts for political economy or find these terminological debates to be more squabbling than substance.[7]

Attention to the Anthropocene also entails a risk of overlooking a major motif of environmental history scholarship: a focus on place that opens a window to human/nature interactions and imaginings. Historian Kate Brown has meditated on this issue and evocatively asked scholars to consider that 'history occurs in place, not, as historians commonly believe, in time. Or rather, time and place have been mixed together metaphorically so that everything, past and present, *takes place* in a particular *space* of time'.[8] In part the Anthropocene abstracts away from the local, and even the ecological, in favour of the global and geological. For anthropologist David Lipset the issue is even thornier. Based on ethnographic research on the Murik Lakes region of Papua New Guinea, he contends that the Anthropocene 'calls into question

---

3. LeCain, 'Against the Anthropocene', p. 4.

4. Davies, *The Birth of the Anthropocene*, p. 7.

5. Bonneuil and Fressoz, *The Shock of the Anthropocene*; Wark, *Molecular Red*; Moore, *Capitalism in the Web of Life*.

6. While I believe there are many reasons to focus on the environmental commonalities among capitalist and communist countries, I also think it is important to attend to communism as its own form of political economy. For this reason, I wrote of the 'Communist Anthropocene' in Bruno, *The Nature of Soviet Power*, pp. 15–18.

7. Davies, *The Birth of the Anthropocene*; McNeill and Engelke, *The Great Acceleration*; Purdy, *After Nature*.

8. Brown, *Dispatches from Dystopia*, p. 6.

the optimistic view that privileges place as a timeless medium through which people sense and understand nothing less than who they are as moral persons'. Instead, 'Anthropocene ethnography must first and foremost acknowledge the prospect, if not the fact, of place loss, the loss of sovereignty, loss of property, and loss of identity'.[9]

Places are certainly lost in the Anthropocene, but they are also made. Can there still be a way to tell stories of the Anthropocene that reveal global change whilst staying focused on the local? Must we sacrifice the concrete for the general? My answer in this essay is hopefully not. I seek to strike balances between the local and the global and between loss and creation by concentrating on a different lake than Lipset. A biography of a water body – or other specific landscape features such as mountains, forests or deserts – provides a promising avenue for interweaving place and the Anthropocene into a historical narrative. Certain elements of waterscapes, including the fact that people can be in them but not dwell in them, seem conducive to thinking about the global and the local synthetically. This essay tells the modern story of Lake Imandra with the aim of elucidating the relationship between worldwide trajectories and local histories in Russia's past.

In general, rivers have featured more prominently in global environmental histories than lakes. Prominent works by Richard White and Mark Cioc established river stories as a fruitful avenue for understanding societies' engagement with water.[10] In the Russian field, Randall Dills and Dorothy Zeisler-Vralsted productively employ this approach to study the Neva and Volga rivers, respectively, whilst Klaus Gestwa, Paul Josephson, Julia Obertreis and Maya Peterson orient their riparian histories more toward the hydroelectric and irrigation technologies adopted by the state.[11] Commenting broadly on the meanings of water in Russian culture, Jane Costlow and Arja Rosenholm note that a major theme from this scholarship is 'a history of the often violent desire to remake the country's geographies of water, allied to dreams of development and the "overcoming" of the past'.[12]

9. Lipset, 'Place in the Anthropocene', pp. 237–38.

10. White, *The Organic Machine*; Cioc, *The Rhine*; Mauch and Zeller (eds), *Rivers in History*.

11. Zeisler-Vralsted, *Rivers, Memory, and Nation-Building*; Dills, 'The River Neva and the Imperial Façade'; Obertreis, 'Soviet Irrigation Policies in Central Asia under Fire'; Josephson, *Industrialized Nature*; Peterson, *Pipe Dreams*; Gestwa, *Die Stalinschen Grossbauten des Kommunismus*. For an overview of river history that prominently highlights Russia's experience, see Roe, 'Riverine Environments', pp. 297–318.

12. Costlow and Rosenholm, 'Introduction', p. 4.

Andy Bruno

Development, dumping and despoliation are important themes in lake histories as well. But so are conservation, wilderness and efforts at amelioration. The Great Lakes of North America and, increasingly, Lake Baikal in Siberia have garnered the bulk of historians' attention. They have told stories of human disregard and folly, but also the deep cultural esteem, even sacredness, that people attribute to these lakes.[13] Smaller bodies like Imandra also deserve to be researched, since they can play just as prominent a role in a region's trajectory as rivers, seas and oceans and thereby help us better see local manifestation of larger trends. For instance, historian Erika Monahan has demonstrated the underappreciated function of Lake Iamysh in Siberia in fostering trade in the seventeenth and eighteenth centuries and Harriet Ritvo has written compellingly about how disputes around Thirlmere in the Lake District near Manchester shaped British environmentalism in the twentieth century.[14]

My biography of Lake Imandra similarly stresses its pivotal role in the development of the Kola Peninsula. Whilst scholars have justifiably highlighted the effect of the White and Barents Seas on the history of the territory, I contend that Imandra's influence has been nearly as important.[15] The lake has shaped how people have settled the region, how they have exploited its natural resources and how they have experienced it. Consider the fact that today some 300,000 people live in the nearby vicinity of Imandra – about the same number as reside in the regional capital of Murmansk on the coast.[16] Foregrounding different functions of the lake over the long run, my narrative will examine transportation and fishing, the use of the lake as a sink for industrial wastes and Imandra's place in the energy sector. To begin, however, let us turn to the earliest history of the lake and how scientists came to know it.

---

13. Angel, *The Scars of Project 459*; Ashworth, *The Late, Great Lakes*; Feldman, *A Storied Wilderness*; Kehoe, *Cleaning up the Great Lakes*; Feldman and Heasley, 'Recentering North American Environmental History'; Macfarlane, *Negotiating a River*; Langston, *Sustaining Lake Superior*; Breyfogle, 'The Fate of Fishing in Tsarist Russia'; Breyfogle, 'Sacred Waters'; Thomson, *Sacred Sea*.

14. Monahan, *Merchants of Siberia*, pp. 175–206; Ritvo, *The Dawn of Green*.

15. On the influence of the White and Barents Seas on the development of the Kola Peninsula, see Aleksandrov, Dmitreva, Laius and Laius, 'More – *nashe pole*'; Yurchak and Petter Nielsen (eds), *In the North My Nest is Made*.

16. Voinov, 'Understanding Human and Ecosystem Dynamics in the Kola Arctic', p. 377.

Polluted Pearl of the North

Early Knowledge of the Lake

Before there was a lake or people to interact with it, geological forces were at work – moving continents, lifting mountains, weathering in lowlands, creating water bodies and more. The moulding of the Imandra basin extends back into deep time. During the Precambrian eon, which encompasses four billion years of the earth's earliest history until around 541 million years ago, the basic complex of rock, including granite, gneiss, crystals and metal, that make up the territory of the future the lake formed. Volcanic activity later created igneous intrusions on several sides of what would become Imandra as well as varying hills and depressions that contributed to the jagged shoreline. Streams cut through these uplands, which also shaped the shores of Imandra, and filled in the sizeable depressions in the landscape. The rolling topography on top of a tectonic depression resulted in numerous islands interrupting the water body and a unified Imandra consisting of three thinly connected sections that together make a backward L. Bol'shaia Imandra takes up a north-south line nestled between the Khibiny Mountains in the east and the Monche tundra in the west. Below it sits Iokostrovskaia Imandra as an oval at the southern end of the lake. Then Babinskaia Imandra extends eastward along the southern foot of the lake.[17]

As a consequence of these geological and hydrological processes, Lake Imandra became the largest freshwater body in the Murmansk region, within the top twenty largest lakes in Europe by area and among the two hundred biggest lakes in the world.[18] As of the early 2000s, it occupied about 880 square kilometres in area, had an average depth of less than fifteen metres and reached as low as 67 metres below the surface. In terms of volume, Imandra held just under eleven cubic kilometres of freshwater, collected from a catchment basin totalling 12,300 square kilometres in area. Water entered Imandra from many small streams and rivers, but only drained out through the Niva River in the south, making its way into the Kandalaksha Bay of the White Sea. The length of the lake was 109 kilometres, whilst its varying width averaged a little over three kilometres across.[19]

17. Koshechkin, *Zhemchuzhina v ladonakh Laplandii*, pp. 9–13.
18. Weyhenmeyer, Psenner and Tranvik, 'Lakes of Europe', pp. 567–76; Herdendorf, 'Large Lakes of the World', pp. 382, 387.
19. Moiseenko, *Antropogennye modifikatsii ekosistemy ozera Imandra*, pp. 14–16.

Andy Bruno

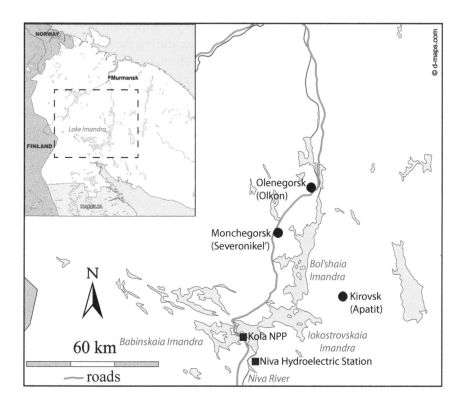

Map 3.1. Map of Lake Imandra with surrounding industrial facilities and cities. Kola NPP refers to the Kola Nuclear Power Plant. Source: Created by Andrew Johnson at The White Horse Press using d-maps. com: © d-maps http://www.d-maps.com/m/europa/russia/ murmansk/murmansk33.pdf.

Knowledge of these basic features of the lake developed fairly slowly. Of course, the indigenous Sami of the central corridor of the Kola Peninsula, whose ancestors arrived in the area as early as 9000 BCE, have known Lake Imandra for much of the Holocene. Yet most of their accumulated wisdom has been lost to posterity. Outsiders, for their part, became acquainted with the lake comparatively late. Maps of the territory even into the eighteenth century frequently failed to include a body that corresponded with what came to be called Lake Imandra. When it did appear in cartographic representations, Imandra, or sections of it, often had the names Lago Bianco, Lacus alba, Imantero and Akilliavr. The final one of these was an older Sami term that seems to have fallen out of favour over the centuries. Scholars debate the origin of the name

'Imandra', with one proposal being that it came from the Sami words for 'ice-continent', owing to its large frozen flat surface during the long winter, and another positing that it refers to a 'lake with a strongly indented coastline'.[20]

Scientific endeavours to understand Lake Imandra began with the onset of the industrial era elsewhere in the world, but turned to a thorough systematic assessment of its properties only with the industrialisation of the Kola Peninsula at the end of the 1920s. Expeditions under Alexander von Middendorff, Wilhelm Ramsay and N.V. Kurdriavtsev in the middle of the nineteenth century charted some details about the geography and geology of the Imandra basin, providing much greater detail than earlier depictions of explorers or postal route agents.[21] Nevertheless, one geographer at the beginning of the twentieth century claimed that 'in many respects Lake Imandra remains a total *terra incognita* … Neither limnological, nor hydrobiological research has been conducted on it and its depth, the structure of shores and its origin are not known'.[22]

This situation changed in the middle of the 1920s as the Soviets started eyeing the territories around the lake for mining development. A team led by Garviil Rikhter conducted several years of thorough research in the physical geography of Imandra, which culminated in newly detailed maps and a book-length study on the lake in 1934.[23] In addition to a number of other scientists participating in Rikhter's fieldwork, the son of Sami resident Kalina Arkhipov – Fedor – aided in the mapping of his homeland. Rikhter described him as 'very observant and inquisitive' and recounted a sophisticated and well-reasoned debate between the two Arkhipovs about the water levels of the lake.[24] Concluding that they both were right in different ways, Rikhter seemed to appreciate the hydrological insights of those indigenous to Imandra.

20. Rikhter, *Fiziko-geograficheskii ocherk ozera Imanda i ego basseina*, pp. 4–5; Moiseenko, *Antropogennye modifikatsii ekosistemy ozera Imandra*, pp. 3–5; Voinov, 'Understanding Human and Ecosystem Dynamics in the Kola Arctic', p. 376.

21. Koshechkin, *Zhemchuzhina v ladonakh Laplandii*, pp. 3–5; Tammiksaar and Stone, 'Alexander von Middendorff and His Expedition to Siberia (1842–1845)', p. 194.

22. Quoted in Koshechkin, *Zhemchuzhina v ladonakh Laplandii*, p. 5.

23. Rikhter, *Fiziko-geograficheskii ocherk ozera Imanda i ego basseina*.

24. Ibid., p. 107.

Andy Bruno

Moving and Feeding

Of the many functions that Lake Imandra came to play for residents and travellers on the Kola Peninsula, transportation and fishing possess the longest histories – ones that extend back before the Anthropocene. In both of these cases, traditional forms of engagement with the lake changed radically with Soviet-era development. Whilst more fish were taken from the lake and more people traversed it than ever before in the recent past, these activities were also, to a considerable degree, outflanked by newer economic endeavours. Long-term reliance on Imandra as a conduit for movement and seasonal sustenance obviously influenced the ecology of the lake, but not as much as the re-engineering and dumping that began around the dawn of the newest geological epoch.

People have been present in the territories around Imandra for thousands of years and fished the lake for much of this period. The Sami who kept seasonal camps nearby took advantage of the bountiful species in the lake and the surrounding streams of its watershed during the five to six months of the year that Imandra typically was not frozen. Hunting and inland fishing dominated the livelihoods of the Kola Sami until the late nineteenth century; it was only at this late point that they started to orient themselves more toward reindeer herding over reindeer hunting. Around this time, Kola residents allegedly possessed fishing grounds in 172 locations on the Imandra watershed.[25]

Meanwhile, Imandra had become just as important for incoming Russian settlers as a transportation entity. Novgorodians made their way up to the Kola Peninsula before Muscovy's fifteenth-century conquest. Over time, migrants gravitated toward a land route that took them from the town of Kandalaksha on the White Sea to the Kola inlet of the Barents Sea in the north and involved traversing the north-south axis of Imandra. Considerable numbers of Pomors of the White Sea region eventually turned to the Imandra route for their annual treks to the Murman coast for summer fishing in the Barents Sea, preferring this inland itinerary to sailing around the Kola Peninsula. The emerging Russian state also found this path useful as authorities created a postal route that went along Lake Imandra in the sixteenth century. Sami with draft reindeer would usually carry goods and information along the lake, which helped place the settlements in the Imandra corridor and on the western part of the Murman coast under state purview.[26] Near the end of the nineteenth century, modernist visions for Imandra emerged. The governor of the region,

---

25. Wheelersburg and Gutsol, 'Babinski and Ekostrovski', p. 224; Krupnik, *Arctic Adaptations*; Koshechkin, *Zhemchuzhina v ladonakh Laplandii*, pp. 51–53.

26. Ushakov, *Izbrannye proizvedeniia*.

Aleksandr Platonovich Engel'gardt, travelled along the lake during a tour of his dominion in the mid-1890s. His expedition plotted out the erection of a line of telegraph poles connecting Kandalaksha and Kola along the eastern side of Imandra. Engel'gardt also recounted sailing on the lake with Sami boats and mentioned the possibility of a railway line along the lake.[27] In this period, the largest settlement along the lake was a Sami outpost that would later become the Imandra railway station, where about 33 families lived at the start of the 1920s.[28]

World War One – that watershed moment for war economies in many parts of the world – triggered the construction of a railway. Divided into three segments, including the northernmost Kandalaksha-Kola section, the Murmansk Railway became operational during the final year of tsarist rule, connecting the new warm water port of Murmansk in the Arctic to the interior of the country. Foreign prisoners of war helped lay tracks along the shores of Imandra, which planners appreciated for its comparatively accommodating features. Unlike swampy Karelia to the south, the right bank of Imandra formed a relatively flat lowland 'almost along a meridian' and possessed sandy and clay soils.[29] For a while in the 1920s, the entire territory of the lake fell under the management of the Murmansk Railway, which not only arranged transportation but also promoted settlement and development, including of the fishing industry, on the territory.[30]

Stalinist industrialisation brought a frenzy of attention and activity to the Imandra basin. In addition to rail service becoming more frequent and stable, the new enterprises surrounding the lake began to occasionally ship items across it in the summer and haul them over the ice in the winter.[31] A highway on the western side of Imandra (opposite the railway) also developed and later came to serve considerable traffic.[32] The Soviet push to quickly become an industrial country in the 1930s was also greeted at the time by calls to develop a major fishing industry on Imandra. Local newspapers exhorted this cause and a new collective farm toyed with setting up a group devoted to

---

27. Engel'gardt, *Russkii sever"*, pp. 73–76.

28. Beliavskii, *Kratkii putevoditel' po Murmanskoi zheleznoi dorogi*, pp. 95–96.

29. *Murmanskaia zheleznaia doroga*, p. 28.

30. Arnol'dov, *Zheleznodorozhnaia kolonizatsiia v Karel'sko-Murmanskom krae*, pp. 42–45.

31. Pozniakov, *Severonikel'*, p. 48.

32. GAMO f. 773, op. 1, d. 55, l. 771.

Andy Bruno

fishing in the lake.[33] At the time one researcher estimated that lake fishing on the Kola Peninsula consisted of '49% whitefish (*sig*), 18.6% pike, 12% perch and 6.6% bull trout (*kumzha*)'.[34]

A few decades of intense industrial activity caused the fish populations of Imandra to noticeably deteriorate. Overfishing was one culprit. Both legally and illegally, many of the tens of thousands of new residents filling in towns like Kirovsk, Apatit, Olenegorsk and Monchegorsk supplemented their diets with catches from Imandra. A report from the mid-1960s by Mariia Vladimirskaia and A.E. Milovanova – scientists at the nearby Lapland nature reserve (*zapovednik*) – attributed a 'sharp reduction of stocks', including 'valuable species such as bull trout, whitefish and grayling', to the 'uncontrolled fishing' in the area. Whilst the whitefish decline came from simple overfishing, bull trout and grayling were threatened by 'amateur fishers' catching young fish as well as by discharges from logging and heavy industry.[35]

Indeed, the pollution that was severely changing the species composition of Imandra's fauna helped turn some of the fishers to the environmentalist cause. In 1966, V. Zhuravlev published a concerned letter in the main regional newspaper about his failures to catch once abundant species. He bemoaned that 'the huge basin of Lake Imandra, which once was replete with first-rate fish, has been depleted' and posited that 'if Imandra is protected from pollution of industrial enterprises, then with reasonable management it will yield so much fresh whitefish, grayling, bull trout, loach and trout that it could supply the population of the Kola Peninsula with fresh fish almost all year round'. Though motivated by a desire to continue fishing, the lesson he took was decidedly environmental: 'Protecting nature is everyone's affair ... People should not – they do not have the right to – pass by and apathetically watch as nature is ruined'.[36] To the extent that the declining stock of fish in Imandra reflected the Soviets shoving this territory into the Anthropocene, it is also noteworthy that some of those engaging most directly with the water body came to develop a more protectionist ethos. Local outpourings of modern environmentalism also accompanied the new geological era.

33. Vorontsov, 'Nachalo', 28 Nov. 1984, p. 2; *Khibinogorskii rabochii*, 'Vziat' sel'd' dlia Khibinogorska', 4 Jul. 1932, p. 1; *Poliarnaia pravda*, 'Sotsial'no-kul'turnyi sektor otstaet', 2 Jun. 1930, p. 3.

34. Bunakov, 'Ekonomicheskoe obosnovanie razvitiia olenevodstva Murmanskogo okruga', p. 114.

35. GARF f. A-358, op. 3, d. 4106, l. 3.

36. Zhuravlev, 'Chelovek i priroda', 11 May 1966, p. 4.

A Pristine Dump

Distinctive materials making their way into strata under the planet's surface provide stratigraphers with much of the evidence of their practice. Glaciation, volcanic activity and changes in the biomass can create distinctive markers in the geological record. In the theory of the Anthropocene, so will the massive quantities of industrial and consumer wastes that have been accumulating at a vastly accelerating scale. Lake Imandra has experienced its share of human dumping as a despoiling array of inorganic and organic chemicals have been transferred into it.

Initial dumping and its negative effects came fast and furious with the creation of a phosphate mining and enrichment enterprise just east of the lake in the Khibiny Mountains in the autumn of 1929. The firm called Apatit quickly drew tens of thousands of migrants – many forcibly relocated peasants – to the new city of Khibinogorsk (later Kirovsk) and its surrounding settlements. With scant municipal provisions, newcomers fouled many waterways with laundry and excrement, including the White River, which drained into Lake Imandra. More consequential was a decision by the leadership of the new enterprise to release materials from their enrichment factory directly into the White River – an avowedly 'temporary' measure that lasted for decades. Tailings from Apatit were later joined by another major source of municipal and industrial water pollution on the other side of Imandra. Located directly on the shores of the lake, Monchegorsk, and the accompanying nickel and copper combine, Severonikel', began to develop in the second half of the 1930s. Further road construction projects and timber operations also caused run-off that reached into the Imandra basin.

Scientists raised concerns about the deteriorating water quality in Imandra as early as the 1930s. Noting that 'the pollution of the water resulting from the development of large settlements and industrial enterprises also represents a small evil', biologist Vladimir Fridolin warned that dusts from apatite production were already changing the colour of the White River. Furthermore 'the influence of these wastes already spreads to Lake Imandra'.[37] In 1939, Rikhter more patiently observed that though 'the microfauna and microflora of water bodies [on the Kola Peninsula] are almost completely unstudied, the role of microorganisms in the purification of sewage and pollution of waters near cities currently has an enormous sanitary significance'.[38] Knowledge of pollution

---

37.   ARAN f. 544, op. 1, d. 161, ll. 40–41.
38.   ARAN f. 544, op. 1, d. 362, l. 7.

and awareness of its specific effects on Imandra amounted to very little until after the reconstruction of the heavy industrial towns after World War Two.

In the late 1940s, Lake Imandra entered 'the period of maximum pollution, when the degradation processes in the ecosystem reached their height', according to a group of later researchers led by Tatiana Moiseenko.[39] In addition to Apatit and Severonikel', Imandra acquired another emitting neighbour to the north in the early 1950s: the iron works of the Olenegorsk combine (Olkon). Together, these three enterprises undertook an assorted array of measures to limit water pollution, such as installing new filters, all whilst increasing production to a point that far outpaced mitigation. Indeed, the water recycling at Severonikel' and Olkon and the establishment of tailing dumps at Apatit did not prevent the pollution into Imandra from spiking into the 1970s.[40] Moiseenko's team has demonstrated that Apatit dumped a peak of 240 million cubic metres of wastes (including sulphates, chlorides, phosphorous, nepheline products and flotation reagents) a year in the late 1970s, Severonikel' emitted over 27 cubic metres of metal-laden liquid wastes in the middle of that decade, and Olkon released iron ore residue through that period.[41] Despite public promises by leadership of the enterprises and internal departments dedicated to nature protection to cut emissions, newspaper articles now declared 'discharges of industrial enterprises' to be a 'serious enemy' of Lake Imandra.[42]

Apatit's relationship with the lake is particularly illustrative of the initial ineffectiveness of these efforts to curb pollution. Around the same time that the enterprise established its first tailing dump in the late 1950s, which prevented it from emitting all of its wastes into Imandra's feeders, Apatit moved forward with a new enrichment plant that would use Imandra as a water supply. Part of the justification for taking Imandra's clear water for the plant's flotation process was that 'all other surface water bodies ... are unsuitable for the water supply, since they are polluted by wastewater discharges'.[43] Trying to balance its treatment of the lake as a sink and a supply led to thorny technical problems for innovating systems to curtail the ways that Apatit 'negatively affected the biological processes in Imandra'. By the middle of the 1970s, observers recognised that the

39. Moiseenko, *Antropogennye modifikatsii ekosistemy ozera Imandra*, p. 5.

40. GARF f. A-482, op. 50, d. 6179, ll. 42–43; Aleinikov and Smirnov, 'Problemy i mneniia', Sept. 1973, p. 2.

41. Moiseenko, *Antropogennye modifikatsii ekosistemy ozera Imandra*, pp. 25–27.

42. Aleinikov and Smirnov, 'Problemy i mneniia', Sept. 1973, p. 2; *Poliarnaia pravda*, 'Chelovek – khoziain prirody', 8 Aug. 1973, p. 2.

43. RGAE, f. 4372, op. 67, d. 1961, l. 180.

'self-cleaning ability' of the lake was inadequate.[44] Yet the enterprise was still releasing an entire 'bouquet of flotation chemicals' and '47,300 cubic metres a day' of purified municipal sewage into the lake. It also failed to implement a system of water recycling that already existed at the neighbouring metal facilities because of the high cost of adapting it to work with apatite-nepheline ore.[45] Staff at Apatit acknowledged that these emissions were 'inconsistent with the active legislation on nature protection'.[46] Henceforth, the firm did reduce its pollution of Imandra by turning to eighty per cent recycled water in the 1980s, which grew to over ninety per cent by the early 2000s. It also improved its removal of flotation reagents and apparently decreased its release of industrial sewage by 4.6 times between 1978 and 2003.[47]

The shift at Apatit and the other firms helped allow Imandra to enter a 'period of reduced anthropogenic loads' from the middle of the 1980s, even if, as an article at the time noted, 'the lake is polluted as before'.[48] There were multiple causes for the lightening of pollution loads into Imandra, but high among them was the economic crisis of the Soviet collapse. Production and pollution from the Kola factories dropped precipitously, and by the time industry recovered better abatement technologies were available, especially at the successful and internationally pressured Noril'sk Nikel' (which owns Severonikel'). This downturn in environmental damage is a significant part of Imandra's local story in the Anthropocene. Countervailing trends toward cleaner water and air are most comprehensible when considering specific places. In this case, the political and economic crisis in Russia helped cause enterprises to pull back from the ecocidal extremes of the 1970s and early 1980s. Or, as I have written elsewhere, Imandra retuned to a situation of 'regular ruin'.[49] Instead of mistaking local improvements for global trends, a perspective that attaches histories of places to trajectories of the Anthropocene helps make sense of nuances without losing sight of the big picture.

Additionally, though the quantity of pollution put into Imandra has been reduced, its effects on the lake's ecosystem were deep and remain some-

44. Aleinikov and Smirnov, 'Problemy i mneniia', Sept. 1973, p. 2.

45. *Priroda i chelovek*, 'Uvy, otpiska!', p. 18; RGAE, f. 4372, op. 67, d. 1961, l. 164.

46. RGAE, f. 4372, op. 67, d. 1961, ll. 81–82.

47. Barabanov and Kalinina, '*Apatit*', p. 95; Markov, P. A. 2005. 'Prirodookhannaia dei-atel'nost' OAO "Apatit"', p. 18.

48. 'Moiseenko, *Antropogennye modifikatsii ekosistemy ozera Imandra*, p. 5; *Priroda i chelovek*, Oct. 1987, p. 18.

49. Bruno, *The Nature of Soviet Power*, pp. 213–219.

what irreversible. Whilst before the 1930s Imandra possessed what scientists call ultrafresh water, with a low quantity of biomass, dumping changed the make-up and amount of species there. Metals and chemical agents accumulated in the sediment near the Belaia and Monche Bays (bordering Apatit and Severonikel', respectively) and wastewater from Olkon caused the formation of hematite slimes. Also the chemistry of the water more generally increased in toxicity from industrial pollutants, whilst biogenic compounds from municipal sources led to extreme eutrophication, and associated algae blooms, near the dump sites. As many of the native species in Imandra disappeared, the quantity of zooplankton, phytoplankton and zoobenthos in the lake increased. Pollution contributed to significant declines in the loach and salmon-trout populations and numerous diseases and growth abnormalities in the fish that remained.[50] Fishing in Imandra rose again with the economic hardships of the Soviet collapse, meaning that people were eating more of these diseased fish than earlier.[51] Human consumers of drinking water from the lake also experienced the accumulation of nickel and other metals in their livers and kidneys, which can cause gastrointestinal, cardiovascular and blood ailments.[52]

During the 1990s and 2000s, water quality in Imandra generally improved on account of reduced concentrations of metals in the water and fish diseases decreased. Though eutrophication processes have continued, water scientists now see a stabilisation of Imandra's ecosystem into a new structure. The local consequences of anthropogenic change of the Anthropocene nevertheless have a permanence. Concerning Lake Imandra, '*the ecosystem recovery* does not mean that the ecosystem regains its original natural state'.[53]

Storing and Releasing

Imandra also became a tool of the regional energy economy during the twentieth century. It served as both a reservoir for hydroelectricity and a cooling pond for nuclear power. Whilst the impact of the Kola energy sector on the water quality of the lake might be less striking than direct pollution, the story of the

---

50. Moiseenko, 'Anthropogenic Transformations of the Arctic Ecosystem of Lake Imandra', pp. 296–309.

51. Moiseenko, 'Long-term Modification of Arctic Lake Ecosystems', p. 10.

52. Moiseenko, 'Water Pollution Effect on Population Health in an Industrial Northern Region', pp. 194–203.

53. Moiseenko, 'Anthropogenic Transformations of the Arctic Ecosystem of Lake Imandra', p. 308.

lake's reconfiguring during the Anthropocene is still quite dramatic. The first attempt to use the territory as an energy source came even before the push for hydropower. In the desperate circumstances at the end of the Russian Civil War, White Army forces planned to collect 20,000 logs from the shores and islands of Lake Imandra for fuel in 1920.[54] Little of this occurred before the Bolsheviks expelled them from the North and later brought their own plans to harvest Imandra.

Enthused about electricity generally and exploiting 'white coal' (hydroelectricity) in particular, Soviet authorities ordered a thorough survey of the Kola Peninsula's streams in the 1920s. As the project to create Apatit got off the ground, planners decided to turn the Niva River, which drains Imandra, into an energy producer. Several thousand ill-equipped forced peasant migrants ('special settlers' in official state parlance) installed an initial unit on the river in the middle of the 1930s – all the while experiencing occasionally lethal exposure to the elements of the harsh North. Two additional units of the Niva cascade were built in the late 1940s and early 1950s. Together, these hydroelectric installations turned Imandra into an indirect natural reservoir, since outflow from the lake fuelled the new hydroelectric stations and filled a constructed reservoir at Lake Pirenga.[55]

The Niva units altered the level of water in Lake Imandra and the cycle of its variation. By controlling the flow of the Niva with dams, the new infrastructure determined the dynamics of Imandra, filling up and draining every year. At first, hydroelectricity raised the water in the lake by half a metre, which led to soil erosion and an increased rockiness along its shores. It also held the lake at its fullest level for several months during the summer, regulating outflow instead of allowing it to occur slowly over time and without interference.[56] Undeterred, the planners plotting additional hydroelectric stations on the Niva at the end of World War Two noted that in further increasing 'the level of water in Lake Imandra … more than fifty hectares of state farm land will be flooded and the subsurface water on the remaining swampy area of the state farm will rise'.[57] Yet a drought at the end of the 1950s conversely led to a sharp decrease in the water level of Imandra, as it was drained to keep the turbines running at the Niva facilities.[58] This dry spell also left local authorities concerned about

54.   GAMO f. R-621, op. 1, d. 22, ll. 73–76a.

55.   Bruno, *The Nature of Soviet Power*, pp. 234–7, 242–3.

56.   Koshechkin, *Zhemchuzhina v ladonakh Laplandii*, pp. 74–75.

57.   RGASPI f. 17, op. 122, d. 104, l. 173.

58.   Koshechkin, *Zhemchuzhina v ladonakh Laplandii*, pp. 74–75.

an electrical dearth and thus factored into a decision to create a different sort of electricity plant on the shore of Imandra – the Kola Nuclear Power Plant.

Abundant freshwater in the lake was just as important for the nuclear plant as for hydroelectric stations. But instead of supplying mechanical energy through river flow, the water held heat energy that allowed fission to occur without triggering an explosion. The need to be able to take in and release massive quantities of water in order to regulate the reactors helped inspire planners to locate the Kola Nuclear Power Plant in the middle of the southern end of the lake, between Iokostrovskaia and Babinskaia Imandra. Accompanying the facility when it came online in the 1970s was another new industry town of the Far North, Poliarnye Zori. Newspapers were quick to celebrate the opening of the power plant, as 'a feat on Imandra', acknowledging the important contribution of the lake to this electrical system.[59] Staff at the facility also tried to assure the public that the water poured back into Imandra did not 'exceed the natural activity of lake water'.[60] Instead they stressed that the heated water, which the plant let out into the Molochnaia Bay through a kilometre-long tube, improved the environment by allowing rainbow trout to grow in a special fish farm.[61] Though water temperature has affected the pH in parts of the lake and the composition of organisms highly sensitive to it, scientists have tended to agree that, despite emissions from the nuclear power plant, the Molochnaia Bay of Imandra 'generally retains features of an oligotrophic water body'.[62]

But, of course, nuclear power acquires its anthropogenic impact more through the entire cycle of mining, enriching, splicing and storing radioactive materials and the risks it poses to landscapes in the case of an accident than through direct emissions. Lake Imandra has already been modified, if not degraded, by the presence of the Kola Nuclear Power Plant. It has also experienced several close calls that might have significantly despoiled the lake.[63] As a place where atomic facilities are set to be located for decades to come, Imandra is entangled in a new geography of risk that is characteristic of the Anthropocene.

59. *Poliarnaia pravda*, 'Podvig na Imandre', 7 Jul. 1973, p. 1.

60. Berlin, 'Kol'skaia AES i okruzhaiushchaia sreda', p. 3.

61. Fedotov and Aleksandrov, 'Bezvrednoe sosedstvo', 5 Jul. 1976, p. 4.

62. Vandysh, 'Specific Features of Zooplankton Community in Industrially Polluted Areas of Subarctic Lake Imandra (Monche, Belaya, and Molochnaya Bays)', p. 396.

63. Bøhmer, *The Arctic Nuclear Challenge*, pp. 39–45.

Conclusion

In 1985 – arguably the moment when pollution in Lake Imandra was at its height – Boris Koshechkin struck an optimistic note about the environmental future of the water body in his short monograph, *Pearl in the Palms of Lapland*. He wrote:

> There is every reason to hope that an end to the gathering of pollutants in the water body and the introduction of a recycled water supply at enterprises around the lake, along with special measures for the reclamation of the water table, can lead to the restoration of the oligotrophic character of the lake. The process of eutrophication will cease, the natural qualities of the water will approach their original conditions and, consequently, the biological resources of the lake will be restored.[64]

Further research, however, has made it clear that Imandra is unlikely to ever return to pre-industrial conditions. Like the Great Lakes in North America, Imandra has instead had the opportunity to acquire a new form of ecosystem stability, which now faces additional pressures from a changing climatic system. The effects of global warming on Imandra remain primarily in the realm of probabilistic forecasts, but warmer water is likely to increase eutrophic conditions and the uptake of toxic metals by fish and plankton.[65] If this is the case, climate change will be working against melioration.

The story I have told here about Lake Imandra has been very much shaped by the deeply local and the deeply global, whilst the specific politics of Russian history have played a secondary role in this account. Imperatives to build socialism through industrial transformation obviously mattered for the explorers, Sami, relocated peasants, fishers, scientists and planners who have engaged with Imandra over the past century or so. But the lake itself experienced many of the changes that the Soviets wrought on its waters at some remove from the specific mid-level ideological motivations that spawned Anthropocene conditions there. What is clear, though, is that by playing its assorted economic functions, Imandra profoundly shaped regional development in this part of the Far North. Political ecologies and environmental histories of places in the Anthropocene stand to offer many insights, including how aquatic localities can facilitate global trajectories.

---

64. Koshechkin, *Zhemchuzhina v ladonakh Laplandii*, p. 82.
65. Moiseenko, 'Long-term Modification of Arctic Lake Ecosystems', pp. 11–12.

Andy Bruno

BIBLIOGRAPHY

Aleinikov, N. and A. Smirnov. 1973. 'Problemy i mneniia. "Apatit" i Imandra. Chto nuzhno dlia dobrogo sosedstva?'. *Poliarnaia pravda*. September.

Aleksandrov, D.A., Z.V. Dmitreva, D.L. Laius and Iu.A. Laius. 2010. *'More – nashe pole': kolichestvennye dannye o rybnykh promyslakh Belogo i Barentseva morei XVII – nachale XX vv.* Saint Petersburg: European University at Saint Petersburg Press.

Angel, Traci. 2014. *The Scars of Project 459: The Environmental Story of the Lake of the Ozarks*. Fayetteville: University of Arkansas Press.

Arkhiv Rossiiskoi Akademii Nauk (ARAN, Archive of the Russian Academy of Sciences).

Arnol'dov, A. 1925. *Zheleznodorozhnaia kolonizatsiia v Karel'sko-Murmanskom krae: Po materialam razrabotannym kolonizatsionnym otdelom pravleniia dorogi*. Leningrad: Pravlenie Murmanskoi zheleznoi dorogi.

Ashworth, William. 1987. *The Late, Great Lakes: An Environmental History*. Detroit: Wayne State University Press.

Barabanov, A.V. and T.A. Kalinina. 2004. *'Apatit': vek iz veka*. Apatity: Laplandia Minerals.

Beliavskii, F. 1923. *Kratkii putevoditel' po Murmanskoi zheleznoi dorogi*.

Berlin, V. 1974. 'Kol'skaia AES i okruzhaiushchaia sreda'. *Kandalakshskii kommunist*. 19 March.

Bøhmer, Nils, Aleksandr Nikitin, Igor Kudrik, Thomas Nilsen, Andrey Zolotkov and Michael H. McGovern. 2001. *The Arctic Nuclear Challenge*. Bellona Report. Vol. 3. Oslo: Bellona.

Bonneuil, Christophe and Jean-Baptiste Fressoz. 2016. *The Shock of the Anthropocene*. London: Verso.

Breyfogle, Nicholas. 2013. 'The Fate of Fishing in Tsarist Russia: The Human-Fish Nexus in Lake Baikal'. *Sibirica* 12 (2): 1–29.

Breyfogle, Nicholas. 2017. 'Sacred Waters: The Spiritual World of Lake Baikal'. In Jane Costlow and Arja Rosenholm (eds), *Meanings and Values of Water in Russian Culture*, pp. 32–50. London: Routledge.

Brown, Kate. 2015. *Dispatches from Dystopia: Histories of Places Not Yet Forgotten*. Chicago: University of Chicago Press.

Bruno, Andy. 2016. *The Nature of Soviet Power: An Arctic Environmental History*. Cambridge: Cambridge University Press.

Bunakov, E.V. 1934. 'Ekonomicheskoe obosnovanie razvitiia olenevodstva Murmanskogo okruga'. *Sovetskoe olenevodstvo* 4: 107–62.

Cioc, Mark. 2002. *The Rhine: An Eco-Biography, 1815–2000*. Seattle: University of Washington Press.

Costlow, Jane and Arja Rosenholm. 2017. 'Introduction'. In Jane Costlow and Arja Rosenholm (eds), *Meanings and Values of Water in Russian Culture*, pp. 1–12. London: Routledge.

Davies, Jeremy. 2016. *The Birth of the Anthropocene*. Berkeley: University of California Press.

Dills, Randall. 2010. 'The River Neva and the Imperial Façade: Culture and Environment in Nineteenth-Century St. Petersburg Russia'. Ph.D. diss., University of Illinois at Urbana-Champaign.

Engel'gardt, A.P. 1997. *Russkii sever: putevye zapiski*. Saint Petersburg: Izdanie A.S. Suvorina.

Fedotov, V. and B. Aleksandrov. 1976. 'Bezvrednoe sosedstvo'. *Poliarnaia pravda*. 5 July.

Feldman, James and Lynne Heasley. 2007. 'Recentering North American Environmental History: Pedagogy and Scholarship in the Great Lakes Region'. *Environmental History* 12 (4): 951–8.

Feldman, James W. 2011. *A Storied Wilderness: Rewilding the Apostle Islands*. Seattle: University of Washington Press.

Gestwa, Klaus. 2010. *Die Stalinschen Grossbauten des Kommunismus*. München: R. Oldenbourg Verlag.

Gosudarstvennyi arkhiv Murmanskoi oblasti (GAMO, State Archive of Murmansk Oblast').

Gosudarstvennyi arkhiv Rossiiskoi Federatsii (GARF, State Archive of the Russian Federation).

Herdendorf, Charles E. 1982. 'Large Lakes of the World'. *Journal of Great Lake Research* 8 (3): 379–412.

Josephson, Paul R. 2002. *Industrialized Nature: Brute Force Technology and the Transformation of the Natural World*. Washington, DC: Island Press.

Kehoe, Terence. 1997. *Cleaning up the Great Lakes: From Cooperation to Confrontation*. DeKalb: Northern Illinois University Press.

Khibinogorskii rabochii. 1932. 'Vziat' sel'd' dlia Khibinogorska'. 4 July.

Koshechkin, B.I. 1985. *Zhemchuzhina v ladonakh Laplandii*. Leningrad: Gidrometeoizdat.

Krupnik, Igor. 1993. *Arctic Adaptations: Native Whalers and Reindeer Herders of Northern Eurasia*. Hanover: University Press of New England.

Langston, Nancy. 2017. *Sustaining Lake Superior: An Extraordinary Lake in a Changing World*. New Haven: Yale University Press.

LeCain, Timothy. 2015. 'Against the Anthropocene: A Neo-Materialist Perspective'. *History, Culture, and Modernity* 3 (1): 1–28.

Lipset, David. 2014. 'Place in the Anthropocene: A Mangrove Lagoon in Papua New Guinea in the Time of Rising Sea-Levels'. *HAU: Journal of Ethnographic Theory* 4 (3): 215–43.

Markov, P.A. 2005. 'Prirodookhannaia deiatel'nost' OAO "Apatit"'. In A.I. Nikolaev (ed.), *Kompleksnost' ispol'zovaniia mineral'no–syr'evykh resursov—osnova povysheniia ekologicheskoi bezopasnosti regiona,* pp. 17–21. Apatity: KNTs AN.

Mauch, Christof and Thomas Zeller (eds). 2008. *Rivers in History: Perspectives on Waterways in Europe and North America.* Pittsburgh: University of Pittsburgh Press.

Macfarlane, Daniel. 2014. *Negotiating a River: Canada, the US, and the Creation of the St. Lawrence Seaway.* Vancouver: University of British Columbia Press.

McNeill, J.R. and Peter Engelke. 2016. *The Great Acceleration: An Environmental History of the Anthropocene.* Cambridge, MA: Harvard University Press.

Moore, Jason W. 2015. *Capitalism in the Web of Life: Ecology and the Accumulation of Capital.* London: Verso.

Moiseenko, T.I., V.A. Dauval'ter, A.A. Lukin, L.P. Kudriavtseva, B.P. Il'iashchuk, L.I. Il'iashchuk, S.S. Sandimirov, L.Ia. Kagan, O.M. Vandysh, Iu.N. Sharova, I.N. Koroleva and A.N. Sharov. 2002. *Antropogennye modifikatsii ekosistemy ozera Imandra.* Moscow: Nauka.

Moiseenko, T.I., N.A. Gashkina, A.N. Sharov, O.I. Vandysh and L.P. Kudryavtseva. 2009. 'Anthropogenic Transformations of the Arctic Ecosystem of Lake Imandra: Tendencies for Recovery after Long Period of Pollution'. *Water Resources* 36 (3): 296–309.

Moiseenko, Tatyana I., Andrey N.Sharov, Oksana I. Vandish, Lubov P. Kudryavtseva, Natalia A. Gashkina and Catherine Rose. 2010. 'Long-term Modification of Arctic Lake Ecosystems: Reference Condition, Degradation under Toxic Impacts and Recovery (Case Study Imandra Lakes, Russia)'. *Limnologica* 39 (1): 1–13.

Moiseenko, T.I., V.V. Megorskii, N.A. Gashkina and L.P. Kudryavtseva. 2010. 'Water Pollution Effect on Population Health in an Industrial Northern Region'. *Water Resources* 37 (2): 194–203.

Murmanskaia zheleznaia doroga: Kratkii ocherk postroiki zheleznoi dorogi na Murmane s opisaniem eia raiona. 1916. Petrograd.

Obertreis, Julia. 2018. 'Soviet Irrigation Policies in Central Asia under Fire: The Ecological Debate in the Turkmen and Uzbek Republics, 1970–1991'. In Nicholas Breyfogle (ed.), *Eurasian Environments: Nature and Ecology in Eurasian History,* pp. 113–29. Pittsburgh: University of Pittsburgh Press.

Peterson, Maya K. 2019. *Pipe Dreams: Water and Empire in Central Asia's Aral Sea Basin.* Cambridge: Cambridge University Press.

Poliarnaia pravda. 1973. 'Chelovek – khoziain prirody'. 8 August.

Poliarnaia pravda. 1973. 'Podvig na Imandre'. 7 July.

Poliarnaia pravda. 1930. 'Sotsial'no-kul'turnyi sektor otstaet'. 2 June.

Pozniakov, V.Ia. 1999. *Severonikel' (stranitsy istorii kombinata 'Severonikel'')*. Moscow: Rud i metall.

Priroda i chelovek. 1987. 'Uvy, otpiska!'. No. 10 (October): 18.

Purdy, Jedediah. 2015. *After Nature: A Politics for the Anthropocene*. Cambridge, MA: Harvard University Press.

Rikhter, G.D. 1934. *Fiziko-geograficheskii ocherk ozera Imandra i ego basseina*. Leningrad: Gosudarstvennoe tekhniko-teoreticheskoe izdatel'stvo.

Rikhter, G.D. 1977. 'Chest' otkrytiia: vospominaniia pervoprokhodtsev'. *Monchegorskii rabochii.* 7 April.

Ritvo, Harriet. 2009. *The Dawn of Green: Manchester, Thirlmere, and Modern Environmentalism*. Chicago: University of Chicago Press.

Roe, Alan. 2012. 'Riverine Environments'. In J.R. McNeill and Erin Stewart Mauldin (eds), *A Companion to Global Environmental History*, pp. 297–318. Chichester: Wiley-Blackwell.

Rossiiskii gosudarstvennyi arkhiv ekonomiki (RGAE, Russian State Archive of the Economy).

Rossiiskii gosudarstvennyi arkhiv sotsial'no-politicheskoi istorii (RGASPI, Russian State Archive of Social and Political History).

Semenov-Tian-Shanskii, O. 1980. 'Pamiati Rikhtera'. *Monchegorskii rabochii.* 30 October.

Subramanian, Meera. 2019. 'Anthropocene Now: Influential Panel Votes to Recognize Earth's New Epoch'. *Nature.* 21 May. https://www.nature.com/articles/d41586-019-01641-5.

Tammiksaar, Erki and Ian R. Stone. 2007. 'Alexander von Middendorff and His Expedition to Siberia (1842–1845)'. *Polar Record* 43: 193–216.

Thomson, Peter. 2009. *Sacred Sea: A Journey to Lake Baikal*. Oxford: Oxford University Press.

Wark, McKenzie. 2015. *Molecular Red: Theory for the Anthropocene*. London: Verso.

Weyhenmeyer, G.A., R. Psenner and L.J. Tranvik. 2009. 'Lakes of Europe'. In G.E. Likens (ed.) *Encyclopedia of Inland Waters*. Vol. 2, pp. 567–76. Oxford: Elsevier.

Wheelersburg, Robert P. and Natalia Gutsol. 2008. 'Babinski and Ekostrovski: Saami *Pogosty* on the Western Kola Peninsula, Russia from 1880 to 1940'. *Arctic Anthropology* 45 (1): 79–96.

White, Richard. 1995. *The Organic Machine: The Remaking of the Columbia River*. New York: Hill and Wang.

Ushakov, I.F. 1997. *Izbrannye proizvedeniia*. Vol. 1, *Kol'skaia zemlia*. Murmansk: Murmanskoe knizhnoe izdatel'stvo.

Andy Bruno

Vandysh, O.I. 2012. 'Specific Features of Zooplankton Community in Industrially Polluted Areas of Subarctic Lake Imandra (Monche, Belaya, and Molochnaya Bays)'. *Russian Journal of Ecology* **43** (5): 390–7.

Voinov, Alexey, Lars Bromley, Elizabeth Kirk, Anatoliy Korchak, Joshua Farley, Tatiana Moiseenko, Tatiana Krasovskaya, Zoya Makarova, Vladimir Megorski, Vladimir Selin, Galina Kharitonova and Robert Edson. 2004. 'Understanding Human and Ecosystem Dynamics in the Kola Arctic: A Participatory Integrated Study'. *Arctic* **57** (4): 375–88.

Vorontsov, N.N. 1984. 'Nachalo: Iz istorii kombinata'. *Metallurg Zapoliar'ia.* 28 November.

Yurchenko, Alexei and Jens Petter Nielsen (eds). 2006. *In the North My Nest is Made: Studies in the History of the Murman Colonization, 1860–1940.* Saint Petersburg: European University at Saint Petersburg Press.

Zeisler-Vralsted, Dorothy. 2014. *Rivers, Memory, and Nation-Building: A History of the Volga and Mississippi Rivers.* New York: Berghahn Books.

Zhuravlev, V. 1966. 'Chelovek i priroda'. *Poliarnaia pravda.* 11 May.

4.

THE VISION AND THE REALITY IN THE TAIGA OF KARELIA AND THE ARKHANGEL'SK OBLAST': OLEG CHERVIAKOV AND VODLOZERO NATIONAL PARK

Alan Roe[1]

'In transforming nature', Maksim Gor'kii famously wrote, 'man transforms himself.'[2] Gor'kii penned these words, which reflected the Promethean world-view of Stalinism and the Communist Party's belief in the malleability of the human spirit, specifically about the convicts who dug the iconic Baltic-White Sea (*Belomor*) Canal and cut vast swathes of forest in Karelia – an autonomous Republic that borders Finland and is the most densely forested part of Euro-pean Russia. Whilst the canal proved too difficult to navigate for productive economic use, central planners increasingly oriented the Karelian economy and the neighbouring Arkhangel'sk Oblast' towards the exploitation of its forests in the decades following the iconic canal's completion. By the late 1980s, Karelia alone accounted for fifteen per cent of the USSR's timber harvest.[3]

This emphasis on transforming northern forest to lumber, paper and other timber-derived products had long discouraged the government of Karelia and the RSFSR from establishing nature reserves (*zapovedniks*) – the most common form of protected territory for the USSR's first several decades – in Karelia. Dedicated mainly to scientific research, the *zapovedniks* imposed strict rules about visitation by the wider public. However, beginning in the late 1960s, geographers, landscape architects, game wardens and many others among the environmentally-concerned public argued that the Soviet Union needed national parks to meet the growing recreation demands of Soviet citizens and

---

1. First published in Roe, *Into Russian Nature*, pp. 206–24. Reproduced here in revised format with permission from Oxford University Press.

2. Gorky, *Belomor*, p. 216.

3. GARF f. A-259, op. 49, d. 3399, l. 42.

Alan Roe

reconcile the goals of landscape protection and economic development.[4] As the discussion about national parks expanded over the following two decades, Karelia became an increasingly popular destination for tourists.[5]

When the RSFSR began establishing national parks in the early 1980s (some other union republics established them during the 1970s), concerned biologists, geographers and foresters saw in national parks, unlike *zapovedniks*, a way to make tourism more profitable for Karelia and thereby direct future economic growth away from timber extraction.[6] As concerns about the RSFSR's natural environment intensified during Perestroika and the RSFSR Committee on Nature Protection discussed expanding significantly the territory under federal protection, many among the environmentally concerned public argued that the establishment of national parks was a task of great urgency for Karelia. In 1988, as this discussion animated Karelia's scientific community, a young university student named Oleg Cherviakov took a life-changing trip on the Illeks River into Lake Vodlozero.

The following pages will tell the remarkable story of Vodlozero National Park in Karelia and the Arkhangel'sk Oblast'. Inspired by the vast swath of old growth forest he saw during his fateful trip, Oleg Cherviakov would over the following three years conceive a park that reflected both his internal spiritual search and the dramatic economic and cultural changes rapidly taking place in the USSR during Perestroika. Cherviakov believed that foreign tourism would revive the region's economy and allow it to rely less on timber harvesting in the future. He envisioned the park as a catalyst for the return to the region's precommunist 'organic development' grounded in its Orthodox Christian traditions. Eventually, he argued, Vodlozero National Park might provide a model for economic development and cultural restoration for all of the Russian North.

Cherviakov's grandiose pronouncements resonated widely during a period of profound transformation in Russia and hope throughout the world – often conveyed through the rubric of 'sustainable development' – about the ability of humankind to come together to solve common environmental problems. However, the park could not have been established at a worse time – just before the collapse of the USSR – for realising this vision. Cherviakov's idealistic declarations about the park's transformative possibilities created unrealistic expectations that could never be met at a time when, in the aftermath of the

---

4. See for example Gerasimov et al., *Teoreticheskie osnovi rekreatsionnoi geographii*, p. 9.

5. Koenker, *Club Red*, p. 279. On the development of National Parks, see Roe, *Into Russian Nature*.

6. NARK f. 6196, op. 1, d. 5, l. 40.

USSR, the fledgling government of the Russian Federation was unable to support national parks as it dealt with economic collapse and a push for greater regional autonomy. Locals who had vested their hopes in Cherviakov and decried the forestry industry quickly became sceptical of the park's prospects for improving their economic situation. Whilst Cherviakov successfully raised the park's international profile and gained financial support from international organisations, he left his position as park director in 2005 after losing faith that the area's inhabitants would ever fully embrace his vision of economic, cultural and spiritual transformation.

The history of Vodlozero's National Park in many ways closely resembles those of many other Russian national parks.[7] Throughout the RSFSR and, after 1991, the Russian Federation, the high expectations set by park founders led to great disappointment when the state did not provide the resources for parks to become fully functional, profit-making establishments. However, perhaps no other founder of a Russian national park has proposed such a broadly transformative vision or experienced such thorough disillusionment as Cherviakov.

A Love of the Forest

'I don't know how to explain this', he said of one of his trips in the forest during early adolescence, 'but one time it happened; it opened fully. I had a mysterious, mystical meeting with nature, a meeting with the forest. This changed my entire life.'[8] Frequently, as he walked through forests near his home of Kharkiv, in present-day Ukraine, and throughout different parts of the Far North of Russia or Siberia during summer vacations, Cherviakov saw markers on trees that indicated impending cuts. 'Every time', he said to me in June 2015 on the island of Varishpelda where he now lives, 'I left a forest, I said goodbye, not knowing whether or not it would be there when I returned.'[9]

Through the nineteenth and early twentieth centuries, Russian writers romanticised northern forests as a broad discussion about the destruction of forests – frequently referred to as 'the forest question' – animated Russian intellectuals and scientists.[10] The 'forest question' largely disappeared from public discourse in the USSR's first decades. Forest harvests, especially in Arkhangel'sk

7. Zabelina et al., *Zapovedniki SSSR*.

8. Interview with Oleg Cherviakov, 20 Jun. 2015.

9. Ibid.

10. Costlow, 'Imaginations of Destruction: The "Forest Question" in Nineteenth Century Russian Culture', pp. 91–118.

Oblast' and Karelia, expanded dramatically under Stalin, with foresters and Soviet leaders largely embracing an 'illusion' that the forests were 'endless'.[11] This perception started changing after Stalin's death in 1953 ushered in a liberalised period of more open discussion under Nikita Khrushchev, commonly known as the 'Thaw'. In the years that followed, Leonid Leonov's novel *The Russian Forest* (1953), which criticised Soviet forestry practices, spurred larger debates about making forestry more sustainable.[12] In the ensuing decades, deforestation became one of the most talked about issues among the environmentally concerned community as forests of Karelia and Arkhangel'sk Oblast' continued to make up a disproportionate share of the Soviet timber harvest.[13]

In taking trips to the eastern part of the Arkhangel'sk Oblast' during his final two years of high school (1984–1985), Cherviakov witnessed first-hand and grew deeply concerned about timber harvesting in the North. The oblast's traditional villages further away from major forestry enterprises, however, left an equally strong impression. There, he met with people who, in his mind, lived as in much the same way as before the revolution. Waxing romantic, he said to me when I met him in 2015:

> They lived in harmony with nature. I saw that the level of spiritual development and the level of knowledge exceeds ours many times. With time I came to understand that it was based on a special relationship to the earth as mother and in the belief in God. These two bases made this traditional world of the village of the Russian North.[14]

Cherviakov's passion for the forest continued to grow stronger after enrolling in the Kharkiv Physics Institute, where he specialised in theoretical nuclear physics. His yearning for the 'ideal' forest led him back to the North during his summer breaks. In the summer of 1987, Cherviakov led a group of fellow students from his Institute to Solovki to help restore a monastery.[15] After leading a group to Solovki again the following summer, Cherviakov had a month free at the end of his work, during which time he took a 150-kilometre float trip on the Ileks River into Vodlozero. He found in this area, which was part of the largest continuous patch of old growth taiga in Europe, the ideal forest that he had long sought.

11. Autio-Sarasmo, 'An Illusion of Endless Forests', p. 125.

12. Leonov, *Russkii les*.

13. Josephson et al., *An Environmental History of Russia*, p. 191.

14. Interview with Oleg Cherviakov.

15. On Solovki, see the chapters by Kraikovski and Lajus and Breyfogle in this volume.

The Vision and the Reality in the Taiga of Karelia and the Arkhangel'sk Oblast'

When Cherviakov made this fateful river trip, the Chernobyl' explosion (in April 1986) had already heightened concerns over myriad environmental dangers, which Gorbachev's reforms allowed to be discussed more openly than at any time in Soviet history.[16] Whilst different branches of the All-Russian Society for Nature Protection and other civic organisations had been proposing national parks for Karelia and Arkhangel'sk Oblast' since the 1970s, the conversation gained momentum in this new cultural climate.[17] Karelia, perhaps more than any other region in the RSFSR, felt a particular urgency to protect landscapes. Whilst it accounted for fifteen per cent of the RSFSR's timber harvest, it had only 0.3 per cent of its territory under protection, which was five times less than the average for the RSFSR.[18] With locations such as Valaam and Kizhi having become increasingly popular with tourists in the previous years, the Institute of the Forest expected tourism to increase two- or threefold by 2000. In turn, it began working on plans for six national parks, including on Kizhi, an island in Lake Onega – the home of a large museum of old wooden churches; and Valaam – the site of a large monastery under restoration on Lake Onega.[19] It called for bringing five per cent of the republic under protection by 2000.[20] In 1988, scientists from Moscow, Leningrad, Arkhangel'sk, Vologda, Petrozavodsk and Syktyvkar met in Arkhangel'sk for a conference dedicated to establishing national parks in northern regions – the Murmansk and Arkhangel'sk Oblast', the Komi ASSR and Karelian ASSR.[21]

One year before this conference, a group of scientists from the Biology Institute of the Karelian Branch of the Academy of Sciences, led by the wetland scientist Vladimir Antipin, had designated 86,000 hectares a landscape *zakaznik* (protected natural area) around Vodlozero.[22] Whilst *zakazniks* were often established at the republic, oblast' or krai level in anticipation of the federal *zapovednik* or national park status, the designation usually allowed

---

16. For more on environmental activism during Perestroika, see Sigman, 'The End of Grassroots Ecology', pp. 190–213; Josephson et al., *An Environmental History of Russia*, pp. 254–86; Weiner, *A Little Corner of Freedom*, pp. 429–440.

17. Pleshak, Ipatov and Danilov (eds), *Problemy organizatsii prirodno-istoricheskikh natsional'nykh parkov*, p. 3.

18. GARF f. A-259, op. 49, d. 3399, ll. 42 and 53.

19. Pleshak, Ipatov and Danilov (eds), *Problemy organizatsii prirodno-istoricheskikh natsional'nykh parkov*, p. 29; GARK, f. 689, op. 1, d. 1461, l. 176.

20. AVNP d. 2, l.59.

21. Pleshak, Ipatov and Danilov (eds), *Problemy organizatsii prirodno-istoricheskikh natsional'nykh parkov*, p. 5.

22. AVNP d. 1, l.2.

Alan Roe

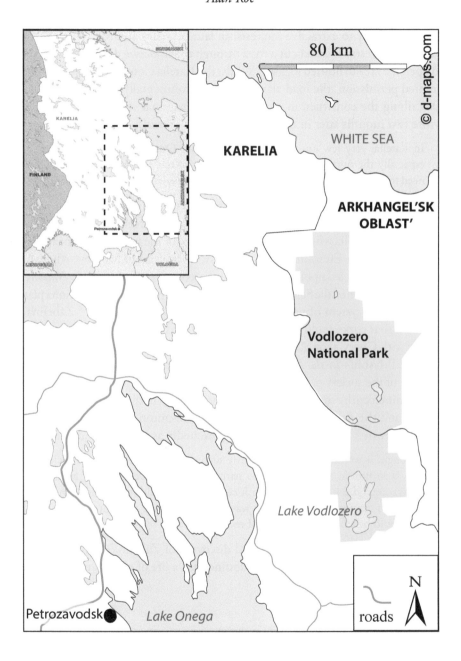

Map 4.1. Vodlozero National Park. Source: Created by Andrew Johnson at The White Horse Press using d-maps.com: © d-maps https://www.d-maps.com/carte.php?num_car=67042&lang=en.

The Vision and the Reality in the Taiga of Karelia and the Arkhangel'sk Oblast'

greater leniency to extractive interests. In late February and March 1988, the Pialmskii Forestry District cut a road through the *zakaznik* directly to the lake to open the area to limited logging. Whilst the Karelia Council of Ministers had granted permission, the road alarmed the environmentally-concerned public. Describing the construction of the road as a 'national calamity', L. Peregud wrote two months later in the newspaper *Znamia truda*:

> In Karelia, very few untouched corners remain. One of them is Vodlozero, especially the northeastern part of this corner of our Pudozh land. Here we need to organise not only a *zakaznik*, but also a *zapovednik* or a national park.[23]

Cherviakov learned about the recent intrusions of the Karelian Timber Cooperative (Karellesprom) into the protected zone as well as larger issues of protected territories in Karelia when he visited the Institute of the Forest in Petrozavodsk after his river trip. En route back to Kharkiv, he stopped in Moscow, where he accidentally stumbled upon Natalia Zabelina's recently published book, *National Park*, which outlined the Scientific Research Institute for Nature Protection's plan for creating of system of national parks for tourists in the USSR.[24] Zabelina's assertion that parks could transform the human-nature relationship resonated deeply with Cherviakov. At the time he found Zabelina's book, he was reading Mikhail Privshin's *In the Place of Fearless Birds*.[25] Prishvin's story is a fictional account of the society of Old Believers, Vygorets, which from late-seventeenth to mid-nineteenth century united several monasteries in the areas of present-day Karelia and the Arkhangel'sk Oblast' into a semi-autonomous economic and political centre.[26] Cherviakov's face lit up excitedly as he told me about this:

> I thought it would be possible to create such an alternative today in a society that is so hostile and aggressive to nature. If Andrei Denisov (the founder of Vygorets) did it in the eighteenth century, why couldn't it be done in the twentieth century? For Denisov, it was a religious idea. I thought about what idea could be a basis for that sort of republic today.[27]

Cherviakov understood his accidental discovery of Zabelina's book as a sign, perhaps from God, that he was not destined for a life of physics research.

---

23. Peregud, 'Doroga v nikuda', 18 May 1988.

24. Zabelina, *Natsional'nyi park*.

25. Privshin, *V kraiu nepugannikh ptits*.

26. See Crumney, *Old Believers and the World of the Anti-Christ*.

27. Interview with Oleg Cherviakov.

Alan Roe

The Campaign

When he returned to Kharkiv, Cherviakov wrote an article 'Desert or National Park', which the Karelian newspaper *Komsomolets* published on 10 November 1988. He asserted that a landscape *zakaznik* could not prevent Karellesprom from penetrating into the 'last ecologically clean region of the republic'. 'I have seen how these loggers work' he wrote. 'They have no mercy on the forests, nor the wetlands. One is left with a depressing impression upon seeing the hundreds of hectares of ruined forest'. After asserting that a national park could transform the regional economy by reviving handicrafts and attracting tourists from throughout the USSR and even other countries, Cherviakov stated that the establishment of the park would also 'clarify the moral health of society'. He concluded the article: 'The logic is simple: empty souls will produce a deserted wasteland around them, rich souls will produce national riches.'[28]

After the Karelian public responded positively to the idea, the editor of *Komsomolets*' told Cherviakov that nothing would come of his idea if the effort did not have a leader. There had, after all, been different proposals for a national park on Vodlozero over the previous fifteen years.[29] His primary academic advisor, Vladimir Volovik, was intrigued and encouraged Cherviakov to spearhead the effort whilst he completed his thesis. He fuelled Cherviakov's imagination by proposing a name for the park that would encapsulate its transformative vision – a *noosphere* park.[30]

The renowned Russian geographer Vladimir Vernadskii (1863–1945) conceived the idea of the *noosphere* during the 1920s.[31] Presaging present-day geological debates about the Anthropocene, Vernadskii argued that human societies throughout the world had become not only agents of biological destruction, but of shaping the geological environment. The noosphere was the sphere of collective human (societal) cognition, which served as the basis for action. Whilst the application of intellect and ingenuity in the name of material progress had caused vast destruction, Vernadskii believed that humans could direct their intellectual energy towards a harmonious and sustainable relationship with nature. The Soviet environmental community rediscovered Vernadskii's ideas during the Brezhnev era, and the noosphere had become a

---

28. Chervkiakov, 'Pustinia ili natsional'nyi park', 10 Nov. 1988, p. 2.

29. Kitsa, 'Bitva za Vodlozero', 21 Feb. 1989.

30. Interview with Cherviakov.

31. Oldfield and Shaw, 'V.I. Vernadsky and the Noosphere Concept', pp. 145–54; V.I. Vernadsky, 'The Biosphere and the Noosphere.'

common trope in Soviet nature protection discourse by Perestroika.[32] Energised by the transformative possibilities, Cherviakov returned to Petrozavodsk just after the New Year holiday in 1989 to rally support for the idea of establishing a national park.

Despite his youth, Cherviakov's charisma, enthusiasm and tireless public outreach helped him win many supporters. He gained the support of the Karelia State Committee on Nature Protection, which had been established the year before.[33] He also quickly won the support of the director of the Institute of Biology, S.N. Drozdov, who would make the case for the park's establishment to the Karelian ASSR Council of Ministers.[34] He met with officials from the Karelian Ministry of Forestry, leaders of newly formed environmental protection organisations, and governmental representatives of the Pudozh District – the most populated area in the territory of the proposed park. Cherviakov organised meetings with village councils and called for members to write petitions to officials at the local, state and union level of government.

Calling forestry 'Karelia's lifeblood', the Karelian Forestry Cooperative opposed the proposal and emphasised the economic harm that its establishment would cause to both the public and the Karelian ASSR Council of Ministers.[35] However, the press largely portrayed widespread support throughout twelve villages, which were home to 3,500 people, in the areas in and adjacent to the park. Throughout the first few months of 1989, the newspaper *Pudozhskii vestnik* received over 750 letters of support with many stating that the park would create new economic opportunities.[36] Because Cherviakov insisted that these villages and their 'authentic' culture were essential to the park, they did not fear forced removal. The population, which was forced to accept the dictates of central economic ministries for decades, was energised by the prospect of having more say in its future.

The park also needed the support of local leaders. The most influential supporter of the park in the Pudozh community was Andrei Beckman, the director of the region's largest employer – the fish-canning factory, Ekodar.

---

32. Josephson et al., *An Environmental History of Russia*, p. 243.

33. NARK f. 6196, op. 1, d. 5, l. 40.

34. Antipin, 'Vodlozerskii natsional'nyi park'. *Priroda glazami uchenikh*, p. 3.

35. Kurnosov, 'Agrolesprom i ne natsional'nyi park', 4 May 1989; Kiriasov, 'Zamili i real'nost: Natsional'nyi park v vodlozero' 20 Dec. 1989; NARK f. R-690, op. 7, d.4926, l. 210. Kitsa, 'Bitva za Vodlozero', 21 Feb. 1989.

36. Fokina, 'Kogda mol'chat nel'zia', 27 May 1989.

Alan Roe

Beckman was sociable and widely trusted throughout the community.[37] He publicly voiced support in an article published in the newspaper *Leninskaia pravda* on 20 October 1989, 'How to Revive Vodlozero'. He wrote: 'The national park is needed not only for our distant descendants but firstly it is necessary for us, those living now.'[38] Embracing the era's renewed emphasis on civic engagement and perhaps concerned about the country's stability, he continued: 'For in protecting the unique historical and natural watershed of Vodlozero and the Ileks River we affirm in our civic-mindedness, our responsibility for the fate of the Fatherland.'[39]

Cherviakov raised the proposed park's profile throughout the RSFSR by writing articles in the more widely circulated magazines *Lesnaia gazeta (Forest Gazette)* and *Priroda i chelovek (Nature and People)*.[40] These articles described the region's forestry practices as 'colonial plunder' led by 'looting central agencies', which were out of step with Perestroika's emphasis on regional economic self-accounting.[41] He argued that tourism would become the largest part of the Karelian economy.[42] Calling for the 'rational' and 'complex' use, Karelian journalists characterised Karelia's forest as a common resource that industry had monopolised at the public's expense.[43] Of the two million cubic metres cut each year, factories in the republic only processed 200,000, resulting in a net loss of thirty to 35 million roubles a year.[44] Tourism, the proposed park's proponents argued, would provide a much more sustainable, diversified and independent basis for the future of the Karelian Republic's economy. Whilst Cherviakov and others were still vague on the specific types of tourism that would take place in the park, he would later fully describe his original, if unrealistic, ideas on the subject.

37.   Interview with Vladimir Antipin, 20 May 2013.
38.   Pimenova, 'Dumaiu, menia poderzhat mnogie', 27 May 1989.
39.   Ibid.
40.   Cherviakov, 'Sobytie obshcherossiskogo mashtaba', 9 May 1990; Cherviakov, 'Eshche ne pozdno', pp. 10-12.
41.   Cherviakov, 'Eshche ne pozdno', p. 10.
42.   Ibid., p. 11.
43.   Peregud, 'Zemlia u okeana', 25 Jul. 1989, p. 3. Also see Viktor Shevchenko, 'Eshche raz o natsional'nom parke', 27 May 1989.
44.   Selivanov, 'O sozdanii vodlozerskogo natsional''nogo parka', 10 Jan 1990.

Cherviakov's Vision

Having developed a close relationship with Natalia Zabelina and influential individuals working in the Main Administration of *Zapovedniks* and Hunting, Cherviakov was offered a position by the head of the Main Administration that would provide him with needed financial support and a place to work as he led the effort. He would live in the Kostomukshckii *Zapovednik* on the Finnish border about 600 kilometres northwest of Lake Vodlozero. His sole responsibility would be to plan the national park. Cherviakov, with the help of his adviser Vladimir Vokolin, put together a team of scientists from the Karelian Institute of the Forest, Ural Division of the Academy of Sciences, the Soviet Geographic Society, Rostov State University and Tambov State University to plan Vodlozero National Noosphere Park.

Cherviakov met with the team of biologists and geographers in the territory of the proposed park during the summer of 1990. They provided the descriptions of the physical territory for the park project report entitled 'The Economic-Ecological Basis for Vodlozero National Park'. Sixty-three per cent of trees in the more than 400,000-hectare park were more than 200 years old, which made it the largest old-growth taiga forest in Europe. Wetland sections within the forests made the territory especially appealing to a variety of avian life and would make road construction for expanding timber harvesting extraordinarily costly and damaging. The abundance of black bears, moose, northern deer, wild boar, rabbits and squirrels, Cherviakov believed, might make the park particularly interesting to foreign hunters.

Much of 'The Economic-Ecological Basis for Vodlozero National Park' articulated Cherviakov's transformative vision, which would have been inconceivable in previous eras of Soviet history. He believed that his conception of a national noosphere park would lay the foundation for environmental sustainability in the region. With words reflecting his utopianism, he wrote:

> These parks provide a symbiosis of protected natural areas and economic development of areas where industry, agriculture, forestry, hunting and fishing, recreation, and other types of nature are based on closed processes and comprehensive use of the local natural resources without any environmental risk.[45]

The revival of 'traditional culture', which Cherviakov largely defined through Orthodox Christianity, would help achieve this ecological harmony and help spur the socioeconomic life of the region.[46] Cherviakov argued that this plan

---

45. AVNP d. 2, l. 206.
46. Ibid., l. 215.

would preserve the area's 'natural evolutionary development' without seeming to consider that the process of development had been profoundly disrupted by Soviet command economy and the state's hostility towards religion.

Cherviakov asserted that the restoration of churches and monasteries provided the foundation for religious revival. 'Restoring ancient temples', he wrote, 'Iliinskii churchyard and the deserted Iur'evskaia Monastery, and their full inclusion into the social life will contribute to the revival of spiritual life in the province and return to the high cultural and moral values of Christianity.'[47] As if by an article of faith, he argued that the return to such a moral atmosphere, in turn, would cultivate a culture in which people valued their work. This would lead to greater creativity.[48] As Vygorets had been a quasi-independent centre of commerce within an increasingly centralised state, Cherviakov believed that Vodlozero National Park would begin a movement that would allow the Russian North to develop a vibrant and independent culture grounded in a strong sense of place and local control.

Harvesting and processing raw wood, wild edible and medicinal plants, fishing and fish processing and agricultural production would help offset economic losses that the logging industry would suffer from the protection of forests. But tourism, especially foreign tourism, would form the economic foundation for the larger vision.[49] Noting that national parks in the United States earned two billion dollars annually, Cherviakov believed that the hundreds of thousands of foreign tourists he expected to visit the park would bring a tremendous source of revenue.[50] He planned the development of paddle tours to the lake's different islands, cross-country skiing trips and excursions on foot and on horseback. Tourists could also take part in tours that focused on the area's local history and literary traditions, scientific tourism oriented around ecological education and 'guest tourism' in which visitors would stay with locals and take part in the collection of berries, mushrooms and medicinal plants. This final sort of tourism would give tourists a glimpse into the 'exotic' of traditional rural life.[51]

Cherviakov asserted that the principle of the 'Ecological Economic Unit' would inform all decisions about the area's development. This model held that the principle of 'ecological stability', which he never clearly defined,

47.   Ibid., l. 216.
48.   Ibid.
49.   Ibid.
50.   Ibid., l. 16.
51.   Ibid., l. 282.

must serve as the basis for all decisions about the region's economic development. Whilst the park administration would determine these 'units' through defining coherent ecosystems, such as watersheds, Cherviakov asserted that a system of monitoring and mathematical modelling could precisely determine the impact of different types of land use.[52] He wrote: 'So, if the scenario does not satisfy the most ecologically acceptable form of development (this is not clearly defined in the report), the option is not allowed for consideration'.[53] Cherviakov believed that this principle of economic organisation would spread to all of Karelia as others in the region looked at Vodlozero National Park as a model (*etalon*). Again, writing with almost a sense of inevitability, he asserted:

> Resources and effort must first be concentrated on model regions most suitable for these goals, transforming them into ecological-economic zones and only then expanding this system to the entire territory of the Republic. The impact would extend beyond the boundaries of Karelia.[54]

According to Cherviakov, the 'Ecological Economic Unit' was 'a task of global, or in any case, European scale'.

These ambitious plans ignored some obvious practical realities. Organised tourism was still almost non-existent in the area of the proposed park, which was far from large population centres.[55] Infrastructure, a qualified staff, improved transportation to the park and marketing the idea abroad would require significant investment. Cherviakov stated that the park could not rely on the state for this investment, given the economic situation in the USSR at the time, but seemed to take as a foregone conclusion that joint enterprises with foreign firms would construct the park's infrastructure.[56] Moreover, Cherviakov never seemed to question how commercialism might undermine the cultural 'authenticity' that he so valued. Could an authentic culture truly be revived and grow 'organically,' as he frequently stated, when it sought for profit to appeal to outsiders who wanted a glimpse of the 'exotic'?

Some of Cherviakov's other ideas demonstrated a profound naiveté with respect to the relationship between money and power and more specifically between economy and culture. He claimed that local power with 'high levels of professionalism and competence' would shape the region's managerial priori-

---

52.   Ibid., l. 41.

53.   Ibid., l. 39.

54.   Ibid., l.37

55.   Ibid., l. 252.

56.   Ibid., l. 261.

Alan Roe

ties. His ideas about competence, however, were based on a particularly narrow and absolutist vision of the proper uses of park territory. Despite his emphasis on local control, he repeatedly argued that the virgin forests of Karelia and Arkhangel'sk were 'universal property' (*obschechelovecheskoe dostoianie*).[57] It followed that the park would prompt the interest of countries of the European community.[58]

Cherviakov was undoubtedly influenced not only by the surge of environmental concern in the USSR, but by his awareness of conservation efforts worldwide. He called for cooperation with the International Union for the Conservation of Nature (IUCN), United Nations Environment Programme (UNEP) and the World Wide Fund for Nature, and compliance with 'proper ecological standards' established by the IUCN and the United Nation's World Conservation Strategy.[59] He never hinted at the fact that such standards might interfere with local autonomy and initiative. Cherviakov also never seemed to consider that outside investors would have leverage to alter his original vision and might obtain advantages with the process of local decision-making. His vision reflected the sense of infinite possibility for the future born out of the broad public questioning of Soviet society's very foundations and the strengthening of the international discourse of 'sustainable development'.[60] At the same time, he demonstrated economic illiteracy. Whilst such economic illiteracy is not uncommon among environmental protection advocates of different countries, it was particularly pronounced in the USSR after decades of a largely centralised and top-down approach to economic decision making.

Establishment and Disappointment

Cherviakov proved more adept at persuasion than in developing a realistic plan. From the publication of 'Desert or National Park' in 1989 to the park's establishment in 1991, he developed relationships not only with scientists, academics and supporters of cultural preservation but with influential government officials whose voice gave the push for the park's establishment significant momentum. 'He had', Natalia Zabelina said, 'a way of crawling into one's heart.'[61] Whilst the Ministry of the Forestry Industry and the State Committee

---

57. Ibid., l. 64.
58. Ibid., ll. 41–2.
59. Ibid.
60. Macekura, *Of Limits and Growth*, pp. 219–260.
61. Interview with Natalia Zabelina, 21 July 2015.

on Forests officially objected to the park's establishment to the special commission on the subject formed by the USSR Council of Ministers, Cherviakov successfully rallied support from ministries, civic organisations and influential environmentalists.[62] The late Aleksei Iablokov, who would later serve as Boris Yeltsin's chief advisor on matters related to the environment, warned in his letter to the USSR Council of Ministers in support of the park that Karelia would exhaust its timber reserves in ten to thirty years.[63] Dmitrii Likhachev, perhaps the USSR's strongest voice for preserving cultural heritage and church restoration efforts in the North, also expressed strong support and visited the site of the proposed park.[64]

Cherviakov also benefited from idiosyncrasies within the Soviet system of allocating forest cuts, which pitted the interests of the Arkhangel'sk Oblast' and the Karelian Republic against one another. Despite the fact that the entire Ileks River and its surrounding old-growth taiga forests were located in the Arkhangel'sk Oblast', the Karelian Forestry Cooperative had the rights to cut these forests long before Cherviakov called for the establishment of a national park.[65] The Arkhangel'sk Executive Committee realised that allowing Karelian Forestry Cooperative to harvest them would bring no economic benefit to the Arkhangel'sk Oblast'. Moreover, by designating a *zakaznik*, the oblast' administration would reach its yearly quota for designating new protected territory set by the Main Administration of Hunting and *Zapovedniks*. Accordingly, in the late 1990s, the Arkhangel'sk Oblast' Executive Committee declared the 274,000 hectares of the proposed park in the oblast' a temporary *zakaznik*.[66] The Karelian ASSR Council of Ministers had been vacillating in its support of the national park in large part because of the projected benefits that timber cuts in this region would bring to the economy of the republic. Now, with the largest portion of the proposed forests inaccessible, regardless of whether or not the RSFSR Council of Ministers established the national park, Vladimir Razonov, who became chair of the Karelian ASSR Council of Ministers in early 1991, expressed his support for the park to the State Committee on Forests (*Goskomles*).[67]

62.   GARF f. A-259, op. 49, d. 3399, l. 57.

63.   Ibid., l, 53.

64.   Ibid., l. 90.

65.   Interview with Oleg Cherviakov, 20 June 2015 in Vodlozero National Park. Cherviakov explained these dynamics to me in my interview with him.

66.   GARF f. A-259, op. 49 d. 3399, l. 5.

67.   NARK f. R-690, op. 7, d. 5089,

Alan Roe

Establishing the park required only the signature of the Deputy Chair of the RSFSR Council of Ministers, Vitalii Trifonovich Gavrilov, if it gained unanimous support from the State Committee on Ecology (*Goskompriroda*), the Ministry of Economy, the State Committee on Forests and the Ministry of Finance. If even one of these agencies opposed its establishment, the park would demand the signature of the head of the RSFSR Council of Ministers, Ivan Silaev. Stating that the creation of a national park would cost the Karelian Forestry Cooperative half of its harvestable territory and result in the loss of 2,000 jobs in the Karelian ASSR, the Association of Workers of the Wood Processing Industry, which was a RSFSR-wide organisation, expressed strong opposition to the park.[68] The Ministry of Economy and the State Committee on Forests, sharing this concern, did not support its establishment. After receiving signatures from Goskompriroda and the Ministry of Finance, Cherviakov depended on Gavrilov to secure Silaev's signature and feared not obtaining it immediately might lead him to reconsider his stated support. Cherviakov waited for three days as Gavrilov was preoccupied with a strike of miners from the Kuzbass region of western Siberia. Knowing that Silaev would be leaving the country the following day, Cherviakov told me that he prayed as he had never before on the night of 19 April 1991. On 20 April, as Silaev was preparing to board the plane, Gavrilov obtained his signature, which officially established the park. To this day, Cherviakov believes that something more powerful than luck was at work.[69]

Whilst the territory of the 490,000-hectare park had been legally established, Cherviakov's vision remained in his head and on paper. Because he despised the USSR for, among other things, its attempts to extirpate religious belief, the fall of the Soviet Union at the end of 1991 intensified Cherviakov's sense of mission and purpose. Moreover, for Cherviakov, the strengthening discourse of 'sustainable development', which was the foundational principle of the Rio Earth Summit of 1992, seemed to confirm that the park was at the vanguard of a new epoch in world history. Local support remained strong for the first year and a half after the park's establishment. One journalist, perhaps with some exaggeration, asserted that 'all residents' of the region supported the park a little less than a year after the RSFSR established it.[70] Others still

---

68. GARF, f. A-259, op. 49, d. 3399, l. 2.
69. Interview with Oleg Cherviakov.
70. Pervunskii, 'Natsional'nyi park ili eshche odin kompleksnyi lespromkhoz?', 19 Mar. 1992, p. 2.

wrote with confidence that interest in the park would 'grow headlong' in other countries, and that it would become a national park 'of the highest category'.[71]

Cherviakov and the national park were working on little more than enthusiasm, whilst the villages of Kugavalanok and the wider Pudozh region's support was based on hope for the future. During the year and a half after the park's establishment, the state provided almost no funding for infrastructural development, and few tourists visited. Moreover, as the state divested itself of many of the responsibilities that it assumed under socialism, the park found itself in the position of exclusive provider of many basic social services for the region – kindergartens, electricity, water – without receiving the necessary funds from an increasingly dysfunctional and financially crippled government.[72] The park also inherited all the area's agricultural enterprises without receiving subsidies from the Ministry of Agriculture. Moreover, the largest employer in Kugavalonok, the fish-canning factory Ekodar, went bankrupt in early 1993, which left the majority of the working population unemployed. Andrei Beckman, who had long been one of the most influential community members and initially a strong supporter of the park, moved to Petrozavodsk.[73] Whilst the population was increasingly looking to the park as a source of employment, it was accruing almost no revenue and therefore could not expand its personnel. Although there could not have been a better time than Perestroika for Cherviakov to inspire others with his transformative vision, the economic collapse that followed created the worst possible conditions for him to realise it.

Whilst Cherviakov's charisma gave him an ability to sell his vision, he seemed uninterested in the everyday social interactions necessary to build and sustain strong relationships and trust with members of the community. They increasingly viewed him, if articles in the press are an accurate indication, as imperious and uncompromising. Whilst many, including Cherviakov, had initially considered the park a means of exerting greater independence from Moscow, the local press began describing it as another imposition from Moscow.[74] Whilst Cherviakov had emphasised empowerment of the local population, many inhabitants of the territory in and around the park accused

---

71. Agarkov, 'Pora brat'sia za inostranni v natsional'nom parke', 11 Aug. 1992, p. 2.

72. Interview with Cherviakov.

73. Interview with Vladimir Antipin, 20 May 2013.

74. Tamm and Peregud, 'Legendy i byli Vodlozer'ia, 11 Jun. 1992; see also Sidirova, 'Po povodu sporov o natsional'nom parke', 28 Apr. 1992; Dobrinina, 'V krivom zerkale Vodlozer'ia', 9 Dec. 1994; Smirnov, 'Komu nuzhni mal'chiki dlia byt'ia', 23 Dec. 1994.

Alan Roe

Moscow of sending 'incompetent people' to govern the region.[75] Moreover, as was the case throughout the Russian Federation, the worsening economic situation made environmental protection seem like an unaffordable luxury.[76]

Cherviakov sought to obtain territory adjacent the park to establish a buffer zone without, according to the community, input from area's inhabitants. Moreover, locals expressed frustration about the fact that the park had not brought the promised economic benefits. They also expressed scepticism that foreign 'moneybags' would want to ever spend their money in the park, doubt about whether the state would ever fund infrastructure and sympathy for the forestry industry, which most had strongly criticised in the lead-up to the park's establishment. [77] At a meeting of the Kugavalanok Council on 30 March 1993, one participant, ignoring the park's new responsibilities for supporting different social services, stated that the national park had not given 'a kopeck' to the region and that the village's residents would not see economic benefits for at least fifteen years.[78] Another attacked the 'science' behind the national park whilst suggesting that its propagandists had deceived the residents of the region. Echoing the sort of suspicions held by local populations towards some national parks in the United States and the world over[79] in the twentieth century, he stated:

> The national park has its professional writers, who can prove whatever they want. But the heart of the matter is that the national park wants to be the master of the region. In deciding the question, concerning the life of the region, only one side is present. Non-objective information has been given to us. The creeping annexation of the territory of Kubovski and Pialmsi complex forestry district is underway, all under the name of science. My personal relationship to science is that whoever pays more will have science prove what they want.[80]

These suspicions towards science reflected the local population's longstanding alienation from the decision-making processes – for decades controlled by 'experts' and scientists from outside the region – that determined the fate of the region. The deputy N.D. Durnev of the Kugavalonok Council perhaps summed

---

75. Agarkov, 'Ekodar na pasput'e', 24 Mar. 1993.

76. Ibid.

77. Ibid.

78. Mikhailova, 'Vokrug natsional'nogo parka Vodlozerskii.'

79. Stevens (ed.), *Indigenous Peoples, National Parks, and Protected Areas.*

80. Ibid.

up the growing distrust between the people in the park best: 'The interests of the region and the interests of the national park are quite different.'[81]

The park administration sought to reassure the local population that it would bring lots of new jobs to and that a 'flood of tourists thirsting for the beauty of wilderness' would soon begin arriving to the park.[82] However, Cherviakov did not always seem to understand the impact of his words, and his occasional lack of tact made it difficult for such appeals to the future to assert a placating influence. In early 1994, he went on a radio programme called 'Hostage to the Village' and remarked, perhaps truthfully but insensitively, that the park had inherited not only an 'unprofitable enterprise' and a 'destroyed economy', but also a 'demoralised collective'.[83] Long one of the park's strongest supporters in the local press, L. Peregud seemed to take offence at this remark and retorted in the newspaper *Severnyi kur'er*: 'It turns out that the park has it bad because of the village. But what does the village get from the park?'[84]

A Vision Unrealised

National parks throughout the Russian Federation found themselves hamstrung by a lack of funds, but no national park had presented such a transformative vision, and few others had assumed so much responsibility for the livelihood of the surrounding population.[85] The funding situation became worse throughout the 1990s. Wages of park employees hovered at subsistence levels. Cherviakov noted in 1996 that the park had tattered infrastructure, no good roads and a transportation fleet that was hardly functional. He estimated that the park needed more than 225 million roubles (US$50,000) more than it received from the state in 1996 in order to fulfil its basic responsibilities.[86] There was no state money for infrastructural development, the absence of which he believed had prevented the park from becoming a popular destination for foreign tourists. At mid-decade, fewer than 3,000 tourists were visiting the national park each

81. Ibid.

82. Rusinov, 'Lesom zhivi', 13 Jul. 1993.

83. 'Legendy i byli Vodlozer'ia'.

84. Ibid.

85. Simonov and Stepanitsky, 'Leaders of Russia's Protected Areas Take Desperate Measures in a Desperate Situation', p. 3.

86. Dobroshin, Personal Archive. Dobroshin's personal archive contains documents from the All-Union Landscape Research-Design Institute, Soiuzgiproleskhoz.

year.[87] As he told me, 'It seemed as though we were moving against the current. It seemed that we were going nowhere.'[88]

Cherviakov did successfully establish foreign contacts and raised the park's international profile, which he had always maintained was necessary for its development. In early 1993, he established a cooperative relationship with the United States National Park Service through which he visited several American parks and hosted superintendents of several US national parks.[89] He received a grant of 2.5 million dollars in 1997 from TACIS (Technical Assistance to the Commonwealth of Independent States).[90] With this grant, the park established an office with an ecological education centre in Petrozavodsk, built an ecological trail, initiated the restoration of old churches and chapels and developed an extensive strategic plan and system of ecological monitoring. However, accessibility remained a problem, and tourism infrastructure remained rudimentary. In 1998, a UNESCO delegation visited the park to determine if it would be designated a World Heritage Site (it was not).[91] It was, however, named a UNESCO biosphere reserve in 2001.

Whilst Cherviakov led an international team in planning the establishment of several more national parks in Karelia and Arkhangel'sk Oblast' in 1998, these parks remained proposals, and Vodlozero National Park was still largely undeveloped as the end of the millennium approached. He said to me:

> I came to the understanding that it was a dead end. Because most of what existed were just plans and documents ... We developed ecological trails, including a forty-kilometre trail. We made booklets and carried out landscape planning, but it is not interesting to anyone. Tourists are only interested throwing out a fishing line and drinking vodka.[92]

Whilst the Soviet tourism movement incorporated a broad range of leisure activities from outdoor recreation to visits to spas, Cherviakov, as a result of his disappointments, came to view the interests of tourists in much more limited terms.[93]

---

87. Ibid.
88. Interview with Oleg Cherviakov.
89. Agarkov, 'Teper' vi nam park-pobratim', 30 Mar. 1993.
90. Dobroshin, Personal Archive.
91. Ibid; Interview with Oleg Cherviakov.
92. Interview with Oleg Cherviakov.
93. For more on Soviet tourism, see Koenker.

The Vision and the Reality in the Taiga of Karelia and the Arkhangel'sk Oblast'

As Cherviakov successfully restored small chapels, a monastery and a small abandoned village, Varishpelda, where he and his wife Natasha lived, he became increasingly devoted to his religious practice (he had been ordained a priest in 1992) and more pessimistic about the park's prospects. Moreover, as he sought to live out his ideal of a life in harmony with the natural world, he was becoming resigned to the fact that 'local residents don't want to return to the motherland of their ancestors', which for him meant the restoration of locally-based economy and deep devotion to Orthodox Christianity and its rituals.[94] In 2005, realising that his utopian vision would never be realised, he left his official position as head administrator of the national park. The new administration has supported and continues to support the development of tourism and educational outreach programmes to the extent that its resources allow, but has abandoned Cherviakov's transformative vision.[95]

Figure 4.1. Il'inskii Vodlozerskii Pogost. Photograph by the author.

---

94. Ibid.

95. *Vodlozerskii natsional'nyi park*

Alan Roe

Figure 4.2. View of Varyshpelda. Photograph by the author.

Figure 4.3. Cherviakov in Vodlozero National Park. Photograph by the author.

Alan Roe

Timber and wood processing industries remain by far the largest part of the Karelian economy. With nearly 765,000 tourists visiting Karelia every year, the tourism industry accounts for almost five per cent of the economy.[96] Though hardly insignificant, tourism has not brought about the economic transformations expected during the late 1980s. With only 7,000 visitors a year, Vodlozero National Park hosts a tiny fraction of what Cherviakov predicted.[97] Although his interaction with the outside world is limited and his focus is local, he maintains an international perspective. Moreover, in assessing how far the park fell short of his vision, his words strongly echo the criticisms of many in the West who have lamented the nature-culture dichotomy born mainly out of a particular cultural understanding of wilderness.[98] On that summer afternoon in 2015, he told me:

> It is not possible to remember without a slight smirk that pathos and inspiration at the time of signing the Rio de Janeiro convention. It is clear that the world has not gone in that direction that was defined as sustainable development. In the world, the tendencies are mostly similar. There is forming an all-world Babylon. This is an entirely different worldview. People are becoming urban. Nature is only a place for recreation, but not a sphere of life. And from this, we have so many cultural, spiritual and ecological problems. Of course, Russia takes part in this process, which is leading us all to the end. The world of the 1990s was vacillating between the direction of sustainable development, or an all-world Babylon. It seems that we made a strong choice towards Babylon.[99]

Cherviakov's evocation of Babylon, which stood as a metaphor for wickedness and false religion throughout the Old and New Testaments, explains much about his continued retreat from the modern world.

Today, the forests in Vodlozero National Park undoubtedly have far more protection than if the park had never been established. Stopping the ongoing destruction of northern forests had been, initially, Cherviakov's foremost concern. But like many Russian national parks, the infrastructure in Vodlozero National Park remains too undeveloped to accommodate large numbers of tourists, which Cherviakov and other park founders believed would make national parks profitable. The relative inaccessibility of many Russian parks and the ability of Russians to travel internationally have also discouraged mass visitation. For Cherviakov, however, the failure of the park

---

96. *Karelinform*, 'Dolia turizma v VVP Karelii otsenivaetsia primerno v 5%'.

97. *Vodlozerskii natsional'yi park*, 'Federal'nye OOPT na territorii Karelii'.

98. See William Cronon (ed.), *Uncommon Ground*.

99. Interview with Oleg Cherviakov.

to become a popular tourist destination is a small part of a larger failure that he understands in apocalyptic terms. He sees in the reluctance of the area's residents to embrace a more traditional lifestyle, which he views as more in 'harmony' with the earth, as symptomatic of an increasingly morally depraved world, expressed by him through the biblical reference to Babylon. Sobered by disappointment, Cherviakov seems now to acknowledge that reclaiming an idealised version of a 'traditional' past was as unrealistic as the Communist Party's aspiration to be the engineers of human souls, as Gor'kii's words once conveyed. Living out these ideals provides him some solace for the fact that few others wanted to do the same.

BIBLIOGRAPHY

Agarkov, Vladimir. 1992. 'Pora brat'sia za inostranni v natsional'nom parke'. *Pudozhskii vestnik*. 11 August.

Agarkov, Vladimir. 1993. 'Ekodar na rasput'e'. *Pudozhskii vestnik*. 24 March.

Agarkov, Vladimir. 1993. 'Teper' vi nam park-pobratim'. *Pudozhskii vestnik*. 30 March.

Antipin, Vladimir. 2007. 'Vodlozerskii natsional'nyi park'. *Priroda glazami uchenikh*. Petrozavodsk: Vodlozero National Park.

Arkhiv Vodlozerskogo natsional'nogo parka (AVNP, Archive of the Vodlozero National Park).

Autio-Sarasmo, Sari. 2005. 'An Illusion of Endless Forests: Timber and Soviet Industrialization during the 1930s'. In Arja Rosenholm and Sari Autio-Sarasmo (eds), *Understanding Russian Nature*, pp. 125–145. Helsinki: Aleksanteri Institute.

Chervkiakov, O. 1988. 'Pustinia ili natsional'nyi park'. *Komsomolets*. 10 November.

Chervkiakov, O. 1990. 'Sobytie obshcherossiskogo mashtaba'. *Lesnaia gazeta*. 9 May.

Chervkiakov, O. 1989. 'Eshche ne pozdno'. *Priroda i chelovek*. No. 10: 10–12.

Costlow, Jane. 2012. *Heart Pine Russia: Walking and Writing in the Nineteenth Century Russian Forest*. Ithaca, NY: Cornell University Press.

Costlow, Jane. 2003. 'Imaginations of Destruction: The "Forest Question" in Nineteenth Century Russian Culture'. *The Russian Review* **62** (1): 91–118.

Cronon, William (ed.), 1996. *Uncommon Ground: Rethinking the Human Place in Nature*. New York: W.W. Norton and Company.

Crummey, Robert O. 1970. *Old Believers and the World of the Anti-Christ*. Madison: University of Wisconsin Press.

Dobrinina, I. 1994. 'V krivom zerkale Vodlozer'ia'. *Servernaia kur'er*. 9 December.

Alan Roe

Dobroshin, Julius. Personal Archive. Documents of Soiuzgiproleskhoz. St Petersburg, Russia.

Fokina, V.P., 1989. 'Kogda mol'chat nel'zia'. *Komsomolets*. 27 May.

Gerasimov, I.P., V.S. Preobrazhenskii, A.S. Abramov, D.L. Armand, S.V. Zon, I.V. Komar, G.M. Lappo, N.F. Leontev and Ia. G. Mashbisch (eds). 1975. *Teoreticheskie osnovi rekreatsionnoi geographii*. Moscow: Nauka.

Gorky, Maxim (ed.). 1935. *Belomor: An Account of the Construction of the New Canal between the White Sea and the Baltic Sea*. New York: Harrison Smith and Robert Haas.

Gosudarstvennyi arkhiv Rossiiskoi Federatsii (GARF, State Archive of the Russian Federation).

Josephson, Paul, Nicolai Dronin, Ruben Mnatsakanian, Aleh Cherp, Dmitry Efremenko and Vladislav Larin. 2013. *An Environmental History of Russia*. New York: Cambridge University Press.

Leonov, Leonid. 1953. *Russkii les*. Moscow: Molodaia gvardiia.

Karelinform. 'Dolia turizma v VVP Karelii otsenivaetsia primerno v 5%'. 2010. 28 September. http://karelinform.ru/?id=20335.

Koenker, Diane. 2013. *Club Red: Vacation Travel and the Soviet Dream*. Ithaca, NY: Cornell University Press.

Kiriasov, A. 1989. 'Zamili i real'nost: Natsional'nyi park v vodlozero'. *Leninskaia Pravda* . 20 December.

Kitsa, L. 1989. 'Bitva za Vodlozero'. *Komsomolets*. 21 February.

Kurnosov, A. 1989. 'Agrolesprom i ne natsional'nyi park,' *Komsomolets*. 4 May.

Natsional'nyi arkhiv Respubliki Kareliia (NARK, National Archive of the Republic of Karelia).

Oldfield, Jonathan and Denis J.B. Shaw. 2006. 'V.I. Vernadsky and the Noosphere Concept: Russian Understandings of Society-Nature Interaction'. *Geoforum* **37** (1): 145–154.

Peregud, L. 1988. 'Doroga v nikuda'. *Znamia truda*. 18 May.

Peregud, L. 1989. 'Zemlia u okeana'. *Znamia truda*. 25 July.

Pervunskii, Nikolai. 1992. 'Natsional'nyi park ili eshche odin kompleksnyi lespromkhoz?' *Pudozhskii vestnik*. 19 March.

Pimenova, A.I. 1989. 'Dumaiu, menia poderzhat mnogie'. *Znamia truda*. 27 May.

Pleshak, T.V., L.F. Ipatov and M.A. Danilov (eds). 1988. *Problemy organizatsii prirodno-istoricheskikh natsional'nykh parkov i razvitiia seti okhraniaemykh prirodnykh territorii na russkom severe*. Arkhangel'sk: Arkhangel'sk Council of the All-Russian Society for Nature Protection.

Privshin, Mikhail. 1907. *V kraiu nepugannikh ptits'*. Saint Petersburg: A.F. Devrien.

Roe, Alan D. 2020. *Into Russian Nature: Tourism, Environmental Protection, and National Parks in the Twentieth Century*. New York: Oxford University Press.

Rusinov, Pavel, 1993. 'Lesom zhivi'. *Pudozhskii vestnik*. 13 July.

Selivanov, I. 1990. 'O sozdanii vodlozerskogo natsional'nogo parka'. *Sel'skaia zhizn'*. 10 January.

Shevchenko, Viktor. 1989. 'Eshche raz o natsional'nom parke'. 27 May.

Sidirova, E. V. 1992. 'Po povodu sporov o natsional'nom parke'. *Pudozhskii vestnik*. 28 April.

Sigman, Carole. 2013. 'The End of Grassroots Ecology: Political Competition and the Fate of Ecology during Perestroika, 1988–1991'. *The Soviet and Post-Soviet Review* **40** (2): 190–213.

Simonov, Eugene and Vsevolod Stepanitsky. 1995. 'Leaders of Russia's Protected Areas Take Desperate Measures in a Desperate Situation'. *Russian Conservation News*, no. 2 (January): 3.

Smirnov, V. 1994. 'Komu nuzhni mal'chiki dlia byt'ia'. *Pudozhskii vestnik*. 23 December.

Sokolov, V.E. and E.E. Syroechkovskii. 1991. *Zapovedniki SSSR: Natsional'nye parki i zakazniki*. Moscow: Mysl'.

Stevens, Stan (ed.). 2014. *Indigenous Peoples, National Parks, and Protected Areas: A New Paradigm Linking Conservation, Culture, and Rights*. Tucson: University of Arizona Press.

Tamm, A. and L. Peregud. 1992. 'Legendy i byli Vodlozer'ia: V zalozhnikakh natsional'nogo parka' *Severnyi kur'er '*. 11 June.

Vernadsky, V.I. 1945. 'The Biosphere and the Noosphere'. *American Scientist* **33** (1): 1–12.

Vodlozerskii natsional'yi park. 2017. 'Federal'nye OOPT na territorii Karelii – eto tochka razvitiia regiona'. 2 May. https://web.archive.org/web/20170707085413/http://vodlozero.ru/ru/news/11058.html.

Weiner, Douglas, 1999. A *Little Corner of Freedom: Russian Nature Protection from Stalin to Gorbachev*. Berkeley: University of California Press.

Zabelina, Natalia. 1987. *Natsional'nyi park*. Moscow: Mysl'.

5.

'THERE, WHERE THEY HAVE GROWN ACCUSTOMED TO FLOODING': COMPARING THE ST PETERSBURG FLOOD OF NOVEMBER 1824 AND THE LENINGRAD FLOOD OF SEPTEMBER 1924

Robert Dale

On the evening of 23 September 1924, hurricane-strength winds blowing along the Baltic Sea and up the Gulf of Finland pushed a huge wall of water back up the River Neva, flooding Leningrad. Although the day began calmly, by the afternoon darkening clouds, strengthening winds and rising waters threatened the city. So ferocious was the storm that at its peak, between 7:00 and 8:00 p.m., the level of the Neva rose 380 centimetres above its normal level. The floodwaters swept through the grand architectural ensembles of the city's historic centre as well as outlying residential and industrial districts. Approximately two-thirds of the city, including the whole of the Vasil'evskii Island, the Petersburg Side, the Vyborg Side and Volodarskii district, was submerged. Factories, workers' housing, public spaces, parks, theatres, scientific laboratories, museums and their collections all suffered extensive damage. Yet, once the wind direction changed, the waters quickly subsided. By the morning, the Neva was back within its channel. This urban cataclysm, however, was not without precedent in the northern capital. Indeed, many Leningraders would have been forgiven for thinking that history was repeating itself. One hundred years earlier, on 7 November 1824,[1] St Petersburg experienced the highest, most destructive and most important flood in its history. On that occasion an even more forceful storm caused the Neva to rise 421 centimetres above normal levels.

The following morning, Leningraders began to connect the floods of September 1924 and November 1824, an event deeply inscribed on the city's physical, social and cultural landscape. Many were drawn towards buildings bearing flood markers, so that comparisons with the level of the 1824 flood

---

1.   This date corresponds to 19 Nov. 1824 in the Gregorian calendar.

could be made. Indeed, photographers and journalists documented these precise moments.[2] Through these means and others, a dialogue was quickly established between the two floods. However, in the hundred years between these catastrophic floods, the two highest in St Petersburg's history, much had changed. The city had experienced enormous economic, political, social and cultural turmoil. Industrialisation, urbanisation and modernisation had expanded the city's footprint, altered its physical fabric, increased its population and transformed the lives of its inhabitants. Since the revolutions of 1917, the city's tsarist rulers had been overthrown, it had lost its capital city status and it had been renamed. Nevertheless, important continuities with the past persisted; Leningrad remained an urban landscape at the mercy of the elements.

This chapter seeks to compare the floods of November 1824 and September 1924, exploiting comparisons made at the time, as a means of exploring St Petersburg/Leningrad's urban landscape. The comparison focuses upon the events of the floods, the destruction they wrought and the response of municipal authorities and urban residents to natural disaster. Although the floods were generated by similar climatic and environmental forces, they affected the city in different ways, demonstrating how the city had changed over the intervening century. Urban floods were moments of danger, destruction and disruption for people in the past, and remain so for many in the present, but they provide historians with invaluable opportunities for examining human interactions with physical space, urban landscapes and environmental forces.[3] Once rivers burst their banks, floodwaters do not make conscious choices; they flow across space bound only by physical relief, revealing how whole communities respond to natural disasters. Flooding was nothing new in St Petersburg/Leningrad. Between its foundation in 1703 and 2004 the city experienced floods, defined as 160 centimetres above normal river level, on 324 occasions, making flooding an almost yearly event.[4] This long history of flooding, then, allows historians to take regular snapshots of how floods affected the city and how its residents responded to periodic inundation. The chapter argues that, because of its susceptibility to flooding, the city and its inhabitants grew accustomed to the challenges presented by this riverine location, developing resilience, as well as

---

2. *Krasnaia gazeta (vechernii vypusk)*, 'Istoricheskaia doska', 24 Sept. 1924, p. 1.

3. For comparative examples, see Kelman, *A River and its City*; Clark, *Deep Water*; Jackson, *Paris under Water*; Dagupta et al., *Urban Flooding of Greater Dhaka in a Changing Climate*; Courtney, *The Nature of Disaster in China*.

4. Pomeranets, *Neschast'ia nevskikh beregov*, 10; Piaskovskii, Pomeranets and Chernysheva, 'Povtoriaemost' navodnenii v Peterburge'.

Robert Dale

practical strategies for combatting or at least mitigating its worst effects. This was particularly apparent in the aftermath of the September 1924 flood, when past experiences and the historical memory of flooding proved important in understanding, explaining and responding to the flood. Indeed, the flood of November 1824, so central to the city's literary landscape and cultural memory, provided a ready-made framework for making sense of natural disaster.

Environmental and Historiographical Context

The city's vulnerability to flooding was the result of a convergence of geography, landscape and decisions taken in urban planning and development. The River Neva had been flowing from Lake Ladoga into the Gulf of Finland through a watery landscape of islands, inter-connected rivers and marshlands long before the city's foundation. Flooding in this low-lying, waterlogged environment was a normal part of the ecosystem; it only became problematic after Peter I's decision in May 1703 to establish a new city of Sankt-Piter-Burkh on the Neva delta. Within months, by August 1703, the fledgling city was already under water, something that would become a regular occurrence in the city's early years.[5] Peter's decision ignored basic principles about where to situate cities.[6] 'A less auspicious place', as James H. Bater writes, 'for a large number of people to live is difficult to imagine', leaving aside the region's dreary climate, 'whatever man might labour months to build could succumb in a matter of hours to tempestuous autumn flood waters'.[7] This view owes much to a long-established narrative that blamed the city's challenges on Peter's hubris, something that locked the city into a primordial struggle with nature.[8] Literary representations of the city associated it with 'wind, storms, rain, snow, dark fogs, "gloomy darkness" (*mrak*), and, especially, uncontrollable floods'.[9] Although these tropes are deeply ingrained in St Petersburg's history and culture, there were sound economic and strategic considerations for establishing a city at the mouth of the Neva delta. Despite its shortcomings, as Robert Jones argues, this location had a decisive advantage, 'it combined access to the sea on one side with access to the Russian interior on the other'. In addition to its strategic importance, the city and port could be connected to a wider riverine network,

5.   Hughes, *Russia in the Age of Peter the Great*, p. 221; Anisimov, *Iunyi grad*, pp. 332–5.
6.   Lincoln, *Sunlight at Midnight*, p. 20.
7.   Bater, *St. Petersburg*, p. 17.
8.   Steinberg, *Petersburg Fin de Siècle*, p. 20.
9.   Ibid., p. 21.

including the fertile Volga region, which allowed Russian and Asian goods to enter the world market.[10] The resilience of the city and its inhabitants in the face of nature's onslaught was not simply bloody-mindedness, but a reflection of the economic advantages offered by this location. Although the river could be capricious, it also brought prosperity.

Throughout its history, the appearance and character of St Petersburg has been shaped by the River Neva and its delta.[11] Many histories of St Petersburg naturally acknowledge flooding as an important theme in the city's history. However, even some of the most influential studies of the city devote relatively little attention to how flooding and responses to it shaped the city and its residents' lives.[12] With the exception of the hydrologist and historical geographer Kim Pomeranets's detailed chronicles of flooding in the northern capital, little work has focused exclusively on the city's vulnerability to flooding.[13] Recent urban and environmental studies of the close relationship between the city and the river have examined how channelling the Neva, in part as a means of flood prevention, fundamentally shaped the layout and material fabric of the city.[14] Literary and cultural histories of St Petersburg and Leningrad have also foregrounded the huge reservoir of writing about, 'the watery onslaughts endured by Petersburg', which flowed into a Petersburg Text, shaping literary landscapes as well as urban identities.[15] Accounts of the 1824 flood, in particular Pushkin's 1833 poem *The Bronze Horseman*, the principal text of the Petersburg myth, structured how subsequent floods were discussed. Katerina Clark and Polina Barskova have both noted the correlation between cultural responses to the September 1924 flood and the literary frameworks created by the November 1824 flood.[16] Accounts of the September 1924 flood frequently owed a debt to narratives that could be traced back to November 1824, if not earlier. Descrip-

---

10. Jones, *Bread upon the Waters*, p. 10.

11. Barskova, 'Celebrating the Return of the Flood', p. 158; Kraikovski and Lajus, 'The Neva as a Metropolitan River of Russia', p. 349.

12. Bater, *St. Petersburg*, pp. 1–16; Lincoln, *Sunlight at Midnight*, pp. 17–52.

13. Pomeranets, *Navodneniia v Peterburge*; Pomeranets, *Tri veka peterburgskikh navodnenii*; Pomeranets, *Neschast'ia nevskikh beregov*.

14. Dills, 'The River Neva and the Imperial Façade'; Dills, 'Cracks in the Granite'; Kraikovski and Lajus, 'The Neva as a Metropolitan River of Russia'.

15. Buckler, *Mapping St. Petersburg*, p. 232.

16. Clark, *Petersburg*, pp. 183–4; Barskova, 'Celebrating the Return of the Flood'.

Robert Dale

tions of these two floods bore striking similarities, in part, because the poetics of flooding remained one of disaster, destruction and dislocation.[17]

A Man-Made Riverine Landscape

Without a valley or floodplain, whenever the Neva burst its banks the city was threatened. The many tributaries and distributaries fanning across the delta ensured that floods quickly spread. Given the regularity with which this happened, it is tempting to view the landscape and environment within which St Petersburg was situated as natural or unchanging. However, over the course of its history repeated alterations were made to this landscape. Creating a model modern city and conquering nature required land to be drained and the flow of waterways regulated and controlled. Canals and drainage systems were dug from Peter I's reign onwards. The scale of groundwork undertaken over the course of the eighteenth and nineteenth centuries was remarkable. The Catherine and Obvodnyi Canals, for example, were amongst the most impressive engineering projects of their day, which reconfigured the city and its environment.[18] Spoil from the new channels dug was used to raise the surrounding relief, or fill large wooden boxes and create new banks and plots of land.[19] By 1824, then, this was a highly engineered landscape, the object of repeated geo-engineering projects, which reconfigured the city and its hydrology. The 'aquatic squares' created by embankments, grand architectural ensembles and the network of artificial canals were intended to bring order to the city, creating rational, modern, well-ordered spaces.[20] Yet in certain weather conditions, water backed up through the man-made hydrological network and was rapidly distributed across the city. Systems designed to control nature could make things worse. As Buckler reminds us, 'the reverse movement of the Neva caused Petersburg's internal waterways – its canals and hydraulic systems – to join forces with the advancing deluge from the sea and turn against the city'.[21]

---

17. Buckler, *Mapping St. Petersburg*, p. 233.

18. Dills, 'The River Neva and the Imperial Façade', pp. 80–112, Anisimov, *Iunyi grad*, pp. 114–19.

19. Kraikovski and Lajus, 'The Neva as a Metropolitan River', pp. 350–2.

20. Ibid., pp. 348–50.

21. Buckler, *Mapping St. Petersburg*, p. 230.

Map 5.1. St Petersburg flood, 7 November 1824. Source: Brockhaus and Efron Encyclopaedic Dictionary / Wikimedia Commons.

In the nineteenth century, as the city rapidly expanded and land became more precious, drainage projects became increasingly important. Residential and urban development was concentrated in low-lying city districts and suburbs especially vulnerable to flooding. Only in 1935, thanks to Lev Il'in's general city plan, was urban expansion directed towards higher ground in the south and south-west, both as a means of reducing flood risk and as a symbolic re-

Robert Dale

focusing of the city away from its tsarist centre.[22] Nevertheless, large parts of the city centre afforded little or no protection against flooding. When strong winds and storms blew water up the Gulf of Finland, pushing a tidal wave of water back into the city, or when river levels rose due to snow melt, the city remained at nature's mercy.

Observing the September 1924 Flood

It was the first of these scenarios, cyclonic winds pushing water from the Gulf of Finland back in the city that caused river levels to rise throughout the morning and afternoon of 23 September 1924. The first warning signals of a flood came at 1:20 p.m. when cannon shots were fired from the Peter and Paul fortress. These began to be repeated first at thirty-minute intervals, and then every fifteen minutes. From 3:00 p.m. as the storm intensified, river levels rose dramatically, and coastal parts of the city, especially at the westerly tip of Vasil'evskii Island, flooded.[23] Leningraders' familiarity with flood risk, combined with the unexpected weather, meant there were still plenty of observers across the city. O.J. Frederiksen, an American aid worker living in Leningrad, for example, described how a friend had gone to post a letter at 4:00 p.m.

> Water was rising in the canals, but was still well below the street level as he went into the post office. As he came out there were already children crying on the post office steps and the water was ankle deep in the streets. After fifteen minutes' walk he found the water nearly knee deep and tried to persuade a *droschky* to take him home.[24]

In low-lying parts of the city, most vulnerable to flood waters, the un-forecast storm and the rapidly rising waters caught many residents unprepared. At the Gavan' harbour, 'where they have grown accustomed to flooding', as the title of an article published in *Krasnaia gazeta* put it, 'previously they had days to prepare for flooding, but now they had half an hour if not less'. The strong north-westerly winds sent people rushing from basements, scrambling to move their children and meagre belongings to the upper floors of buildings, in anticipation of the tidal surge. But the storm hit at a time of day when many residents were at work in factories and workplaces across the city, cutting them

---

22. Ruble, *Leningrad*, pp. 42–5.
23. *Leningradskaia pravda*, 'Vchera v Leningrade', 24 Sept. 1924, p. 1.
24. Frederiksen, p. 1.

off from their homes and families.[25] On Vasil'evskii Island, where floodwaters were at their deepest, nine-year-old Dmitrii Fridrikhsberg was let out of school early. Rather than heading straight home, he and some friends watched the rising waters. At the Andreevskii market he observed:

> People were running about abandoning their stalls and goods. Watermelons were floating by, we caught as many of them as we could hold. At home I met my father, who was as white as a sheet. He didn't approve of my excitement.

From their window that evening they could see sheets of roofing steel flying past, trees snapped in half, and people picking their way through the floodwaters suddenly disappearing down holes.[26]

By 5:00 p.m., the flood was causing disruption across the city. With every passing minute, the water level rose. Uritskii Square (Palace Square) and Prospekt 25 October (Nevskii Prospect) were soon under water.[27] The trams stopped running, and as the flood reached knee height it became impossible to walk the city's main thoroughfare. Before long the Moika and Fontanka rivers had burst their banks. Cut off by the flood, pedestrians were forced to wade through the waters, many choosing to undress before entering the water.[28] For many Leningraders this was a spectacle not to be missed. A crowd, for example, gathered at the Republican Bridge (Palace Bridge) curious to watch the river break its banks.[29] As the poet Mikhail Zenkevich put it, 'Leningrad came out by the thousands to watch the raging of the obdurate river, the fast coursing of its foamy waves; to see the barges and scows break the fetters that had constrained them and, carefree, dance their dying dance.'[30]

Memories, Narratives and Responses

For many memoirists, diarists and letter writers this extraordinary spectacle could not pass without comment. As winds ripped roofs from buildings, rivers raged through the streets and water poured into basements, the norms of

25. *Krasnaia gazeta (vechernyi vypusk)*, 'Tam, gde privykli k navodneniiam', 25 Sept. 1924, p. 3.

26. Quoted in Pomeranets, *Tri veka Peterburgskikh navodnenii*, p. 81.

27. Many street names and the names of bridges were changed after the October Revolution.

28. *Ekonomicheskaia zhizn'*, 'Iz Leningrada – Buria na Neve', 24 Sept. 1924, p. 1; *Leningradskaia pravda*, '23-e sentiabria v Leningrade', 24 Sept. 1924, p. 2.

29. *Leningradskaia pravda*, 'Na ulitsakh', 24 Sept. 1924, p. 2.

30. Quoted in Barskova, 'Celebrating the Return of the Flood', p. 164.

urban life were suspended. Beer barrels, firewood, furniture, uprooted trees, signs, lampposts and all manner of things were washed past Leningraders as they made their way across the city. In places the atmosphere bordered on the carnivalesque; uncanny or absurd sights stuck in the memory. Frederiksen recalled how a well-dressed couple calmly waded through deep water: 'Only two bobbing heads showed above the water, the man's sporting a derby and the lady's nearly hidden under a wide lace hat with a bright feather.'[31] But these stories also captured how calmly Leningraders met the disaster. According to Frederiksen, 'Even during the flood itself people who floated by on scraps of planking or sections of fence called out jokes to those leaning out of upper windows to enjoy the scene.'[32] Other correspondents commented upon the stoicism of their fellow citizens. As one put it in a letter intercepted by the military censor:

> Having been on the street the whole time as the water rose, one needs to note that people did not lose their heads, there was total calm, thoughtfulness, and self-confidence. There was so much self-sacrifice that evening, as those drowning and dying from fire were rescued. The same mood and behaviour can be observed after the flood amongst the city's inhabitants ... brave and selfless Leningraders have stood before danger more than once.[33]

The newspapers ran stories of how ordinary life continued even as the floodwaters rose.[34] By 1924, many Leningraders, having lived through world war, revolution and civil war, had learned to take adversity in their stride. 'The experiences (*perezhivanie*) of the Russian people (*narod*) as whole', as one correspondent put it, 'are the experiences of the much suffering Jehovah – in the last decade it is as if the horn of plenty is pouring unhappiness after unhappiness on the heads of the Russian people.'[35] The flood was just another setback to be overcome.

Only rarely did isolated incidents of emotional agitation intrude on a picture of a calm and organised flood response.[36] The most arresting of these concerned a panicked crowd of 'hysterical women' (*klikushi*) who had gathered on the colonnade of the St. Isaac Cathedral. 'These women', as *Krasnaia gazeta* reported, 'hysterically screamed of the end of the world, of the great deluge,

---

31. Letter written by O.J. Frederiksen, 30 Sept. 1924 (Leningrad Flood), p. 1.
32. Ibid.
33. TsGAIPD–SPb f. 16, op. 5, d. 5915, l. 87.
34. *Leningradskaia pravda*, '23-e sentiabria v Leningrade', 24 Sept. 1924, p. 3.
35. TsGAIPD-SPb f. 16, op. 5, d. 5914, l. 75.
36. 'Organizovannyi otpor strikhii – Bez paniki', p. 3

and several of them threw themselves from the colonnade into the raging waves and dashed themselves on slabs of pavement and the cathedral's foundations.' A group of pioneers and Komsomol members were on hand in boats to rescue around 150 women and children.[37] Similar stories were repeated in letters intercepted by the military censor.[38]

The narratives that emerged after the flood owed much to deeply ingrained tropes within the Petersburg literary landscape. 'The 1824 flood in particular', as Julie Buckler observes, created, 'a distinct literary tributary – an entire corpus of verse and memoir tributes, Pushkin's 'Bronze Horseman' amongst them, flowing into the Petersburg text'.[39] Alongside Pushkin's masterpiece, literary descriptions of the 1824 flood by Adam Mickiewicz, Aleksander Griboedov, Dmitrii Khvostov and Sergei Glinka structured a discourse about urban flooding. Although strict censorship prevented newspapers from reporting detailed information about the flood of 7 November 1824, many personal accounts of the flood were published in the second half of the nineteenth century, which kept memories about catastrophic flooding in circulation.[40]

Narrating and Responding to the November 1824 Flood

The parallels between the two floods were not purely literary. The floods of November 1824 and September 1924 were created by similar meteorological and hydrological forces. On the night of 6 and 7 November 1824, a storm gathered in the Gulf of Finland. By the morning, cyclonic winds were ripping roofs from buildings and trees from their roots and a wave of water surged from the sea towards the city with surprising speed and force. Around 10:00 a.m. the Neva burst its banks, and within approximately thirty minutes a flood of unprecedented magnitude engulfed the city. By noon, at least two thirds of the city was under water. Flooding hit districts in the west of the city, as well as low-lying island regions, and parts of the central districts hardest. The deluge dissipated almost as quickly as it came; by 5:00 p.m. the flood was subsiding.

---

37. *Krasnaia gazeta (vechernyii vypusk)*, 'Spasena na vodakh', 24 Sept. 1924, p. 2; Dmitrii Shedrikh, *1924*, pp. 206–7; Barskova, 'Celebrating the Return of the Flood', p. 163. On the *Klikush* see Worobec, *Possessed*.

38. TsGAIPD-SPb, f. 16, op. 5, d. 5914, l. 176; TsGAIPD-SPb, f. 16, op. 5, d. 5915, l. 82.

39. Buckler, *Mapping St. Petersburg*, p. 231.

40. Sorokina, 'Navodnenie pod tsezurnym zapreshom', pp. 407–23; Sorokina, 'Peterburgskoe navodnenie 1824 goda na stranitsakh literaturnykh al'manakhov 20-kh gg. XIX v., pp. 206–20.

Robert Dale

Enormous damage had been wrought upon the city in little over five hours.[41] Alexander Bestuzhev-Marlinksii, the editor of *Polar Star* and future Decembrist, subsequently described the flood and its aftermath in a letter to his mother:

> The scene was terrible – the sea raged along the streets. Horses and people saved themselves, (some) drowned and soon there were homes, firewood, furniture and corpses floating everywhere. No living soul could be seen anywhere – everywhere was like one damp grave. At 6 o'clock the water went down, and the next day the sunrise threw light on the terrors of destruction. Ships and barges lay on the streets, embankments weren't standing, broken windows and crying faces, groans and pity everywhere. The harbour and the low-lying parts of the island were completely wiped away, not a single straw of the surroundings was preserved, all the trees were even wiped and carried away.[42]

Wooden buildings were swept away and deposited intact across the city. The contents of homes, shops, factories and warehouses were displaced and deposited at random. Stone buildings collapsed after their foundations were damaged. 'Bridges and embankments', as Dills writes, 'symbols of Russia's modernity crumbled under water pressure.'[43] At the Smolensk cemetery, centrally located on Vasil'evskii Island, gravestones, metal railings, wooden crosses, coffins and even corpses were washed away.[44] One British observer, having picked his way through the wreckage the following morning, wrote home cataloguing the death and destruction; 'as I approached nearer I found the most appalling causes for so much distress – a plain thickly strewn with dead bodies, particularly women. I walked over confused heaps of devastation intermixed with the corpses of men and animals.'[45] Calculating the loss of life and the extent of material damage to public infrastructure and private property was a complicated task, and, unsurprisingly, estimates vary. Whilst Dills's suggests that 700 people perished in the flood, Samuel Aller's detailed contemporary account calculated 3,625 deaths.[46]

The flood relief efforts were coordinated by Tsar Alexander I, and charitable work by his mother Mariia Feodorovna, although official documents

---

41. Aller, *Opisanie navodneniia byvshago v Sankt-Peterburge 7 chisla Noiabria 1824 goda*, pp. 1–3; Dills, 'The River Neva and the Imperial Façade', pp. 28–56; Pomeranets, *Neschast'ia nevskikh beregov*, pp. 24–40; Pomeranets, *Navodneniia v Peterburge*, pp. 22–44.

42. 'Pis'mo A.A. Bestuzheva-Marlinskogo k materi', p. 219.

43. Dills, 'Cracks in the Granite', p. 482.

44. Aller, *Opisanie navodneniia*, pp. 5–16.

45. *Durham Chronicle*, 'The Late Dreadful Inundation at St. Petersburg. [Extract of a Private Letter. Dated St. Petersburg, Nov. 12(24).]', 25 Dec. 1824, p. 2.

46. Dills, 'Cracks in the Granite', p. 483; Aller, *Opisanie navodneniia*, p. 21.

may overlook the responses of ordinary people, privileging the actions of the government and a political and social elite. Alexander's initial concern was providing shelter, clothing, food and warmth to flood victims. The responsibility for immediate reconstruction was delegated to Governor-General M.A. Miloradovich, with responsibility for the worst affected parts of the city devolved to Adjutant-General Benkendorff on Vasil'evskii Island, Adjutant-General Komarovskii on the Petersburg Side and Adjutant-General Depreradovich on the Vyborg Side. One hundred thousand roubles were made available to each for reconstruction.[47] On 11 November 1824, a committee to aid those ruined by the flood (*Komitet o posobii razorennym navodneniem Sankt-Peterburga*), known colloquially as the Kurakin Committee after its director A.B. Kurakin, was established.[48] This was just one of a number of public, humanitarian and charitable bodies that provided financial and material assistance and collected and distributed funds, some of which continued to operate until early 1826.[49] Alongside the charitable impulse, however, official reports demonstrated a desire to count, record and categorise damage. This, according to Randall Dills, revealed much about the need to reassert autocratic prestige and the vision of the well-ordered city that the flood had so damaged.[50] Yet these reports also highlight where and on whom the impact of the flood fell most heavily. People living in wooden buildings were more vulnerable to flooding than more affluent residents located in stone or brick structures. Indeed, the number of damaged wooden buildings and even the number of cattle and horses drowned within central districts were good indications of St Petersburg's level of urbanisation.[51]

Connecting the Floods

Given the magnitude of the flood, the common geography of devastation and the convenient hundred-year interlude, it is easy to understand why comparisons between 1824 and 1924 were quickly made. In other circumstances, a natural disaster of this magnitude might have shocked residents and destabilised

---

47. E.N. Pogozhev, 'K istorii navodneniia v S. Peterburge v 1824 gody', *Russkaia starina*, 117 (No.1231), January 1904, pp. 231–39 (p. 231).

48. Ibid., 232–3;

49. *Obshchii otchet Tsentral'nogo komiteta o posobii razorennym navodneniem S. Peterburga*; Kononova, 'Blagotvoritel'nost' Rossiiskogo Imperatorskogo doma v period pandemii (na primere likvidatsii posledstveii navodneniia 1824g.)', pp. 10–23.

50. Dills, 'The River Neva and the Imperial Façade', pp. 39–47.

51. Bater, *St. Petersburg*, pp. 155–7; Aller, *Opisanie navodneniia*, pp. 19–20.

Robert Dale

municipal government. The prominence of the November 1824 flood in the city's cultural fabric, however, gave Leningraders a readymade framework to make sense of potentially traumatic experiences. Within days the press began publishing articles drawing connections between November 1824 and September 1924.[52] Books and pamphlets explaining and contextualising the 1924 flood frequently contained lengthy historical surveys of past inundations.[53] At the end of October 1924, *Krasnaia gazeta* published an account of the 1824 flood based on archival documents from the Chancellery of His Imperial Majesty the Tsar, which were hardly ideologically acceptable sources.[54] It devoted an entire page to recounting the history of the November 1824 flood on its hundredth anniversary.[55] The cultural resources created by previous floods bolstered the response to the September 1924 inundation by placing exceptional events into a context, helping to normalise an extreme event and remind citizens that the city had recovered from previous disasters.

Despite the persistence of cultural tropes about flooding, the same low-lying districts of the city were hit by the deluge, but were affected differently. A century of urban and industrial development had altered the urban landscape, creating new infrastructure, industries and institutions, which proved vulnerable to flooding. The construction of tramlines, plumbing for clean water supply and sewerage disposal, the laying of telephone and telegraph cables, as well as electrification projects, helped establish St Petersburg as a modern European capital city. These systems, all introduced since 1824, suffered extensive damage and disruption in September 1924. It took weeks to re-establish these services and utilities; water damage was compounded by devastating electrical and chemical fires. For example, at the Bolshevik factory, one of the city's leading armaments manufacturers, a broken electrical cable started a fire in the shell assembly workshop, which threatened to spread. The raging waters made it difficult for firefighters to reach and access burning buildings. Many fires burned untended whilst fire crews were preoccupied with saving lives.[56]

---

52. *Krasnaia gazeta (vechernyi vypusk)*, 'Navodnenie v 1824 gody', 25 Sept. 1924, p. 2; *Krasnaia gazeta (vechernyi vypusk)*, 'Literatura navodneniia', 27 Sept. 1924, p. 5.

53. Matseino, 'Istoriia Leningradskikh navodnenii i ikh povtoriaemost'', pp. 164–70; Stolpianskii, 'K istorii Peterburgskikh navodnenii', pp. 13–21.

54. *Krasnaia gazeta (vechernyi vypusk)*, 'Navodnenie 1824 g.', 28 Oct. 1924, p. 3.

55. *Krasnaia gazeta (vechernyi vypusk)*, 'Stoletie navodnenia v peterburge. 1824 g. – 7/19 Noiabria – 1924 g.', 19 Nov. 1924, p. 2.

56. TsGAIPD-SPb, f. 16, op. 5, d. 5381, l. 2; TsGAIPD-SPb, f.16, op. 5, d. 5914, l. 87; *Krasnaia gazeta (vechernyi vypusk)*, 'Pozharnye v bor'be so stikhiei', 25 Sept. 1924, p. 3.

The ever-growing complexity of urban life, then, made repairing flood damage more difficult and expensive. Whilst residents were often resilient in the face of natural disaster, urban and industrial infrastructure was often poorly protected, easily disrupted and difficult to repair.

Confronting the Aftermath of Flooding

A commission established to calculate the damage estimated that the total cost of repair might eventually exceed 25 million roubles, approximately US$183 million in 2018 values.[57] Reports about the scale of the flooding indicated not only the extent of destruction, but the priorities for re-establishing normal life. Approximately 10,000 people, who had lost all of their clothing, furniture and personal property, were flooded out of basements and had to be re-housed.[58] Although the extent of wooden housing declined over the century, the number of people living in cellars, which regularly flooded, had increased.[59] As in 1824, the urban poor were the most vulnerable to flooding. Public health concerns dictated that drowned livestock and corpses disinterred from the Smolensk cemetery were quickly reburied.[60] Embankments and bridges had to be repaired or rebuilt, and an estimated 250 ships and barges deposited on embankments or streets had to be removed, to enable the normal flow of people, vehicles and goods across the city.[61] Amongst the most pressing tasks was replacing the 90,000 square *sazhens* or approximately 100 acres, of wooden blocks (*tortsovaia mostovaia*), which surfaced Leningrad's central thoroughfares. According to Frederiksen, 'There (were) millions of them, so many and so scattered that it seem(ed) impossible that anyone could ever had laid them all in place, or that anyone can ever do it again.'[62]

When Leningrad's municipal authorities began counting the cost of flood damage, they paid particularly close attention to the harm inflicted on industrial enterprises and their production. In mid-October 1924, the economic journal *Promyshlennost' i torgovlia* calculated that the total industrial

57. *Krasnaia gazeta (vechernyi vypusk)*, 'Ubytki ot navodneniia svyshche 20.000.000 rub. – Uvlechenie platy za kvartiry', 27 Sept. 1924, p. 2.

58. *Leningradskaia pravda*, 'Kvartiry postradavshim', 30 Sept. 1924, p. 3.

59. Bater, *St. Petersburg*, pp. 176–8.

60. *Leningradskaia pravda*, 'Vsplyvshie trupy pokoinikov', 25 Sept. 1924, p. 3; TsGA-SPb f. 1000, op. 8, d. 130, l. 10; TsGA-SPb f. 1000, op. 8, d. 131, l. 3.

61. GARF f. R-3316, op. 46, d. 26, l. 41–2; TsGA-SPb f. 1000, op. 8. d. 129, l. 6–7.

62. Letter written by O.J. Frederiksen, 30 Sept. 1924 (Leningrad Flood), p. 1.

losses amounted to 10,808,000 roubles, or approximately US$79 million today.[63] The municipal authorities' detailed reports about the impact of the flood on factories provide a fascinating insight into how the city's economy had developed since 1824. More than one hundred factories and industrial plants were flooded. Amongst the worst affected was the Putilov Factory, which manufactured armaments, railway equipment and tractors, situated near the harbour in the south-west of the city. Approximately eighty per cent of its huge territory was flooded, production lines were damaged and its archives ruined.[64] Factories manufacturing precision engineered products, such as dynamos and radios, or the Russkii Dizel' (diesel engines), Sevkabel' (electrical cable) and the Lieutenant Schmidt Electric-Battery factories, which had not existed in 1824, were badly disrupted. More traditional industries, like textiles, shoe manufacturing and food processing, which had adopted modern technologies, proved no less vulnerable. Entire supplies of raw materials, including leather, cotton, paper, flour, firewood, coal, oil and even the sand used by foundries to create moulds, were washed away. At one tobacco factory more than fifteen million cigarettes were water-damaged.[65] This catalogue of destruction was a function of decisions about industrial zoning. Since the 1860s, many factories had been located in vacant plots of land in central districts, particularly places connected to waterways and in close proximity to workforces.[66] There appears to have been little concern about their vulnerability to flooding.

Leningrad was, however, more than just an industrial powerhouse; cultural, scientific and educational institutions, many of them situated in prestigious waterside locations, also suffered. The Academy of Arts on University Embankment, for example, had its basements flooded, damaging seventeen apartments and the moulding and mosaic workshops.[67] At the State Academic Theatre (Mariinskii Theatre), situated on the embankment of the Catherine Canal, lighting, heating and electrical systems, as well as collections of scenery, costumes and musical instruments, were all badly damaged.[68] According to Frederiksen:

63. *Promyshlennost' i torgovlia*, 'Promyshlennost' posle navodneniia', p. 36.

64. TsGAIPD-SPb, f. 16, op. 5, d. 5381, l. 3; 'Promyshlennost' posle navodneniia', p. 32.

65. TsGAIPD-SPb, f. 16, op. 5, d. 5381, ll. 3–10; *Leningradskaia pravda*, 'Leningradskaia promyshlennost' i navodnenie', 27 Sept. 1924, p. 4.

66. Bater, *St. Petersburg*, pp. 107–10.

67. TsGAIPD-SPb, f. 16, op. 5, d. 5381, l. 12.

68. GARF, f. A-259, op. 9b, d. 4323, ll. 25–25ob; *Krasnaia gazeta (vechernyi vypusk)*, 'Posledstviia navodneniia v Ak.-teatrakh', 25 Sept. 1924, p. 3; Clark, *Petersburg*, 183.

... the grand piano had floated from the orchestra pit upon into the parterre and a 15,000 ruble (*sic*) harp was under water. The next morning the square in front of the theatre was a bizarre sight with hundreds of blue silk and gilt chairs set out to dry and great expanses of scenery laid out under the brilliant sun that followed the storm.[69]

The morning after the flood a similar scene could be seen in the courtyard of the Mikhailovskii Palace, where priceless textiles and canvases were being dried by Russian Museum staff.[70] Institutions as diverse as the Botanical Gardens, the Institute for Eastern Languages and the Electro-Technical Institute all suffered damage to buildings and collections. At the Russian Academy of Sciences, 62,000 volumes in the library needed to be dried and restored. In the ichthyology department, more than 25,000 glass jars that had either been smashed or suffered water ingress, part of an irreplaceable collection of zoological samples, had to be rebottled.[71] The flood's impact on the experimental work of Ivan Pavlov was particularly significant. His laboratories at the Academy of Sciences on Vasil'evskii Island and the Institute of Experimental Medicine on the Petrograd Side were both inundated.[72] The central government subsequently awarded Pavlov 10,000 roubles to repair the damage.[73] At the Institute for Experimental Medicine, approximately one hundred dogs had to be rescued from the rapidly rising water. The experience of being dragged to safety from their kennels, through the floodwaters, was reported to have affected the dogs' characters, something which prompted Pavlov and his team to begin researching traumatic reactions and nervous pathologies.[74] This catalogue of disaster and destruction was not simply evidence of the scale of the flooding, but also a statement of the continued flourishing of cultural, scientific and educational activity within the city since 1824. The prominence of these institutions within the cultural landscape, as indicated by the reporting and accounting of flood damage, and the physical environment, often reflected in their prominent but vulnerable waterside locations, reflected the development of the city as a modern capital city.

---

69. Letter written by O.J. Frederiksen, 30 Sept. 1924 (Leningrad Flood), p. 2. The harp would have cost approximately US$100,000 today.

70. Isachenko, *Rabota nad tkaniami, postradavshshimi v etnograficheskom otdele vo vremiia navodneniia.*

71. *Otchet o deiatel'nosti Rossiiskoi Akademii Nauk za 1924 goda*, pp. i–ii, 96–8.

72. Todes, *Ivan Pavlov*, p. 503.

73. TsGAIPD-SPb, f. 16, op. 5, d. 5907, l. 85.

74. Todes, *Ivan Pavlov*, 503–9; Pavlov, *Lectures on Conditioned Reflexes*, pp. 363–9.

Robert Dale

Although Pavlov's dogs began to exhibit traumatic reactions, Leningraders on the whole demonstrated great resilience in the face of disaster. Compared to the dislocation experienced after the November 1824 flood, when the effects were felt many months later, the flood response in the weeks and months after 23 September 1924 was remarkably successful. One of the biggest differences between the two floods was that efforts to prevent deaths and save lives appear to have been more effective in 1924 than 1824. In the immediate wake of the flood, *Leningradskaia pravda* reported that sixteen people had perished in the flood.[75] In the following days the press reported further deaths, the discovery of bodies and the passing away of the critically ill.[76] A week after the flood, the most detailed archival sources stated that the death-toll did not exceed 25 people.[77] Individual correspondents doubted such low estimates, but even if massaged, the death toll was far lower than in 1824.[78] This was a remarkable achievement in a city the size and complexity of Leningrad.

Bolshevik Initiative

One explanation for the relatively low loss of life was the speed and energy with which the early Bolshevik party-state coordinated its flood response. By 5:00 p.m. on 23 September, even before the full extent of the emergency was apparent, the Leningrad Party Executive Committee and city Soviet had established an emergency troika, with equivalents in every district, to maintain order and organise flood relief. Martial law was swiftly declared, and the police and military were mobilised. The population was warned of the oncoming danger, the streets were cleared, and Leningraders were moved to the upper floors of buildings.[79] In Moscow on 25 September, the Politburo established a special commission, consisting of M.I. Kalinin, L.B. Kamenev, G.E. Zinoviev, V.M. Smirnov, N.P. Komarov, P.A. Zalutskii and K.E. Voroshilov, to assist Leningrad and its population. It met the same day and assigned emergency funds for reconstruction

75. 'Organizovanno i poriadka', p. 1.

76. 'Pogibshie pri navodnenii 23-go Sentiabria', p. 1; *Leningradskaia Pravda*, 'Zhertvy navodneniia', 2 Oct. 1924, p. 3; *Krasnaia gazeta (vechernyi vypusk)*, 'Obval s chelovecheskimi zhertvami', 4 Oct. 1924, p. 2.

77. TsGAIPD-SPb, f. 16, op. 5, d. 5381, l. 2.

78. TsGAIPD-SPb, f. 16, op. 5, d. 5914, l. 75, 77, 78, 85, 86, 87.

79. *Leningradskaia pravda*, 'Postanovleniia Prezidiuma Leningradskogo Gubispolkoma', 24 Sept. 1924, p. 1; *Vestnik Leningradskogo Soveta*, 'O bor'be s navodneniem i merakh po likvidatsii ego posledstvii', 27 Sept. 1924, p. 1.

work.[80] The following day the commission was reinforced with the addition of G.M. Krzhizhanovskii as a representative of the State Planning Committee, N.M. Shvernik on behalf of the Central Control Commission, M.I. Frumkin as a representative of People's Commissariat of Finance and V.M. Molotov on behalf of the Party Central Committee. Along with Kalinin, these four new members were dispatched to Leningrad to assess the damage and formulate a reconstruction plan.[81] Local and central government prioritised maintaining law and order, planning reconstruction efforts and making emergency funds available to those who had lost their homes.

The authoritarian impulses of the early Bolshevik state had their advantages in a natural disaster. At a meeting of the Leningrad Soviet, i.e. the city council, convened on 3 October 1924, the intellectual and revolutionary Moritz Vinchevkii, who had recently returned from America, praised the clean-up efforts: 'I saw a similar flood in the south of America about nine years ago, and I believe, despite the perfection of American technology, in three weeks they didn't achieve the same level of reconstruction or bring about the same level of order as we did in three days.'[82] Although the official and public setting of these comments might explain their optimism, similar sentiments were expressed in private correspondence intercepted by the military censor. Many letters praised the city's Bolshevik leaders for the speed with which martial law was announced and rescue efforts organised. 'The energy and strict organisation', according to one correspondent, 'reduced the disaster by 75 per cent.'[83] A report examining the political and economic conditions of Leningrad's factories found that workers supported the regime's attempts to prevent food speculation in the flood's aftermath and expressed faith in the government's plans to support flood victims.[84] Indeed, the success of the Bolshevik response increased the regime's credibility and shifted political opinion. In a letter to relatives overseas, Nils Rasmusen expressed disbelief at the, 'rapid, efficient and energetic action and labour from the Bolsheviks. In Denmark, and in England, we wouldn't have achieved in such a short time as the "Bolsheviks" have achieved here.'[85] As another letter put it: 'I have heard many people who

---

80. RGASPI f. 17, op. 3, d.465, l. 4; d. 466, l. 4.

81. RGASPI f. 17, op. 3, d. 466, l. 6.

82. *Ekonomicheskaia zhizn'*, 'Na mestakh – Posle navodneniia (Leningradskie pis'ma)', 4 Oct. 1924, p. 4.

83. TsGAIPD-SPb f. 16, op. 5, d. 5915, l. 182.

84. TsGAIPD-SPb f. 16, op. 5, d. 5905, ll. 107–32.

85. TsGAIPD-SPb f. 16, op. 5, d. 5915, l. 182

Robert Dale

frequently curse the Bolsheviks, now praise them for their energy'.[86] Natural disaster not only disrupted municipal government and everyday life, but had the capacity to transform political attitudes and allegiances.

Growing Accustomed to Flooding

The success of the flood response, however, owed as much to the exertions, experience and resilience of ordinary Leningraders as to the mobilising power of the Bolshevik party-state. Some workers heroically stayed on in their factories ensuring that valuable materials, equipment and finished products were moved to upper floors.[87] Students who had recently formed themselves into experimental communes, particularly the 'Red Student' Artel and the Commune of the 133, were active in forming emergency relief teams, saving lives, recovering property and launching clean-up operations.[88] Newspapers were full of campaigns that mobilised people to repair the damage. Local and national titles appealed to collect funds to assist flood victims, to which people from across the city and nation donated.[89] These actions were the product of the decisions and agency of ordinary people, independent of political authorities.

The reaction of Leningraders, and the decisions taken by their political leaders, owed much to the historical experience of flooding and long-established practices about how to respond to flooding. People had been interacting with the river and living within this marshy environment for over two hundred years, benefitting from the advantages it conferred and periodically experiencing its capriciousness. Through sustained interaction with the river, people had come to understand its flows and habits, its annual routines and cycles, which became embedded within the everyday and customary life of the city.[90] Writing in 1840, for example, the ethnographer I.I. Pushkarev detailed how residents understood flooding patterns and learnt to judge and normalise flood risk.[91]

---

86. TsGAIPD-SPb f. 16, op. 5, d, 5914, l. 73.

87. *Leningradksaia pravda*, 'Leningrad – na postu', 25 Sept. 1924, p. 4; *Leningradskaia pravda*, 'Razrushennoe stikhiei – vosstanovim kollektivnym rudom – Nashi geroi', 25 Sept. 1924, p. 4; *Leningradskaia pravda*, 'Na boevom postu', 27 Sept. 1924, p. 6.

88. Andy Willimott, *Living the Revolution*, pp. 65–6; M. Iankovskii, *Kommuna sta tridtsati trekh*, pp. 31–2; Richard Stites, *Revolutionary Dreams*, p. 213.

89. *Leningradskaia pravda*, 'Na pomoshch' postradabshshim ot navodnenia', 25 Sept. 1924, p. 1; *Leningradskaia pravda*, 'Nash fond pomoshchi', 23 Dec. 1924, p. 7.

90. Kraikovski and Lajus, 'Living on the River', pp. 235–52.

91. Dills, 'Cracks in the Granite', p. 490. See also Pushkarev, *Nikolaevskii Peterburg*, pp. 27–35.

'There, Where They Have Grown Accustomed to Flooding'

Recurrent flooding and fires, as Julie Buckler argues, resulted in, 'a constant awareness of the sword of Damocles hanging over the city in the here and now, and a sense of impending doom that [was] itself as terrible as the anticipated cataclysm'.[92] Flooding for many Leningraders was part of normal life; part of the price paid for living in the northern capital, something to be endured, confronted, mitigated and eventually eradicated.[93] By 1924, direct memories of 1824 and earlier catastrophic floods were no longer in living memory, but the risks presented by more regular less dramatic flooding were well established. Between 1824 and 1924, the city experienced 124 floods of over 160 centimetres. In the seven years after the February Revolution, the city flooded eleven times; all but one of these floods were the result of autumnal storms.[94] Cyclonic winds and the rising water levels were a normal part of this season.

Most Leningraders, then, were conscious of flood risk and understood when and where to anticipate it. This awareness was especially acute in vulnerable low-lying or coastal parts of the city, such as the Admiralty, the Petersburg Side, Vasil'evskii Island and the Nevskii districts. In these and other locales, even a relatively modest rise in river levels, which barely registered in more central areas, could prove disruptive and dangerous.[95] In these and other places the regularity of flooding necessitated the development of warning systems, drills for moving people and property to upper floors, and methods for combatting rising waters. By November 1833, the city had developed a detailed set of practices, codified in imperial legislation, for warning of floods and responding to natural disaster. Cannon shots and red warning flags would signal when to move to safety, teams of oarsmen were instructed to rescue people and evacuation points would be established in barracks for the displaced.[96] Likewise, a detailed set of instructions on how to respond to future floods, explained on a district by district basis, were issued on 20 November 1925.[97] Despite the intervening years, there was much continuity between these measures. By September 1924, fundamental shifts in national politics and local administration prompted by the political revolutions of 1917 had exerted little influence

---

92. Buckler, *Mapping St. Petersburg*, p. 229.

93. Dills, 'The River Neva and the Imperial Façade', p. 56.

94. Pomeranets, *Tri veka peterburgskikh navodnenii*, pp. 193–205; Pomeranets, *Neshchast'ia nevskikh beregov*, pp. 399–415.

95. Kraikovski and Lajus, 'Living on the River', p. 246.

96. *Polnoe sobranie zakonov Rossiiskoi imperii* VIII, no. 6575, 16 November 1833, pp. 668–9; Dills, 'Cracks in the Granite', p. 489.

97. *Leningrad v bor'be s navodneniem*, pp. 11–64.

Robert Dale

on the city's riverine landscape, or on the environmental vulnerabilities that it brought. Over the course of a century, urbanisation, industrialisation and economic and technological modernisation substantially altered the fabric of the city and land use patterns, but different political systems sought broadly similar solutions.

Conclusion

The long-term solution to eliminating flood risk was sought in further human modification of the landscape. A dam across the Gulf of Finland that would protect the city from periodic low-level floods as well as another catastrophic inundation was mooted in the wake of both the November 1824 and September 1924 floods.[98] Over time, engineers' proposed interventions became increasingly sophisticated, technocratic and expensive. These visions of a flood-proof city, however, were unrealised, thwarted by the scale of the engineering project and projected cost. Yet the impulse to conquer nature and protect the city from tidal storms never disappeared. Discussion of a flood prevention dam resurfaced in the 1970s, culminating on 2 August 1979 with a joint resolution of Central Committee of the Communist Party and the Council of Ministers of the USSR entitled 'On the construction of a structure to defend Leningrad from flooding'.[99] The project, and the extent of risk posed by floodwaters, became the subject of increasingly heated debate between environmentalists, politicians, hydrologists and engineers during Perestroika.[100] Work on the construction of a 25-kilometre dam began in 1981, but after various interruptions and delays the project was mothballed in 1995.[101] It was not until October 2004 that work resumed on a revised scheme, renamed the Saint Petersburg Flood Prevention Facility Complex. Much of the previous structure had to be

---

98. On examples of plans for dams across the Gulf of Finland, see *Kriticheskii obzor' proektov dlia predokhraneniia S.-Peterburga ot navodneniia*; Dills, 'The River Neva and the Imperial Façade', p. 102; *Krasnaia gazeta (vechernyi vypusk)*, 'Kak borot'sia s navodneniiami', 25 Sept. 1924, p. 3.

99. *Pravda*, 'V TSK KPSS i Sovete Ministrov SSSR', 19 Aug. 1979, p. 1; Council of Ministers of the SSSR, 'O stroitel'stve sooruzhenii zashchity g. Leningrada ot navodnenii'.

100. G. Tziafetas, 'The Ecologists versus the Builders, pp. 182–9.

101. Senin, *Leningrad bez navodnenii*.

rebuilt, but the completed dam was finally inaugurated by Vladimir Putin in mid-August 2011.[102]

The realisation of this long-held ambition, something that thwarted both the Russian Empire and the Soviet Union, has rescued the city from the immediate blight of flooding, although rising sea-levels and the deterioration or failure of the dam might threaten the city in the future.[103] In the process, however, it caused far-reaching environmental damage and altered one of the defining features of the city's cultural landscape, its vulnerability to flooding. Living behind the protection of the dam, the regularity of flooding and its catastrophic consequences, as well as the resilience and adaptability of residents in the face of natural disaster, are likely to fade from memory. Although the floods of 1824 and 1924 affected the city differently, in the intervening one hundred years the urban landscape remained at nature's mercy. In both cases citizens understood the potential for flooding and the risks posed by the city's precarious location. By the time of the centenary and bicentenary of the city's two worst floods in 2024, this link with the past, through interaction with the city's watery landscape, is likely to have been weakened, if not entirely eroded.

ACKNOWLEDGEMENTS

This research was made possible by a Santander International Connections Award (Travel Grant) awarded at the University of York in July 2012. I am indebted to the editors of this volume, and my colleagues Ben Houston, David Saunders and Felix Schulz for their comments, suggestions and encouragement. Remaining weaknesses and errors remain my responsibility.

BIBLIOGRAPHY

Aller, Samuil. 1826. *Opisanie navodneniia byvshago v Sankt-Peterburge 7 chisla Noiabria 1824 goda.* St Petersburg: Tipografiia Departamenta Narodnago Prosvysheniia.

Anisimov, E.V. 2003. *Iunyi grad: Peterburg vremen Petra Velikogo.* St Petersburg: Dmitrii Bulanin.

---

102. Tziafetas, 'The Ecologists Versus the Builders', p. 187; *Kommersant"*, 'Damba budet zhit' v dolg', 25 Oct. 2004; *BaltInfo.ru*, 'Putin otkryl kompleks zashchitnykh sooruzhenii Peterburga ot navodnenii', 12 Aug. 2011.

103. See Directorate of FPFC, *Flood Prevention Facility Complex;* Semiotic.ru, 'Kompleks Zashchitnykh Sooruzhenii Sankt-Peterburga ot navodnenii'.

Robert Dale

Avvakumov, S.I. et al. (eds). 1964. *Ocherki istorii Leningrada*. Vol. 4, *Period Velikoi Otkiabr'skoi sotsialisticheskoi revoliutiss i postroeniia sotsializma v SSSR 1917–1941 gg.* Moscow and Leningrad: Nauka.

BaltInfo.ru. 2011. 'Putin otkryl kompleks zashchitnykh sooruzhenii Peterburga ot navodnenii'. 12 August. http://www.baltinfo.ru/2011/08/12/Putin-otkryl-kompleks-zaschitnykh-sooruzhenii-Peterburga-ot-navodnenii-222438

Barskova, Polina. 2017. 'Celebrating the Return of the Flood'. In Jane Costlow and Arja Rosenholm (eds), *Meanings and Values of Water in Russian Culture,* pp. 158–74. Abingdon: Routledge.

Bater, James H. 1976. *St Petersburg: Industrialization and Change.* London: Edward Arnold, 1976.

Brockhaus and Efron Encyclopedic Dictionary. 1907. 'Map of St. Petersburg Flood, 7 November 1824'. https://commons.wikimedia.org/wiki/File:Floods_in_Saint-Petersburg.jpg

Buckler, Julie. 2005. *Mapping St. Petersburg: Imperial Text and Cityscape.* Princeton: Princeton University Press.

Clark, Katerina. 1995. *Petersburg: Crucible of Cultural Revolution.* Cambridge, MA: Harvard University Press.

Clark, Robert. 2008. *Deep Water: Art, Disaster, and Redemption in Florence.* New York: Doubleday.

Council of Ministers of the USSR. 1979. 'O stroitel'stve sooruzhenii zashchity g. Leningrada ot navodnenii'. Postanovlenie No.745. 2 August. http://docs.cntd3.ru/document/901737037.

Courtney, Chris. 2018. *The Nature of Disaster in China: The 1931 Yangzi River Flood.* Cambridge: Cambridge University Press.

Dagupta, Susmita, Asif Mohammed Zaman, Subhendu Roy, Mainul Hug, Sarwar Jahan and Ainun Nishat. 2015. *Urban Flooding of Greater Dhaka in a Changing Climate: Building Local Resilience to Disaster Risk.* Washington, DC: The World Bank.

Dills, Randall. 2010. 'The River Neva and the Imperial Façade: Culture and Environment in Nineteenth Century St. Petersburg Russia'. Ph.D diss., University of Illinois at Urbana-Champaign.

Dills, Randall. 2014. 'Cracks in the Granite: Paternal Care, the Imperial Façade, and the Limits of Authority in the 1824 St. Petersburg Flood'. *Journal of Urban History* **40** (3): 470–96.

Directorate of FPFC of the Saint Petersburg Ministry of Construction Industry, Housing and Utilities Sector of the Russian Federation. 2014. *Flood Prevention Facility Complex.* http://www.dambaspb.ru/en/#intro

Durham Chronicle. 1824. 'The Late Dreadful Inundation at St. Petersburg [Extract of a Private Letter. Dated St Petersburg, Nov. 12(24).]'. 25 December.

'There, Where They Have Grown Accustomed to Flooding'

Ekonomicheskaia zhizn'. 1924. 'Iz Leningrada – Buria na Neve'. 24 September.

Ekonomicheskaia zhizn'. 1924. 'Na mestakh – Posle navodneniia (Leningradskie pis'ma)'. 4 October.

Gosudarstvennyi arkhiv Rossisskoi Federatsii (GARF, State Archive of the Russian Federation).

Hoover Institution Archives, O.J. Frederiksen Collection, Letter written by O.J. Frederiksen, 30 September 1924 (Leningrad Flood).

Hughes, Lindsey. 1998. *Russia in the Age of Peter the Great*. New Haven and London: Yale University Press.

Jackson, Jeffrey H. 2010. *Paris under Water: How the City of Light Survived the Great Flood of 1910*. New York: Palgrave Macmillan.

Jones, Robert E. 2013. *Bread upon the Waters: The St. Petersburg Grain Trade and the Russian Economy, 1703–1811*. Pittsburgh: University of Pittsburgh Press.

Iankovskii, M. 1929. *Kommuna sta tridtsati trekh*. Leningrad: Priboi.

Isachenko, N.V. 1926. *Rabota nad tkaniami, postradavshshimi v etnograficheskom otdele vo vremiia navodneniia*. Leningrad: Izdanie Gosudarsvennogo Russkogo Muzeia.

Kelman, Ari. 2006. *A River and its City: The Nature of Landscape in New Orleans*. Berkeley, CA: University of California Press.

Kipriianov, V. 1858. *Kriticheskii obzor' proektov dlia predokhraneniia S.-Peterburga ot navodneniia*. St.Petersburg: Tipografiia Glavnogo Upravleniia Putei Soobshcheniia.

Kommersant''. 2004. 'Damba budet zhit' v dolg: Ee profinansiruiut zapadnye banki'. 25 October. https://www.kommersant.ru/doc/519047

Kononova, T.B. 2007. 'Blagotvoritel'nost' Rossiiskogo Imperatorskogo doma v period pandemii (na primere likvidatsii posledstveii navodneniia 1824g.)'. In L.V. Shvedova (ed.), *Blagotvoritel'nost' v Rossii kak sotial'nyi institut: istoriia, vozrozhdenie, razvitie*, pp. 10–23. Moscow: Knizhnyi dom universitet.

Kraikovski, Alexei and Julia Lajus. 2010. 'The Neva as a Metropolitan River of Russia: Environment. Economy and Culture'. In Terje Tvedt and Richard Coopey (eds), *A History of Water*. Series II, Vol. 2, *Rivers and Society: From Early Civilizations to Modern Times*, pp. 339–64. London, New York: I. B. Tauris.

Kraikovski, Alexei and Julia Lajus. 2017. 'Living on the River: The Significance of the Neva to Imperial Saint Petersburg'. In Martin Knoll, Uwe Lübken and Dieter Schott (eds), *Rivers Lost, Rivers Regained: Rethinking City-River Relations*, pp. 235–52. Pittsburgh: University of Pittsburgh Press.

Krasnaia gazeta (vechernii vypusk). 1924. 'Istoricheskaia doska'. 24 September.

Krasnaia gazeta (vechernyi vypusk). 1924. 'Kak borot'sia s navodneniiami'. 25 September.

Krasnaia gazeta (vechernyi vypusk). 1924. 'Literatura navodneniia'. 27 September.

Robert Dale

Krasnaia gazeta (vechernyi vypusk). 1924. 'Navodnenie 1824 g. (Po dokumentam arkhiva sobstvennoi E. I. V. kantseliarii)'. 28 October.

Krasnaia gazeta (vechernyi vypusk). 1924. 'Navodnenie v 1824 gody'. 25 September.

Krasnaia gazeta (vechernyi vypusk). 1924. 'Obval s chelovecheskimi zhertvami'. 4 October.

Krasnaia gazeta (vechernyi vypusk). 1924. 'Posledstviia navodneniia v Ak.-teatrakh'. 25 September.

Krasnaia gazeta (vechernyi vypusk). 1924. 'Pozharnye v bor'be so stikhiei'. 25 September.

Krasnaia gazeta (vechernyi vypusk). 1924. 'Spasena na vodakh'. 24 September.

Krasnaia gazeta (vechernyi vypusk). 1924. 'Stoletie navodneniia v peterburge. 1824 g. – 7/19 Noiabria – 1924 g.'. 19 November.

Krasnaia gazeta (vechernyi vypusk). 1924. 'Tam, gde privykli k navodneniiam'. 25 September.

Krasnaia gazeta (vechernyi vypusk). 1924. 'Ubytki ot navodneniia svyshche 20.000.000 rub. – Uvlechenie platy za kvartiry'. 27 September.

Leningrad v bor'be s navodneniem. 1925. Leningrad: Redaktsiia i izdanie Leningradskogo komendantskogo upravleniia.

Leningradskaia pravda. 1924. '23-e sentiabria v Leningrade'. 24 September.

Leningradskaia pravda. 1924. 'Kvartiry postradavshim'. 30 September.

Leningradksaia pravda. 1924. 'Leningrad – na postu'. 25 September.

Leningradskaia pravda. 1924. 'Leningradskaia promyshlennost' i navodnenie'. 27 September.

Leningradskaia pravda. 1924. 'Organizovannyi otpor strikhii – Bez paniki'. 24 September.

Leningradskaia pravda. 1924. 'Na boevom postu'. 27 September.

Leningradskaia pravda. 1924. 'Na pomoshch' postradabshshim ot navodnenia'. 25 September.

Leningradskaia pravda. 1924. 'Nash fond pomoshchi'. 23 December.

Leningradskaia pravda. 1924. 'Na ulitsakh'. 24 September.

Leningradskaia pravda. 1924. 'Pogibshie pri navodnenii 23-go Sentiabria'. 25 September.

Leningradskaia pravda. 1924. 'Postanovleniia Prezidiuma Leningradskogo Gubispolkoma'. 24 September.

Leningradskaia pravda. 1924. 'Razrushennoe stikhiei – vosstanovim kollektivnym rudom – Nashi geroi'. 25 September.

Leningradskaia pravda. 1924. 'Vchera v Leningrade'. 24 September.

Leningradskaia pravda. 1924. 'Vsplyvshie trupy pokoinikov'. 25 September.

Leningradskaia pravda. 1924. 'Zhertvy navodneniia'. 2 October.

'*There, Where They Have Grown Accustomed to Flooding*'

Leningradskaia pravda (Ekstrennyi vechernyii vypusk). 1924. 'Organizovanno i poriadka'. 24 September.

Lincoln, W. Bruce. 2001. *Sunlight at Midnight: St. Petersburg and the Rise of Modern Russia*. Oxford: Perseus.

Vestnik Leningradskogo Soveta. 1924. 'O bor'be s navodneniem i merakh po likvidatsii ego posledstvii. Postanovleniia Leningradskogo Gubispolkoma ego prezidiuma i Chrezvychainoi komissii'. 27 September.

Obshchii otchet Tsentral'nogo komiteta o posobii razorennym navodneniem S. Peterburga, podnesennyi gosudariu imperatory, 23 genvaria 1826 goda. 1826. St Petersburg: Tipografii departamenta narodnogo prosveshcheniia.

Otchet o deiatel'nosti Rossiiskoi Akademii Nauk za 1924 goda sostavlennyi nepremennym sekretarem akademikoi S. F. Ol'denburgom i chitannyi v publichnom zasedanii 2 fevralia 1925 goda. 1925. Leningrad.

Pavlov, I.P. 1928. *Lectures on Conditioned Reflexes: Twenty-Five Year of Objective Study of the Higher Nervous Activity (Behaviour) of Animals*. Vol. 1, pp. 363–9. London: Lawrence and Wishart.

Piaskovskii, R.V., K.S. Pomeranets, E.S. Chernysheva. 2003. 'Povtoriaemost' navodnenii v Peterburge'. *Priroda*. No. 9.

'Pis'mo A.A. Bestuzheva-Marlinskogo k materi'. 1994. *Literaturnyi arkhiv: materialy po istorii russkoi literatury i obshchestvennoi* mysli. pp. 219-20. St Petersburg: Nauka.

Polnoe sobranie zakonov Rossiiskoi imperii VIII, no. 6575, 16 November 1833.

Pomeranets, K.S. 1998. *Navodneniia v Peterburge, 1703–1997*. St.Petersburg: Baltrus-buk.

Pomeranets, K.S. 2005. *Tri veka peterburgskikh navodnenii*. St.-Petersburg: Iskusstvo–SPb.

Pomeranets, Kim. 2009. *Neschast'ia nevskikh beregov: Iz istorii peterburgskikh navodnenii*. Moscow: Tsentropoligraf.

Pravda. 1979. 'V TsK KPSS i Sovete Ministrov SSSR'. 19 August.

Promyshlennost' i torgovlia: Ezhenedel'nyi zhurnal posviashchennyi voprosom ekonomiki. 1924. 'Promyshlennost' posle navodneniia'. No. 38–39: pp. 32–7.

Pushkarev, I.I. 2000 [1840]. *Nikolaevskii Peterburg*. St Petersburg: Liga-Plius.

Rossiiskii gosudarstvennyi arkhiv sotsial'no-politicheskoi istorii (RGASPI, Russian State Archive of Social and Political History).

Ruble, Blair A. 1990. *Leningrad: Shaping a Soviet City*. Berkeley: University of California Press.

Semiotic.ru. 2007. 'Kompleks Zashchitnykh Sooruzhenii Sankt-Peterburga ot navodnenii.' http://www.semiotic.ru/d/index.html

Senin, V.T. 1984. *Leningrad bez navodnenii*. Leningrad: Lenizdat.

Sherikh, Dmitrii. 2004. *Iz Petrograda v Leningrad. 1924*. Moscow: Tsentropoligraf.

Robert Dale

Sorokina, L.A. 2001. 'Peterburgskoe navodnenie 1824 goda na stranitsakh literaturnykh al'manakhov 20-kh gg. XIX v.: k postanovke voprosa'. In N.I. Priimak and E.V. Letenkova (eds), *Istoriografiia i istochnikovedenie otechestvennoi istorii: Sbornik nauchnykh statei v soobshchenii*, pp. 206–20. St Petersburg: Tehnika.

Sorokina, L.A. 2003. 'Navodnenie pod tsezurnym zapreshom: osveshenie peterburgskoi katastrofy 1824 g v literaturno-khudozhestvennykh al'manakhakh'. In Iu.V. Krivosheeva and M.V. Khodiakov (eds), pp. 407–23. *Univertetskie peterburgskie chteniia. 300 let Severnoi stolits. Sbornik Statei*. St Petersburg: Izdatel'stvo – Znamenitnye universanty.

Steinberg, Mark D. 2011. *Petersburg Fin de Siècle*. New Haven and London: Yale University Press.

Stites, Richard. 1989. *Revolutionary Dreams: Utopian Vision and Experimental Life in the Russian Revolution*. Oxford: Oxford University Press.

Stolpianskii, P. 1924. 'K istorii Peterburgskikh navodnenii'. In *Navodnenie v Leningrade 23 sentiabria 1924*, pp. 13-21. Leningrad: Tipografiia Otkomkhoza.

Todes, Daniel P. 2014. *Ivan Pavlov: A Russian Life in Science*. Oxford: Oxford University Press.

Tsentral'nyi gosudarstvennyi arkhiv istoriko-politicheskikh dokumentov Sankt-Peterburga (TsGAIPD–SPb, Central State Archive of Historical-Political Documents for St Petersburg).

Tsentral'nyi gosudarstvennyi arkhiv Sankt-Peterburga (TsGA-SPb, Central State Archive of St Petersburg).

Tziafetas, G. 2014. 'The Ecologists Versus the Builders: The Conflict Over the Leningrad Dam in the Nineteen Seventies and Eighties'. *Peterburgskii istoricheskii zhurnal*. No. 1: 182–9.

Willimott, Andy. 2017. *Living the Revolution: Urban Communes and Soviet Socialism, 1917–1932*. Oxford: Oxford University Press.

Worobec, Christine. 2001. *Possessed: Women, Witches and Demons in Imperial Russia*. DeKalb: Northern Illinois University Press.

PART II.

BEING THERE:
PHOTOGRAPHIC ESSAYS

6.

FAITH AND NATURE ON SOLOVKI

Nicholas B. Breyfogle[1]

Figure 6.1. First sighting: The Solovetskie Islands (a.k.a. Solovki) and the Solovetskii Monastery as they come into view from the ferry. Photograph by the author.

I stand at the bow of the ferry as the water of the White Sea comes in, wave after wave, through the hole in the gunwale for the anchor chain. Stepping up on the coiled ropes lying on the deck, my feet stay dry and I look out with excitement at the outstretched sea in front of me. The weather could not be more perfect – sun, light winds, calm seas, easy sailing across a sea known for its nausea-inducing swells. A mother and son play in the running water beside me whilst a young couple stands draped over each other. A middle-aged man

---

1. First published as Breyfogle, 'A Postcard from Solovki'. Reproduced in revised format with permission from the editors.

Faith and Nature on Solovki

discusses cameras with a young photographer taking 'art' photos. Then, about an hour and half into the trip, we all see it. The Solovetskie Islands (a.k.a. Solovki) and the spires of its amazing Monastery complex appear on the distant horizon.

Figure 6.2. Coming closer: The Solovetskii Monastery as the ferry enters the harbour. Photograph by the author.

I marvel at the approaching human and environmental wonder of Russia's Solovetskie Islands – an archipelago of six major islands (and about 100 smaller ones) in the White Sea not far to the south of the Arctic Circle. A centre of Russian Orthodoxy for centuries, the islands are a Russian national park and have been a UNESCO World Heritage Site since 1992.[2]

A Bit about the Islands

People have come to Solovki for thousands of years, but it was not until the late fifteenth century that humans began to live full-time on the island. For centuries, fishermen took boats to the islands in the summer months to take advantage of the rich fishing in the waters nearby. When winter came, they

---

2.   UNESCO, *Cultural and Historic Ensemble of the Solovetsky Islands.*

Nicholas B. Breyfogle

returned to their homes on the mainland with fish aplenty for the long, cold months ahead. These pre-historic fishers have left behind amazing stone constructions: labyrinths and burial mounds.

In 1429, the first two permanent settlers on the island were Orthodox monks – Savvatii and German. They sought out the islands not for the fish but for solitude; to be able to worship God more fully without any of the distractions of humanity. The Solovetskie Islands were hardly an easy place to live, and Savvatii was an old man. But they sought the most distant point imaginable where they might live an ascetic life. They searched for a place where they could pray and work without interruption, and where the forces of nature and the cold climate would test their spirits and their bodies each day.

Map 6.1. *Map of the White Sea and Solovetskie Islands (Solovki) in Russia. Created by Bill Nelson on behalf of the author.*

Figures 6.3 and 6.4. A diverse landscape: The forest on Solovki (top) and the tundra-like landscape of Bol'shoi Zaiatskii Island (bottom). Photographs by the author.

Nicholas B. Breyfogle

Whilst I stood comfortably on the ferry as it ploughed the waters to Solovki, I could not stop thinking that these two men so many centuries before had rowed out across the sea to an island they had never seen before to start a life as distant from other people and as physically gruelling as possible. The historian Roy Robson, who has written a marvellous book on Solovki asks, 'What would make someone leave life behind, seeking an existence of unremitting toil and prayer, where sleep and food were considered weaknesses of the flesh?'[3] What indeed?

In one of the great paradoxes, word spread quickly of the holiness of these two men and soon others wished to join them or live nearby, to learn from them and their ascetic life. And so began one of the great struggles of the religious community on Solovki: whether to search for complete isolation, so better to pray and to live a godly life of renunciation, or to share and spread the asceticism and to build a larger religious community. As the years passed, the monks on Solovki laboured with the question of how best to serve God. In the end, it was the latter view that won the day. One of the most glorious monasteries exists now as a result.

Figure 6.5. View of the Solovetskii Monastery. Photograph by the author.

---

3.   Robson, *Solovki*, p. 7.

Figure 6.6. The Solovetskii Monastery's massive stone walls were initially built stone on stone without any bonding between them – a beautiful rearranging of nature for human needs. Photograph by the author.

Nicholas B. Breyfogle

In the sixteenth and seventeenth centuries, the monastery expanded rapidly. It attracted more and more monks, and more and more pilgrims. There were ups and downs to be sure (especially during the great Russian religious Schism of the seventeenth century, when the monastery was at war with the Orthodox Church). Nevertheless, the monastery grew, becoming one of the most impressive monastic complexes in the Orthodox world. A spiritual centre for generations, it also became one of the most economically successful ventures in the region – especially through the sustainable and immensely profitable fishing industry. Then in the 1920s and 1930s, the monastery became the stage for one of the darkest stories of the twentieth century: the Gulag. Today it is a working monastery once again, a destination for large numbers of pilgrims and tourists alike.

Figure 6.7. Solovetskii Monastery: Sunset across the harbour. Photograph by the author.

Labyrinths

I have spent my career studying and teaching modern history – events and processes from the sixteenth century on and especially after the mid-eighteenth century, when industrial change began. Yet, as I travel, I find myself ever more fascinated by the creations and constructions that humans erected thousands of years ago. Standing at Stonehenge, I was amazed at the thought and care (not to mention muscle power) that it took to conceive and build the complex.

These stone structures are monuments to human ingenuity and vision – like the menhirs in Brittany (France) or the native mounds in Ohio, not to mention the pyramids and Valley of the Kings and Queens in Egypt, Göbekli Tepe in Turkey and any number of sites in Australia, China, India and Central America. They are a reminder that human history is so much longer than we usually care to remember; that our current industrial moment in the human story is just a tiny sliver in the longer run of *Homo sapiens* on the planet. Of course, we may never know how humans in the past built these amazing structures, or perhaps more importantly, why, but build them they did.

Solovki offers its own prehistoric stone structures. On the Zaiatskie Islands, there are some twenty labyrinths and about 900 stone piles and funeral mounds. Whilst no two of these fascinating labyrinths are the same design, they are usually spiral figures with a system of intricate paths lined with stones. They were made, it appears, by first tracing the patterns in the dirt and then placing the stones along the sketched designs. The largest of the labyrinths has almost 5,000 stones. The stones are now covered in plant growth that shows off the circular patterns.

Figure 6.8. A view of the labyrinths (1). Photograph by the author.

Nicholas B. Breyfogle

Figure 6.9. A view of the labyrinths (2). Photograph by the author.

Схема конструирования лабиринта
Scheme of creating a labyrinth

Figure 6.10. Diagram of labyrinth designs found on Bol'shoi Zaiatskii Island (Solovki). From Zaiatskii ostrov, p. 31. Reproduced with permission of the publisher.

Faith and Nature on Solovki

No one knows for sure what they were for or why they were built. But there they are nonetheless, challenging us today to wrap our insufficient brains around what fishing communities in the first millennium before the Common Era might have been thinking as they took time out of their days to move these stones into concentric shapes. Some have argued that they were designed as part of the fishing experience; that fishermen began the fishing season by walking through the labyrinth to the centre. The hope was to help the fisherman find his way to an abundant catch and then return from the sea safely. For others, the fact that the labyrinths are so close to burial mounds indicates that these labyrinths were somehow connected to the spiritual world; and the circular paths were the paths that a spirit would walk to make it to the spiritual world.

Near the burial mounds is a much more recent layout of stones: a cross laid out near the burial mounds in an effort to consecrate and Christianise what the monks saw as an unacceptably pagan site. It is of course not unusual in Christian history for priests and others to erect, carve, paint or draw crosses over prehistoric sites in an effort to consecrate them. But I was struck at Bol'shoi Zaiatskii Island how the priests had laid out stones to materially endow the place with specific meanings – just as the people before them. The shapes may have been different – crosses versus labyrinths – but the effort to use stones for cultural and religious purposes remained in many ways constant, reflecting the similar building materials these people – separated by so many centuries – found available for their purposes on the island. That the cross and the labyrinths have both similarly been covered over in plant growth reflects, Ozymandias-style, the way that the best laid plans and aspirations of humans disappear, collapse or are engulfed over time. More recently, larger, standing wood crosses have been erected on the shores.

Our Ever-Changing World

On Solovki, I am reminded at every turn of the ever-changing, ever-shifting world in which we live. Even the rock under our feet is not always as solid and sedentary as we like to believe. It is now centuries since the last glaciers retreated from atop the geological formations that now make up the Solovetskie Islands. Yet the effect of the glaciers is still being felt. As in many places, the weight of the glaciers compressed the stone of the islands. When the glaciers receded, the islands experienced a rebound effect. They rose, and continue to rise, ever so slowly as the weight of the ice no longer holds them down. As a result, the islands are ascending, bit by bit, a little higher out of the water. (And scientists

Nicholas B. Breyfogle

Figure 6.11. Christianising the labyrinths: Cross of stones on Bol'shoi Zaiatskii Island. Photograph by the author.

Faith and Nature on Solovki

Figure 6.12. Cross on the shores of Bol'shoi Zaiatskii Island. Photograph by the author.

regularly talk about this phenomenon with Greenland and Antarctica. As the ice cover melts away there, freed from the weight, Greenland and Antarctica will rise up.)

Now, you cannot see or feel this rise day-to-day, but you can see its effects on things that humans have built. When Russians built a church on Bol'shoi Zaiatskii Island, they also built a little harbour of stone walls for boats to weather storms. Once there were five slips for boats, but today the island has rebounded to the point that but a trickle of water runs through the entryway. The picture below (Figure 6.13) shows the now-narrow entryway to the harbour and the berths for the boats, outlined in stone, are now dry land. It is a reminder that as we plan for our future on this planet, we have to plan for change: in the climate, in the flora and fauna and in the landscapes and geologies we move on. Change, Solovki reminds us, is as constant in the non-human world as the human.

Figure 6.13. Old harbour on Bol'shoi Zaiatskii Island. Photograph by the author.

Faith and Nature on Solovki

Lakes and Canals

I was glad I chose to rent the high-performance mountain bike as I bounced my way up the roads of the main island to spend an afternoon rowing, paddling and otherwise exploring the remarkable system of lakes and canals that run through the island. This was one of the most beautiful and peaceful systems of water I had been to in years, spreading a calm serenity through me each time I pulled with the oars. At the boat rental dock, the young man handed me two oars and a paddle. 'Why all three', I asked, cursing yet again that I only had two arms. The oars were for rowing the lakes, the paddle for the narrow canals. 'Lifejacket?' I inquired. 'As you like', he shrugged.

If the White Sea offered the monks a seemingly endless bounty of fish to eat, they had to work a little harder to ensure fresh water for their communities. And they did so through extensive hydrological engineering systems that connected the different lakes together to provide both fresh water and also water transport possibilities up and down the island. (Even today, plying the water in a small rowboat was much more pleasant than bumping my way along the roads on a bike).

There are no rivers on Solovki, but some 500 lakes overflow each spring from the melting snow. The waters then run overland from one lake to another. Over the course of the fifteenth to nineteenth centuries, some twenty lake-canal systems were developed across the archipelago. As the first parts of the monastery complex were being built in the fourteenth century, the monks needed to ensure a constant supply of potable, fresh water. They dug out a lake on one side of the monastery to capture water and then filled it with water that flowed down the island in canals dug through the forests. The water was channelled in pipes and other water transport systems into the monastery (where a water wheel for milling was eventually set up and where a collection tank was kept to ensure water in times of attack). The water went back out through a weir to the harbour and sea. Eventually, the system of lakes and rivers that flowed down into the Sacred Lake next to the monastery connected seventy lakes and canals up the island.

Nicholas B. Breyfogle

Figure 6.14. The Sacred Lake providing fresh water storage for the monastery. Photograph by the author.

The system worked well. It ensured that the collected water did not sit stagnant but moved through the mill canal, powering the wheels, and then out to the harbour. The hydrological works of the monks are a reminder to those of us accustomed to water appearing as if by magic from a tap that extended effort was so often needed to ensure sufficient, usable water for communities. Great physical effort reconfigured landscapes and waterways to meet the monastery's needs. Perhaps most remarkable for me as I paddled along were the canals between the lakes that the monks built in the early twentieth century for transportation purposes. Over the years, the monks had watched the natural flows of water when the lakes overflowed in the spring. When they decided to carve connector canals between the lakes, they followed these paths of least water resistance.

Figure 6.15. View of a stone-lined canal, Solovki. Photograph by the author.

Figure 6.16. View of a stone-lined canal, Solovki. Photograph by the author.

Nicholas B. Breyfogle

The canals were a marvel. The monks dug them out to allow rowboats and small steam powered boats to go through. They lined the banks of the canals with large stones. They built underwater wood and stone foundations to keep the canals open and navigable. They were both form and function. Boats could now navigate their ways up and down the islands through the lakes. And fresh water would be in uninterrupted supply. The canals also created tree-covered aqua-pathways. As I paddled through, I felt a certain warm embrace of the trees and green shores on either side.

The Botanical Gardens

In addition to the canals and the monastery complex, perhaps the most marvellous site on the islands was the Botanical Gardens, about four kilometres from the main village.

Figure 6.17. The trees and flowers of the Botanical Gardens, Solovki. Photograph by the author.

Founded in 1822 by Archimandrite Makarii, the Gardens are located in a little ravine-valley that produces its own micro-climate (a micro-climate within the micro-climates that are Solovki). Here, the walls of the ravine block out the wind and the temperature during the year is warmer than other parts of the island. This micro-climate allowed the monks to grow all sorts of plants and trees that were non-native to the region and would otherwise be unable to survive such a northern location. Here, both monks and others experimented with what sorts of plants and trees might grow, and learned a great deal about the effects of temperature, latitude, wind, water and other factors on the growth patterns of this flora.

Figure 6.18. Visitors stroll in the Botanical Gardens, Solovki. Photograph by the author.

The monks grew a range of medicinal herbs and plants, which they sold on the mainland. They also planted trees from different parts of the Russian empire. Some trees that grew out of the protective shield of the valley had their tops knocked off again and again. A lovely tree-lined pathway was planted, but too close together and the branches grow primarily to the outside of the alley.

Nicholas B. Breyfogle

Figures 6.19 and 6.20. A tree with wind-damage and re-growth of two trunks (left) and the path of the Botanical Gardens, with branches mostly facing out because the trees were too closely planted together (right). Photographs by the author.

Figure 6.21. Botanical Gardens, Solovki (1). Photograph by the author.

Faith and Nature on Solovki

Figure 6.22. Botanical Gardens, Solovki (2). Photograph by the author.

The Gulag Prison Camp

I have taught the history of the Gulag – the forced prison system of the Soviet Union – for many years now. And as many of my students will attest, I often have a hard time getting through the discussion without tears in my eyes. For all the years I have studied the past and wrestled with what it means to be human, I have never quite come to terms with the horrifyingly deep capacity of humans to unleash terrible and unspeakable cruelty on others. We are gluttons for our doom, and particular gluttons for the doom of others.

Solovki played a special role in what Aleksandr Solzhenitsyn famously called the 'Gulag Archipelago'. It was in many ways at Solovki that the Gulag got its start and began its horrifying expansion. It was also at Solovki that the idea filtered into the minds of certain members of the Soviet leadership that the camps could be economically profitable. They never were, but they held tightly and ever hopefully to the idea of profit from penal labour.

The monastery was shut in 1920 – not an unexpected decision from the atheist Soviet state. But then what to do with the marvellous buildings and infrastructure? The monastery had been used for centuries as a place of banishment and exile for opponents to the tsarist regime and to the Orthodox

Nicholas B. Breyfogle

Church – and some prisoners had lived for decades cramped into tiny, dark stone cells. There had never been that many prisoners, and the prison function was a minor part of the larger monastic religious purpose. However, it set a precedent and it was not a huge leap of imagination to turn the entire monastic complex on a distant island into a prison camp.

In 1923, the Solovetskii Monastery became known as the Solovetskii Camp of Special Designation (SLON in its Russian acronym, a word that means 'elephant' in Russian. There were endless plays on words.) The camp saw some 80,000 people arrive, about half of whom perished there and are now part of the Solovki ecosystem. There are archaeological digs going on in the mass graves – but the guide on the tour I was on was uninterested in taking us there.

The types of prisoners that came to Solovki tended to be elite ones: political opponents of the Bolsheviks (especially members of other socialist parties), former tsarist nobles, officers of the Imperial Army or the White Army that fought the Bolsheviks in the Civil War and Russian intellectuals and cultural icons. In the words of our tour guide: 'the very light of the Russian nation'. And they were horribly mistreated. The savagery of humanity was once again on nauseating display. Who would do these things, I kept asking myself, and how can we avoid a repeat? (And just how naïve a question is that?) Daily life was extraordinarily hard and abusive. Cold, poorly clothed (if clothed at all), they were jammed into cells to sleep and then marched through the islands to carry out various forms of work (logging in particular) with insufficient food and clothing and broken, inappropriate tools.

On Sekirka, one of the hills of Solovki, a Church stands (with a lighthouse on top) and during the Gulag period it was used as a place of special punishment. As Robson describes in his book: 'there, men were made to sit perfectly still atop the "perch" or "pole" – about an arm's width wide – for hours on end, stripped almost naked, teetering on the high-ceilinged, unheated Church of the Beheading of St. John. Though they shivered and caught frostbite, the slightest movement was reason for falling off and a beating. At night, the prisoners lay three or four atop another, hoping to stay warm.'[4] Savage creatures we humans are. And there are so many hundreds more of these cruel stories. Dead or almost dead bodies were strapped to a log and sent careening down the staircase on the far side of the hill – 365 stairs to the bottom. Ironically, these stairs had long before had a different meaning. They were the way that pilgrims would walk up to the Church, and the word was that for every step one walked up a sin was forgiven. With the Gulag, it was the world turned upside down.

4.　Robson, *Solovki*, p. 227.

Figure 6.23. Church and lighthouse on Sekirka. Photograph by the author.

Nicholas B. Breyfogle

Figure 6.24. Pilgrim stairs, Gulag stairs: Looking down Sekirka. Photograph by the author.

Here too the human-nature relationship was transformed. The cold climate, geographic location and very physical characteristics that had kept humans from the islands for so long (and had made the archipelago such a good place for monks seeking solitude and fortitude) met up with human aspirations to punish and torture those who might challenge the dominant political ideology. Over the centuries, people had come for fish and in search of God. Now they came because they were arrested and coerced. Now they were forced to come to endure the pain that Solovki's nature – manipulated by humans – might unleash on them.

I went to see Sekirka with a group of Russian tourists who were coming face to face with the terrors of their history. All peoples and countries have moments of horror in their past, where violence and cruelty saturated society. We humans share this tendency. What is different is how we then deal with the memories and the legacies of the mercilessness, and how we make amends.

Faith and Nature on Solovki

Figure 6.25. Pilgrim Stairs, Gulag Stairs. Looking up Sekirka. Photograph by the author.

Nicholas B. Breyfogle

The guide spared no horrible detail for the group. There were tears all around as she told story after story of torture and the wanton brutalisation of some humans by others. I do not know what these tourists knew or did not know about the Gulag and Solovki before arriving, but they left with their souls weighed heavy by the knowledge. Interestingly, the tour guide never discussed any details about the Gulag system that did not directly relate to Solovki. So, any sense of the broader political context was not discussed – of the Bolshevik efforts to hold power, later of Stalin, the purges, collectivisation, forced deportations or of the larger Gulag system that stretched across the whole Eurasian landmass. The focus here was only local: on the terrifying treatment of the people who came to Solovki between 1923 and 1939. But perhaps that was enough.

BIBLIOGRAPHY

Breyfogle, Nicholas B. 2016. 'A Postcard from Solovki'. *Origins: Current Events in Historical Perspective*. 26 January. http://origins.osu.edu/connecting-history/postcard-solovki

Robson, Roy R. 2004. *Solovki: The Story of Russia Told Through Its Most Remarkable Islands*. New Haven: Yale University Press.

UNESCO. 2020. 'Cultural and Historic Ensemble of the Solovetsky Islands'. http://whc.unesco.org/en/list/632

Zaiatskii ostrov fotoputevoditel'. Arkhangel'sk: OAO 'IPP "Pravda Severa"'.

7.

INDUSTRIAL HERITAGE IN THE URALS

Catherine Evtuhov[1]

When our group of sixteen historians and geographers (from the Russian Federation, the United Kingdom, United States and Norway) arrived on the banks of Russia's Kama River on 11 July 2016 for an intense five-day excursion through the Perm'-Ekaterinburg region, we followed a venerable tradition of Urals travel and exploration. Naturalist Johann Gmelin (1709–55) was so captivated by the industrial sites of 'Catharinenburg' that he visited twice – on his path to and from Siberia in 1734 and again in September 1742 – commenting from Nev'iansk: 'I had little interaction with humans here, and didn't desire any, because other matters were more useful. The foundries, mines, factories and animals were for me more reasonable objects of interest, and more fit to shape and illuminate my mind.'

Our interests were quite similar to Gmelin's: our group[2] was pursuing the themes of 'industry, mining, transport and industrial heritage tourism'. The site of early modern Russian industrial production, the Urals tell a rich tale of mineral resources and their exploitation from the sixteenth century to the Gulag labour-staffed chemical and metallurgical plants of the twentieth century. The Urals made Russia into Europe's primary iron exporter in the eighteenth century, as well as a key producer of iron and steel for domestic use in the railway age of the nineteenth century. Urals industry received a new, albeit grim, lease on life with the massive evacuation of industry from Ukraine and the Donbass during the World War Two. The 'factory-cities' of the Urals region today form a unique cultural space, with a vibrant international commercial life and a powerful presence on the literary and theatrical scene.

---

1.   First published as Evtuhov, 'A Postcard from the Ural Mountains'. Reproduced in revised format with permission from the editors and author.

2.   See University of York, *Exploring Russia's History and Natural Resources*.

Catherine Evtuhov

Figure 7.1: Modern chemical factory in Berezniki, across the Kama River from Usol'e. Photograph by the author.

Perm' and the Salt Works

On the morning of 12 July, we set off for Solikamsk and Usol'e to the north of Perm', where we were instructed in early modern techniques of salt extraction.

Crucial to the preservation of food, salt was in high demand throughout Russia for every social class. Before the discovery of Lake Elton near the Caspian Sea, the Kama region was one of the richest in salt deposits, which were often located, however, at a distance of 200 or more metres below the earth's surface. Master artisans at the salt works, now concentrated in a special Salt Museum at Ust'-Borovsk, extracted salt and water from underground, boiled the viscous mixture using special ovens and dried out the salt crystals on wooden planks.

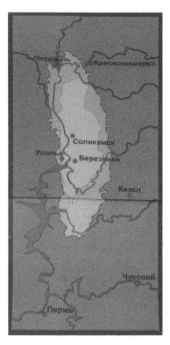

Figure 7.2. The geographic distribution of salt (purple) and potassium salts (pink) in the upper Kama region. From the History of Salt Museum, Ust'-Borovsk. Photograph by the author.

Figure 7.3. Mechanism for extracting salt (left) and boards on which the salt crystals evaporated (right). From the History of Salt Museum, Ust'-Borovsk. Photographs by the author.

Catherine Evtuhov

The salt was transported to market by barge, and loaded by men and women with enormous bags on their backs. The norm is said to have been 48 kilograms for women and eighty for men. We also visited the residence of the Urals salt magnates, the Stroganov family, at Usol'e, narrowly missing a huge downpour as we arrived. The Stroganovs were the virtual lords of the Perm' region in the sixteenth and seventeenth centuries. Granted privileges and lands based on their success in salt production by Tsar Ivan IV (the Terrible, 1633–84), they vied with the great monasteries for control over the salt business in all the Muscovite lands, and expanded their vast commercial empire into agriculture, fishing, hunting and mining.

Figure 7.4. Church and bell tower at Usol'e. Photograph by the author.

Figure 7.5. Stroganov residence at Usol'e, 1720s. Photograph by the author.

The material culture of the Perm' region has for centuries been linked to industrial production and commerce. The following day, we visited the nearby outdoor museum of wooden architecture, with its fascinating reconstruction of middling and rich Komi and Russian peasant houses, adapted to frigid climes; we also saw the docks where the salt sacks were loaded on barges for the long journey to central Russia. Capital and industrial development are reflected in the region's 'high culture' as well. We had time to drop in at the Perm' Museum of Contemporary Art with its original and clever post-modern installations, and the Perm' campus of the Higher School of Economics.

Figure 7.6. The Perm' Museum of Contemporary Art logo, public domain image. Source: Evtuhov, 'A Postcard from the Ural Mountains'.

Catherine Evtuhov

Kungur

One of the unexpected gems of our voyage was the picturesque town of Kungur, about a third of the way on the main road between Perm' and Ekaterinburg. Kungur's heyday was in the nineteenth century, when wealthy merchants built opulent wooden and stone houses along the inclines overlooking the Sylva River. We didn't want to miss our chance to see the world from on high, and climbed up the bell tower of the Saviour Cathedral, which itself perches on the tallest hill of the town.

Figure 7.7. View from the Saviour Cathedral bell tower, Kungur. Photograph by the author.

After climbing to Kungur's highest point, nothing could make us happier than to descend equally far into the earth's depths at the area's most famous tourist attraction: the Kungur caverns, mapped already by geographer Semen Remezov in 1703 and then V.N. Tatishchev in the 1730s. We pulled on parkas and silk underwear to spend ninety minutes underground. Perhaps most impressive were the perfectly still and limpid underground lakes – so clear that we needed convincing that they were actually filled with water. Even they have an inhabitant – a tiny shrimp-like mollusc.

Figure 7.8. Underground lake in the Kungur caverns. Photograph by Arkady Kalikhman. Reproduced with permission.

Ekaterinburg and Iron Production

Like Gmelin, I am particularly interested in the iron foundries and factories of his own time – the large-scale enterprises that catapulted Russia into its place as the biggest iron exporter in Europe on the eve of the 'industrial revolution'. Thus our final two days were a highlight, dedicated to Ekaterinburg and the almost mythically famous (so far as industrial lore goes) Nev'iansk and Nizhnii Tagil. Several of us stared incredulously out the windows of our bus as we entered the metropolis of Ekaterinburg with its impressive skyscrapers, towering construction cranes and fashionably dressed young people, after many kilometres of nearly unbroken forest. Ekaterinburg arguably represents a unique type of urban formation – the 'city-factory' of the Urals. The city grew up around the iron factory of the 1720s, strategically placed on the Iset River to maximise hydropower. The characteristic immense factory reservoir, narrowing into a thin stream beyond the dam, lies at its centre.

Catherine Evtuhov

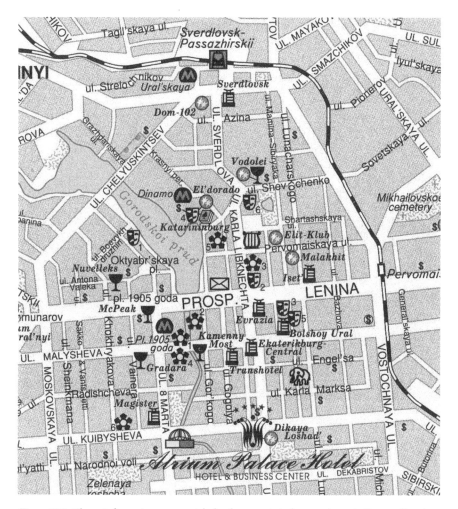

Figure 7.9. Ekaterinburg city centre, with the characteristic factory reservoir. Source: Evtuhov, 'A Postcard from the Ural Mountains'.

Our final travels took us to the leaning tower of Nev'iansk – the site of the Demidov family ironworks of the early eighteenth century, where one can observe firsthand the extremely high quality of cast iron from that time. Nikita Demidov (1656–1725), son of a Tula blacksmith, founded the ironworks during the reign of Peter I (the Great, 1682–1725). The business eventually expanded far beyond its original purpose of military production, and the Demidov dynasty became one of the wealthiest and most influential noble families in Europe. It was fun, and illuminating, to see the moving replica of an eighteenth-century iron factory in the local museum.

Figure 7.10. Russia's famous leaning tower of Nev'iansk, 1720s–40s. Photograph by the author.

And the trip would not have been complete without the remarkable Factory-Museum of Nizhnii Tagil – a metallurgical plant that had functioned consistently from the first half of the eighteenth century up until the 1980s, and where one may now wander cautiously, invading the old industrial structures along with the plant life that has largely taken over. Nizhnii Tagil also boasts a local history museum originally established at the unusually early date of 1840.

Our day concluded with a small hike up the 'High Mountain' (*Gora Vysokaia*), which has the distinction of being some fifty metres less high than it was before industrial mining got to it – but at least it is not a crater in the ground, as is a copper-rich former hill on its southern slope (see Figures 7.11 and 7.12).

Catherine Evtuhov

Figure 7.11. A pipe for diversion of spring floods at the factory (left) and the Factory-Museum at Nizhnii Tagil (right). Photographs by the author.

Figure 7.12: Copper crater, seen from atop the High Mountain. Photograph by the author.

We returned to St Petersburg on 17 July, somewhat crumpled from countless hours in the bus, but thrilled by the intensity of our experiences and encounters with the heritage of the Ural Mountains' industrial and mining past.

BIBLIOGRAPHY

Evtuhov, Catherine. 2016. 'A Postcard from the Ural Mountains'. *Origins: Events in Historical Perspective.* 24 October. http://origins.osu.edu/connecting-history/postcard-ural-mountains.

University of York. 2016. 'Exploring Russia's History and Natural Resources'. http://www.york.ac.uk/history/research/majorprojects/russiasenvironmentalhistory/

8.

NEW DAMS, WARMING WATERS, FOREST FIRES: LAKE BAIKAL IN PERIL

Bryce Stewart[1]

Sweat ran down my face and the scalding air stung my lips as I struggled to breathe in. 'Russia sure is a land of extremes', I gasped to the people either side of me.

It seemed appropriate. On this occasion I was in a *bania*, the Russian version of sauna, somewhat nervously awaiting the traditional experience of being whipped with birch leaves.

But only a few days earlier I had felt very similar as I struggled up the near vertical slopes of the Barguzin mountain range in Siberia, in temperatures topping thirty degrees centigrade.

When you mention Siberia to most people, they think of snow, ice and extreme cold – a remote place people were exiled to in the past as a punishment. Maybe they might mention a Siberian husky if they are *au fait* with the canine world.

But we experienced a beautiful natural landscape, inhabited by incredibly friendly people, and glorious summer weather that compelled us to take a swim in the crystal-clear waters of Lake Baikal nearly every day.

I had travelled to Siberia, and Lake Baikal in particular, as part of the Leverhulme-funded project 'Exploring Russia's Environmental History and Natural Resources'.[2] This three-year project is the brainchild of Professor David Moon from the University of York.

---

1.   This chapter originally appeared as Stewart, 'New Dams, Warming Waters, Forest Fires – Lake Baikal in Peril'.

2.   University of York, *Exploring Russia's Environmental History and Natural Resources*.

New Dams, Warming Waters, Forest Fires

Figure 8.1. The author on bow of the boat Sekret, in Chivyrkui Bay on the eastern shores of Lake Baikal, setting off on the expedition, July 2015. Photograph by Nicholas Breyfogle.

By bringing together colleagues from the UK, Russia, the United States, Canada and Romania, it aims to unveil a more realistic view of Russian environmental history and conservation than the predominately negative stereotype that is commonly perceived in the western world.

There were sixteen people on our field trip, the second in a series to several key areas of Russia, with almost all of the others being environmental historians. I am a marine biologist, so what was I doing on a trip to Lake Baikal, which is pretty much as far from the sea as anywhere on Earth? Well, to slightly misquote James Bond, 'Where there is water a marine biologist is never on holiday.'

The ecological principles that apply in marine and freshwater environments are very similar, so I had been asked to accompany the group to give my perspective on the state of fish stocks in the lake and to make suggestions for future management. In reality, I had the amazing opportunity to do most of the learning on the trip.

Bryce Stewart

An Aquatic Wonderworld

Lake Baikal is arguably the largest lake in the world, at least in terms of volume, due to both its large surface area and immense depth of over 1,600 metres.[3] In fact it is estimated to hold over twenty per cent of all the unfrozen freshwater in the world. Being formed due to a continental rift over 25 million years ago, it is also the world's oldest lake.

This combination of size, age and isolation has blended together to produce a unique environment, both geologically and biologically. Surrounded by high mountain ranges and with crystal clear waters, it is stunningly beautiful. It is also incredibly biodiverse, and many of the species that occur there exist nowhere else in the world.

Figure 8.2. Nerpa seal on the Ushkan'i Islands, July 2015. Photograph by Nicholas Breyfogle.

Along with the nerpas, the world's only true freshwater seals, and possibly the cutest, over half of the 56 fish species present are also endemic. The lake also contains over 350 species of amphipod shrimps, most of them endemic and also gigantic in size (for amphipods!). Of its 2,500 known species, 75 per cent are endemic – unknown anywhere else.

---

3.   Bww.irk.ru, *Comprehensive Data about Lake Baikal in Siberia.*

The lake's fisheries centre on the omul, *Coregonus migratorius*, which is a member of the salmon family and another endemic species.[4] It is revered as a delicacy throughout Russia, and rightly so. We ate it on at least half a dozen occasions – each time prepared in a different way and each time delicious.

Annual commercial catches have amounted to over 10,000 tonnes per year in the past, which is a sizeable fishery in anybody's eyes. However, the fishery for omul, along with the lake's other targeted species such as sturgeon, whitefish and grayling, have a chequered and widely fluctuating history.

In fact, things got so bad that in 1969 the entire commercial fleet was closed down until 1982. The declining fortunes of the lake's fisheries have certainly been driven by overfishing to a certain extent, but environmental factors also play a large role.[5]

Beautiful but Fragile

Water level in the lake, controlled by both changes in precipitation and hydroelectric dams, particularly on the Angara, the only river flowing out of the lake, has long been known to be a crucial factor. This affects the amount and quality of fish spawning habitat in the shallow waters around the lake's edge and in the deltas of inflowing rivers.

Likewise, changes in water temperature affect both the survival of young fish and the behaviour of adults. When the summer temperatures are warmer than usual, the omul swim deeper and therefore are more difficult to catch.

We travelled around Lake Baikal by a combination of train, road, boat and foot, from Irkutsk in the west, to Ulan-Ude in the east and then north and back via the Zabaikal National Park, Ushkan'i Islands and Ol'khon Island. One of the real highlights of our trip was the opportunity to spend three days at the remote Barguzin nature reserve on the northeast side of the lake.

Barguzin is a *zapovednik*, the oldest type of nature reserve in Russia, and is reserved primarily for scientific research. Established in 1916, it covers almost 2,500 square kilometres of rich mountainous landscape along with taiga forests, gurgling streams and part of the lake itself.[6]

---

4.   Smirnov, Smirnova-Zalumi and Sukhanova, 'Fishery Management of Omul', p. 203.

5.   Kozhova and Silow, 'The Current Problems of Lake Baikal Ecosystem Conservation'.

6.   See the chapter by Nicholas Breyfogle in this volume on the beginnings of the Barguzin Nature Reserve.

Bryce Stewart

Figure 8.3. The pristine forests of the Barguzin Zapovednik, July 2015. Photograph by Nicholas Breyfogle.

This joined up approach to conservation was well ahead of its time. The reserve was originally established to revitalise sable populations in the area, a species of marten which was highly prized for its 'soft gold' fur at the time.

The reserve was zoned into areas offering different levels of protection – in the southern half, hunting was completely banned, while in the northern half, controlled hunting was allowed in order to determine sustainable levels of exploitation.

A farm was also established in order to breed sable in captivity for release into the reserve. On hearing this, I immediately thought of the zonal approach to conservation applied by Great Barrier Reef Marine Park off Australia. This is held up as highly innovative and the gold standard model for the rest of the world to follow. But the idea was actually first pioneered in Siberia nearly three-quarters of a century earlier.

Along with holding several workshops during our time at Barguzin, we hiked the forests, hills and shores of the lake and were regaled with tales of bears, who appear to be the main local inhabitants these days. We never actually saw a bear in the flesh, but we saw plenty of signs of their presence in the form of scat, bear pits and claw marks on trees.

At one point while catching my breath along another forest path I asked if the bears were asleep during the day. 'No, no', I was told, 'They are up there, in the trees, watching us.'

Extreme Weather is Creating Ecological Havoc

If I have painted a picture of Lake Baikal as a unique and beautiful environment, then I've done my job. But the future is far less rosy. The area is a climate change hotspot, warming up much faster than the global average.

The average temperature of the lake increased by 1.2 degrees between 1946 and 2004, which has had dramatic effects on the plankton community and no doubt the rest of the aquatic ecosystem.[7] On land, the ice-free season has increased in length by sixteen days since the late 1800s. Continued warming could start to melt the permafrost, changing land-atmosphere gas fluxes, damaging roads and infrastructure, and flooding the lake with excess nutrients.[8] The growth of invasive algae is already a problem in southern parts of the lake.[9]

Extreme weather conditions brought on by climate change are also wreaking havoc. The beautiful warm and dry weather and extraordinary sunsets we were blessed with on our trip were not entirely natural.

An usually warm and dry summer had produced the perfect conditions for forest fires, which raged around us on most days, resulting in an omnipresent haze and destroying untold hectares of pristine forest.

These are still burning out of control in many areas as fire fighters struggle with limited resources and the inaccessibility of many areas. Things are only likely to get worse in future years. In fact, wildfires in the summers of 2019 and 2020 have burnt unprecedented areas of forest and tundra across Siberia.[10]

Due to its outstanding natural scenery and biological diversity Lake Baikal was declared a World Heritage area in 1996, leading many to think its future would be secure. Even the infamous pulp and paper mill which pumped poisonous dioxins and other waste into the southern waters of the lake for nearly half a century was closed down in 2013.

---

7. Hampton et al. 'Sixty Years of Environmental Change in the World's Largest Freshwater Lake'

8. Moore et al. 'Climate Change and the World's "Sacred Sea"'

9. Timoshkin et al. 'Mass Development of Green Filamentous Algae of the Genera *Spirogyra* and *Stigeoclonium* (Chlorophyta) in the Littoral Zone of the Southern Part of Lake Baikal'.

10. Thomas, 'Arctic Wildfires' and Alberts, 'Photos Show Scale'.

Bryce Stewart

Figure 8.4. A Baikal sunset through thick smoke from the forest fires. Taken from shore of the Barguzin Zapovednik, July 2015. Photograph by the author.

Now a New Threat Looms: A Giant Dam in Mongolia

International non-governmental organisations (NGOs) started to move away and turn their attention to other areas, figuring the battle to protect the lake had been won. But World Heritage legislation has limited power in Russian law, and climate change is a global issue, which needs all of us to take action.

Now a new threat is emerging: the proposed construction of the Shuren Dam, on the Selenga River in Mongolia, and an associated pipeline taking more water from one of its tributaries.[11] The Selenga subsequently flows into Russia to supply Lake Baikal with almost half of its water.

The dam and pipeline would undoubtedly further decrease the already record low water level of Baikal and irretrievably damage the Selenga Delta – a vital spawning and feeding area for the lake's fish and bird life.

Given the multitude of other threats already facing the incredible natural jewel that Baikal represents, I can only hope that the current campaign by the

---

11. McKay, 'Lake Baikal: World Heritage Ecosystems at Risk'; McKay, 'Lake Baikal: Incredible Ecosystem Threatened'.

NGO Rivers without Boundaries,[12] along with diplomatic pressure from Russia, will stop this potentially catastrophic project from going ahead.

BIBLIOGRAPHY

Alberts, Elizabeth Claire. 2020. 'Photos Show Scale of Massive Fires Tearing through Siberian Forests'. *Mongabay: News & Inspiration from Nature's Frontline.* 23 July. https://news.mongabay.com/2020/07/photos-show-scale-of-massive-fires-tearing-through-siberian-forests/.

Bww.irk.ru. 'Comprehensive Data about Lake Baikal in Siberia'. http://www.bww.irk.ru/index.html.

Hampton, Stephanie E., Lyubov R. Izmest'eva, Marianne V. Moore, Stephen L. Katz, Brian Dennis and Eugene A. Silow. 2008. 'Sixty Years of Environmental Change in the World's Largest Freshwater Lake – Lake Baikal, Siberia'. *Global Change Biology* **14** (8): 1947–1958.

Kozhova, Ol'ga M. and Eugene A. Silow. 1998. 'The Current Problems of Lake Baikal Ecosystem Conservation'. *Lakes & Reservoirs: Research & Management* 3 (1): 19–33.

Mackay, Anson. 2015. 'Lake Baikal: World Heritage Ecosystems at Risk from Mongolian Dam and Pipeline'. *The Ecologist.* 19 April. https://theecologist.org/2015/apr/19/lake-baikal-world-heritage-ecosystems-risk-mongolian-dam.

Mackay, Anson. 2015. 'Lake Baikal: Incredible Ecosystem Threatened by Mongolian Dam and Pipeline'. *The Conversation.* 14 April. https://theconversation.com/lake-baikal-incredible-ecosystem-threatened-by-mongolian-dam-and-pipeline-40025.

Moore, Marianne V., Stephanie E. Hampton, Lyubov R. Izmest'eva , Eugene A. Silow, Ekaterina V. Peshkova and Boris K. Pavlov. 2009. 'Climate Change and the World's "Sacred Sea" – Lake Baikal, Siberia'. *BioScience* **59** (5): 405-417.

Rivers without Boundaries: Saving Transnational Rivers. 2015. 'RwB Mongolia Explains the Reasons for Compliant to the World Bank Inspection on Selenge Basin Dams'. 28 February. http://www.transrivers.org/2015/1498/.

Smirnov, V.V., N.S. Smirnova-Zalumi and L.V. Sukhanova. 2012. 'Fishery Management of Omul (*Coregonus autumnalis migratorius*) as Part of the Conservation of Ichthyo-Fauna Diversity in Lake Baikal'. *Polish Journal of Natural Science* 27 (2): 203-214.

Stewart, Bryce. 2015. 'New Dams, Warming Waters, Forest Fires – Lake Baikal in Peril'. *The Ecologist: The Journal for the Post-Industrial Age.* 17 September. https://theecologist.org/2015/sep/17/new-dams-warming-waters-forest-fires-lake-baikal-peril

---

12. Rivers without Boundaries, 'RwB Mongolia Explains the Reasons for Compliant to the World Bank Inspection on Selenge Basin Dams'

Bryce Stewart

Thomas, Tobi. 2020. 'Arctic Wildfires Emit 35% more CO_2 so far in 2020 than for Whole of 2019'. *The Guardian*. 31 August. https://www.theguardian.com/world/2020/aug/31/arctic-wildfires-emit-35-more-co2-so-far-in-2020-than-for-whole-of-2019.

Timoshkin, O.A., N.A. Bondarenko, Ye.A. Volkova, I.V. Tomberg, V.S. Vishnyakov and V.V. Malnik. 2015. 'Mass Development of Green Filamentous Algae of the Genera *Spirogyra* and *Stigeoclonium* (Chlorophyta) in the Littoral Zone of the Southern Part of Lake Baikal'. *Hydrobiological Journal* 51*(1): 13-23.*

University of York. 2016. 'Exploring Russia's History and Natural Resources'. http://www.york.ac.uk/history/research/majorprojects/russiasenvironmentalhistory/

9.

A SHAGGY-BEAR STORY: AN ENVIRONMENTAL HISTORY FROM A REMOTE REGION

David Moon[1]

As we made our way through the primeval forest above the lake's clear waters, our guide pointed to fresh bear tracks and scratch marks on tree trunks where male bears had marked their territory. He advised us that the bears were higher up the slope, and that they could see and smell us, even if we could not see them. Our way was blocked by fallen trees which, while they decayed, provided habitats for wildlife. Younger trees were thrusting upwards, competing for sun light amid the canopy. Lichens covered the trees, evidence for the air's cleanliness. We asked when people had last been in this forest: the answer was two to three years ago.

Our guide told us about extreme hardships the bears had experienced in a very harsh winter two decades earlier. Deprived of their usual food by the severe cold, bears had approached the settlement, where the inhabitants had shot them in self defence. When they cut open the bodies, they found that, in their desperate hunger, the bears had been eating each other. By the winter's end, only the smaller bears, which needed less food, had survived. Their human neighbours noticed that the females were having more cubs than usual, but that the cubs were smaller than average. Our guide stretched out the shaggy-bear story to build up the tension to the punch line: one of the smaller male bear cubs was observed climbing up a tree to scratch out its territory, higher than it could reach from the ground, to give the impression to potential rivals that he was taller than he really was.

---

1. This chapter originally appeared as Moon, 'A Shaggy-Bear Story'.

David Moon

Figure 9.1. Hiking through the forest. Photograph by Voicu Ion Sucala. Reproduced with permission.

Figure 9.2. Trees with lichen in forest. Photograph by Voicu Ion Sucala. Reproduced with permission.

Figure 9.3. Bear scratch marks on trees. Photograph by Voicu Ion Sucala. Reproduced with permission.

We were in the Barguzin *Zapovednik* (nature reserve) on the remote northeastern shore of Lake Baikal in Eastern Siberia. Our guide, Aleksandr Ananin, was the reserve's scientific director. The area is so remote that some of our group were horrified to find there was no phone signal. Or mains electricity. Or running water. Or road to the outside world. To get there, we had three options: hire helicopters (beyond our budget); hike for two weeks over the mountains carrying forty-kilogram packs; or charter boats to meet us at the end of the road from Ulan-Ude, the capital of the Russian Republic of Buriatiia. We took the last option and enjoyed several days on the lake.

David Moon

Baikal is well known to environmental historians, not primarily for its natural riches, but for how it was endangered by Soviet economic development. Spurred to overtake the capitalist west, Soviet planners subjected their environments to ruthless, wasteful exploitation. Global environmental historians compare the environmental impact of communist, capitalist and colonial states, and while there is disagreement, many argue that communism was most harmful.[2] Baikal's pristine waters and unique ecosystem were threatened by pollution from cellulose plants built on its shores from the 1960s. After a long struggle, they have finally been closed. A dam built in the 1950s at Irkutsk, on the Angara River, which flows out of the lake, remains. Further dams planned for tributaries of the Selenga River, which flows into the lake from Mongolia, may pose further threats. While we were there, we witnessed the lake shrouded with smoke from forest fires caused by lightning strikes, which are natural, but also by careless tourists and in conditions more prone to fire due to a changing climate, which are threats caused by humans. Thus our bears, like their fellow bears and human neighbours around the globe, face a constellation of threats from both natural and anthropogenic sources.

Figure 9.4. Smoke from forest fires over Lake Baikal. Photograph by Mark Sokolsky. Reproduced with permission.

---

2.   For instance Weiner, 'The Predatory Tribute-Taking State'.

A Shaggy-Bear Story

Why don't more environmental histories of Russia and the Soviet Union start in remote regions and pay more attention to areas that people have not yet utterly transformed, but in which they, and even bears, struggle to survive? A leading environmental historian expressed surprise that 'the Soviet Union was … the first country where nature protection sought to avail itself of the authority of science'.[3] However, the Barguzin *Zapovednik* was founded in 1916 and was the first of a network of state reserves established throughout the Soviet Union that had roots in late-nineteenth-century Russia. Its global importance was marked by its designation as a UNESCO biosphere reserve, and it is part of the UNESCO World Heritage Site of Lake Baikal: 'the most outstanding example of a freshwater ecosystem'.[4] Accounts of Russian or Soviet environmental history typically characterise it as 'a deadening litany of environmental disasters' such as Chernobyl'.[5] While this declensionist narrative conveys the undeniable damage inflicted during the Soviet period, there are wider stories to be told about this part of the world, such as: the diversity of environments away from the centres of population and industry; the long-standing commitment of scientists and conservationists to protect such environments; and the resilience of even fragile environments and their inhabitants if they are given a chance. Thus, from the perspective of our bears in a remote region, who kept away from Soviet planners and nuclear power stations, as well as from us, the environmental history of Russia takes a different hue.

BIBLIOGRAPHY

Breyfogle, Nicholas B. 2015. 'At the Watershed: 1958 and the Beginnings of Lake Baikal Environmentalism'. *Slavonic and East European Review* **93** (1): 147–180.

Josephson, Paul, Nicolai Dronin, Ruben Mnatsakanian, Aleh Cherp, Dmitry Efremenko and Vladislav Larin. 2013. *An Environmental History of Russia.* New York: Cambridge University Press.

Moon, David. 2018. 'A Shaggy-Bear Story: An Environmental History from a Remote Region'. *Arcadia: Explorations in Environmental History.* No. 4. http://www.environmentandsociety.org/arcadia/shaggy-bear-story-environmental-history-remote-region

Radkau, Joachim. 2008. *Nature and Power: A Global History of the Environment.* Cambridge: Cambridge University Press.

---

3.   Radkau, *Nature and Power,* p. 275.

4.   UNESCO, 'Lake Baikal'.

5.   Josephson et al., *An Environmental History of Russia,* p. 236.

Shtilmark, Feliks. 2003. *The History of Russian Zapovedniks, 1895–1995*, translated by G.H. Harper. Edinburgh: Russian Nature Press.

Weiner, Douglas R. 1988. *Models of Nature: Ecology, Conservation and Cultural Revolution in Soviet Russia*. Pittsburgh: University of Pittsburgh Press8.

Weiner, Douglas R. 2009. 'The Predatory Tribute-Taking State: A Framework for Understanding Russian Environmental History'. In Edmund Burke III and Kenneth Pomeranz (eds), *The Environment and World History*, pp. 276–315. Berkeley: University of California Press.

RELATED LINKS

BaikalInfo. 2010. 'F.A.C.T. – Watch out – Bears!' http://www.baikalinfo.com/html/english_gbt_fact_bears.xml.php

The Siberian Times. 2015. 'World's Deepest Lake Shrouded in Smoke, Swimmers Covered in Ash'. 10 August. http://siberiantimes.com/ecology/casestudy/news/n0350-worlds-deepest-lake-shrouded-in-smoke-swimmers-covered-in-ash/

Stewart, Bryce. 2015. 'New dams, warming waters, forest fires – Lake Baikal in peril'. *The Ecologist: The Journal for the Post-Industrial Age*. 17 September. https://theecologist.org/2015/sep/17/new-dams-warming-waters-forest-fires-lake-baikal-peril

UNESCO. 2020. 'Lake Baikal'. http://whc.unesco.org/en/list/754/

University of York. 2016. 'Exploring Russia's History and Natural Resources: Lake Baikal in Siberia. 25 July–4 August 2015'. http://www.york.ac.uk/history/research/majorprojects/russiasenvironmentalhistory/

Zapovednoe Podlemore. 2013. Barguzinskii gosudarstvennyi prirodnyi biosfernyi zapovednik imeni K.A. Zabelina (The K.A. Zabelin Barguzin State Nature-Biosphere *Zapovednik*). http://zapovednoe-podlemorye.ru/territory/barguzin

PART III.

SIBERIA AND THE PACIFIC FAR EAST

10.

TRANS-SIBERIAN 'LANDSCAPES OF TRANSPORTATION' THROUGH THE LENS OF TRAVEL GUIDEBOOKS IN LATE IMPERIAL RUSSIA

Alexandra Bekasova and Ekaterina Kalemeneva

Along with the development of a vast transportation network, the spread of rail services and the introduction of new railway tariffs in 1894, the number of travellers in the Russian Empire increased by the beginning of the twentieth century. All those people required reliable information, instructions and advice on how to organise and complete their journeys, which they increasingly found in tourist guidebooks. Guidebook authors and publishers helped them master the fears arising from the uncertainties of travel. As tourist guidebooks acquired practical dimensions and evolved into popular publications for a broader audience, travellers widely sought and used them. Responding to travellers' demands, publishers increased guidebook production and circulation, cooperating with entrepreneurs to stay profitable whilst keeping prices low for their readers. Entrepreneurs, in turn, began to consider guidebooks an effective advertising space for travel-related services and commodities.[1]

    Along with advertisements and practical articles, guidebooks contained descriptions of routes and landscapes, transport infrastructure and services and economic development in the regions and cities. They contained historical and geographical reviews as well as visual materials – photographs, maps and plans – that, together, we term 'landscapes of transportation'. Inspired by the seminal book by Wolfgang Schivelbusch, *The Railway Journey: The Industrialization of Time and Space in the Nineteenth Century,*[2] and publications by Thomas Zeller on the history of autobahn construction in Europe from an 'envirotech' stud-

---

1.   For more detailed analysis of the close interrelations between the development of transportation networks, commercialisation of travel and the travel guidebook market in Russia in the nineteenth and the beginning of the twentieth century, see Anisimov, Bekasova and Kalemeneva, 'Books that Link Worlds'.

2.   Schivelbusch, *The Railway Journey.*

ies perspective, we approach these landscapes as a physical phenomenon and a kind of rhetorical resource.[3]

As Denis Cosgrove has pointed out, landscapes privilege a particular 'way of seeing' and are socially constructed through assemblages of cultural practices.[4] From about the end of the 1990s, cultural geographers and environmental historians began to see landscapes and their appreciation as more than a dialogue, a view embedded within the long literary and philosophical tradition of dealing with intersecting sets of discourses. This new scholarship holds that the perception of landscapes is both technologically constructed and charged with various values. The redefinition and shaping of landscapes for transportation have been studied in the context of a fundamental process of continuous transformation through production, consumption and appropriation. Focusing on how transportation infrastructure changed the topography, historians analyse how local landscapes were invested with different and often contested meanings by creators and consumers.[5] They also study how the development of transportation technologies created new ways of framing the world, shaping the notions of what travellers ought to see; and how various locations such as beaches and mountains were transformed from places of trepidation into desirable spaces and purchasable commodities during the emergence of tourism and mass consumption.[6] Recent historiography demonstrates an important shift in the understanding of space from neutral territory to socially constructed entity.[7] Interest in singling out space as a category of analysis enabled a new appreciation of geographical space as a vital factor that defined Russian development in historical perspective[8] and the mastering of Siberia in particular.[9] The notion

---

3.   Zeller, *Driving Germany*; Mauch and Zeller, *The World beyond the Windshield*; Lekan and Zeller, *Germany's Nature*.

4.   Cosgrove, *Social Formation and Symbolic Landscape*; Gailing and Leibenath, 'The Social Construction of Landscapes'.

5.   Zeller, *Driving Germany*, pp. 13–19.

6.   Zuelow, *A History of Modern Tourism*, pp. 30–59.

7.   Livingstone, *Putting Science in Its Place*; Schillings and van Wickeren, 'Towards a Material and Spatial History'; Withers, 'Place and the Spatial Turn'.

8.   For example, see Bassin, Ely and Stockdale, *Space, Place, and Power in Modern Russia*; Baron, 'New Spatial Histories of Twentieth-Century Russia and the Soviet Union'.

9.   Bassin, 'Russia between Europe and Asia: The Ideological Construction of Geographical Space'; Stolberg, 'The Siberian Frontier between "White Mission" and "Yellow Peril," 1890s–1920s'; Remnev, 'Siberia and the Russian Far East in the Imperial Geography of Power'; Schenck, 'Mastering Imperial Space?'

of far-flung, rich but undeveloped territories that, like a sleeping beauty, were waiting to be awakened, animated various descriptions of Siberia for centuries.[10]

The formation of the travel and tourism industry in the Russian Empire was a prolonged process. It unfolded over several decades in the second half of the nineteenth century and the beginning of the twentieth century, maturing during the Soviet period.[11] Although it started later there than in other parts of the world, the general directions and tendencies of its development were similar.[12] The commodification of travel was shaped by the development of transportation, the tourist service sector and the hotel industry, and was accompanied by the emergence of new social practices. The system was largely shaped by the activities of voluntary associations and societies, transportation companies and entrepreneurs, all of whom became actively engaged in publishing travel guides, reference literature and visual materials.

Intensive growth in the guidebook publishing market reflected new trends in economic and social development and a noticeable rise in mobility flows. The dynamics of that process were different in each region of the Russian Empire. Whilst the Volga River area and the Black Sea region, including the Crimean peninsula and the Caucasus were transformed rapidly into touristic and recreational spaces soon after rail services were introduced, Siberia and the Far East, where railway construction started later, lagged behind.[13] The opening of the Siberian railway network, which facilitated flows of colonists, settlers, migrants and tourists, significantly changed the situation.[14]

---

10. Kusber, 'Mastering the Imperial Space'.

11. On the history of travel and tourism in Russia and the Soviet Union, for example see Koenker, *Club Red*; Gorsuch and Koenker, 'Turizm'; McReynolds, *Russia at Play*.

12. There are several works that stand out noticeably in the vast scholarship on the history of tourism, including the collection of articles edited by Baranowski and Furlough, *Being Elsewhere* (especially its comprehensive introductory essay), even though it was published in 2001. On the travel and tourism industry in Europe, see also Zuelow (ed.), *Touring beyond the Nation*; Tissot, 'Construction d'une industrie touristique'; Koshar, *German Travel Cultures*.

13. On the history of tourism in Russia during late imperial period, see McReynolds, 'The Prerevolutionary Russian Tourist'.

14. On the history of migration in Russia and the Soviet Union, see Siegelbaum and Moch, *Broad Is My Native Land*. On resettlement to Siberia in the end of the nineteenth and the beginning of the twentieth centuries, see pp. 19–31. On political and economic issues of territorial colonisation in Siberia and the Far East from imperial history point of view, among other publications, see Remnev, 'Rossiia i Sibir' v meniaiushchemsia prostranstve imperii (19–nachalo 20 veka)'; Marks, 'Conquering the Great East'.

Trans-Siberian 'Landscapes of Transportation'

A number of scholars have focused on the role of guidebooks as a phenomenon of mass culture, closely connected to the social and economic development of particular areas of the Russian Empire.[15] Historians use guidebook narratives to analyse the Russian landscape as a cultural construction, proposing the emergence of new aesthetic norms to accommodate its perception.[16] In this chapter, we approach travel guides as complex artefacts that combine social interaction and marketing logistics. They integrate diverse elements from the present and the past, including various geographical locations and diverse professional activities of authors, publishers, state bureaucrats and entrepreneurs. Focusing on how travel guides functioned within the context of the burgeoning travel industry, we analyse them as a kind of boundary object that enabled different communities to intersect and communicate with one another and to articulate their goals. We argue that in the process of (re)making railway landscapes – which we consider as a material stage on which actions took place – perception of these landscapes was shaped by the natural environment in the process of its transformation, by transportation technologies and infrastructure, by services and conveniences, comfort and safety. As we shall demonstrate, it was easier for travellers to enjoy the railway panorama, with its changing views of 'wild' nature complemented by grandiose infrastructure, when they were safely transported in express trains with all sorts of modern conveniences. Being a highly contested rhetorical resource, authors, compilers and publishers of guidebooks debated, negotiated and constantly changed the Trans-Siberian 'landscapes of transportation'. By analysing travel guides on Siberia as complex artefacts and focusing on the transportation landscapes as a historical phenomenon, we hope to shed more light on the complex intersections of mobility, transport technologies and environment in the Russian Empire at the end of the nineteenth and the beginning of the twentieth century.

Travel Guidebooks and Practical Dimensions of the Trans-Siberian 'Landscapes of Transportation'

The construction of the Trans-Siberian Railway, which connected St Petersburg and Moscow with Vladivostok and Port Arthur on the Pacific coast, started in the 1890s and continued for about two decades. Sections of the railway were

---

15. Rutzinskaia, *Putevoditel' kak fenomen massovoi kul'tury*; Kiseleva, *Putevoditel' kak semioticheskii ob"ekt*.

16. Ely, *This Meager Nature*; Hausmann, *Mütterchen Wolga*; Lywood, 'From Russia's Orient to Russia's Riviera'.

put into operation, step-by-step, as soon as they were ready. Separate sections of the railway, which were to pass through hard-to-reach mountainous areas (around Lake Baikal and some others), continued to be built (and repeatedly reconstructed) until 1916.[17] Spurred by this construction, travel guides devoted to the eastern part of Russia – Siberia and the Far East – proliferated in the late 1890s.

Indeed, the publishing dynamics of guidebooks intensified substantially with the construction of the Trans-Siberian Railway network, which included several connecting lines. Among about 400 original travel guidebooks on various parts of the Russian Empire published in Russian since the 1800s (half of them appearing between 1900 and 1917), 39 guidebooks (not counting re-editions and translations into other languages) were focused on Siberia and the Far East. Though the first travel guides were issued in the 1880s, before the construction of the railway, about two-thirds of travel guides on Siberia and Russian Far East were issued between 1900 and 1914 by printing houses in St Petersburg, Moscow, Irkutsk, Tomsk and Vladivostok. As the construction of the Siberian railway network continued for decades, several travel guidebooks were republished annually, indicating that they were in demand and sold out quickly. Not much is known about the number of copies published because it was not customary at that time to indicate this information in print. Thanks to the fact that sometimes authors did keep records, it is known that some guides were printed in runs of more than 10,000 copies.[18]

As the construction of the Trans-Siberian Railway was a long process, new railway sections, stations along railway lines and other infrastructure facilities were put into operation gradually. At the beginning of the railway's operation, carriages sometimes went off the rails and became detached from the locomotive, and trains sometimes got stuck in heavy snow. Whilst spacious railway stations were still being built according to modern plans, passengers had to huddle in temporary premises that were not well adapted for holding travellers. The establishment of continuous traffic by rail over several thousand kilometres, reconciliation of timetables and other important functional details,

17. On the history of the railway network in Siberia, the Russian Far East and Manchuria in late nineteenth and early twentieth centuries from different perspectives, among other publications, see Schenk, 'Mastering Imperial Space?'; Hsu, 'Frontier Urban and Imperial Dreams'; Hsu, 'A Tale of Two Railroads'; Lukoianov, *'Ne otstat' ot derzhav…' Rossiia na Dal'nem Vostoke v kontse XIX – nachale XX vekov*, esp. pp. 64–116; Il'in, *Sozdanie velikogo sibirskogo puti*; Borzunov, *Transsibirskaia magistral' v mirovoi politike velikikh derzhav*.

18. Audze, *Putevoditel' po Sibiri*, p. 38.

as well as dealing with troubleshooting, required time and constant effort. The passenger service system was also being adjusted and improved systematically. In practice, distant travel through the vast Siberian transportation network at the beginning of the twentieth century was possible using a combination of different modes of transportation, including not only railway, but also icebreakers or steamships and even horse-drawn carriages.

Travellers, especially those who were going to distant regions, required reliable information, instruction, advice and help to them plan their journey. Guidebook authors and publishers helped them mitigate the fears that arose from the uncertainties of travel and enabled them to control the unknown with practical information. Mikhail Stozh, who was an experienced railway employee as well as an author and publisher,[19] included a list of basic rules of behaviour for railway passengers in his 'Sputnik'[20] guides. He explained: 'With "Sputnik" in hand and being familiar with these rules you will not feel in a quandary ... you will not travel groping about, but with open eyes, and will not harass employees of the railway (who are often very busy) with bothersome questions.'[21] Reminding travellers about difficulties and uncertainties, which could not be avoided during long journeys, he advised passengers 'to be equipped with patience, to prepare for the worst ... not to get lost under any circumstances, [and] to trust only themselves'. He reminded his readers about the risk of being robbed during railway journeys and recommended caution and awareness of swindlers. Stozh considered it necessary give passengers practical advice on how to behave: '... it is worth remembering the number of the wagon ... maintain cleanliness and do not allow the wagon to turn into a pigsty'.[22] These seemingly obvious tips demonstrate that Stozh oriented his writing toward passengers with low income and little experience travelling by rail.

Responding to a significant demand for reliable, practical travel information, authors and compilers of guides to Siberia, the Russian Far East and Manchuria supplied their publications with diverse material for tourists. They often included lists of addresses of administrative and postal offices and commercial firms, with short reviews on services provided and hotels available in the cities. Recent timetables and ticket prices, information about operational details of postal routes, reviews of railways and steamship services, customs

---

19. We will discuss Stozh and his publications in depth later in the chapter.
20. In the era before satellites orbiting the earth, *sputnik* meant simply travelling companion.
21. Stozh, *Sputnik po Zabaikail'skoi zheleznoi doroge*, p. 27.
22. Ibid., p. 27.

regulations, maps and plans of the cities were regularly published in the pages of travel guides. Authors not only reprinted useful information obtained from other publications but regularly edited and recombined it to simplify and facilitate the use of rather complicated data on the functioning of the railway system and services that were constantly changing. They published actual railway timetables for each edition, for example, and they indicated the stations where trains stopped longer and passengers could have snacks or eat meals at restaurants and buffets that were available at only some stations on the Trans-Siberian.[23]

Time itself was a challenge when taking a long journey across the continent.[24] As Wolfgang Schivelbusch demonstrated, travellers' engagement with and understanding of landscapes crucially depends on forms of movement, speed and travel time. In order to help passengers deal with different railway time regimes, authors and compilers of guides summarised the various timetables and included them in the travel books. They reminded readers about the coexistence of different time zones inside and outside the trains on different rail lines along routes to the Russian Far East or China. St Petersburg time was used on trains that operated on the Siberian railway up to Irkutsk, whilst inhabitants of the cities on the route kept their local times. The trains of the Trans-Baikal Railway (which ran to the east of Lake Baikal) and the Circum-Baikal Railway (which ran around the southern shores of Baikal) operated according to the Irkutsk time, whilst Harbin time was used in the trains of the Chinese-Eastern Railway. Finding themselves at the Manchurian station, where the two lines crossed, passengers transferring from one line to another had to remember to adjust their watches.[25]

The Ministry of Ways and Communication began to issue official editions of combined railway timetables of all lines operated in the Russian Empire and current tariffs for passenger and freight traffic, but did not always cope with the rapid update of information. Being commercially oriented, authors and publishers of travel guides often managed to do this more efficiently, a fact that helped promote their publications to potential customers.[26] Authors of guides notified their readers that, regardless of how different timetables for

---

23. *Kratkii putevoditel' na Dal'nii Vostok po sploshnomu zheleznodorozhnomu puti*, pp. 9, 65; Stozh, *Zheleznodorozhnyi sputnik po Zabaikal'skoi zheleznoi doroge*, p. 8.

24. For more details on the railway operation and clock time regimes in the Russian Empire, see Schenk, 'Universal'noe vremia versus local'nye vremena: zheleznye dorogi i spory o vremiaischislenii v Rossii (1870–1910)'.

25. For example see, Stozh, *Sputnik po Zabaikal'skoi zheleznoi doroge*, p. 8

26. For example see, *Kratkii putevoditel' na Dal'nii Vostok po sploshnomu zheleznodorozhnomu puti*, p. 1.

express trains were coordinated, in practice there could be intervals of several hours between connected trains running on different railway tracks. Describing the route from Irkutsk to the station on the border with China in his guide published in 1906, I. Klark – who was not only a travel guide publisher, but also a railway employee on the Ussuri Railway – pointed out that passengers who came by train on the Trans-Siberian Railway to Irkutsk had to wait several hours before they could transfer to the connecting train on the Circum-Baikal Railway. He warned travellers about the inconvenience caused by the fact that waiting rooms for first- and second-class passengers at the central railway station in Irkutsk were too small and inconvenient. Furthermore, there was no left-luggage office at the station at that time. Despite these difficulties, he recommended travellers to leave hand luggage to the care of owners of houses situated close to the railway station.

Advising them not to waste time at the station, he inspired them to go sightseeing in the city and gave detailed advice on how to behave properly. In his description, Irkutsk's urban elements were closely intertwined with the issues of safety and other practicalities. Reviewing the main city attractions, he pointed out the panoramic view of the Angara River, the 'civilised' and attractive centre of the city with cobbled and lit streets, triumphal gates erected in 1868 with the inscription 'The Way to the Great Ocean' and buildings housing the museum and the city theatre, as well as many cathedrals and churches. Klark compared these sites to the neglected, dark and dirty outskirts of Irkutsk. He also described the high cost of living and traditions of charity as characteristic features of the city's image.[27]

When the railway line around Lake Baikal was opened for operation in 1904–1905, its throughput was rather small, because it was only single track until the line was reconstructed in 1911–1914. For this reason, two icebreaker ferries, The *Baikal* and the *Angara*, which were built in Newcastle upon Tyne in Britain,[28] continued to transport cargo and passengers across the lake.

---

27. Klark, *Sputnik po Manchzhurii, Amuru i Ussuriiskomu kraiu*, pp. 1–3.

28. For more details on the construction of the icebreakers for the Russian Empire in Britain, see Saunders, 'Icebreakers in Anglo-Russian Relations (1914–21)'.

Alexandra Bekasova and Ekaterina Kalemeneva

Figure 10.1. View of the Baikal station of the Circum-Baikal Railway and icebreaker marinas, printed on a postcard. Source: Private collection of Alexandra Bekasova.

When it froze during the winter, a sledge way was set up and used inten-sively for transportation.[29] The author of the travel guide informed his readers about these two alternatives for continuing the journey from Irkutsk to the Far East. Each of these possibilities (by ferryboat or by train) had advantages and disadvantages. Among the advantages of taking the icebreaker across the lake were noticeable savings of travel time, picturesque mountainous landscapes and familiarisation with the grandiose transport infrastructure. At the same time, that kind of journey was complicated by two tiresome changes from the train to the ship and from the ship back to the train. Going by the railway around Lake Baikal was easier but much longer. 'As if in a sealed envelope the train delivers you in about three days through the railway around the lake to Manchuria', the author wrote.[30]

29. For more details on ferry-icebreakers' infrastructure and crossing Lake Baikal, see Kolo-tilo, Anrienko, *Transbaikal'skii perekrestok.*

30. *Sputnik po Manchzhurii, Amuru i Ussuriiskomu kraiu,* p. 5.

Figure 10.2. View of a cliff near the source of the Angara River and Lake Baikal, printed on a postcard. Source: Private collection of Alexandra Bekasova.

Concerning the railway line that was built around the lake, he noted that 'far from flattering reviews about it existed', that it was being built 'hastily and unsatisfactorily', that one of the nineteen tunnels on the road had already collapsed and that, therefore, 'to go this way not providing a family with a testament is risky'.[31]

He described the route from the station of Mysovaia to Verkhneudinsk (Ulan-Ude) and then to Chita and on to Manchuria as very picturesque and worth seeing. The author represented the singular beauty of that transportation landscape: 'Scenic views do not leave you until Chita ... through the Iablonovyi [mountain] Range the train keeps zigzagging all the time amidst wild nature, in a dense, majestic taiga and rises in a tunnel along a high embankment. On the portal at the entrance to the tunnel there is an inscription – "To the Great Ocean" and on the portal at the exit from the tunnel – "To the Atlantic Ocean".'[32]

---

31. Ibid., p. 4.
32. Ibid., p. 6.

Alexandra Bekasova and Ekaterina Kalemeneva

Figure 10.3. View of the Trans-Baikal Railway where it crosses the Tolacha River, printed on a postcard. Source: Private collection of Alexandra Bekasova.

Steamers and icebreakers, the wild taiga of the mountainous region surrounding a vast lake, railway tracks, bridges, piers and other objects of impressive transport infrastructure did not just enchant authors and compilers of guidebooks. They had become favourites for photographers and painters as well. For all of them the motive of conquering 'wild' nature had become extremely popular.[33] Spectacular panoramic views of transportation landscapes were in great demand. They appeared regularly on pages of guidebooks. Moreover, they were printed on postcards and circulated widely in large numbers.[34] Travellers who could afford first- or second-class tickets on the so-called 'Siberian Express' – luxurious express trains of the International Society of Sleeping Carriages (*Companie International des Wagons Lits*, or CIWL) – had a chance to taste these

---

33. Among these painters was Pavel Paisetskii, who made a Siberian panorama for the World Fair in Paris in 1900. For more details about him and his works, see Printseva, *Sibirskii put' Pavla Piasetkogo*. The railway motif was often encountered in the works of artists Konstantin Pomerantsev and Vladimir Ettel', who collaborated with Stozh's private publishing house in Irkutsk. About Pomerantsev and Ettel', see Lykhin and Khenok (eds), *Khudozhnik Konstantin Pomerantsev*; Deviat'airova, *V.K. Ettel'*.

34. Bochenkov and Miasnikov, *Rossiiskie zheleznye dorogi na starinnoi pochtovoi otkrytke*, pp. 127–202.

impressive panoramas along with delicious dishes prepared by experienced chefs in the dining carriage and to enjoy all sorts of modern conveniences during the long journey, including electricity and warm water for bathing.[35] The company widely advertised its services in the guidebooks and other reference literature. It offered the possibility to order not only an individual compartment for travellers, but even an entire carriage. Passengers enjoyed services and comfort in individual compartments, the restaurant and the library, where they could read books, look through illustrated journals and play chess. They could also send telegrams in foreign languages whilst on board the train. Moreover, to ease further the way to China and Japan, the company advertised steamboats from Vladivostok to the seaports of Nagasaki or Tsuruga and back, relating their schedules to the railway timetables.[36]

Thus, acting as mediators of reliable practical information, authors, compilers and publishers of the travel guides did important intermediary work to help travellers cope with the difficulties and uncertainties during a long journey across the continent. Promptly informing potential travellers about the opening of new railway lines and other opportunities accordingly, as well as supplying them with up-to-date railway timetables, the guidebook authors helped them to plan their journeys more rationally. They linked and adapted the dizzying ideas of transport planners to the daily routine of a multimodal and complex transportation network. Addressing passengers in first and second class, who enjoyed modern services and conveniences on board the trains, they promoted the practice of admiring the panoramas of transportation landscapes.

Marketing Siberian 'Landscapes of Transportation': Authors and Their Publishing Strategies

The authors and compilers of guidebooks on the Trans-Siberian Railway had different social and professional backgrounds: among them were journalists, state bureaucrats, employees of the Trans-Siberian Railway, owners of publishing houses and entrepreneurs. Therefore, they pursued different goals by issuing travel guides. They targeted various audiences, reflecting the structure of the

---

35. On Companie International des Wagons Lits (CIWL) and its business activities in the Russian Empire, see Kel'ner, 'Liternyi poezd "Severnyi ekspress" – mezhdu mirom i voinoi (1884–1914)'. On the duties of the Siberian express train team and the services they provided for passengers see *Instruktsiia nomer 1*. Some practical information was also published along with timetables, for example, see *Mezhdunarodnoe obshchestvo spal'nykh vagonov i skorykh poezdov*.

36. Putnik (N.N. Lender), *Vseobshchii illiustrirovannyi putevoditel'*, pp. 9–10.

Alexandra Bekasova and Ekaterina Kalemeneva

material composition and strategies of knowledge production about Siberia and the Far East. Competing for the readers' attention, authors used various strategies to promote their guides. Whilst some of them highlighted practical dimensions of their volumes, others focused on illustrations or 'comprehensiveness' of information presented.

The character of the narratives of Siberian landscapes in guidebooks largely depended on the motives of the publication. The first guidebooks that demonstrated quasi-official narratives on the railway and on Siberia itself were issued for big international events in the late nineteenth century. The travel guidebook 'Siberia and the Great Siberian Railway' was prepared for the World's Columbian Exposition in Chicago in 1893 and the 'Guide to the Great Siberian Railway', which ran to almost 600 pages, was presented at the World's Fair in Paris in 1900, where the Trans-Siberian Railway was presented in the Russian pavilion – an opportune moment to champion a grand narrative on the history and development of the region.[37] From the beginning, these guides, with advertisements for numerous Russian industrial companies, private enterprises and travel agencies, were seen as an explanation and supplementary literature for the international audience at the exhibitions.[38] The Ministry of Ways and Communication initiated publication of these books, which soon became influential: from 1900 to 1914, the 'Guide to the Great Siberian Railway', was reissued along with translations more than ten times.

The publication of these guides for international trade fairs predetermined the format of a guide's narrative and its orientation toward a wealthy public. The guides looked more like reference books and were intended to inform readers broadly about the region and the railway's continuing construction and operation. The 'Guide to the Great Siberian Railway' contained comprehensive geographical, historical, scientific and ethnographic reviews of Siberia and short descriptions of cities and settlements situated on the route of the railway lines. The publication was richly illustrated and contained more than 350 photo-gravures with views of Siberian landscapes, cities and objects of the Great Siberian railway's infrastructure, portraits of important political and cultural figures and ethnographical typologies of local inhabitants, as well as maps and plans.

---

37.   Dmitriev-Mamonov and Zdiarskii, *The Guide to Great Siberian Railway*.

38.   On the presentation of the Trans-Siberian Railway at the World Fair in Paris, see Schenk, *Poezd v sovremennost'*, pp. 97–103; Remnev, 'Uchastie Komiteta Sibirskoi zheleznoi dorogi vo Vsemirnoi vystavke 1900 goda v Parizhe'.

The railway itself was represented not only as an instrument of colonisation, but also as a grandiose technological system that transformed the natural environment. It was described as the 'safest, quickest, cheapest and the most convenient route' from Europe to the Pacific Ocean.[39] Numerous photographs represented huge bridges, tunnels and railway stations. The 'Guide to the Great Siberian Railway' placed Siberia geographically as 'an area possessing a very diversified relief and geological structure, and a most varied climate, flora and fauna'. These guides provided general descriptions of the entire region, rather than practical information for travellers. As a result, they were widely used as informational resources by other authors and compilers of travel guides. The references to these editions can be found in guidebooks and other publications, printed during the twentieth century and even more recently.[40]

Another influential type of narrative of the Trans-Siberian Railway was in the 'Guide to all of Siberia and Russia's Middle-Asian Domains', first published in 1895 and issued in seven editions up to 1903.[41] The author of this guide – a former prince, Vsevolod Dolgorukov, who was exiled in Tomsk, Siberia, where he became a journalist and a bureaucrat at the local court – explained that the rapidly increasing numbers of travellers to Siberia necessitated publishing a travel guidebook. In the introductory sections, he explicitly highlighted that, with the construction of the railway, Siberia was attracting the attention of 'the educated world', but the only published guidebooks at that time were brief reference books with lists of stations. He justified the need for his new publication in the following way: 'There are no business reference books that would give travellers to Siberia the necessary information about the transportation system and at least brief descriptions of the main cities and local attractions.'[42] Providing each subsequent reissue of his guidebook with short translations of its materials into French, German and English, he wrote in the preface to the seventh edition, published in 1903–1904: 'About ten years ago a trip to Siberia was considered almost a feat and not everyone would have decided to take it. Now Siberia is willingly visited not only by the inhabitants of European Russia, but also by foreigners.'[43] The guide covered general information about

39. Dmitriev-Mamonov and Zdiarskii, *The Guide to Great Siberian Railway*, p. 77.

40. See, for instance, Klark, *Sputnik po Manchzhurii, Amuru i Ussuriiskomu Kraiiu*; Iudin, *Transsibirskaia magistral'*.

41. Gur'ev and Dolgorukov, *Putevoditel' po vsei Sibiri i Sredne-Aziatskim vladeniiam Rossii s podrobnym dorozhnikom*.

42. Ibid., pp. i–xii.

43. Dolgorukov, *Putevoditel' po vsei Sibiri i Aziatskim vladeniiam Rossii*, pp. i–iii.

Alexandra Bekasova and Ekaterina Kalemeneva

the construction of the railway and the history of the region, and gave a lot of practical details about travel.

The case of Mikhail Stozh, a publisher, entrepreneur and railway employee, demonstrates another strategy for publishing travel guides. He was born in Vitebsk, in present-day Belarus, in 1880 and came to Irkutsk in 1900 from Ashkhabad, in contemporary Turkmenistan, where he had worked on the Trans-Caspian Railway.[44] He wrote in a romantic tone in an edition of his 'Illustrated Companion to Siberia and the Far East', that in 1900 he suddenly fell ill at Irkutsk station, and a lady with 'blue eyes beaming with incomprehensible kindness' took him to a hotel and cared for him until he recovered.[45] He settled in Irkutsk and started to work on the railway, where he held a variety of jobs: ticket sales agent, clerk, accountant, telegraph operator, stoker, locksmith, train inspector and even express train-master.

Stozh's printing activities started in 1903 when he established the first private publishing house in Irkutsk, later known as 'Irises'.[46] He published a variety of literature and materials on Siberia: guidebooks, postcards with Siberian landscapes, poetic brochures on Lake Baikal, literary journals, fiction novels, etc. He organised competitions for the best poetry and prose about Lake Baikal with a valuable prize for the winner – 50 roubles or a gold medal with an emblem of his publishing house. Stozh published 'The Dictionary of Siberian Poets, Writers and Scientists',[47] which was widely criticised for unchecked information, irrational structure and unsatisfactory typographical quality.[48] In 1903, Stozh published his first guidebook on the Trans-Siberian Railway called 'Timetables of Postal, Passengers and Express Trains or Companion of a Passenger to Siberian Railways'.[49] Besides timetables it contained short reviews of Siberia and its regions and cities, railway construction and practical tips for travellers as well as a range of other practical information. He printed 'Companions' on various parts of the Trans-Siberian Railway twice a year until the 1920s. He

---

44.   Stozh, *Illiustrirovannyi sputnik po Sibiri i Dal'nemu Vostoku*, p. 56.

45.   Ibid., pp. 56–58.

46.   For more about publishing enterprises in Irkutsk, see Shinkareva, *Stanovlenie i razvitie izdatel'skogo dela v Irkutske (XIX – nachalo XX veka)*; Shinkareva, 'Knizhnoe izdatel'stvo M.E. Stozha 'Irisy' i ego rol' v kul'turnoi zhizni Irkutska nachala XX veka", pp. 148–63.

47.   Stozh, *Slovar' sibirskikh pisatelei, poetov i uchenykh.*

48.   V.G., 'Sibirskaia bibliografiia'.

49.   Stozh, *Raspisanie poezdov pochtovykh, passazhirskikh, a ravno i skorykh (ekspress) ili Sputnik passazhira po sibirskim zheleznym dorogam.*

actively supported Siberian poets and writers, including information about them or fragments of their works in his guides.

Stozh ambitiously represented himself as a local expert whose aim was to promote knowledge of and interest in the region both among its inhabitants and travellers. He claimed that since his *Companion to the Trans-Baikal Railway* was free of useless information, 'one can find it in the hands of the majority of advanced travellers'.[50] However, his guidebooks were far from professional in composition. He actively used them for self-promotion, advertising all his publishing activities in the guidebooks and brochures and including panegyric reviews of his works and even a letter of support written by his mother.[51] His guidebooks were cheap (from ten to twenty kopecks), and included updated train timetables and information about prices for various public services in cities and towns along the railway lines and promotional illustrated post cards with each edition. His active self-advertisement made him a remarkable narrator of Siberia and the Lake Baikal region. As he wrote in his books, his '*Companion* [was] so well-established, that it no longer [had] any serious rivals'.[52]

Even critical reviewers of his guides, whilst recognising their low quality, had to confirm the popularity of his publications:

> Stozh's works are usually considered as waste paper, and this is ¾ true. However ... whilst 'good' literature is lying in fug, the number of Stozh's 'waste papers' is ever increasing ... Whilst competent Siberians are just dreaming, Stozh comes and having understood the demand of Siberian readers or travellers to have certain types publication, he immediately publishes them and announces them a year in advance.[53]

The various reasons for publications as well as the different publishing strategies of authors of travel guides described above substantially influenced the content of their books and the formats of the guides' narratives. Each book was oriented toward different reading audiences and constructed specific views on the transportation landscapes.

---

50. Stozh, *Sputnik po Zabaikal'skoi zheleznoi doroge*, p. 85.

51. Stozh, *Illiustrirovannyi sputnik po Sibiri i Dal'nemu Vostoku s kartoiu*, p. 59.

52. Stozh, *Zheleznodorozhnyi sputnik po Zabaikal'skoi zheleznoi doroge*, p. 85.

53. V.G., 'Sibirskaia bibliografiia', pp. 368–9.

Alexandra Bekasova and Ekaterina Kalemeneva

Narrating Siberia and the Trans-Siberian Railway: Strategies of Regional Promotion

Narrating the Trans-Siberian, authors and compilers of travel guides emphasised close connections between Siberia with its various geographical localities and the functioning of the transportation network. In the process, they did a lot to shape railway construction, Siberian transportation infrastructure and the route itself, which went through diverse Siberian spaces and noticeable points of interest for Russian and foreign travellers.[54]

Siberia had long been associated in the public imagination with exile, deportations or business activities. However, the construction of the Trans-Siberian Railway and the circulation of mass literature contributed to the transformation of its image into a wonderland with numerous attractions, mineral resorts and sightseeing possibilities awaiting discovery. The rapid development of transport infrastructure in the Russian Empire in the nineteenth century made regions situated far from the capital much more accessible for diverse groups of travellers. It also stimulated the rise of interest in distant parts of the empire among a broader audience. The author of an article published in the journal *Russkaia Mysl'* in 1895 wrote: 'Until now, the only people who went [to Siberia] freely were those attracted by bureaucratic or trade advantages. But now a substantial part of Asian Russia is freely accessible to ordinary tourists, ordinary curious people, and not limited to specialists and scientists.'[55]

Guides' narratives on Siberia and its transportation landscapes could be roughly divided into three groups according to the scale of representation of the region: local, national and transnational perspectives. The national perspective is characterised by a centralist view of Siberia as a vast, wild part of the Russian Empire with boundless plains, forests and big rivers, rich with natural resources. The railway was presented as a powerful key to the further development and integration of the region.

In the preface to the English translation of the publication 'Siberia and the Great Siberian Railway', which addressed an international bureaucratic and business audience at the Chicago World's Fair, the compilers expressed the official tsarist government's vision of the importance of railway construction in Siberia:

> Of that great expanse of territory reaching all the way from the Ural Mountains to the Pacific Ocean and from the frozen seas to the borders of the Celestial Empire there is perhaps little more than the name, Siberia, authentically known

---

54. For example, see Audze, *Putevoditel' po Sibiri*.
55. Kostin, Iakovenko and Bykova, *Vsevolod Alekseevich Dolgorukov*, p. 25.

to the public. Yet with its wide-stretching plains, its magnificent water systems and its unknown wealth of noble metals and other valuable mineral deposits buried in its bosom, there is for such a land a future too great to be overlooked at the present day. With the steel rails of the Great Siberian Railway piercing their steady way through the vast country to the Far East, thus completing the arc of the circle that in direct lines, winding about the 50th parallel of north latitude, will steam around the world.

A similar view on Siberia and the 'civilising role' of the railway can be found in memoirs of travellers. For instance, John Foster Fraser, a British traveller on the Trans-Siberian Railway, noted in his travelogue published in 1902:

> I confess the railway, a twin thread of steel spreading over the continent, began to fascinate me as nothing had done for a long time. Here is a land, one and a half times as large as Europe – forty times, indeed, as big as the United Kingdom – that has lain dormant through the ages, but is at last being tickled into life, as it were, by the railway, as a giant might be aroused from slumber by a wisp.[56]

In a distinct, local type of narrative, some guidebook authors focused in more detail on regional localities and represented Siberia not only as a colonised region, but as place worth visiting.[57] For example, D. Bogdanov's comprehensive guidebook on Vladivostok and the surrounding area contained an overview of geographic characteristics of each part of the Primorskaia Oblast' and Sakhalin Island along with description of the city, and practical information concerning administrative institutions, commercial firms, communications and transportation. Seeing his task as acquainting a wide layer of local society and travellers with the region and its riches and narrating briefly, clearly and without using special scientific terminology, the author paid attention to descriptions of the fishing industry, fur trade and hunting, the timber industry, mining, cattle breeding and agriculture. He focused specifically on such local industries as whaling and seal fisheries, collecting sea cucumbers and seaweed and harvesting deer antlers, among others, all of which were described as important for the economic development of the region. Emphasising that those industries and trades were flourishing in Alaska and Japan, Bogdanov considered it absurd that the Far East of the Russian Empire lived at the expense of state appropriations. He considered it his civil duty to popularise the province and its riches

---

56. Fraser, *The Real Siberia*.

57. For example, see Bogdanov, *Putevoditel' po Vladivostoku i promysly Primorskoi Oblasti, Kamchatki i Sakhalina*; Fomenko, *Sputnik po Dal'nemu Vostoku*.

among local residents and to promote the importance of intensive use of local resources.[58]

Stozh's *Companion* books demonstrate an even stronger insider's view of the region. Addressing consumers with lower incomes, he recounted advantages of travel to Siberia. He described the beauty of Siberian landscapes, augmenting his claims with numerous illustrations and poetry. He also tried to develop the image of Siberia as a recreational resort by including information about its mineral waters. Nevertheless, the main theme of many of his narratives was praising Lake Baikal. Romanticised descriptions of the lake as a 'natural miracle of Siberia' appeared in his guides alongside mystical narratives on its 'severe character' and damaging storms which led to 'superstitious fear and homage of local people'.[59] Stozh constantly described it as the 'sacred sea', compared it with 'a miracle in a deep frame of its abrupt green shores'. He explained the absence of poems on Baikal only by 'the lack of poetic gift among local inhabitants'.[60] To fill this gap, Stozh even published a 125-page-brochure entitled *How Lake Baikal is Praised in Poetry and Prose*. He explained his mission to develop knowledge about Lake Baikal among local inhabitants:

> I could have been blamed for including many weak works in this volume ... But my goal was to collect everything told in poetry by native Siberians and newcomers about the beauty of Lake Baikal regardless of the level of their talent. ... A poet who can praise the beauty of it and compose laudatory hymns in its honour would be a great Siberian poet.[61]

In his guides, Stozh compared Siberian natural beauty to famous European landscapes, considering them to be the highest reference points for evaluating local landscapes. Just as the Caucasus Mountains in mass literature narratives were usually associated with the Swiss Alps, Lake Baikal was usually associated with Lake Geneva, despite the marked difference in size.[62]

---

58. Bogdanov, *Putevoditel' po Vladivostoku i promysly Primorskoi Oblasti, Kamchatki i Sakhalina*, pp. xvi–xviii.

59. Stozh, *Kak vospet Baikal v stikhakh i proze*, p.1.

60. Ibid.

61. Ibid., p. 124.

62. Ibid.

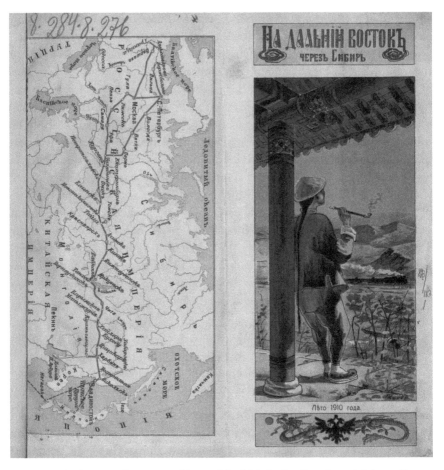

Figure 10.4. The cover illustration of the guidebook To the Far East through Siberia. Source: Na Dal'nii Vostok cherez Sibir' (1910).

    A transnational focus was the third scale of narrating the Trans-Siberian Railway. This type of narrative constructed the image of Siberia (and a railway) first as a transit route from Western Europe to China and Japan. For instance, at the very beginning of the guidebook 'To the Far East through Siberia', the author claimed that 'construction of the Great Siberian Route and its continuation – the Chinese-Eastern railway – was aimed to create a transit route from West European states through Russia to the Far East and the Great Ocean'.[63] The cover illustration echoed this theme by depicting a person dressed in tradi-

---

63.   *Na Dal'nii Vostok cherez Sibir'. Leto 1910*, p.1.

tional Chinese costume looking at a mountainous landscape with a locomotive in the distance. This image of Siberia as a transit route to the east was mainly oriented toward foreigners who travelled to or through Russia, as special attention was paid to the details of customs and passport control regulations for those travelling to Russia by train. European railway systems at that time already connected Paris with St Petersburg by 'Nord-Express' trains, and the construction of the Trans-Siberian Railway created a nearly direct overland connection between major European and Asian capitals.

Travel from Moscow to Vladivostok with comfortable sleeping cars took ten days or more, but the tickets were valid for three months, so passengers had the opportunity to get off at any stop and to explore Russian cities and towns during their journeys. Thus, in a transnational perspective, the Trans-Siberian Railway was advertised as the fastest and the cheapest way from London to Shanghai (the world's biggest trading centres in the early twentieth century).[64] Another guidebook specifically highlighted that the route Paris – Berlin – Moscow – Beijing could be completed in just twelve days.[65] Different scales of presenting Siberia – as an integral part of the Empire, as a region which differed from other parts of the country, or as a transnational bridge between 'West' and 'East' – are traceable not only in guidebook narratives, but also in other materials published in these books. The structure of guides, their prices and their advertisements shed more light on this issue. For instance, *Travel Guide to the Great Siberian Railway*, which went through its twelfth reprint in 1914, contained 84 pages of advertising before the text itself (even before the title page).[66] The fact that many advertisements had no connection to the region featured in the publication meant that the editor of a guide used the services of a dense network of agents who collected advertisements from companies and firms in various cities of the Russian Empire. These advertisers were interested in the wide geographical distribution of their products and services. Despite different scales of narration and presentation, the number of travel publications, which was increasing annually over the early twentieth century, helped transform Siberia into a notable destination by creating recognisable images of the region and the railway.

---

64. Ibid., pp.1–2.

65. Putnik (N.N. Lender), *Vseobshchii illiustrirovannyi putevoditel'*.

66. Dmitriev-Mamonov and Zdiarskii, *Putevoditel' po Velikoi sibirskoi zheleznoi doroge*.

Conclusions

Travel guides proved to be highly sensitive to technological, social and aesthetic changes. Many types of information found a home in the pages of these books and brochures: large-scale geological prospecting works, the construction of grandiose transport infrastructure in Siberia, economic development of regions and specific features of the daily functioning of that huge multimodal transport network. Moreover, these books reflected the interests of diverse social and professional groups that interacted with one another regarding both the creation and the use of such publications. Focusing on requests and tastes of different readership audiences, they acted as commercial mediators, promoting the circulation of diverse configurations of images, visions and informational bricolage, which were in demand among those wishing to travel to this vast, untamed region. Sensitively responding to readers' requests, they picked up ideas and views that were 'in the air', packaged them and promoted their goods on the printing market.

These books and brochures, of distinct size and quality, contained short reviews on Siberia, the Russian Far East and Manchuria and their major cities and natural sights. They combined geographic descriptions with a variety of practical information: timetables, tariffs, time ratio tables, customs regulations, rules of conduct for railway passengers, photographs, maps and plans. Furthermore, advertisements for many types of products and services were published in the pages of travel guides. They added new dimensions to the composite mosaic of informational space through which 'landscapes of transportation' were constructed and perceived.

This case study of Siberian 'landscapes of transportation' reveals the technological, social and aesthetic changes connected with the construction of the Trans-Siberian Railway network. They were located at the intersection of culture, the built environment and what is usually called 'nature'. The construction brought intensive scientific exploration of the region, large-scale technological intervention and physical intrusions into landscapes. Whilst the railway was represented as a symbol of prestige, progress and power, the territories through which it ran, with their dense forests, mountains, rivers and lakes only lightly brushed by human habitation, were described as 'wild'. Thus, the railway was represented as a crucial tool for the transformation of the natural environment. At the same time, it made distant areas and landscapes, like Lake Baikal, accessible for larger numbers of business travellers, settlers and tourists. The operation of the railway with a length of more than 8,000 kilometres, which spanned the Eurasian landmass, reduced both the time and cost of travel. It had a profound impact not only on the concepts of space and time but also on habits of visual perception. Along with rail services and modern conveniences offered on board express trains, impressive views and panoramas from the railway around Lake Baikal evolved into a demandable good and purchasable commodity. Being actively involved in the replication and circulation of these images, authors and publishers of guides invested in the process of transformation of Lake Baikal into an object of natural and cultural heritage. Pursuing commercial interest, they attracted public attention to a vast range of Siberian places as beautiful, valuable and worth visiting.

BIBLIOGRAPHY

Anisimov, Evgenii, Alexandra Bekasova and Ekaterina Kalemeneva. 2016. 'Books that Link Worlds: Travel Guides, the Development of Transportation Infrastructure, and the Emergence of the Tourism Industry in Imperial Russia, Nineteenth–Early Twentieth Centuries'. *Journal of Tourism History* **8** (2): 184–204.

Audze, L. 1914. *Putevoditel' po Sibiri. S raspisaniem passazhirskikh poezdov ot S.-Petersburga i Moskvy do Vladivostoka (I sokrashchenno do: Kryma, Kavkaza, Varshavy, Granitsy, Aleksandrovo i Verzhbolovo). S kartoi zheleznykh dorog.* Tomsk: Tovarishchestvo 'Pechiatnia S.P. Iakovleva'.

Baranowski, Shelley and Ellen Furlough (eds). 2001. *Being Elsewhere: Tourism, Consumer Culture, and Identity in Modern Europe and North America.* Ann Arbor: University of Michigan Press.

Baron, Nick. 2007. 'New Spatial Histories of Twentieth-Century Russia and the Soviet Union: Surveying the Landscape'. *Jahrbücher für Geschichte Osteuropas* **55** (3): 374–401.

Bassin, Mark. 1991. 'Russia between Europe and Asia: The Ideological Construction of Geographical Space'. *Slavic Review* **50** (1): 1–17.

Bassin, Mark, Christopher Ely and Melissa K. Stockdale (eds). 2010. *Space, Place, and Power in Modern Russia: Essays in the New Spatial History.* DeKalb, Illinois: Northern Illinois University Press.

Bogdanov, D. 1909. *Putevoditel' po Vladivostoku i promysly Primorskoy oblasti, Kamchatki i Sakhalina.* Vladivostok.

Bochenkov, V. and A. Miasnikov. 2012. *Rossiiskie zheleznye dorogi na starinnoi pochtovoi otkrytke. Al'bom,* Moscow: Izdatel'skii dom 'Zheleznodorozdnoe Delo'.

Borzunov, Valentin F. 2001. *Transsibirskaia magistral' v mirovoi politike velikikh derzhav, v 2-kh tomakh.* Moscow: MIIT.

Cosgrove, Denis E. 1997. *Social Formation and Symbolic Landscape,* 2nd ed. Madison, WI: University of Wisconsin Press.

Deviat'airova I.G. 1994. 'V.K. Ettel'. K biographii illiustratora omskikh izdanii'. In *Tret'i Makushenskie chtenia 12–14 Maia v Omske*, pp. 239–242. Novosibirsk.

Dmitriev-Mamonov, Aleksandr and A.F. Zdiarskii (eds). 1914. *Putevoditel' po Velikoi sibirskoi zheleznoi doroge.* St Petersburg: Tipografiia I. Shurei.

Dmitriev-Mamonov, A.I. and A.F. Zdiarskii (eds). 1900. *The Guide to Great Siberian Railway. Published by the Ministry of Ways of Communication.* St Petersburg: Typography of the Artistic Printing Society.

Dolgorukov, V.A. 1903–1904. *Putevoditel' po vsei Sibiri i Aziatskim vladeniiam Rossii: God 7.* Tomsk: Parovaia tipo-litografiia P.I. Makushina.

Ely, Christopher. 2002. *This Meager Nature: Landscape and National Identity in Imperial Russia.* DeKalb: Northern Illinois University Press.

Fomenko, S.M. 1910–1911. *Sputnik po Dal'nemu Vostoku: Zabaikal'e, Amurskii krai, Primorskaia oblast', Kamchatka i Sakhalin, Man'chzhuria, Mongolia, Kitai, Koreia i Iaponiia. Goroda i porty: Adresno-Spravochnyi Otdel. Angliiskie i iaponskie slova i frazy: Plany Vazhneishikh Gorodov.* Kharbin: Tipographiia Kitaisko-Vostochnoi Zheleznoi Dorogi.

Fraser, John Forster. 1902. *The Real Siberia.* London: Cassell and Company, Ltd. http://www.friends-partners.org/oldfriends/mes/books/fraser/siberia.htm

Gailing, Ludger and Marcus Leibenath. 2015. 'The Social Construction of Landscapes: Two Theoretical Lenses and Their Empirical Applications'. *Landscape Research* **40** (2): 123–138.

Gorsuch, Anne E. and Diane P. Koenker (eds). 2006. *Turizm: The Russian and East European Tourist under Capitalism and Socialism.* Ithaca, NY: Cornell University Press.

Gur'ev, N.A. and V.A. Dolgorukov (eds). 1895. *Putevoditel' po vsei Sibiri i Sredne-Aziatskim vladeniiam Rossii s podrobnym dorozhnikom. Opisanie gorodov i raznykh mestnostei. Dostoprimechatel'nosti. Svedeniia o rechnykh i sukhoputnykh soobshcheniiakh. Sudoproizvodstvo i sudoustroistvo. Sputnik po mineral'nym vodam Aziatskoy Rossii s prilozheniiami.* Tomsk: V.A. Dolgorukov.

Hausmann, Guido. 2009. *Mütterchen Wolga: Ein Fluss als Erinnerungsort vom 17. bis zum frühen 20. Jahrhundert.* Frankfurt: Campus Verlag.

Hsu, Chia Yin. 2006. 'A Tale of Two Railroads: "Yellow Labor," Agrarian Colonization, and the Making of Russianness at the Far Eastern Frontier, 1890s–1910s'. *Ab Imperio* **3**: 217–53.

Hsu, Chia Yin. 2012. 'Frontier Urban and Imperial Dreams: The Chinese Eastern Railroad and the Creation of a Russian Global City, 1890s–1917'. In J. Randolph and E.M. Avrutin (eds), *Russia in Motion: Cultures of Human Mobility Since 1850*, pp. 43–62. Urbana, IL: University of Illinois Press.

Il'in, Iu. I. (ed.). 2005. *Sozdanie velikogo sibirskogo puti. V 2-kh tomakh.* St Petersburg: Gruppa kompanii 'Evrosib'.

Alexandra Bekasova and Ekaterina Kalemeneva

Instruktsiia nomer 1. Zaveduiushchim i brigadam sibirskikh poezdov priamogo uskoren- nogo soobshcheniia. 1905. St Petersburg: Tipografiia Kraiz.

Iudin, A.V. 2009. *Transsibirskaia magistral'. Putevoditel'.* OOO Krasivaia strana. https:// lib.rin.ru/book/transsibirskaja-magistral-putevoditel_aleksandr-judin/text/

Kel'ner, Andrei. 2015. 'Liternyi poezd "Severnyi ekspress" – mezhdu mirom i voinoi (1884–1914)'. *Quaestio Rossica.* No. 1: 109–128.

Kiseleva, Liubov' (ed.). 2008. *Putevoditel' kak semioticheskii ob"ekt.* Tartu: Tartu Ülikooli kirjastus.

Klark, I.S. 1906. *Sputnik po Man'chzhurii, Amuru i Ussuriiskomu kraiiu. Vypusk 1. Let- nee dvizhenie 1906 goda. Sostavil nachal'nik kontory dvizheniia ussuriiskoi zheleznoi dorogi.* Vladivostok: Tipografiia Primorskogo oblastnogo pravleniia.

Koenker, Diane. 2013. *Club Red: Vacation Travel and the Soviet Dream.* Ithaca, NY: Cornell University Press.

Kolotilo, L.G. and V.G. Anrienko. 2005. *Transbaikal'skii perekrestok: problemy trans- portnykh putei i zheleznodorozhnoi paromnoi perepravy cherez ozero Baikal na rubezhe XIX – XX vekov.* St Petersburg: Nauka.

Koshar, Rudy. 2000. *German Travel Cultures.* Oxford: Berg.

Kostin, V.M., Iakovenko, A.V. and S.S. Bykova (eds). 2013. *Vsevolod Alekseevich Dol- gorukov: Sbornik materialov.* Tomsk: TOUNB im. A.S. Pushkina.

Kratkii putevoditel' na Dal'nii Vostok po sploshnomu zheleznodorozhnomu puti. Moskva- Vladivostok-Port-Artur-Pekin i Obratno. 1902. St Petersburg: Tipografiia E.E. Novitskogo.

Kusber, Jan. 2008. 'Mastering the Imperial Space: The Case of Siberia. Theoretical Approaches and Recent Directions of Research'. *Ab Imperio* 4: 52–74.

Lekan, Thomas and Thomas Zeller (eds). 2005. *Germany's Nature: Cultural Landscapes and Environmental History.* New Brunswick, NJ: Rutgers University Press.

Livingstone, David N. 2003. *Putting Science in Its Place: Geographies of Scientific Knowledge.* Chicago: University of Chicago Press.

Lukoianov, I. V. 2008. *'Ne Otstat' ot Derzhav…' Rossiia na Dal'nem Vostoke v kontse XIX – Nachale XX vekov.* St Petersburg: Nestor-Istoriia.

Lykhin, Iu. P. and I.R. Khenok (eds). 2001. *Khudozhnik Konstantin Pomerantsev: Pis'ma. Dokumenti. Vospominania.* Irkutsk, Izdatel'stvo IGEA.

Lywood, William G. 2009. 'From Russia's Orient to Russia's Riviera: Reimagining the Black Sea Coast Caucasus from Romantic Literature to Early Tourist Guidebooks'. Master's thesis, Ohio State University.

Marks, S.G. 1995. 'Conquering the Great East: Kulomzin, Peasant Resettlement, and the Creation of Modern Siberia'. In Stephen Kotkin and David Wolff (eds), *Rediscovering Russia in Asia*, pp. 23–39. Armonk, NY: M.E. Sharpe.

Trans-Siberian 'Landscapes of Transportation'

Mauch, Christof and Thomas Zeller (eds). 2008. *The World beyond the Windshield: Roads and Landscapes in the United States and Europe.* Athens: Ohio University Press.

McReynolds, Louise. 2003. *Russia at Play: Leisure Activities at the End of the Tsarist Era.* Ithaca, NY: Cornell University Press.

McReynolds, Louise. 2006. 'The Prerevolutionary Russian Tourist: Commercialization in the Nineteenth Century'. In A.E. Gorsuch and D.P. Koenker (eds), *Turizm: The Russian and East European Tourist Under Capitalism and Socialism,* pp. 17–42. Ithaca, NY: Cornell University Press.

Mezhdunarodnoe obshchestvo spal'nykh vagonov i skorykh poezdov. Raspisanie 1908–09. Zimnee dvizhenie sibirskogo ekspressa. Moskva. Irkutsk. Dal'nii. Vladivostok. Port-Artur. Pekin. 1903–1909. St Petersburg: Tipo-litografiia Ts. Kraiz.

Na Dal'nii Vostok cherez Sibir'. Leto 1910. 1910. St Petersburg: Tipografiia A.F. Shtol'tsenburga.

Printseva, G. A. 2011. *Sibirskii put' Pavla Piasetskogo.* St Petersburg: Izdatel'stvo Gosudarstvennogo Ermitazha.

Putnik (N.N. Lender). 1914. *Vseobshchii illiustrirovannyi putevoditel'. Glavneishie zheleznodorozhnye marshruty i morskie puteshestviia.* St Petersburg: Tipografiia Suvorina 'Novoie Vremia'.

Remnev, A.V. 2007. 'Rossiia i Sibir' v meniaiushchemsia prostranstve Imperii (XIX – nachalo XX veka)'. In L.M. Dameshek, A.V. Remnev (eds), *Sibir' v sostave Rossiyskoy imperii.* Moscow: Novoe Literaturnoe Obozrenie, pp. 286–319.

Remnev, A.V. 2007. 'Siberia and the Russian Far East in the Imperial Geography of Power'. In Jane Burbank, Mark von Hagen and Anatolyi Remnev (eds), *Russian Empire: Space, People, Power, 1700–1930,* pp. 425–454. Bloomington: Indiana University Press.

Remnev, A.V. 1991. 'Uchastie Komiteta sibirskoi zheleznoi dorogi vo Vsemirnoi vystavke 1900 goda v Parizhe'. In *Khozaistvennoe osvoenie Sibiri. Istoriia, istoriografiia, istochniki. Vypusk 1.* Tomsk: Izdatel'stvo Tomskogo Universiteta.

Rutzinskaia, Irina. 2014. *Putevoditel' kak fenomen massovoi kul'tury: Obrazy Rossiiskikh regionov v provintsial'nykh putevoditeliakh vtoroi poloviny XIX – nachala XX veka.* Moscow: URSS.

Saunders, David. 2016. 'Icebreakers in Anglo-Russian Relations (1914–21)'. *The International History Review* **38** (4): 814–829.

Schenk, Frithjof Benjamin. 2010. 'Mastering Imperial Space? The Ambivalent Impact of Railway Building in Tsarist Russia'. In J. Leonhard and U. von Hirschhausen (eds), *Comparing Empires: Encounters and Transfers in the Long Nineteenth Century,* pp. 60–77. Göttingen: Vandenhoeck & Ruprecht.

Alexandra Bekasova and Ekaterina Kalemeneva

Schenk, Frithjof Benjamin. 2013. 'Universal'noe vremia versus local'nye vremena: zheleznye dorogi i spory o vremiaischislenii v Rossii (1870–1910)'. In E.Vishlenkova and D. Sdvizhkov (eds), *Izobretenie veka. Problemy i modeli vremeni v Rossii i v Evrope XIX stoletiia*, pp. 131–147. Moscow: NLO.

Schenk, Frithjof Benjamin. 2016. *Poezd v sovremennost': mobil'nost' i sotsial'noe prostranstvo Rossii v vek zheleznykh dorog*. Translated by M. Lavrinovich. Moscow: Novoe literaturnoe obozrenie.

Schillings, P. and A. van Wickeren. 2015. 'Towards a Material and Spatial History of Knowledge Production. An Introduction'. *Historical Social Research / Historische Sozialforschung* **40** (1): 203–218.

Schivelbusch, Wolfgang. 1987. *The Railway Journey: The Industrialization of Time and Space in the Nineteenth Century*. Berkeley: University of California Press.

Shinkareva, A.P. 1989. 'Knizhnoe izdatel'stvo M.E. Stozha 'Irisy' i ego rol' v kul'turnoi zhizni Irkutska nachala XX veka'. In *Kniga v Sibiri (konets XVIII – nachalo XX vekov). Sbornik nauchnykh trudov*. Novosibirsk: GNTB.

Shinkareva, A.P. 2011. 'Stanovlenie i razvitie izdatel'skogo dela v Irkutske (XIX – nachalo XX veka)'. Kand. Diss. (Avtoreferat). Irkutsk State University.

Siegelbaum, Lewis H. and Leslie P. Moch. 2014. *Broad Is My Native Land: Repertoires and Regimes of Migration in Russia's Twentieth Century*. Ithaca, NY: Cornell University Press.

Stolberg, Eva-Maria. 2004. 'The Siberian Frontier between "White Mission" and "Yellow Peril", 1890s–1920s'. *Nationalities Papers* **32** (1): 165–182.

Stozh, Mikhail. 1903. *Raspisanie poezdov pochtovykh, passazhirskikh, a ravno i skorykh (ekspress) ili Sputnik passazhira po sibirskim zheleznym dorogam: Sibirskoi, Zabaikal'skoi, Kitaiskoi-vostochnoi, Ussuriiskoi. Zimnee dvizhenie 1903–1904*. Irkutsk: Tipolitigrafiia M.P. Okuneva.

Stozh, Mikhail. 1904. *Zheleznodorozhnyi sputnik po Zabaikal'skoi zheleznoi doroge*. Irkutsk: Irisy.

Stozh, Mikhail. 1910. *Sputnik po Zabaikail'skoi zheleznoi doroge s raspisaniem vsekh poezdov*. Irkutsk: Irisy.

Stozh, Mikhail. 1910. *Zheleznodorozhnyi Sputnik po Zabaikal'skoi zheleznoi doroge*. Irkutsk: Tipografiia Irkutskogo tovarishchestva pechatnogo dela.

Stozh, Mikhail. 1914. *Slovar' sibirskikh pisatelei, poetov i uchenykh: v 4 chastiakh*. Irkutsk: Irisy.

Stozh, Mikhail. 1915. *Kak vospet Baikal v stikhakh i proze*. Irkutsk: Irisy.

Stozh, Mikhail. 1917. *Illiustrirovannyi sputnik po Sibiri i Dal'nemu Vostoku s kartoiu*. Irkutsk: Irisy.

Tissot, Laurent. 2003. 'Construction d'une industrie touristique au 19e et 20e siècles. Perspectives internationales'. In L. Tissot (ed.), *Development of a Tourist Industry in the 19th and 20th Centuries. International Perspectives*. Neuchâtel: Editions Alphil.

V.G. 1916. 'Sibirskaia bibliografiia'. *Sibirskaia letopis'. Zhurnal istorii, arkheologii, geografii, etnografii, kul'tury i obshchestvennosti Sibiri, Srednei Asii i Dal'nego Vostoka.* No. 6–8: 368–71.

Withers, Charles W. J. 2009. 'Place and the Spatial Turn in Geography and in History'. *Journal of the History of Ideas* 4 (70): 637–58.

Zeller, Thomas. 2007. *Driving Germany: The Landscape of the German Autobahn, 1930–1970*. New York, Oxford: Berghahn Books.

Zuelow, Eric G.E. 2015. *A History of Modern Tourism*. Basingstoke: Palgrave Macmillan.

Zuelow, Eric G.E. (ed.). 2011. *Touring beyond the Nation: A Transnational Approach to European Tourism History*. Farnham: Ashgate.

11

THE ENVIRONMENTAL HISTORY OF LAKE BAIKAL

Arkady Kalikhman and Tatiana Kalikhman

Translated by Chase McDaries with Angela Brintlinger

In 1991, a Soviet-American-Canadian expedition called 'Superior-Baikal Connect' undertook its first stage of cooperative research, as members paddled kayaks around the oldest, deepest, and largest (by volume) freshwater lake on the planet. They aimed to acquaint themselves with Lake Baikal, inspecting its natural features and learning how the people in surrounding cities and towns lived. The following year, having become a Russian-American-Canadian expedition after the end of the Soviet Union, the group undertook a second stage of cooperation with a similar tour of Lake Superior.[1] During the circumnavigation of Baikal, we – the leaders of the Soviet, later Russian, team – hoped to compare the testimony of scientists and specialists who worked to protect the lake with our own observations as well as the stories of local people, whose concerns formed the basis of our inquiry. An analogous programme was carried out at Lake Superior, where we visited several universities, metallurgical and pulp factories, residents of cities and towns and representatives of the indigenous peoples.[2]

The Superior-Baikal Connect expedition on the sister lakes made it clear that Lake Baikal had been greatly preserved in comparison to Lake Superior by the inaccessibility of a sizable part of its shore and, to a lesser extent, by human efforts to protect its ecosystem. It became obvious that, over the past several decades, the sister lakes had moved in opposite directions in terms of environmental policy. If the Clean Water Act, adopted in the United States in 1972, had helped reduce the number of polluting industries on the banks of Lake Superior with the closing of two dozen pulp and paper mills, then on Baikal, the opposite was true. The most serious blow to the latter's ecosystem was the construction of the Irkutsk Hydroelectric Power Station (Irkutsk GES)

---

1.   Huntoon, 'Superior-Baikal Connect', p. 2.
2.   Rennicke, 'Montana with an Ocean', pp. 38-47.

dam on the Angara River 65 kilometres from its source in Lake Baikal, which increased the level of water in the lake by more than a metre in 1960. Other environmentally damaging events included the opening in 1966 of the Baikal'sk Pulp and Paper Plant, which discharged conventionally-treated production effluents into the lake;[3] the use of cigar-rafts for transporting timber along the lake, a practice which continued almost until the end of the Soviet era; and the extension in 1978 of the Baikal-Amur Mainline (BAM) to the banks of Lake Baikal and the simultaneous construction of Severobaikal'sk, a city intended to house 30,000 inhabitants.

Our American and Canadian colleagues were surprised that we could not see solutions that seemed obvious to them. If the damage from the Baikal plant was apparent to everyone, as even its deputy director agreed when he met with us, then why not close the plant and have people move to other cities such as Bratsk and Ust-Ilimsk with analogous industries? On Lake Superior, similar factories had been closed in ten towns. Our colleagues were also surprised that we objected to the construction of a main road around Baikal, which would permit the monitoring of environmentally sensitive territories and the swift removal of waste from coastal settlements. But we believed that the more difficult it was to access the shore, the better.

We in turn could neither understand nor agree with our North American colleagues' views on the activities of public environmental organisations around Lake Superior. Not only national and provincial parks officials, but also public organisations were supporting the Lake Superior Center expedition from Duluth, Minnesota, in carrying out our mission. At the time, we simply did not understand the significant role such organisations could play in the governments of democratic countries. On the other hand, we did marvel at the huge grain elevators we saw on the banks of Thunder Bay, Ontario, where the Canadian organisers of our expedition met our kayaks. For many years these powerful elevators stored grain for shipment to the Soviet Union on dry cargo ships, and we remembered that in 1984 alone our country purchased more than 46 million tons of grain from abroad.

We were struck by the fact that many of those we met in Canada and the United States knew about Lake Baikal's origins, its geology and especially its depth. The *National Geographic* magazine photographer who accompanied us for several days explained why: one month earlier, the June 1992 issue had included an article entitled 'The World's Great Lake'.[4] No such article about

---

3.   See the chapter by Elena Kochetkova in this volume.
4.   Belt, 'The World's Great Lake'.

Arkady Kalikhman and Tatiana Kalikhman

Lake Superior had appeared for Russian readers, and thus we were surprised that everyone in the United States called Lake Superior the largest freshwater lake in the world.

Before the expedition, of course, we knew the main characteristics of the sister lakes well, but only after closely comparing Lake Baikal with Lake Superior over the expedition's two years did our understandings of Lake Baikal change significantly. This study altered our view of its condition, of its role in people's lives and the role of people in the life of the lake, and most importantly, of the problems of ecological conservation.

The history of human interaction with Baikal has long attracted researchers in the natural sciences and humanities. We have spent the majority of our careers travelling and studying the lake and its watershed. In this chapter we explore the history of economic development around Lake Baikal and the growth of new ideas on environmental policy and the protection of the lake. We examine these topics with the help of a table of historical events, which permits us to combine both synchronic and diachronic research methods. The strict boundaries of each of the table's cells permit an objective consideration that leaves the sacred, mystical, emotional and mythical aspects of the lake to one side in favour of scientific ones.

Humans and Baikal: A Matrix of Historical Events

Russia's only federal law devoted to a specific geographic location protects Lake Baikal. And on 7 December 1996, at its 20th session, in Merida, Mexico, UNESCO's World Heritage Committee named Lake Baikal a World Heritage Site.[5] The history of the development of Lake Baikal and the lives of people on its shores, as described in archaeological and written sources, can be systematised using a historical matrix (see Table 11.1, below). This arrangement has helped us to discover:

- The arbitrary or pre-determined nature of events, phenomena and institutions
- The timeliness, prematurity, or belatedness of events, phenomena and institutions
- The reasons for zero content in certain cells of the matrix
- Predictions of future phenomena and events

---

5.   T. Kalikhman and A. Kalikhman, 'Lake Baikal', pp. 122-7; UNESCO, 'Lake Baikal'.

The Environmental History of Lake Baikal

Table 11.1. Humans and Baikal: A matrix of historical events.

Time Period	Peoples and Empires	Notable Individuals	Economic Development, Fishing/Boating Technology	Environmental Impacts	Research and Science	Protection, Safeguards	Laws and Legislation
200 BCE– 200 CE	Huns		The ancient settlement Ivol'ginsk				
6th– 10th centuries	Turkic khanates		Kurumchinsk blacksmiths				
10th– 12th centuries	Kurykans		Ol'khon Island				
13th– 16th centuries	Mongol Empire		Gorodishcha (fortified settlements), burial sites				
1600s	Evenks (Tungus), Ekhirit, Bulgat, Khori, Cossacks and Russians	K. Ivanov, V. Kolesnikov, I. Pokhabov, I. Galkin	Verkholensk, Verkhnean-garsk, Barguzin and Kabansk forts. Row boats		N.G. Spathari, E.Y. Ides, P. Golovin, S.U. Remezov		Siberian *Prikaz*
1700s	Buriats, Evenks and Russians		The Siberian Road (*Trakt*). Seines, boats, fish production		D.G. Messerschmidt, J.G. Gmelin, P.S. Pallas, J.G. Georgi, A. Pushkarev		The decrees of Peter I, Catherine II
1800– 1850	*Inorodtsy* (non-Russian minorities in Imperial Russia)	M.M. Speranskii G.S. Batenkov, the Decembrists, S. Petőfi, W. Küchelbecker, exiled Poles	South Shore Road (*Trakt*), Bol'shie Koty – gold mining, lime extraction, Baikal Shipping Company	Sable extermination	G.S. Batenkov, G. Radde		The Siberian decree, Charter on the management of *inorodtsy*

Arkady Kalikhman and Tatiana Kalikhman

Time Period	Peoples and Empires	Notable Individuals	Economic Development, Fishing/Boating Technology	Environmental Impacts	Research and Science	Protection, Safeguards	Laws and Legislation
19th century up to 1900	Polish exiles, Old Believers (separatists from Russian Orthodox Church)		Trans-Siberian Railway, monasteries, bishophouses – fishing, steamboats	Deforestation, the decline of the fur-bearing animals and fish, the earthquake of 1861	I.D. Cherski, A.L. Chekanovskii, B.T. Dybowski, V.A. Godlewski, V.A. Obruchev		Fishing Rules
1900–1917		G.G. Doppel'mair, K.A. Zabelin, M.A. Novomeiskii	The Circum-Baikal Railway, *Baikal* and *Angara* ice-breakers	The decline of Omul, Baikal sturgeon and taimen	V.B. Shostakovich, V.Ch. Dorogostaiskii, G.Iu. Vereshchagin	Barguzin *Zapovednik*	
1940		G.Iu. Vereshchagin	Iaroslavskii Shipyard, Komsomolets and Khuzhir Fisheries	Plan for damming the Angara River	The Baikal Commission, Baikal Limological Station		
1960		M.M. Kozhov	Sliudianka and Listvianka (port towns)	Rise of the water level	Irkutsk Scientific Centre of the Academy of Sciences	Reduction in the size of the Barguzin *Zapovednik*	Decree on the closure of *zapovedniks*
1970	Baikal'sk Pulp and Paper Plant builders/workers		Irkutsk GES, Baikal'sk Pulp and Paper Plant	Molev timber rafting, waste from the Baikal'sk Pulp and Paper Plant		Baikal *Zapovednik*, Frolikha and Kabansk federal *zakazniks*; Kochergatsk and Kurtunsk regional *zakazniks*	

The Environmental History of Lake Baikal

Time Period	Peoples and Empires	Notable Individuals	Economic Development, Fishing/Boating Technology	Environmental Impacts	Research and Science	Protection, Safeguards	Laws and Legislation
1980	North Baikal builders, BAM (Baikal–Amur Mainline)		BAM, Severobaikal'sk, the vessels *Comet, Meteor* and *Komsomolets*	Decline in Omul fishing, Baikal–Amur Mainline outlet to shore	Dives by Pisces VII and XI submersibles1	Verkhneangarsk, Pribaikal and Ol'khon regional *zakazniks*	
1990			Listvianka, Malomor'e, Ol'khon and Vydrino hostels	Molev timber rafting		The Baikal-Lena *Zapovednik*, the Pribaikal and Zabaikal national parks, the liquidation of the Peschanaia and Ol'khon *zakazniks*	The 1987 Resolution, Maximum Permissible Impact (MPI) standards
1996		M.A. Grachev			Neutrino telescope	TerSKOP (Territorial complex scheme for nature protection)	
2000					Baikal deep drilling		The World Heritage Site; Law on the Protection of Lake Baikal
2005			Production of drinking water			GBT (Great Baikal Trail), volunteers, liquidation of the Kurtun *zakaznik*	
2010					Dives by Mir-1 and Mir-2 submersibles		Baikal Natural Territory (BNT) boundaries
2015			Closure of the Baikal'sk Pulp and Paper Plant	Forest fires		Joint directorates of PAs (Protected Areas)	

Arkady Kalikhman and Tatiana Kalikhman

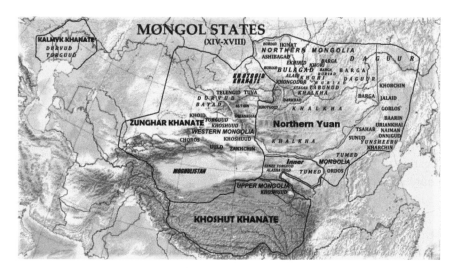

Map 11.1. Distribution of Mongolian-speaking peoples around Lake Baikal and in Siberia in the Fourteenth to Seventeenth Centuries. Source: Wikimedia Commons, 'Mongolia XVII'.

The first tribal alliance south of Lake Baikal was the Hun Empire, a confederation of Turkic-speaking nomadic people who inhabited territories north of China from the second century BCE until the second century CE. In the tenth century and the beginning of the eleventh century, the Turkic khanates were replaced by the Khitan Empire, which united the Mongolian-speaking tribes. At the beginning of the thirteenth century, it was transformed into the Mongol Empire by the conquests of Temujin, who proclaimed himself the ruler of the empire, 'Chinggis Khan'. The main groups of Mongol-speaking peoples who lived around Lake Baikal included the Khori, Bulagat, Ekhirit, Ashibagat, Hongodor and Khalkha (see Map 11.1).

During the second half of the seventeenth century, following much ethnic consolidation, the Bulagat, Ehirit, Ashibaght and Hongodor tribes (joined in the early eighteenth century by the Khori) began to call themselves Buriats, while the Khalkha became the primary foundation of the people who took the general name of Mongols. This uniting of Mongolian-speaking peoples around Baikal took place against the background of the arrival of Russians in Siberia and Baikal from the middle of the seventeenth century. Three waves of human in-migration occurred in the Baikal region. After the Turkic khanates in the fifth through seventh centuries and the Mongolian domination in the twelfth through fifteenth centuries, Russia began to 'expand via Siberia', in the well-known phrase of Mikhail Lomonosov.[6]

Lake Baikal and the Colonisation of Siberia

A look at the earliest surviving documents creates a reliable picture of the state of the territories around Baikal. In a book about his journey through Siberia in 1675, Nicolae Milescu Spathari, a Moldovan noble who headed the Russian legation to Beijing, gave the first description of Lake Baikal and its natural resources. Baikal, though a lake, Spathari wrote, 'can be called a sea', for 'it is great in its length, its width and its depth', and was connected, via the Enisei, with the sea.[7] Ysbrants Ides, a Dutch merchant famously close to Peter I, who was sent in 1692 to Beijing with the next Russian legation, describes Baikal's winter and the people around the lake. Like Spathari, Ides noted that although Baikal's water was fresh, from a distance 'it looked marine-green (*zelenovato-morskoi*) and bright, like in the ocean', and contained seals and large and plentiful fish.[8]

By the end of the seventeenth century, the military actions of tsarist atamans and servicemen (*sluzhilye liudi*)[9] on the lands around Lake Baikal led to the complete suppression of all centres of indigenous resistance that had emerged over the course of the century, using violent tactics such as robbery, extortion, murder, bullying and hostage-taking. According to the historian G.F. Miller, who visited Siberia, forts – the strong points of colonisation – were built in order to bring the recalcitrant people 'under the hand of the high sovereign'.[10] In 1619, a fort was built on the Enisei, another at Ilimsk in 1630, and at Bratsk and Ust'-Kutsk in 1631. Closer to Lake Baikal, more forts were built: Verkholensk in 1641, Verkhneangarsk in 1647, Barguzin in 1648, Irkutsk in 1652 and Verkhneudinsk (Ulan-Ude) in 1666.

Starting in the middle of the seventeenth century, the integration of new lands into the Russian state permitted the country to almost triple its territory, and the term Siberia began to denote the area from the Ob' River to the shores of the Pacific Ocean. Administration of Siberia was entrusted to a special Siberian government department, the Siberian *Prikaz*, created in 1637. In the territories

---

6. Lomonosov, 'Kratkoe Opisanie raznykh puteshestvii po severnym moriam…', p. 498.

7. Spafarii, *Puteshestviia cherez Sibir'*, pp. 99–100.

8. Ides, *Zapiski o russkom posol'stve*, p. 140.

9. A category that included Cossacks, musketeers (strel'tsy) and state servitors of various ranks.

10. Miller, *Istoriia Sibiri*, Vol. 1, p. 365.

near Lake Baikal, the Siberian department was supplemented by steppe offices (*kontors*) – Buriat self-government bodies – created in 1743. In the Baikal area, Balagansk, Verkholensk, Kudinsk, Idinsk and Ol′khon steppe offices emerged, while in the Transbaikal region Oninsk (Khorinsk), Kudarinsk, Selenginsk and Barguzin steppe offices were founded, operating as such from 1743 to 1822.

Thus, by the end of the seventeenth century, Siberia had been completely colonised, the lands and peoples around Baikal becoming a source of revenue for the Russian state. Such an assessment allows us to appraise the transition leading to many years of unsustainable environmental management at Lake Baikal.

Development and Research

The eighteenth century witnessed the development of Lake Baikal, particularly sable hunting, timber harvesting, fishing and research expeditions conducted by Russian and foreign scientists. By decree of Peter I, fisheries became sources of quitrent (*obrok*) not only for the treasury, but also for monasteries and bishops' houses. The Posol′skoe Monastery of the Transfiguration of the Saviour, the very first on Baikal, owned the Selenga Delta fisheries; the Holy Trinity Selenga Monastery owned the fisheries on the southern coast of Lake Baikal; the Kirensk Monastery owned the ones on Chivyrkui Bay; and the Irkutsk Ascension Monastery owned the fisheries north of the Selenga Delta. Intensive sable trading and the legal redefinition of the fur trade for Evenk hunters from a 'duty' into a market commodity led to a sharp decline in the local sable populations in the middle of the century. Similarly, the development of agriculture led to a reduction in forested areas, which was in part connected to a decree issued in 1762, 'On Collecting Taxes in Money from Siberian Peasants', at the beginning of Catherine II's reign. At the same time, timber was cut for mining operations.[11] Despite these substantial changes, traditional practices of careful, sparing use of natural resources were preserved through the end of the century, allowing for the natural restoration of bio-resources.

The politics of punishment and criminal exile, the means of settling Siberia for over three centuries, affected the environmental management of Baikal. From the time Russians appeared there, exile was an important element of colonial expansion. One of the first exiles to Siberia was the archpriest Avvakum, who on his way to the Transbaikal region, crossed the lake in 1654

---

11. *Polnoe sobranie zakonov Rossiiskoi imperii s 1649 goda*, XVI, no. 11633, 28 June 1762, p. 39.

and gave a detailed description of its natural features. The number of exiles in Irkutsk Province continually increased, reaching 17,819 by 1823.

Exiles played a special role in the first fundamental research on Lake Baikal, most especially prominent Polish scientists who were sent there after taking part in the 1863 Polish uprising. The most famous of these is Benedykt Dybowski, who worked with Wiktor Godlewski to describe the region's diverse and numerous species. The two men also studied the relief of the lake-bed, its currents and its water temperature. Geologist Aleksander Czekanowski proposed one of the first tectonic schemes of the Baikal basin and gave a description of the geology of Irkutsk province. Jan Czerski, a geologist and palaeontologist, drafted the first geological map of the shores of Lake Baikal.

In the historical matrix above, the nineteenth century cells include various events, phenomena and institutional transformations. Only one cell remains blank – the one connected with conservation of Lake Baikal's natural habitats and resources. By the end of the century, scientists began to talk about how the extensive and even predatory use of natural resources could not continue. Regulations of that time include: 'Rules for the Fishing Industry during the Run of Omul in the Upper Angara and Kichera Rivers', approved by the Governor-General of Eastern Siberia on 6 May 1872; and 'Rules for the Fishing Industry in Lake Baikal and on the Selenga River', approved by the Amur governor-general on 23 August 1900. In the Barguzin office, timbering at the mouths of the tributaries of the Barguzin River was forbidden, as those forests prevented erosion of the sandy banks. These restrictions cannot be characterised as conservation measures, but they reflected an understanding of environmental consequences.

The first industrial revolution in Russia became a time of anthropogenic transformation of Lake Baikal's southern shoreline and dealt the first blow to the lake's ecosystem. By the end of the century, the Trans-Siberian Railway had come close to the shores, setting in motion various processes: surveying a route for the Circum-Baikal Railway (which was difficult to design and construct, due to the topography); the employment of two large icebreaking vessels as temporary ferry transportation for railway cars; the creation of the village of Sliudianka on the banks of Lake Baikal to serve as a railway junction; and the construction of a floating wooden sectional dock at the village of Listvenichnoe.[12]

South Baikal's pristine shoreline was significantly disturbed by the construction between 1902 and 1904 of more than 300 kilometres of the Circum-

---

12. On the Trans-Siberian and Circum-Baikal Railways, see the chapter by Bekasova and
     Kalemeneva in this volume.

Arkady Kalikhman and Tatiana Kalikhman

Baikal Railway from Port Baikal to Mysovaia. The section between the Port Baikal and Kultuk stations underwent the greatest transformation, although with its 39 tunnels, galleries and retaining walls built into rock cliffs, this section came to be called a 'masterpiece of engineering art'. On the coastline between the Kultuk and Mysovaia stations, the station towns of Sliudianka, Utulik, Murino, Vydrino, Tankhoi, Pereemnaia, Mishikha and Mysovaia were built. The last four of these stations, like the Port Baikal station, were equipped with mooring walls with a 'fork' for mooring an ice breaker-ferry, railway tracks, transitional bridges for loading wagons and locomotives and depots.

The largest vessels on Lake Baikal were the *Baikal* ferry-icebreaker and the cargo-carrying icebreaker *Angara*, which were constructed at the Armstrong Whitworth works in Newcastle upon Tyne, Britain, and assembled and launched at the shipyard in the village of Listvenichnoe in 1900. The *Baikal* was recycled as scrap after being damaged during the Civil War in 1918, and the *Angara* later became a floating museum in Irkutsk. No larger vessels have ever sailed on Lake Baikal.[13]

Figure 11.1. The icebreaking train ferry steamer SS Baikal, Lake Baikal. Source: Tyne & Wear Archives & Museums. Reprinted with permission from Bridgeman Images.

13.   Saunders, 'Icebreakers in Anglo-Russian Relations (1914–21)', p. 818.

Figure 11.2: Plaque to the Baikal indicating its construction in Newcastle upon Tyne. Source: From the collection of the Museum of the Circum-Baikal Railway, Port Baikal. Photograph by the authors.

Transition to Environmental Policy

Even as the railway took shape, F.K. Drizhenko carried out a hydrographic expedition between 1896 and 1902. The expedition provided data for the first complete navigational chart, atlas and general map of Lake Baikal. It also installed two dozen lighthouses and conducted deep-water, magnetic and astronomical observations. The scientists A.V. Voznesenskii and V.B. Shostakovich from the Irkutsk Magnetic and Meteorological Observatory established meteorological stations on the shores in Listvenichnoe, Bolshoe Goloustnoe, Upper Mishikha, Mysovaia and Kabansk for conducting periodic climate observations. The work of ichthyologists helped explain the reduction of fishing yields and other problems of the industry. The reasons for the trending decrease of the omul[14] in size and weight remained unclear, but the results of predatory sturgeon fishing were obvious. The population of sturgeon in Baikal has not been restored to this day. V.A. Obruchev, the first state geologist of Siberia, continued geological studies of the Baikal basin. The Academy of Sciences established the Commission for the Study of Baikal, which included academicians L.S. Berg, V.A. Obruchev

---

14. The omul (*Coregonus migratorius georgi*) is an endemic and iconic fish species that served as a staple food for people around Baikal.

and A.N. Severtsov, as well as their young colleagues G.Iu. Vereshchagin and V.Ch. Dorogostaiskii.

The year 1916 is considered to be the beginning of systematic ecological preservation of Lake Baikal, after the Russian government established the Barguzin *Zapovednik* (nature reserve) by decree on 29 December 1916 (11 January 1917 new style).[15] This continued, with some changes in emphasis, after the Bolshevik Revolution and subsequent establishment of the Soviet government. In 1925, a permanent expedition, based at Maritui Station, was organised by the Academy of Sciences of the USSR. In 1928, the expedition was named the Baikal Limnological Station of the USSR Academy of Sciences, and G.Iu. Vereshchagin became its director. In 1930, the station moved to the village of Listvianka, where scientific work was conducted year-round by three dozen researchers.

Turning to the table of historical events, it should be noted that, in parallel with the extensive scientific studies of Baikal's natural resources, activities of an opposite nature were planned. This can be characterised by the words of the geneticist V.I. Michurin, who was decorated by both tsarist and Soviet authorities: 'We cannot wait for favours from nature. Our task is to take them from her. Man can and must create new forms of plants better than [those created by] nature.' On the slightest pretext, Bolshevik propaganda would cite the first part of this phrase to justify and implement the purposeful 'conquest' of Baikal. The historical synchronism of the events identified in the Baikal table for the two decades after the revolution in Russia is probably coincidental rather than deterministic. But in our opinion, such an assessment of the events, which were directly related to the final victory of the Bolsheviks in Siberia three years after the Petrograd coup (what the Bolsheviks called the October Revolution of 1917), permits a more accurate evaluation of the results of the subsequent intensive resource exploitation of Lake Baikal, and of the absence before the revolution of conditions that might have led to active conservation.

The Resource Curse of Lake Baikal

We borrow this phrase, the 'resource curse' of Lake Baikal, from the 2003 book by US scholars Fiona Hill and Clifford Gaddy, whose work was retitled for Russian-language publication as *The Siberian Burden: Miscalculations of Soviet*

---

15. On the origins of the Barguzin Nature Reserve, see the chapter by Breyfogle in this volume.

Planning and the Future of Russia.[16] Ol'khon Island offers an excellent example of why the phrase works for Baikal. For the residents of Ol'khon, the rise of the Bolsheviks and the establishment of Soviet power in the country turned out to be a continuation and intensification of the former colonial policy, now with a communist ideology. The offensive label *inorodets* – meaning 'foreigner' or 'non-Russian,' the term coined by M.M. Speranskii for subjects of non-Slavic origin and the indigenous peoples of Siberia – finally disappeared. The Bolsheviks introduced a new status for collective farmers with compulsory labour service. Ten years later, the labour shortage was augmented by drafting people and by establishing a forced labour camp (still not officially recognised as such), an approach that had been planned by the tsarist authorities back in 1910 but was not developed at that time.[17]

The Soviet government imposed its own economic priorities on the island, leading to the seizure of vital natural resources from the island's inhabitants. This policy differed little from that of the tsarist government, which used the term *iasak* (a tax paid in kind), retitled by the Bolsheviks as a 'tax'. For example, the fish resources of the Maloe More Strait were placed at the disposal of the newly created Goslov-Malomor'e State Fishery Factory and Trust. The previous grant of exclusive control of the fish to the Ol'khon Buriats, as requested by local representatives in early 1917, became irrelevant. In 1932, in order to develop a 'highly productive raw material base', the Goslov-Malomor'e fish processing factory was constructed and facilities with equipment for pickling, smoking and packing fish were built in Zagli Bay, located in the coastal zone of the Tashkai *ulus* (settlement). Peripheral fish processing docks were established near the *uluses* of Semisosensk and Khuzhir. On the other shore, similar stations appeared near Kurma and Onguren, which also processed fish from collective farm brigades. The population was forced to collectivise all livestock, land cultivation tools and fishing equipment. By the end of 1932, a number of collective farms had been created: 'Ulan-Khushin', 'Land Reform', '10 years of the Buriat Central Executive Committee' and the fish *artel* (cooperative work unit or association) 'Ulan Ol'khon' ('Red Ol'khon'). These collective farms, together with 'Victory' in Khadai, 'Heroes of the Arctic' in Ialga, 'Kirov' in Semisosna, and 'Kaganovich' in Kharantsi (which appeared later), remained unprofitable and were subsidised up until the end of the Soviet Union.

In 1937, fish processing plants were built in Khuzhir Bay, north of the Khuzhir *ulus*, and the Goslov office was transferred there from Tashka. The

---

16. Hill and Gaddy, *The Siberian Curse.*
17. A. Kalikhman, Bencharova and T. Kalikhman, *Ol'khon*, pp. 63–6.

Arkady Kalikhman and Tatiana Kalikhman

constant growth of fish production led to plans to create a large fish processing enterprise with factories for freezing, pickling, smoking and canning. This plant was to become the lead station, combining small production facilities on the western shore of Lake Baikal, including the Malomorsk fish processing plant in Onguren, the Sarma fish farm in Sarma, and the motor and fishing station in Sahurte. In all these efforts, Goslov was struggling to find a resolution to the main and only task posed by the Bolshevik Party for the state fishing industry: increased, more efficient production of fish for wide distribution.

The transformation of the island into a site for uninterrupted, industrial fishing was supplemented by the creation of a mandatory labour zone, or forced labour colony, by the Soviet regime. In 1910, the Governor-General of Eastern Siberia, A.I. Selivanov, had proposed a plan to Tsar Nicholas II entitled 'On the Establishment of a Penal Colony on the island of Ol'khon, the Most Significant of the Islands on Lake Baikal'. Selivanov wrote: 'A very suitable place for such an establishment of supervised exiles could be two islands on Lake Baikal. Namely, Ol'khon Island for political, less important exiles, and the Ushkan'i Islands for more important ones; it would be necessary to build barracks for them, prepare food stores and create a guard regime'. The tsar's resolution stated: 'Establish now the necessary arrangements on the island of Ol'khon, so as to exempt other areas of Siberia from the settlement of a criminal element'.[18] However, the prison colony on Ol'khon was not built at this time. In a report for 1910 and 1911, the governor of Irkutsk Province, L.M. Kniazev, stated that 'the treasury expense to maintain and guard such colonies, in particular an Ol'khon colony, given the natural conditions, is not feasible, nor can the labour of such colonists be productively exploited'. Only in 1937 did a colony for prisoners on the island of Ol'khon begin to form in Semisosna, and later that year it was moved to the Peschanaia Road (*Trakt*) near Niurgan Guba Bay. Thus, some thirty years later, a correctional labour colony was finally built that was to partially realise the penitentiary plans of the tsarist authorities. The first 'colonists' were de-kulakised peasants from the European part of the country, later joined by 'enemies of the people' from the Baikal region.

Another example of the resource curse of Lake Baikal was the potential of its water energy, as the source of the Angara River. In the first 'Plan for the

---

18. Kolosok, 'Usloviia otbyvaniia nakazaniia zakliuchennimi Irkutskoi gubernii v kontse XIX–nachale XX vv.', pp. 26–7.

Electrification of the RSFSR',[19] adopted in 1920, the Angara River is mentioned once, ranking second after the Lena River in the list of the country's sources of potential water energy. In 1930, I.G. Aleksandrov and V.M. Malyshev, well known scientists of hydraulic engineering and hydropower, published an article entitled 'The Angara River Challenge' in the journal *Planned Economy* (*Planovoe khoziaistvo*) wherein they stated: 'An ideal reservoir for the Angara is Lake Baikal, which allows for almost unlimited regulation and ensures the maximum amount of primary (constant) energy ... Of particular interest is the area of the source of the Angara, where it is necessary to build a dam in order to use Baikal as a reservoir'.[20] In 1931, the book *The Angara Challenge* issued a specific verdict on the fate of the Angara River and Lake Baikal.[21]

V.M. Malyshev's 1935 book *A Hypothesis for Resolving the Angara Problem* laid out a plan to build hydroelectric power stations on the Angara River and its tributaries and to permit Lake Baikal to rise and flood its shores and the Angara.[22] Without hesitation, the author articulated the consequences of raising the water level of Lake Baikal on the ecosystem:

> Given the lake's control value, it is highly desirable to raise its level, which on the one hand will save a considerable amount of water for use and, on the other hand, will facilitate manipulation of control. The rise will increase the pressure at the Baikal (Irkutsk) hydropower station ... We take the mark of the average multi-year level raised by 2 m against its norm, that is, the normal raised level of the lake Baikal with a full reservoir – 457.37 m ... Flooding the mouths of the rivers Selenga, Barguzin, Upper Angara should not affect the omul run (omul is the main fish product of Lake Baikal). Flooding the isthmus separating Chivyrkui Bay from Barguzin Bay and creating shallow-water areas there should have a positive effect on fish farming ... Twelve settlements along the Angara, consisting of a total of 500 households, will be in the flood zone. The villages of Larchivnichnoe, Goloustnoe, Ust'-Barguzin and Dushkachan on the shores of Lake Baikal, several villages near the Proval Gulf in the delta of Selenga and some Buriat *uluses* will be affected. Cultivated and arable land will fall into the flood zone only within the residential settlements.[23]

---

19. This plan was overseen by the State Commission for the Electrification of Russia (Gosudarstvennaia komissia po elektrifikatsii Rossii, GOELRO).

20. Aleksandrov and Malyshev, 'Problema reki Angary', p. 215.

21. Aleksandrov, *Problema Angary*.

22. Malyshev, *Gipoteza resheniia*.

23. Malyshev, *Gipoteza resheniia*, pp. 82–3.

The execution of this judgement on Lake Baikal and the valley of the Angara River was postponed by the beginning of World War Two. But the Soviets would return to these plans after the war, when the so-called industrialisation of Lake Baikal began.

Industrialisation

In the pre-war period, the term industrialisation referred to a transition to accelerated production in territories that traditionally had been areas of development. The Soviet government continued to implement plans for industrial expansion in Siberia, but now closer to the shores of Lake Baikal. The shipyard in Listvianka, for example, was capable of building up to five vessels simultaneously, and before its closure, after the fall of the Soviet Union, more than 100 ships were assembled and built there, half of which were barges. So-called 'Iaroslavets' multi-purpose boats were delivered by rail from production facilities in Iaroslavl'. Currently on Lake Baikal there are about 100 of this type of vessel out of more than 400 total vessels, most engaged in servicing tourists.

After the war, the fishing industry maintained very high catch levels for Lake Baikal. Beginning in 1960, the fishing yields began to decrease and, since then, there have been no gains. The correlation between periods of high yields and periods of high water levels in Baikal is well known. These observation data make it possible to distinguish three century-long cycles of lake level fluctuations: 1710 to 1814, 1815 to 1903 and 1904 to the present. The graph below shows yields of omul between 1900 and 2000, compared to the average water levels over the same period.[24]

The step-like rise in the water level by more than one metre from 1958 to 1962 is associated with the construction of the Irkutsk GES dam. According to the graph, it follows that yields above 5,000 tonnes per year were recorded between approximately 1935 and 1960. Fragmentary archival data demonstrate that in the period between 1830 and 1850 catches reached 7,000 to 8,000 tonnes, and 100 years later in 1942 the yield was more than 9,000 tonnes. It is possible that by 2040 there will be another increase in yield, although there are no scientifically substantiated prerequisites for this. Specialists believe that, after the rise in water level in Lake Baikal from 1963 to 1982, the size, weight and total mass of the omul decreased. Subsequently a slow increase in these indicators began and continues to the present.

---

24. Atutov et al., *Gidroenergetika i sostoianie ekosystemy ozera Baikal*, pp. 43, 71; Mamontov, 'Otsenka obshchikh ulovov omulia v Baikale', pp. 76–7.

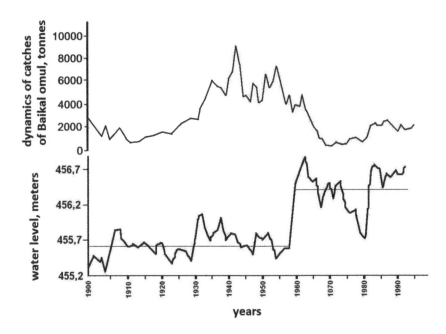

Figure 11.3. Dynamics of omul catches and average water levels from 1900 to 2000. Source: Created by Arkady Kalikhman.

The next stage in the industrialisation of Lake Baikal according to V.M. Malyshev's plan was hydropower.[25] It seems surprising that none of the lake researchers at that time warned about the environmental catastrophe looming over Lake Baikal. Only ten to fifteen years later did they begin to refer to what had happened as a terrible blow to the ecosystem of Lake Baikal and the most significant event in the history of environmental monitoring there. Since 1959, the Irkutsk dam has raised the levels in Baikal and created a new hydrological regime. The lake's fate has since become more dependent on hydropower requirements and less on natural factors.

The technological zone of the hydroelectric complex comprises a flooded area of about 1,230 square kilometres, of which about 600 square kilometres contains valuable economic and natural resources. The flood zone eradicated 141 settlements and 1,712 private homes. Both the shores of the lake and the many coastal geologic forms, which had long been stable, began to erode and collapse, and landslides and screes increased. In the first four to six years, the average annual rate of erosion of the lower banks was three to four metres,

25. Malyshev, *Gipoteza resheniia.*

and the maximum erosion as much as twelve metres. An area measuring 28.5 square kilometres of the lacustrine-litter systems was flooded, which significantly changed environmental conditions for reproduction among shallow-water fish, birds and waterfowl. The natural seasonal cycle of fluctuations in the water level changed significantly, and over the subsequent fifty years the resultant change has forced the fish to adapt to different food supplies and to move spawning grounds. Many scientists directly link the omul's decreasing size and the decline in its yield in the period from 1965 to 1975, clearly visible on the graph, to the increase in Baikal's water level.[26]

We can turn to a book of memoirs dedicated to the scientist G.I. Galazii to see how scientists perceived the events of energy industrialisation.[27] Academician M.N. Kuzmin, author of the first article, writes:

> In connection with the design and construction of the Irkutsk hydroelectric power station – the head power station of the Angarsk cascade – and the anticipated rise in the water level in Lake Baikal, there was a need to predict how its shores would be altered in accordance with the change in the lake's water level. Participating in the multi-purpose expedition of the East Siberian Branch of the USSR Academy of Sciences, G.I. Galazii developed a botanical method for determining the dates of the highest lake levels in the past. With the help of this method, patterns in lake levels and in the alterations of its shores were elucidated, which facilitated the appropriate engineering calculations and necessary forecasts.[28]

Galazii, a future Academician, gave a scientific justification for raising the water level. Both a botanist and a dendrologist, he nonetheless failed to assess the consequences of rising water levels and the regulation of runoff from the lake and the resulting damage to almost all components of the Baikal ecosystem. V.A. Fialkov, director of the Baikal Museum, writes:

> The Baikal station in the 1940s and 1950s performed a large amount of work for the energy ministry and Angarstroi [the Angara Construction Administration], including a huge construction site (a cascade of hydroelectric power stations on the Angara was under construction). The ministry agreed to build a laboratory building and a residential town.[29]

26. Atutov et al., *Gidroenergetika i sostoianie ecosystemy ozera Baikal*, pp. 43, 71; Mamontov, 'Otsenka obshchikh ulovov omulia v Baikale', pp. 76–7.

27. Matiashenko (ed.), *Grigorii Ivanovich Galazii.*

28. Kuzmin and Matiashenko, 'Zhizennyi put' G.I. Galaziia', p. 6.

29. Fialkov, 'Da budet dom!', p. 135.

The Environmental History of Lake Baikal

In 1961, while the water level in Baikal continued to rise, the station was renamed the Limnological Institute of the Siberian Branch of the Academy of Sciences, and Galazii became its director. The builders of the Irkutsk GES thanked Galazii and helped in the construction of the scientific settlement. It is understandable that under this director the institute did not investigate and did not analyse the damage inflicted on Lake Baikal. However, other researchers did.

Another blow to Baikal's ecosystem and another stage in industrialisation came with the construction of the Baikal'sk Pulp and Paper Plant on the southern shore. In 1954, the idea was born to produce high-strength viscose cord for aviation purposes, something only the United States was producing at that time. Over the course of several years, locations were designated on freshwater lakes, near timber sources, for its production in the Soviet Union. In 1959, a site on the shore of Lake Baikal a kilometre east of the mouth of the Solzan River was selected, and construction of the plant began later that year. To the west of this site, the city of Baikal'sk emerged, eventually with a population of about 17,000. In 1966, the plant began to produce viscose pulp, and in 1976 it became the Baikal'sk Pulp and Paper Plant. It is important to note that the Bratsk Cord Cellulose Plant opened in 1965 and the Ust'-Ilim Pulp and Paper Plant – with more than five times the capacity of Baikal plant – opened in 1980. With so many other options, the utter senselessness of having a city and cellulose production on the shores of Baikal is obvious.

This was discussed in 1958, when many scientists for the first time in the history of the Soviet Union opposed plans to locate harmful manufacturing plants on the shore of Baikal. They raised their concerns about the unlimited use of clean water for technological purposes and discharges of treated sewage back into the lake. Against this background, fears that the quality of pulp products would be reduced due to the possible contamination of Baikal water – as a consequence of the erosion of the banks when the water level rose after the construction of the dam at the Irkutsk GES – looked particularly cynical. The authorities promised to create the most effective water treatment facilities in the country, which would prevent the lake's pollution. Monitoring of pollution was conducted by a Baikal'sk laboratory, later named the Institute of Ecological Toxicology. Its task was to demonstrate the absence of significant changes in the composition of phytoplankton and zooplankton under the influence of supposedly treated sewage waters and to show there were no irreversible changes in the ecosystem of the lake as a whole. The conclusions of O.M. Kozhova and the director of the Institute, A.M. Beim, in the book *Ecological Monitoring of Baikal* are characteristic: anthropogenic influence on the lake area adjacent to the city of Baikal'sk is assessed as creating a state of 'ecological well-being'.[30] These scientists made a bold but far from scientific conclusion: 'The condition which has been characterised as environmentally safe is due to the significant dilution of treated sewage in the lake due to the effect of hydrodynamic factors and active self-purification processes of the water'.[31]

The activities of the Baikal'sk Pulp and Paper Plant in the south of the lake during the first decade after its launch and the subsequent regular discharge of treated effluents into Lake Baikal resulted in an area of about thirty square kilometres with a disturbed hydrochemical regime and pollution of bottom sediments. It also changed the hydrobiological and microbiological characteristics of the waters. In terms of discharged sewage volumes, the plant contributed significantly to the overall anthropogenic impact on the coastal water areas. The plant ceased operations at the end of 2008, but started up again in 2010, by decision of the government headed by then Prime Minister Vladimir Putin. The main production and pulping were finally stopped on 13 September 2013. But the territories of the former plant have yet to be reclaimed. In an area of about one square kilometre around the plant's territory, there are fourteen slag-lignin storage tanks with a mass of more than 6.5 million tons, including ash from incineration of sewage sludge and unused chemicals. So far, no optimal technology for processing hazardous waste has been found, and two options were rejected in 2016.

We studied the future of the city of Baikal'sk after the closure of the Baikal'sk Pulp and Paper Plant within the framework of the European TACIS project (Technical Assistance for the Commonwealth of Independent States), which recommended the creation of a tourist infrastructure and a recreation industry based on downhill skiing as an alternative to cellulose production. In 1999 and 2000, a business plan for the development of tourism was developed and the first stage of its implementation was completed. The groundwork laid in 2000 and 2001 for the year-round operation of tourist firms, recreation centres and service enterprises of Baikal'sk remains relevant today.[32]

Construction of BAM was the next disruption of the Baikal ecosystem. A year after the work began on the northern shore of the lake in 1975, a workers' settlement appeared, becoming the city of Severobaikal'sk, with a population of about 30,000 by 1980. After the railway reached Lake Baikal, two fundamen-

---

30. Kozhova and Beim, *Ekologicheskii monitoring Baikala*, p. 75.

31. Ibid., p. 331.

32. A. Kalikhman et al. *Assessment of Business Potential for Tourism in the Southern Lake Baikal Region.*

tally different variants for running the rails were proposed: laying the rails near the lake's coastline or at a distance from the shore through tunnels in the cliffs of the Baikal Ridge spurs. As a temporary solution, the path along the coast was chosen and operated from 1976 to 1989. In 1989, four cape tunnels with a total length of more than five kilometres were opened, moving the railway from the shore of the lake and reducing the risk of oil and other substances spilling into the water because of train accidents. Interestingly, eighty years before the tunnels were built, a coastal section of the Circum-Baikal Railway was laid south of Baikal, which comprised 39 tunnels with a total length of 8.5 kilometres. By comparing the type of portals and tunnels in photographs from 1904 and 1984 (see Figure 11.4), it is possible to judge the change in people's attitudes toward the quality, beauty and aesthetics of coastal structures and toward the preservation of the primordial nature of Baikal's coastline over the years of Soviet power.

Figure 11.4. Portals of the tunnels in the southern (1904, left) and northern (1984, right) Baikal region. Photographs by Arkady Kalikhman.

Returning to our table of historical events, we can give the following assessment of this period of Baikal's industrialisation. The rise in water level and the regulation of the flow from Baikal had a severe impact on its ecosystem, lasting even to this day. The appearance of cellulose production in the south of Baikal can be considered somewhat arbitrary and unnecessary, but, on the other hand, the Baikal'sk Pulp and Paper Plant has become a kind of limiting factor – to use biological terminology – that has deterred the construction of new harmful industries. The plant spurred public environmental movements in the region and the country and caused scientists to begin monitoring discharges into the lake.

Arkady Kalikhman and Tatiana Kalikhman

During the construction of BAM, which began as far back as 1938 and resumed in 1974, the largest city on the shore of the lake appeared. The construction of Severobaikal'sk was utterly ill-conceived. BAM was projected to reach Lake Baikal at the mouth of the Tyia River. The village of Nizhnean-garsk was located only twenty kilometres from that spot and could easily have assumed the functions of a larger transport hub, as it was already a regional centre with a reliable airport and sufficient flatlands at the mouth of the Kichera River. To this day none of the towns and villages on the shore of Lake Baikal, including Severobaikal'sk and Nizhneangarsk, has sufficient wastewater treatment facilities to prevent discharges into the lake, nor do they have sufficient garbage and waste disposal plants, confining themselves rather to landfills for the collection and accumulation of solid domestic waste. Called by alarmists an ecological catastrophe, the anthropogenic pollution in the past few years has been clearly documented.[33]

Concepts of Nature Protection

Discussions of the environmental conservation of Lake Baikal occurred at the end of the nineteenth century and beginning of the twentieth century. Scientists noticed that natural resources had already been partially depleted, and most importantly, no state system existed for protecting the lake. Projects for creating a system of reserves and the actual creation of the Barguzin *Zapovednik* in 1916 happened because of this first concept of protecting the ecosystem of Lake Baikal.

The results of industrial development in the 1950s and 1960s and the exploitation of natural resources in the Baikal and Trans-Baikal regions began to manifest themselves in the degradation of a number of natural complexes in the Baikal basin. Public opinion and scientists' arguments directed against industrial expansion on the shores of Lake Baikal competed with periodic decisions by the Council of Ministers of the USSR. State authorities cleverly used in their declarations the words 'protection and use of natural resources', although in the case of Lake Baikal these should have been separated: *either* protection *or* use. In May 1960, the Soviet Council of Ministers issued Resolution No. 652, 'On the Protection and Use of Natural Resources in the Baikal Basin', with the obligatory installation of treatment plants before the launch of the Baikal'sk Pulp and Paper Plant. In 1969, Decree No. 52, 'On Measures

---

33. Timoshkin, 'Rapid Ecological Change in the Coastal Zone of Lake Baikal (East Siberia)', pp. 487–97.

for the Conservation and Rational Use of Natural Complexes of the Lake Baikal Basin', determined the water protection zone of Lake Baikal within its basin, but lacked mechanisms for its creation. Therefore, in 1971 the Council of Ministers issued a resolution jointly with the Central Committee of the Communist Party of the Soviet Union, 'On Additional Measures to Ensure the Rational Use and Conservation of the Natural Resources of the Lake Baikal Basin', wherein the authorities tried to smooth out the contradiction between environmental conservation and the activities of plants with low efficiency and high energy costs. By resolution of the Central Committee of the Communist Party of the Soviet Union (CPSU) and the Council of Ministers of 1977, 'On Measures to Further Ensure the Rational Use of the Natural Resources of the Lake Baikal Basin', the discharge of untreated sewage into water bodies was to cease altogether and air emissions were to be reduced by 1985. By 1995, all transportation of timber across the lake was to be discontinued. These conditions were not realised. Transportation of wood via cigar rafts required that each raft have a volume of at least 1,000 cubic metres, since with smaller volumes the rafts broke up during stormy conditions. According to data from the press, by 1980 there had been 32 raft accidents with an accumulated loss of 73,000 cubic metres of timber. Log driving was discontinued after the end of the Soviet regime.[34]

Effective concepts of Baikal environmental conservation have been utterly lacking, but, in the very last years of Soviet rule, change finally came by a return essentially to the very first concept. In 1986, the Baikal-Lena *Zapovednik* and the Pribaikal and Zabaikal national parks were created on the shores of Baikal. Earlier, in 1969, the Baikal *Zapovednik* was established. The creation of new and significant protected areas was fundamentally different from 'the use of natural resources'. But the Soviet authorities continued to use their own language, and in 1987, the Central Committee of the CPSU and the Council of Ministers issued Resolution No. 434, 'On Measures to Further Ensure the Rational Use of the Natural Resources of the Lake Baikal Basin in 1987–1995'. Along with this resolution, the Soviet Academy of Sciences presented 'Norms of Permissible Impacts on the Ecological System of Lake Baikal (for the period 1987–1995)'. Although these norms did not reduce negative impacts, they did serve as a conceptual and methodological basis for subsequent developments. The same resolution (No. 434) provided for the creation of a 'territorially-integrated scheme for the protection of nature in the Lake Baikal basin' (*Territorial'naia kompleksnaia skhema okhrany prirody basseina ozera Baikal*, TerKSOP), a funda-

---

34. T. Kalikhman. 'Federal'nyi zakon "Ob okhrane ozera Baikal"', p. 74.

mentally new concept where environmental protection became the dominant focus, and only after this main task was solved would exploitative resource management be allowed.[35]

Our participation in the work on TerKSOP helped us understand that nature protection requires huge financial outlays relative to the entire economy of the region: about one third of revenue would need to be spent on environmental protection. The Baikal basin served as an example of why the global imperative for nature protection, on one hand, and regional needs for industrial and social development, on the other hand, contradict each other. However, the implementation of a large-scale project could not begin in 1990 due to the impending collapse of the Soviet Union and the formation of a new state.[36]

UNESCO World Heritage Site

Our participation in the Baikal TerKSOP project gave us valuable international context and introduced us to a form of grant financing for projects – new to us – provided by US and international environmental funds. The first work with American ecologists was the creation in 1990–1992 of 'A Comprehensive Program of Land Use Policies for the Russian Portion of the Lake Baikal Region', which also was given the ambitious name *Lake Baikal in the Twenty-First Century: A Model of Sustainable Development or Continued Degradation*.[37] In the absence of land legislation at that time in Russia, it was difficult for us to agree with proposals for new land use conditions similar to those in the United States. But we enthusiastically accepted such programme goals as: preserve the purity of Lake Baikal's water for all time; inextricably link sustainable development and environmental protection; preserve the natural ecological processes and biological diversity of the Lake Baikal watershed; achieve UNESCO World Heritage Site designation to reflect the global significance of the Baikal region.[38]

The next international project in which we participated was commissioned by the World Bank and carried out in 1994. It was called the 'Ecotourism Master Plan and Development Plan for Lake Baikal, Russian Federation'. The key underlying objective was to plan ecotourism development such that it:

---

35. *Territorial'naia kompleksnaia skhema okhrany prirody basseina ozera Baikal.*
36. Ibid.
37. Davis (ed.), *The Lake Baikal Region in the Twenty-First Century.*
38. Ibid.

- Did not exceed the ecological, socioeconomic or cultural carrying capacity of fragile – and in some cases unique – plant, animal and human communities of the region

- Provided maximum opportunities and economic benefits to local communities

- Provided maximum benefit to natural areas, particularly the national parks and *zapovedniks* in the Baikal area and Lake Baikal itself, by increasing the incentives and funds available to protect these areas

The project helped to assess the current capacity for six optimal ecotourism areas around Lake Baikal and offered a detailed analysis of the entire study area of 350,000 square kilometres. The overall ecotourism-carrying capacity of the Lake Baikal study area exceeds two million visitors per season, or an average of 18,500 visitors per day. We are still using these figures today as the guideline for building tourist infrastructure for visiting natural areas near Baikal.

The history of the inclusion of Lake Baikal in the list of World Natural Heritage sites began in 1988, when the Soviet Union became the 98th country to sign the 1972 Convention for the Protection of World Heritage. The initiator of the work on the inclusion of Baikal was M.A. Grachev, director of the Limnological Institute. After two earlier appeals, in 1990 Lake Baikal was visited by a group of experts headed by Bernd von Droste, now founding director of the UNESCO World Heritage Centre. Von Droste wrote:

> Our advocacy of World Heritage nomination was well received, but it then took years of preparatory work to settle many outstanding problems concerning the lake's protection. Finally, in 1996, Lake Baikal was inscribed on the World Heritage List as one of the planet's outstanding natural sites.[39]

Baikal was inscribed in the list after one final hurdle was overcome. In early 1996, it was clear that Baikal could not become a World Heritage site as long as the Baikal'sk Pulp and Paper Plant continued to operate. However, hope remained for American investment in a retooling programme for the plant through the Gore-Chernomyrdin Commission, which was designed to enhance Russian-American cooperation in technology, trade and defence. The January session of the commission allocated funds to the American corporation CH2M Hill Companies, Ltd., through USAID, to examine the possibility of converting the plant to other economic activities. The Russian organisation 'Baikal Centre for Environmental and Civil Initiatives' together with the group 'Baikal Watch'

---

39.   von Droste, 'Empowerment of the Convention'; UNESCO, 'Lake Baikal'.

Arkady Kalikhman and Tatiana Kalikhman

of the NGO 'Earth Island Institute' (San Francisco), also received a grant to support local retooling initiatives for the plant.

Working with Academician V.A. Koptiug, Chairman of the Siberian Branch of the Russian Academy of Sciences, and CH2M Hill, along with the Baikal'sk Pulp and Paper Plant, allowed us to identify as optimal a conversion of the plant from pulping technology to chemical thermo-mechanical mass (initialised as CTMM in Russian and CTMP in English). In October 1996, USAID provided information about supporting the proposal of the Koptiug Group for the transition of the plant to the production of CTMP via technology from the Canadian Millar Western Pulp plant. However, on 9 January 1997, Koptiug's report at the meeting of the Governmental Commission for Baikal under the Ministry of Environmental Protection was received negatively, despite substantial arguments in the project's favour. This became Koptiug's last speech, and that evening he died. This loss of supporters for the project to convert the Baikal'sk Pulp and Paper Plant and cease waste discharges into the lake turned out to be irretrievable, and thus the plant 'successfully' continued to operate for another sixteen years.

Against this background, the inclusion of Lake Baikal in the list of World Heritage sites in December 1996 seemed quite deserved, although a lack of information about this in the local media for several months was surprising. It should be emphasised that the size of the new heritage site – Lake Baikal – now an internationally protected natural area, was about 90,000 square kilometres, with a population of about 150,000 on the shores belonging to two regions: the Irkutsk Region and the Republic of Buriatiia. The departmental affiliations of the constituent lands thwarted the effort to find legal approaches to solving problems of unified management, unified legal and institutional conditions. The exact boundaries of the heritage site were not defined, nor were the urbanised regions with towns and villages on the shore included: Kultuk, Sliudianka, Baikal'sk, Babushkin and Severobaikal'sk. For help in solving these problems, we turned to the World Heritage Centre. In the summer of 1997, Baikal planned an official nomination by UNESCO representatives and a methodological seminar for a broad discussion of the problems that had arisen.

This seminar and consultations with representatives of the World Heritage Centre showed that the inclusion of Lake Baikal in the list of World Heritage sites had been somewhat premature. In 1995, the State Duma of the Russian Federation adopted the law 'On the Protection of Lake Baikal', but the law remained in draft status. Therefore, the conventionality and limitations of the applicability of international law for the management of land outside then current Russian legislation was understandable. As a result, the seminar emphasised the urgency of completing work on the law about Baikal, on the maximum permissible impact (MPI) standards and on the definition of exact boundaries, without which the status and protection of the World Heritage site remained uncertain and could not be taken into account in federal level documents.

Figure 11.5. The official recognition of Lake Baikal as a UNESCO World Heritage site (inset) and representatives of UNESCO and other participants of the Baikal Seminar at the Shaman's Rock, Khuzhir, October 1997. The authors are seen to the right. Source: Photograph by Arkady Kalikhman.

The Law on the Protection of Lake Baikal and Tourism

The law 'On the Protection of Lake Baikal' was adopted in 1999. Key to the law is the article that introduced the concept of the Baikal Natural Territory (BNT). BNT includes Lake Baikal, the adjacent water protection zone, its catchment area on the territory of the Russian Federation, specially protected natural areas (PA) adjacent to Lake Baikal and an area up to 200 kilometres

Arkady Kalikhman and Tatiana Kalikhman

wide to the west and northwest of Lake Baikal. The BNT zoning distinguishes three areas:

- The Central Ecological Zone (CEZ) includes Lake Baikal with its islands, the water protection zone adjacent to Lake Baikal and the PAs near Lake Baikal
- The Buffer Ecological Zone (BEZ) encompasses the territory outside the CEZ, which includes the drainage basin of Lake Baikal within Russia
- The Ecological Zone of Atmospheric Influence (EZAI) includes an area outside the drainage basin of Lake Baikal, up to 200 kilometres wide to the west and northwest of it, where economic facilities are located that have a negative impact on the unique ecological system of Lake Baikal

The scheme of BNT ecological zoning uses the Baikal structure defined earlier in TerKSOP and implies the creation of a protected territory with a new status. BNT replaces the usual regulations of nature with the preservation of the natural environment in ecological zones. In 2006, the borders of the BNT, CEZ, BEZ and EZAI were approved. The water protection zone for Lake Baikal under the Water Code of the Russian Federation from 2006 was a 500-metre-wide coastal strip. In 2015, its borders were combined with the borders of CEZ and, accordingly, with the boundaries of the World Heritage site. Strict requirements for the water protection zone restrict the development of settlements in the CEZ and on the shores of Lake Baikal but, so far, the Ministry of Natural Resources and the Environment of the Russian Federation have not permitted the water protection zone to be reduced in size. In reality, these problems will not be solved by changing the width of the water protection zone, but by small changes in the water protection legislation.

After the approval of the CEZ borders, it became possible to continue working on the normative acts necessary to implement the content of all 25 articles of the law 'On the Protection of Lake Baikal'. The 'List of Activities Banned in the CEZ of the BNT', adopted back in 2001, was justified. For more than fifteen years, we have been working on a report entitled 'The organisation of tourism and recreation in the CEZ'. To assess the recreational capacity and tourist loads on natural areas, we use the methodology of Limits of Acceptable Change (LAC), recommended by the UNESCO World Heritage Centre. The methodology was developed by the U.S. Forest Service and tested on Lake Baikal from 1998 to 2016.[40]

In 2003, our research entered a practical stage: building and equipping trails on the shores of Lake Baikal. The first international projects with the participation of forest trail specialists from the U.S. Forest Service made it possible to create a public organisation called the Great Baikal Trail, which, during the period of 2003– 2016, built and equipped more than 700 kilometres of trails, mainly in the specially protected areas (PA) of Baikal. In 2017, we completed the Sarai Ring trail project and built its main part.[41]

Figure 11.6. The Sarai Ring Trail in a pine forest on the shore of the Sarai Bay, Ol'khon Island. Photographs by Arkady Kalikhman.

In 2011–2016, we developed trails and assessed recreational capacity and visitor loads in natural areas for the Pribaikal and Zabaikal national parks and for the Baikal-Lena *Zapovednik*. For Ol'khon Island, the maximum number of visitors in excursion mode according to the LAC method is distributed as: Cape Shamanka – 80 people, Kobyl'ia Peninsula Head – 120 people, Cape Khoboi – 100 people, Sagan Khushun Cape – 60 people, Khankhoi Lake – 50 people, Lake Shara-Nur – 40 people. A typical example of the effects of exceeding the number of visitors can be witnessed at Cape Khoboi, where the beauty of the natural landscape is marred by footpaths featuring trampled grass and abandoned campfire sites and rutted roads from excessive vehicle traffic.

---

40.   A. Kalikhman et al., *Metodika predelov dopustimykh izmenenii na Baikale.*

41.   The expedition members of Exploring Russia's Environmental History and Natural Resources, including many of the authors in this book, were in Sarai Bay on Ol'khon Island in July 2015.

Arkady Kalikhman and Tatiana Kalikhman

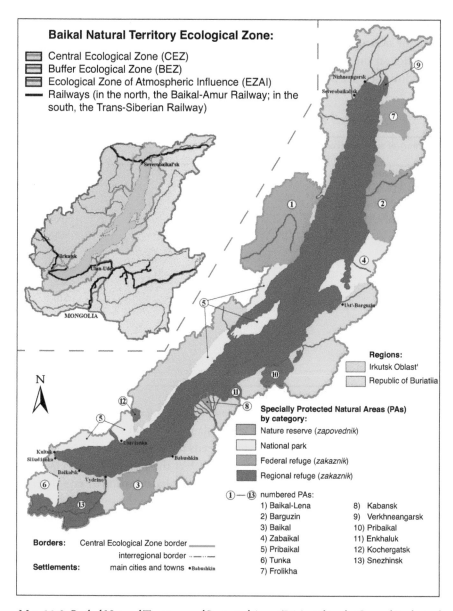

Map 11.2. Baikal Natural Territory and Protected Areas (PAs) within the Central Ecological Zone (CEZ). At the top is left is the BNT structure with the different ecological zones. The larger map shows the CEZ with PAs of all categories. One PA – Tunka National Park – is not fully included in the CEZ (one-tenth of the total park area). Source: T.P. Kalikhman, Territorial'naia okhrana prirody v Baikal'skom regione, p. 238.

Below are brief results of our inventory of the state of tourist infrastructure for overnight stays within the CEZ at the present time. The table gives statistics on the number of facilities and the number of available beds within the administrative areas and settlements included in the CEZ.

Table 11.2. Tourist facilities in the Central Ecological Zone (CEZ)

Territory of recreational use	Tourist centres, campsites, recreation facilities	Accommodation beds
Kabansk District	142	4,779
Pribaikal District	58	1,980
Barguzin District	40	1,614
Severobaikal'sk District	11	496
City of Severobaikal'sk	18	665
Ol'khon District	61	4,891
Ol'khon Island	82	3,217
Goloustnensk District	26	475
Irkutsk District	11	510
Listvianka Settlement	40	2,340
Sliudianka District	31	798
Utulik Settlement	11	1,276
Baikal'sk city	21	970
Total	552	24,011

From the table it follows that tourism and recreation are the primary activities for the inhabitants of Ol'khon Island, Listvianka and Utulik, where the number of accommodation places exceeds the population. For other areas, such a prospect is expected in a few years. Over the past five years, efforts to create infrastructure for tourists and vacationers have expanded rapidly. This is largely due to the increase in Russian tourists during the summer, as well as increasing numbers of tourists from China and elsewhere in Asia year-round.

Returning to the law 'On the Protection of Lake Baikal', it should be noted that it has not yet become an integrated environmental mechanism that will permanently alleviate the threat to the ecological system of the lake. Regional and federal authorities clearly have minimal interest in fulfilling the law by creating the essential regulatory acts to protect nature and to facilitate the planned recreational development within the CEZ. At the same time, the adoption of a special law for all UNESCO World Natural Heritage sites in Russia, including the definition of strict prohibitions and permitted activities, would be timely.

Arkady Kalikhman and Tatiana Kalikhman

Conclusions

Lake Baikal is a geographical object, closely associated with human history for almost two millennia. Baikal found itself in the path of several civilisations and eras. Not all details are known about events in the territories around Baikal during the sequential succession of three frontiers – Turkic, Mongolian and Russian. It is difficult to find a refutation or confirmation of the prediction of a fourth frontier – Chinese – although it is often spoken about in connection with the discussion of problems of clean water and lack of territories. The most recent discussions concern a projected pipeline for transporting drinking water from Lake Baikal to China and the construction of a hydroelectric power station in Mongolia on the main tributary of the Baikal, the Selenga, and the rivers flowing into it.

In our opinion, the table of historical events associated with Lake Baikal offers important insight. The last two centuries in the life of Lake Baikal can be considered key in terms of the degree of anthropogenic impact. They were also quite different as far as people's attitude toward the natural aspect of the lake and the use of its resources are concerned. If the nineteenth century showed examples of depletion of fish resources, which was almost complete for sturgeon and taimen, then the twentieth century, after the establishment of the communist regime, saw the results of the 'Baikal industrialisation'. The severe consequences of the development of hydropower and the water level rise in Baikal were worsened by log driving, the construction of the Baikal'sk Pulp and Paper Plant and the city of Baikal'sk, the extension of BAM to the lake and the construction of the city of Severobaikal'sk. Events of this time can be considered arbitrary, not logical economic and social developments of the territories around Lake Baikal. Soviet history remembers the slogan 'the conquest of the Angara', which culminated in the Irkutsk, Bratsk and Ust'-Ilimsk hydroelectric stations, but no-one now remembers the excess of electricity produced and its use primarily for aluminium production. The last example is the Boguchansk Hydroelectric Station (Boguchansk GES), which was launched in 2014 after being under construction for forty years. This energy will also be used for aluminium production, but the aluminium plant in Taishet, which began construction in 2006, has not yet been completed.

As far as choosing a site for the construction of a pulp plant and organising the production of mythical high-strength cellulose cord, Baikal could also have been left alone. It was senseless to build and operate the Baikal'sk Pulp and Paper Plant on the southern shore of Lake Baikal for almost fifty years, since pulp mills with much higher capacity were built almost at the same time in Bratsk and then in Ust'-Ilimsk. In the end, after the closure of the Baikal'sk Pulp and Paper Plant, the technology for processing millions of tons of sludge-lignin has not yet been worked out, and abandoned production sites are not being reclaimed.

Our observations and participation in environmental programmes at Baikal over more than thirty years allow us to draw some conclusions. As a result of the more than hundred-year history of the network of specially protected natural areas (PAs), a significant part of the Baikal coast is provided with territorial protection of the lake ecosystems. At the same time, there is a clear lack of PA at a distance from the coastal territory. On Baikal itself, the water area enters the PA system in a very limited manner: a three-kilometre strip along the Barguzin *Zapovednik*, the Chivyrkui Bay and part of Barguzin in the Zabaikal National Park. Therefore, the inclusion of lake ecosystems in PA boundaries is important and timely in order to preserve the nature of the lake. These include the islands of the Maloe More and their surrounding waters, the Bay of Posol'skii Sor, the waters of the Selenga delta, the joint delta of the rivers Kichera and the Upper Angara, the source of the Angara and the protection zones of all PA adjacent to the lake.

The creation of joint directorates, which changed the management structure of groups of contiguous PAs, has not contributed to the development of nature protection on Lake Baikal. The first, created in 2012, was the Podlemor'e Reserve (*Zapovednoe Podlemor'e*) directorate, formed from the Barguzin *Zapovednik* combined with the Zabaikal National Park and the Frolikha Federal *Zakaznik* (temporary reserve). In 2013, the Pribaikal Reserve (*Zapovednoe Pribaikal'e*) directorate emerged, which includes the Baikal-Lena *Zapovednik*, the elongated and difficult to manage Pribaikal National Park, as well as the Krasnyi Iar and Tofalar Federal *Zakazniks*, the latter of which is quite far from the others, and finally the Baikal Reserve (*Zapovednoe Baikal'e*) directorate, to which was added the Kabansk Federal *Zakaznik* and the very remote Altachei *Zakaznik*. The problem of the 2014–16 forest fires, when nearly 1.5 million hectares of forest burned on the slopes of the shores of Lake Baikal and surrounding ridges, illustrates how ineffective these new structures are.[42]

The opinion expressed at the beginning of this chapter – that Baikal has been preserved more by its inaccessibility than by the efforts of those trying to protect it – remains our forecast for the future of the lake.[43] The environmental protection policy for Baikal declared by the current government only reinforces

---

42. On the forest fires, see the essay by Bryce Stewart in this volume.

43. On the theme of inaccessibility, see the essay by David Moon in this volume.

this forecast of continuity, but it leaves room for hope for a future in which people can strive to mitigate the consequences of 'Baikal industrialisation' and rethink the prevailing approach to environmental protection.

BIBLIOGRAPHY

Aleksandrov, I. 1931. *Problema Angary*. Leningrad: Sotsegiz.

Aleksandrov, I. and V. Malyshev. 1930. 'Problema reki Angary'. *Planovoe khoziaistvo*. No. 6: 204–28.

Atutov, A.A. et al. 1999. *Gidroenergetika i sostoianie ekosystemy ozera Baikal*. Novosibirsk: Izdatel'stvo SO RAN.

Belt, D. 1992. 'The World's Great Lake'. *National Geographic* **181** (6): 2–39.

Davis, George (ed.). 1993. *The Lake Baikal Region in the Twenty-First Century: A Model of Sustainable Development or Continued Degradation? A Comprehensive Program of Land Use Policies for the Russian Portion of the Lake Baikal Region*. San Francisco, Ulan-Ude, Wadhams, NY and Irkutsk: Center for Citizen Initiatives-USA; Centre for Socio-Ecological Problems of the Baikal Region; Davis Associates; Russian Academy of Sciences.

Fialkov, V.A. and V.I. Galkina. 2004. 'Da budet dom!'. In G.V. Matiashenko (ed.), *Grigorii Ivanovich Galazii. Rytsar Baikala: Sbornik*, pp. 144–5. Novosibirsk: Izdatel'stvo SO RAN.

Hill, Fiona and Clifford Gaddy. 2003. *The Siberian Curse: How Communist Planners Left Russia Out in the Cold*. Washington, DC: Brookings Institution Press.

Huntoon, J.E. 1991. 'Superior-Baikal Connect: Linking the World's Great Lakes (Abs.).' *Abstracts from the 28th Annual Lake Superior Biological Conference*. Houghton, MI.

Ides, I., Brand, A. 1967. *Zapiski o russkom posol'stve v Kitay (1692–1695)*. Moscow: Glavnaia redakstiia Vostochnoi literatury Izdatel'stvo Nauka.

Kalikhman, T. 2017. 'Federal'nyi zakon "Ob okhrane ozera Baikal": istoriia i trudnosti realizatsii'. In N. Filatov (ed.), *Ozera Evrazii: Problemy i puti ikh resheniia*, pp. 67–74. Petrozavodsk: Karel'skii nauchnyi tsentr RAN.

Kalikhman, A., N. Bencharova and T. Kalikhman. 2017. *Ol'khon: priroda i liudi*. Irkutsk: Institut geografii SO RAN.

Kalikhman, A. et al. 1999. *Metodika predelov dopustimykh izmenenii na Baikale – uchastke vsemirnogo naslediia UNESCO*. Irkutsk: Ottisk.

Kalikhman, A. et al. 2000. *Assessment of Business Potential for Tourism in Southern Lake Baikal Region. TACIS final report*. Irkutsk: TACIS.

Kalikhman, T. and A. Kalikhman. 2012. 'Lake Baikal'. *World Heritage*. No. 64: 122–7.

Kalikhman, T.P. 2007. 'Osobo okhraniaemye prirodnye territorii Baikal'skogo regiona'. *Izvestiia RAN. Seriia geograficheskaia.* No. 3: 75–86.

Kalikhman, T.P. 2011. *Territorial'naia okhrana prirody v Baikal'skom regione.* Irkutsk: Institut geografii SO RAN.

Kolosok, S. 2000. 'Usloviia otbyvaniia nakazaniia zakliuchennymi Irkutskoy gubernii v kontse XIX–nachale XX vv.' *Sibirskii Iuridicheskii Vestnik.* No. 3: 23–9.

Kozhova, O. and A. Beim. 1993. *Ekologicheskii monitoring Baikala.* Moscow: Ekologiia.

Kuzmin, M.I. and G.V. Matiashenko. 2004. 'Zhizennyi put'' G.I. Galaziia'. In G.V. Matiashenko (ed.), *Grigorii Ivanovich Galazii. Rytsar Baikala: Sbornik*, pp. 5–10. Novosibirsk: Izdatel'stvo SO RAN.

Lomonosov, M.V. 1950–1983 [1763]. 'Kratkoe Opisanie raznykh puteshestvii po severnym moriam i pokazanie vozmozhnogo prokhodu Sibirskim okeanom v Vostochnuiu Indiiu'. In *Lomonosov M.V. Polnoe Sobranie sochinenii*, pp. 417–98. Moscow and Leningrad: AN SSSR. http://feb-web.ru/feb/lomonos/texts/lo0/lo6/lo6-417-.htm?cmd=p

Malyshev, V.M. 1935. *Gipoteza resheniia Angarskoi problemy.* Irkutsk: Vostochnosibirskoe kraevoe izdatel'stvo.

Mamontov, A. 2009. 'Otsenka obshchikh ulovov omulia v Baikale'. *Geografiia i prirodnye resursy.* No. 1: 75–80.

Matiasheko, G.V. (ed.). 2004. *Grigorii Ivanovich Galazii: Rytsar Baikala.* Novosibirsk: Izdatel'stvo SO RAN.

Miller, G.F. 1937. *Istoriia Sibiri.* 2 vols. Moscow and Leningrad: Nauka.

Polnoe sobranie zakonov Rossiiskoi imperii 1649 goda (PSZ): Pervoe Sobranie. 1649–1825. 45 vols.

Rennicke, J. 1994. 'Montana with an Ocean'. *Backpacker* 22 (5): 38–47.

Spafarii, N. 1882. *Puteshestviia cherez Sibir' ot Tobol'ska do Nerchinska i granits Kitaia russkogo poslannika Nikolaia Spafariia v 1675 godu.* St Petersburg: Tipografiia V. Kirshbaum.

Saunders, David. 2016. 'Icebreakers in Anglo-Russian Relations (1914–21)'. *The International History Review* 38 (4): 814–829.

Territorial'naia kompleksnaia skhema okhrany prirody basseina ozera Baikal. Osnovnye polozheniia. 1990. Moscow: Giprogor.

Timoshkin, O.A. et al. 2016. 'Rapid Ecological Change in the Coastal Zone of Lake Baikal (East Siberia): Is the Site of the World's Greatest Freshwater Biodiversity in Danger?' *Journal of Great Lakes Research* 42 (3): 487–97.

UNESCO. 2020. 'Lake Baikal'. http://whc.unesco.org/en/list/754/

von Droste, Bernd. 2012. 'Empowerment of the Convention: From the Theory to the Practical Application (1981–2000)'. *World Heritage Review. Special Issue: World Heritage in the Russian Federation*: 12–19.

Wikimedia Commons. 2015. 'Mongolia VII' https://commons.wikimedia.org/wiki/File:Mongolia_XVII.png

12.

THE ORIGINS OF THE BARGUZIN NATURE RESERVE

Nicholas B. Breyfogle

On 29 December 1916 – in what we now know were the dying days of the tsarist empire – the Russian Senate passed into law the Barguzin *Zapovednik* (nature reserve), located on the northeastern shores of Lake Baikal in Siberia.[1] It was the first and only state-sponsored nature reserve to be created in the tsarist period (although there were other private nature reserves of various shapes, sizes and goals set up by individuals and non-governmental organisations).[2] The Barguzin *Zapovednik* began its storied career as an effort to protect the sable population from possible localised extinction – with the ultimate concern that humans might lose this very profitable fur mammal from their hunting repertoire. However, over the past century, Barguzin became much more than just a safe haven for sable. It was also a remarkable site for ecosystem-based nature protection and extensive scientific study, and it served as a model for the structure of nature reserves across the Soviet Union.

This chapter explores a series of interrelated questions about the origins of the Barguzin *Zapovednik*: *why* the *zapovednik* was created at all, *why* it was established *where* it was and with the specific boundaries that it had (Siberia is, after all, a massive place – why in the lands between the northeastern shores of Baikal and the Barguzin Mountains and not somewhere else?) and *why* it was created *at the specific moment* that it was created (in the midst of World War One, no less). In answering these questions, this chapter utilises a methodology that approaches the region's flora and fauna, local socio-ethnic structures and the materiality of local landscapes and ecosystems as causative forces that helped to determine the overall outcome of the human-environment interaction. The

---

1. All dates are given in the Old Style calendar in use in Russia before the Bolshevik Revolution.

2. Shtilmark, *History of the Russian Zapovedniks*; Nasimovich, 'Dorevoliutsionnyi period'; Weiner, *Models of Nature*. On the history of National Parks in Russia, see also Alan Roe, *Into Russian Nature*.

Nicholas B. Breyfogle

story of *zapovedniks* is often told as an intellectual history of science; as a story that focuses on macro-level ideas of conservation and nature protection that a small group of elites developed and applied. And it is often told as a story that concentrates on humans as the primary actors.[3] In contrast, I argue here that in the planning process of the Barguzin *Zapovednik* (and at the core of the decision to develop a nature reserve at all), the influence of the physical characteristics of Lake Baikal and the Barguzin region – the local topography, landscapes, hydrology, flora, fauna and ecologies – was significant. Moreover, and more importantly, sable played a decisive role in their own salvation through their physical characteristics and their habits and patterns. The role of sable was, to be sure, an unwitting and unconscious one – the sable did not themselves choose to create the *zapovednik*. Their impact in the process became manifest through 1) moments of interaction between sables and humans and 2) the intersections of sables with other species (such as viruses and fish) through the mediation of human desires, socio-economic activities and colonial policies.[4]

This attention to non-human causation in the development of the Barguzin *Zapovednik* is not to deny the importance of humans, of course. Throughout, this chapter strives to highlight the intersections and mutual interrelations of larger intellectual/scientific developments and policy agendas from the central halls of power – and of broader ideologies of nature protection and preservation – with local concerns and the specificities of local geographies, landscapes, weather patterns and animal and plant life. The chapter casts a wide historical net over the range of humans that we need to consider as contributors to the creation of the Barguzin *Zapovednik* alongside the scientists and scholars who developed the *zapovednik* idea: regional administrators in Irkutsk, the local inhabitants of the Baikal region (especially Evenks,[5] but also Russian peasant settlers) and the five principle members of a crucial scientific expedition sent to scout out the region in 1914–1915: G.G. Doppel'mair, K.A. Zabelin, Z.F. Svatosh, D.N. Aleksandrov and A.D. Baturin.

3.   Weiner, *Models of Nature*; Weiner, *A Little Corner*; Shtilmark, *History of the Russian Zapovedniks*. An exception is Moon, *The Plough that Broke the Steppes*.

4.   On these theoretical and methodological approaches, see Kohn, *How Forests Think*; Latour, *Reassembling the Social*; Timothy J. LeCain, *The Matter of History: How Things Create the Past*; Mitchell, *Rule of Experts*, pp. 19–53; Nash, 'The Agency of Nature', pp. 67–69; Brown, 'Thing Theory'; Odling-Smee et al., *Niche Construction*; Russell, *Evolutionary History*. On these themes, see also the chapter by Mark Sokolsky in this volume.

5.   In the tsarist period, Russians used the name 'Tungus' to label the Evenk people. For a history of the Evenks, see Shubin, *Evenki Pribaikal'ia*.

The Origins of the Barguzin Nature Reserve

The *zapovednik* that was created in December 1916 initially comprised three different parts. First, there was a large territory set aside for the protection of the sable – a game-management *zapovednik* area that was to be inviolable and in which humans were forbidden to hunt. This zone was created in order to give the sable a permanent reprieve from human hunting that would let the species breed, expand its numbers and improve the health of its communities unmolested. Second, there was to be a special game or hunting zone created as a geographically contiguous area to the north of the game-management reserve. The purpose of this hunting zone was to establish an area in which scientists and hunting specialists could conduct research on sustainable sable hunting practices. In the hunting area, only a highly restricted number of hunters and trappers would be permitted to catch sable. All aspects of the hunt would be subjected to scientific scrutiny: from the number of sable that might be 'harvested' each season (and yet still ensure a stable population), to the way in which they were caught (technologies, systems, traps), the location of the catch, breakdowns by age and sex of the sable, the number of hunters per sable population, the presence or absence of different foods for the sable and the meteorological specificities of a given season. The goal was to learn how to end the unmaintainable hunting practices of previous generations and to manage scientifically the game populations to ensure sable pelts for future generations. Third, a sable farm was to be set up in the *zapovednik* territory to breed and study sable in captivity. The farmed sable would then be used to re-populate areas throughout Siberia where the sable had been hunted to localised extinction and thereby expand the wild population. Here the genetic specificities of the Barguzin sable would be spread by human hand across large swathes of Siberian territory. At the same time, the breeding station would offer scientists opportunities to study and learn about the sable and its place in larger ecological networks.[6]

The origin story of the Barguzin *Zapovednik* is important for several reasons. First, it was the first and the longest lasting of state-sponsored *zapovedniks* in Russian/Soviet history. The *zapovednik* model as it was conceived in tsarist Russia and then widely implemented during the Soviet era represents one of the most important contributions to global conservation efforts of the Russian/Soviet world.[7] As Sergei Zalygin wrote in 1992: 'the word "*zapovednik*"

---

6. Zabelin, 'Promyslovye okhoty', pp. 49–50; Doppel'mair and Zabelin, 'Naselenie Barguzinskogo uezda', pp. 127–270.

7. For global comparison, see Sheail, *Nature's Spectacle*; Kupper, *Creating Wilderness*; Roe, *Into Russian Nature*; Gissibl, Höhler and Kupper (eds), *Civilizing Nature*.

Nicholas B. Breyfogle

means "a parcel of land or marine territory completely and eternally taken out of economic use and placed under the protection of the state'". These segregated, closed lands were then to be used for scientific research: by separating out examples of a wide range of different ecologies, scientists could examine and understand the development of these natural communities absent any human influence. But, more than that, Zalygin continues, 'a *zapovednik* is something sacred and indestructible, not only in nature but in the human being itself; it is also a commandment, a sacred vow [from its root *zapoved'*]'.[8]

Second, the Barguzin Reserve has been, in many ways, successful: it achieved its original aims to save the sable, study the species scientifically and disperse populations of these mammals elsewhere in Siberia. In 1986, it became a UNESCO Biosphere Reserve and, in 1996, part of the Lake Baikal World Heritage Site. Moreover, as a result of the protections to the entire territory, the land, water, air, flora and fauna of Barguzin remain relatively pure and unaffected by humanity.[9] Third, as the first state *zapovednik*, it became a test ground during the Soviet period for some of the foundational ideas of what a *zapovednik* should (or could) be, especially for the 'game *zapovedniks*' designed to protect specific animals. Many of the fundamental principles that would come to define the *zapovednik* system in the Soviet period were delineated and enacted at Barguzin. This chapter will explore these themes through a chronological discussion of rising human concern over the increasingly endangered sable population, the evolution of ideas for creating a nature reserve, the importance of the 1914–15 expedition and the social and environmental process of delimiting the boundaries of the new *zapovednik*.

---

8.   Quoted in Weiner, *A Little Corner*, p. 4. See also Shtilmark, *History of the Russian Zapovedniks*; Nasimovich, 'Dorevoliutsionnyi period'; Weiner, *Models of Nature*.

9.   GARB f. R-562, op. 4, d. 219; GARB f. R-562, op. 4, d. 119; GARB f. R-562, op. 4, d. 143; GARB f. R-562, op. 4, d. 242; GARB f. R-562, op. 4, d. 245; UNESCO, 'Barguzinskyi Biosphere Reserve, Russian Federation'; Barguzin *Zapovednik* Museum exhibit. On the establishment of Lake Baikal as a UNESCO World Heritage Site, see the chapter by Arkady Kalikhman and Tatiana Kalikhman in this volume.

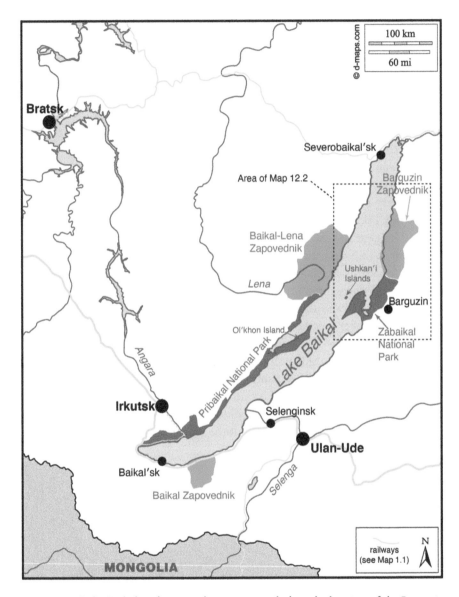

Map 12.1. Lake Baikal and surrounding region, including the location of the Barguzin Zapovednik and a selection of other zapovedniks and national parks marked in green. Source: Created by Andrew Johnson at White Horse Press using d-maps.com: © d-maps.

Nicholas B. Breyfogle

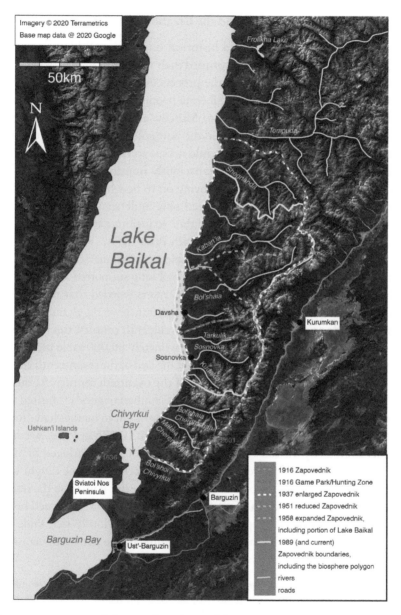

Map 12.2. Location and changing boundaries of the Barguzin Zapovednik, 1916 to today. Source: Created by Andrew Johnson at White Horse Press using d-maps.com: © d-maps; based upon maps from GARB f. R-562, op. 4, d. 143, l. 6; GARB f. R-562, op. 4, d. 113, ll. 3, 24; Savenkova, Atlas okhraniaemye prirodnye territorii, p. 37 and maps at the Barguzin Zapovednik Museum.

The Origins of the Barguzin Nature Reserve

Disappearing Sable and the Creation of a Zapovednik

The sable was a mammal of world historical importance. Sables were among the primary reasons that Russians sprinted their way across to the Pacific Ocean in the seventeenth century and in the process incorporated into their empire the vast Siberian lands and diverse Siberian peoples. The large piles of furs that made their way back across Siberia to Moscow and later St Petersburg made Russian leaders wealthy as they passed the 'soft gold' into the international fur trade. As a result of the riches that could accrue to those in the sable hunting process, there was a long history of rapaciously hunting the sable out of certain geographic locations and then moving on to new hunting grounds. Such unimpeded extraction of sable produced new understandings of humanity's potential impact on nature and led over time to various nature-protection laws for the sable (beginning in a small way with Peter I).[10]

By the late nineteenth century, sable populations across Siberia had decreased markedly. In many regions that had long supported large numbers, sable experienced localised extirpation. Observers worried that the sable was on the verge of extinction and with its disappearance would go one of Russia's most profitable resources. Already in the seventeenth century, catches of sable had declined in eastern Siberia: from approximately 80,000 sable pelts caught annually in mid-century, to 4,500 caught at the end of the seventeenth century, and dwindling to 2,700 at the beginning of the twentieth century. At the Irbit market (through which abundant quantities of Siberian goods transited westward), by the early 1910s, the number of pelts brought to market had dropped five to six times: from 61,000 sable pelts in 1889 to 10,275 in 1910. According to other sources, by the early 1900s, the quantity of sable marketed in Siberia had declined by as much as ten times. A similar decline in sable caught in the Baikal region was part of the overall Siberian decline but it was also the result of specific, localised processes in the Baikal and Irkutsk region (discussed below). In the Barguzin area, one report noted that, in a previously rich sable area, only forty living sable remained by the beginning of the twentieth century.[11]

---

10. For similar worry in other parts of the empire and the germination of ideas of utilitarian conservation and nature protection, see Fisher, *The Russian Fur Trade;* Etkind, 'Barrels of Fur', pp. 164–171; Egorov, *Anatolii Alekseevich Silant'ev*, p. 67; Jones, *Empire of Extinction*; Moon, *The Plough that Broke the Steppes*. For comparison, see Grove, *Ecological Imperialism.*

11. Egorov, *Anatolii Alekseevich Silant'ev*, pp. 57–62, 67. Doppel'mair, *Sobolinyi promysel,* p. 3; Gusev, 'Sobolinyi krai', p. 16; Gusev, *Na ocharovannom beregu*, p. 160; Freidberg, *Baikal, Barguzinskii Zapovednik*, pp. 14–15; Barguzin Zapovednik Museum exhibits.

Nicholas B. Breyfogle

The decline in sable provoked a range of responses from merchants, traders, hunters and both local and central tsarist officials. In 1910, a union of fur-traders, in tandem with the Irbit Market Committee, petitioned the Main Administration of Land Use and Agriculture (GUZZ) with a request for the full prohibition of sable hunting for two years in order to offer sable a respite from the pressures of commercial exploitation. Officials in St Petersburg had been worried for some time about the drop in hunting productivity in general and especially of sable. In 1911, the Department of Agriculture created a new division to deal with their hunting concerns, 'having as its goal the support and regularisation of this important branch of economic activity'. The new division – led by a new generation of specialists from the Forest Institute, trained in the practice, policy and economics of hunting – worked to gather knowledge about hunting as the foundation for developing appropriate laws and practices.[12]

Decreases in the marketing of sable also prompted a response from several successive Irkutsk governors-general. In 1910, the governor-general forbade sable hunting in state forests in Enisei Province and the Trans-Baikal region annually from 1 February to 1 October and also the use of specific hunting tools (including certain types of nets and traps). Moreover, in his 1910–1911 annual report, he highlighted the dramatic drop in the quantity of sable catches and the significant impact of these decreases on the livelihoods of people in the region. He underscored the 'extreme importance of the rapid application in Siberia of a law about hunting in general and about hunting sable in particular'. He argued for the immediate need to set aside parcels of land 'in which hunting of any sort and at all times of the year would be unconditionally forbidden'. The governor-general noted that examples of such protected areas could be found in U.S. national parks, and he highlighted that these parks served multiple goals: they were economically important and not only acted 'as a natural nursery for valued animals of surrounding areas, but also gives rich scientific material'. The report also mentioned that local officials from GUZZ had put forward a plan to set up such a protected area in the Saian Mountains. However, the governor-general underscored the particular need to establish such a park on the shores of Baikal for the protection of the sable because the many rivers that flowed into Baikal hosted particularly productive ecosystems for the Barguzin and the Kultuk sable.[13]

For comparison, on declining fish populations in the Baikal region, see Breyfogle, 'The Fate of Fishing', pp. 1–29.

12. Egorov, *Anatolii Alekseevich Silant'ev*, pp. 59–68.

13. Iankus, *Zenon Svatosh*, pp. 35–36; Egorov, *Anatolii Alekseevich Silant'ev*, pp. 60–63.

This was not the first time that the leadership in Irkutsk had pleaded their case in St Petersburg for protective nature regulations and strict laws on hunting. In 1895, the Irkutsk governor-general issued rules on the use of state forests, including a detailed discussion of hunting birds and animals. These directives were reviewed and then published again in 1910 given the significant drops in the sable population. In both 1893 and 1903, moreover, the governors-general had approached the minister responsible for state domains with proposed new rules for hunting, but neither of these projects were approved.[14]

This time, however, the report provoked a response in St Petersburg. Taking the governor-general's worries seriously, and after much discussion through the bureaucracy, on 9 June 1912, the tsar affirmed a decree that recognised the need for legal intervention to save the sable and highlighted the urgency of setting up *zapovedniks* to protect the land on which sable lived.[15] There were two important outcomes from the 1912 law. First, the decree mandated a three-year moratorium on hunting sable throughout Russia from 1 February 1913 to 15 October 1916. It was optimistically hoped that during this time the sable would re-populate itself, and from that point forward hunting could take place for a restricted period each winter, from 15 October to 1 February annually.[16] The law was welcomed not only by naturalists but also by fur-traders at the Irbit trade fair, who in their 1914 meeting recognised that the 'law, despite certain defects, not only is having a beneficial impact in regards to the preservation of the sable itself, but is also having a beneficial influence on the protection of other animals'.[17] Second, A.A. Silant'ev, an experienced hunter and bureaucrat and the official in charge of the hunting section of the ministry, initiated the 'Project for Studying the Sable Regions of Russia, 1913–1915'. The Project began to organise an expedition to study the sable and sable hunting and to look for locations in Siberia where it might be possible to set up some form of nature reserve for the sable (*zapovedniks* or *zakazniks*).[18] Initially, Silant'ev

---

14. Iankus, *Zenon Svatosh*, pp. 35; Egorov, *Anatolii Alekseevich Silant'ev*, pp. 60–63.

15. Startsev, 'Gosudarstvennoe regulirovanie', pp.152–156; Egorov, *Anatolii Alekseevich Silant'ev*, pp. 61–62;

16. Nasimovich, 'Dorevoliutsionnyi period', p. 17

17. Quoted in Egorov, *Anatolii Alekseevich Silant'ev*, p. 87.

18. In contrast to a *zapovednik*, with its permanent, inviolable protections, a *zakaznik* was defined as a protected territory in which certain economic activities (such as hunting, mining, and logging, among others) were restricted for either a temporary or perpetual period in order to shelter defined components of the natural ecosystems, which might include the entire territory or just certain parts or species. Savenkova, *Atlas: okhraniaemye prirodnye territorii.*

Nicholas B. Breyfogle

chose three locations: the northern Baikal region, the central part of the eastern Saian Mountains and certain regions of Kamchatka.[19]

Why did Silant'ev nominate these three locations of all the possible locations in Siberia? While the sable population had dropped precipitously throughout Siberia, each of these locations had its own, specific reasons to be selected as the focus of a research expedition. Here we start to see the importance of local peculiarities in developing nature protection measures. The decision to focus attention on the northeastern Baikal region for the protection of the sable was particularly a result of three factors. First, the fact that it was the Irkutsk governor's report that set in motion a response in St Petersburg ensured that lands around Irkutsk would receive special attention. Second, the highly prized quality of the Barguzin sable's fur was especially important to the decision to send an expedition to the Baikal region. The sable of the northeastern shores of Lake Baikal (what the locals call Podlemor'e) were a particular type – *Mustela zibellina princeps Bis* – that were among the most valued in the world. Along the Kudalda River in particular could be found 'the best of the best of Barguzin sable, dark-chocolate, almost black, and with blue underfur'. So valued was the Barguzin sable that a single pelt could bring in as much as 1,500 roubles.[20] Here, the specific colour and quality of the fur of the sable in this region – to which humans assigned greater value – offered selective advantage to the Barguzin sable over sable of other regions (as well as other mammals). Inadvertently, their biological qualities helped to save them from extermination.

A third reason for the selection of Podlemor'e as the location for one of the research expeditions was the recent and rapid decline of the sable population. This decrease was the outcome of the complex combination of specific disease patterns (smallpox) and the region's ethno-social structures of commercial hunting (especially who was hunting and how) to increase population pressures on the sable.[21] The impact of an outbreak of smallpox among the Shemagir Evenks of the Podlemor'e region (what they described as 'some sort of large sickness') was transformative for the fate of the sable in the region and for the creation of the Barguzin *zapovednik*. Here, we see the effect of one organism upon another, but mediated or channelled through the actions and views of

19. Nasimovich, 'Dorevoliutsionnyi period', p.17; Egorov, *Anatolii Alekseevich Silant'ev*, pp. 59–97; Solov'ev, 'Zapovedniki', pp. 267–309; Doppel'mair, *Sobolinyi promysel*; GARB f. R-562, op. 4, d. 10.

20. Zabelin, 'Promyslovye okhoty', pp. 49–50; Ustinov, *Zapovednik na Baikale*, p.14; Iankus, *Zenon Svatosh*, p. 42.

21. Egorov, *Anatolii Alekseevich Silant'ev*, p. 62.

humans – particularly the way in which the smallpox virus inadvertently helped to protect the sable in the Barguzin region because of the impact of the virus on the human population there.

The arrival of epidemic smallpox in the region decimated the population of the Evenk communities and fundamentally changed their life patterns and economic activities. Smallpox hit the region particularly severely in the mid-nineteenth century, in the 1890s and then again in 1907–8 (among other times). The epidemic in the mid-nineteenth century took the lives of so many that according to some sources, 'there was no one left to bury them. The neighbouring Kindigirs helped them'. In 1880, there were approximately 500 people among the Shemagir Evenks but another epidemic of smallpox in 1891 took about half of the population. In 1907–08, up and down the river valleys, entire families died and 'people in panic took off for the taiga'. One Evenk who stayed behind and was alive to tell the story in the 1970s noted that this was the moment when, orphaned, he came to live with a Russian family, who raised him. By the end of the epidemic, there were only about nineteen families and 68 people left (of whom only a reported sixteen worked as hunters in 1914).[22]

The smallpox death toll brought about social dislocation and a reconfiguration of traditional lifeways, which in turn had effects on the future of sable and the *zapovednik*. For generations, Evenks had followed an annual cycle of movement up into the hills in the summers (for pasture for the reindeer and to escape the mosquitoes) and in winter they came back down to the shores of Baikal. Throughout the year, they followed the cycles of the animals and fish around them: hunting and fishing what they needed for their communities and to pay *iasak* (tribute) and taxes, and using reindeer for many of their needs. Smallpox changed these practices. The Shemagir Evenks largely stopped hunting the lands to which they had been given legal right by tsarist decree. They also ended their migratory lifestyle, with the few remaining families coming together in a more or less permanent settlement at Sosnovka (with a church, lighthouse, administrative buildings, a store and winter houses).[23]

When these Evenks ceased hunting sable, they almost universally rented their hunting allotments to nearby Russian settlers, primarily to a small number of merchants in Barguzin who then sub-leased these allotments to Russian

---

22. Ustinov, *Zapovednik na Baikale*, pp. 12–14; Egorov, *Anatolii Alekseevich Silant'ev*, p. 65; Freidberg, *Baikal, Barguzinskii Zapovednik*, p. 15; Iankus, *Zenon Svatosh*, pp. 58–75, esp. 65; Shubin, *Evenki Pribaikal'ia*, pp. 36–37. Smallpox arrived in Siberia in the seventeenth century, as part of Russian colonial expansion, and spread death and illness in its wake. See Richards, *Unending Frontier*, 538–41

23. Ustinov, *Zapovednik na Baikale*, pp. 13–14.

Nicholas B. Breyfogle

peasants. The ethnic shift in hunting was important because this commercial rental structure incentivised Russian hunters to extract as many sable pelts as they could in any given year – to take 'everything', in the words of one analyst. They were required to pay a rental fee to the merchants and so needed to be sure that they caught at least that much in furs. At the same time, they were not guaranteed to receive access to the same hunting allotments from year to year, so it was in their best interest to hunt as much as they could whilst they could. Unlike the Evenks, they often did not actually live in the hunting region nor did they necessarily feel much spiritual or cultural attachment to the land, forests, waters and animals that they were hunting.[24] The Shemagir Evenks had control of approximately twenty rivers from the Chivyrkui to Shireglen. In 1908, for example, 48 Russians bought rights to hunt on six rivers at a cost of 12 roubles 50 kopecks per river. Fourteen other rivers were given for hunting for 4518.50 roubles. The merchants did remarkably well from this arrangement. Over nine years, the Barguzin merchant A.D. Novomeiskii obtained 2,686 sable pelts at a cost of 246,604 roubles and sold them for 485,555 roubles, making a handsome profit for the merchant firm. The surviving Evenks also fared well under these agreements. They kept significant savings in money in the state bank and, as scholar N.I. Tsivilev writes, after the 1890s, the life of the Shemagir Evenks was 'a full cup of happiness'.[25]

The Barguzin sable's experience of these new hunting arrangements was something quite different. To be sure, the demands for *iasak* had forced the Evenks over the years to hunt more sables than they might have done otherwise, but the sudden appearance of Russians into the hunting industry lead to an even more rapid drop in the number of Barguzin sable. There was one exception. The surviving Evenks kept for themselves the rights to hunt sable up the Kudalda River. The elder Evenks cherished this river and its flora and described how the light's reflection off the river on a sunny day reminded them of the youth of their tribe, stories of happiness, hunting success and adventures. But it was not just for these memories and the connections with nature that they valued the river valley. In most of Podlemor'e, the sable was almost completely killed off, but the 'grandiose, many-storey, dense' stands of cedars, scattered on 'the

---

24. Doppel'mair and Zabelin, 'Naselenie Barguzinskogo uezda', pp. 197–237; Iankus, *Zenon Svatosh*, 64; Shubin, *Evenki Pribaikal'ia*, pp. 45–65; Ustinov, *Zapovednik na Baikale*, pp. 12–14.

25. Tsivilev, 'Zametki', pp. 8–12.

steep slope in the valley of the Kudalda, saved the sable from the persecution of dogs and hunters'.[26]

Thus, the decision of officials in St Petersburg to choose the northeastern shores of Baikal as one of the locations to try to save the Siberian sable was prompted by a combination of the human desire for the specific qualities of the furs of the Barguzin sable, the frighteningly quick reduction in sable population that accompanied the ethnic shift in hunting from Evenks to Russians and also the fact that there remained one river valley with a healthy population of sable upon which to rebuild the population.

Figure 12.1. The author (on left at head of table) presenting an earlier version of this chapter at a seminar at the Davsha meeting house in the Barguzin Zapovednik, 29 July 2015, almost a century after the establishment of the nature reserve. The seminar was sponsored by the Leverhulme Trust International Network 'Exploring Russia's Environmental History and Natural Resources'. Photograph courtesy of Arkady Kalikhman. Reproduced with permission.

---

26. Zabelin, 'Promyslovye okhoty', pp. 38–50; Doppel'mair and Zabelin, 'Naselenie Barguzinskogo uezda', pp. 197–237; Ustinov, *Zapovednik na Baikale*, p. 14.

Nicholas B. Breyfogle

The Expedition

In 1914, a preparatory expedition was dispatched to the northeastern shores of Baikal in order to explore the conditions under which a sable nature reserve should or could be created. The formation of the Barguzin *Zapovednik* in 1916 was in no small measure the result of the work of a few men who took part in the expedition, especially G.G. Doppel'mair, the leader, A.D. Baturin, K.A. Zabelin, Z.F. Svatosh and D.N. Aleksandrov. The researchers arrived in the summer of 1914 and set up their base of operations in the village of Sosnovka, the small administrative centre that the Evenk peoples had established after smallpox put an end to their migratory lifestyle.[27]

The focus of the expedition was research, and they gathered important data on the landscapes, hydrology, geography, forests, flora, fauna and, particularly, the sable and their hunters. They also captured the region on film for the first time. Over the course of 1914 and into 1915, the members of the expedition, along with Evenk guides and companions, spread out across the region. They travelled extensively in the area: into the hills, along the shores of the lake, and along the different river valleys. In the interests of science, the expedition received permission to ignore the 1912 ban on sable hunting. Accompanied by local Evenk hunters, they set off to hunt and trap in the winter with two goals in mind. First, they wished to capture some male and female sable that would be used as breeding stock for a domesticated farming project that they envisioned. Second, they wanted to see sable hunting in practice. If they were to create a sustainable hunting district contiguous to the *zapovednik*, where they would establish scientifically-based hunting practices, they believed it essential to understand the human patterns and technical mechanics involved in the hunt: how many hunters there were, how many sable did an average hunter catch annually, and from where, and the different methods and tools that Evenk hunters employed to catch sable (from nets to wood structures that crushed sable as they took the bait (*kulemki*) and metal spring traps).[28]

Based on the data collected during the summer of 1914, Doppel'mair returned to Petrograd,[29] where he requested and received permission to proceed

27. Doppel'mair, *Sobolinyi promysel*, pp. 5–22; Egorov, *Anatolii Alekseevich Silant'ev*, pp. 68–70.

28. Baturin, 'Sobol' i sobolinyi promysel', pp. 103–145; Doppel'mair, *Sobolinyi promysel*, pp. 5–22; Egorov, *Anatolii Alekseevich Silant'ev*, pp. 86–92; Iankus, *Zenon Svatosh*, pp. 49–56.

29. Petrograd was the name for St Petersburg between 1914 and 1924. It was changed in World War One to make the then-capital sound less Germanic.

with the creation of a nature reserve. Doppel'mair found a sympathetic ear in the capital. Since the passing of the 1912 laws, many hunters and scientists had come to believe that the brief, three-year moratorium on hunting would not be sufficient to give the sable time and space in which to reproduce and rebuild their population numbers. Instead, in the words of Silant'ev, there was the 'need to have a *zapovednik* that will allow for the quiet existence and expansion in the number of sable and their spread to adjoining regions'.[30] Others added that the problems with the moratorium were more than just its temporary status. For instance, F. Shillinger argued that the more serious problem was the absence of enforcement and oversight. Without agents to enforce the moratorium, hunters simply did as they wished. He believed a *zapovednik* was needed and one with appropriate guards and aggressive supervision.[31]

The Barguzin reserve was created in three parts: 1) a *zapovednik* (inviolable, in which the sable could be left alone to live, thrive, survive – and in which a sable breeding centre could be created); 2) a sable game park, in which researchers would explore how to develop a sustainable hunting system (i.e., hunting would be allowed in these areas, but only in order to advance scientific knowledge about the best principles to ensure a sustainable and ongoing hunt in the future); and 3) a breeding programme/farm to enhance the sable population by breeding in captivity and then re-introducing the sable into the forests to spur on wild populations. The breeding stations would also offer important research opportunities for scientists to understand the sable.

With Petrograd's permission for a nature reserve granted, a race began to get the *zapovednik* up and running before the end of the moratorium on sable hunting. As the expedition members started their 1915 summer research programme, there was approximately a year left until the three-year window closed. They saw six primary tasks ahead of them: 1) to carry out further biological research and data gathering about the landscapes, climate, hydrology, flora and fauna of the region – especially sable, and hunting practices – in order to make informed decisions; 2) to set up a legal foundation upon which to appropriate state lands and forests from other uses and designate them for use by a nature reserve; 3) to delimit the specific boundaries of the two-part nature reserve; 4) to move the Evenks who lived on the land of the *zapovednik* to other locations; 5) to build infrastructure necessary for research and everyday life: houses for guards to live in and for researchers to carry out their examination of sable; fields to grow food for them; boats and scientific equipment; and the pens

---

30.   Gusev, 'Sobolinyi krai', pp. 16–17; Freidberg, *Baikal, Barguzinskii Zapovednik*, p. 13.

31.   Shillinger, 'Sovremennoe sostoiane', No. 6: 142–143 and No. 7: 163–165.

Nicholas B. Breyfogle

and cages for the sable breeding farms; and 6) to determine how the hunting process would work in the game park (who would get to hunt, when, using what technologies and how much would they be able to hunt). These were difficult questions that required information-gathering, extended thought and thorough planning, but the most complicated was the question of boundaries.[32]

Lines on the Landscape: Creating the Boundaries of the Zapovednik

It was one thing to decide to create the nature reserve, it was quite another to actually determine how much territory should be included – which lands and waters exactly – and what to do with the people who already lived in or migrated through that territory. Just where exactly would the nature reserve be and, one might ask, why did they not attempt to set aside for preservation more land than they ultimately did? Many factors went into setting the boundaries of the *zapovednik*. The process is a reminder of the often arbitrary divisions that were supposed to create 'inviolable' nature reserves – and helps us to understand, in part, why the boundaries changed as often as they did in the twentieth century (see Map 12.2). The process also underscores the importance of the region's landscapes, waterscapes, flora and fauna in defining the limits of preservation. These factors included: 1) The size, location and movements of the sable population and the availability of appropriate food and shelter for sable in various locations; 2) the landscape and hydrological systems of the region (the mountains, watersheds, rivers and lakes that offered 'natural' boundaries for the *zapovednik*); 3) the human needs of the local population for hunting and fishing, especially the hunting patterns and traditional territorial rights of Evenks and Russian peasants in the area; 4) the need to ensure a stable guard population who could travel easily through the *zapovednik* and the need to create defensible boundaries for guards to protect; and 5) the location of pre-existing administrative and communal boundaries.

In delimiting the boundaries of the nature reserve, the physical contours of the landscapes and waterscapes were determining factors. That is, whilst humans made the ultimate choices in deciding where the boundaries would be, the actual structures of the land and river systems directly affected their efforts. The initial plan (from 1914) for the Barguzin nature reserve was

---

32. Doppel'mair, *Sobolinyi promysel*, pp. 5–22. It bears remembering that all of this planning took place in the midst of World War One, which complicated matters from access to materials, travel and other logistics, and even to the point that Svatosh, a Czech, was investigated as a potential threat because of his birth in Habsburg territory. Iankus, *Zenon Svatosh*, p. 55.

a great deal more expansive than the final one agreed upon, stretching all the way from the Bol'shaia River in the north down to the Sviatoi Nos peninsula, just north of Ust'-Barguzin. However Doppel'mair and his fellow expedition members considered the original map 'unacceptable' for a variety of reasons: the hydrology of the watersheds, the need to ensure the livelihood of the Evenk population and to protect their rights and also defence against 'predatory' hunters. The eastern and western boundaries remained relatively stable because of geography: to the east stood the Barguzin Mountains, which formed a 'natural' eastern boundary; to the west was the shoreline of Lake Baikal, another 'natural' boundary in their view.[33] In the north, however, the expedition members worried that the boundary deviated too far from the watershed of the Bol'shaia River, did not include important tributaries and did not follow the course of the river through the valley. Ultimately, Doppel'mair believed, the boundary was too disconnected from the natural landscapes and waterscapes to be useful for the *zapovednik*. The research team then re-located the northern boundaries of the nature reserve southward to the right side of the valley of the Tarkulik River. The *zapovednik* was designed to incorporate the river valleys that housed the most dark-furred sable (including the Bol'shaia, the Malaia and Bol'shaia Cheremshana, Kudalda and Sosnovka rivers). By shifting south, they offered a northern border that they thought would be easier to defend from predatory hunters. At the same time, they believed that the *zapovednik* would intervene less in the hunting lives of the local Evenks who had traditionally hunted in the Bol'shaia River area.[34]

The expedition also moved the location of the southern boundary, cutting from the originally-proposed *zapovednik* the entire Sviatoi Nos region and some of the land north of it, a region of about 60,000 *desiatinas*. This large amount of land was dropped from the protected zone for several reasons: 1) there were no sable to be found in the territory at that time; 2) the forest suffered from frequent fires and the forest area was of little meaningful economic value (its rent in 1906–07 was only nineteen roubles); 3) they believed it would be difficult to guard and protect (only sable by the shore areas might be properly guarded); 4) the planners did not want to impede certain economic activities of the local population. Part of the land was used for profitable squirrel hunting and a *zapovednik* would impede those catches. There were also tracts of land

---

33. In 1958, part of the lake itself was included in the *zapovednik*, but not in the original delimitation of the borders.

34. Shillinger, 'Sovremennoe sostoiane', No. 6: 142–143 and No. 7: pp. 163–165; Turov, 'K voprosu', pp. 3–20; Doppel'mair, *Sobolinyi promysel*, pp. 11–15.

and water near Sviatoi Nos that were important fishing grounds (especially in the Barguzin and Chivyrkui bays) that planners did not want to take from the local population's use; and 5) to alienate the native peoples of the Chitkan Volost' (district) from access to this land would be a complicated legal process.[35]

Having decided not to include Sviatoi Nos, they chose instead a southern boundary along the Bol'shoi Chivyrkui River that would run up into the Barguzin range. The planners in the expedition wanted to include the Bol'shoi Chivyrkui River region in the *zapovednik* even though in preceding years very few sable had been noted (or caught) – and the economic importance of these rivers had fallen. They did so because there were important food sources for the sable in the forests along the river valley (especially pine nuts and berries) and very good conditions for the sable to live in. The planners hoped that by including these forests and lands in the *zapovednik*, ultimately sable would make their way south to take advantage of the abundant food. They also judged that the Bol'shoi Chivyrkui River was easy to guard as a boundary. A post could be built at the mouth of the river, where guards could live without too much difficulty because of access to transit routes, to fish in Baikal and because of the possibility of grain growing.[36] Moreover, this river was the northern end of the Chitkan Volost', and only to the north of that boundary was it possible to alienate the native people from their land without legal difficulties. In the end, the size of the inviolable part of the *zapovednik* was to be 198,542 *desiatinas*.

Doppel'mair and his team also had to figure out how sable hunting would work in the hunting zone contiguous to the *zapovednik*. Who would hunt, how and under what rules? In reducing the size of the *zapovednik* in the north, they opened up this land to be used for a restricted game reserve – a place where hunting would take place in such a way as to ensure the long-term health of the sable populations. There would be sufficient sable, they estimated, for 62 to 64 sable hunters in the game reserve. These lands were then subdivided based on older Evenk hunting practices. The hunting reserve was to have an overall size of 325,833 *desiatinas*. The faith of the research team that sustainable sable hunting could be undertaken in the game reserve was bolstered by their belief that the Evenks had for years hunted there without extinguishing the sable and had refined sustainable methods and technologies.

---

35. Turov, 'K voprosu', pp. 3–20.
36. The boundaries of the *zapovednik* were designed to be most easily protected. The expedition team believed the village of Sosnovka, for example, was a location where guards could live and from which they could easily travel up the rivers and into the central parts of the *zapovednik* to protect the sable from poachers.

Losing out to the Sable: Evenks

During the process of creating the *zapovednik*, the Shemagir Evenk communities were relocated northward and given new lands to inhabit. In 1918, they relocated to the village of Tompa and later, in the Soviet period, onto collective farms inland.[37] This environmental relocation is but one of many examples globally of how the fate of indigenous communities was intimately tied up with environmental conservation, and how the native peoples often lost out in the nexus of empire and conservation. Notably, after these people were removed from the land they had utilised for generations, their former territory was re-envisioned by Russian writers as 'untouched taiga' where no humans had lived before. In this way the land became appropriate to fit the model of the *zapovednik* where 'virgin' lands were protected and closed off from human influence.[38]

Yet, tsarist officials did take the needs of the Evenk inhabitants into account during the process of creating the Barguzin *Zapovednik*. From the very outset of the discussions, they were aware of and concerned for the Evenks who lived and hunted the region. When the Irkutsk governor-general first proposed the creation of a *zapovednik*, he emphasised that its establishment would be complicated by the fact that the designated area was in the Evenk domain, 'who, on the foundation of articles 34–35 of the Statute on *Inorodtsy*, have here "full freedom in the economic use of the waters and lands", in addition to which hunting for sable for these inorodtsy serves as the only means of existence'.[39] Moreover, the governor-general worried that because the post-smallpox Evenks only hunted three or four rivers themselves and otherwise rented out the remainder of rivers to local Russians – for a revenue, in his estimation, of about 16,000 roubles – that separating them from these hunting lands would cause serious injury to their communities. In his views, the governor-general echoed those of the Trans-Baikal Oblast' administration, who, when discussing the creation of a sable reserve in 1913, asserted that the land could only be taken from Evenk control if other lands were given to them in the place of these losses. From this effort to compensate the Evenks came a plan to move many of them much further north up Lake Baikal, where they could hunt unimpeded by any

---

37. Iankus, 'Istoricheskii opyt sozdaniia', p. 74.

38. Freidberg, *Baikal, Barguzinskii Zapovednik*, pp. 4, 15–16. For comparison, see Oliver-Smith, 'Evicted from Eden' pp. 141–162; Dowie, *Conservation Refugees*.

39. Iankus, *Zenon Svatosh*, p. 36.

Nicholas B. Breyfogle

state conservation rules, and then allow Evenk hunters to work the northern, restricted hunting areas of the nature reserve.[40]

War and Revolution and the Establishment of the Barguzin Zapovednik

The legal foundation for the Barguzin reserve came in three stages after the preparatory scientific and surveying work was completed. It was set out in a decree of the Irkutsk governor-general on 17 May 1916, which announced the creation of the Barguzin sable *zapovednik*, comprised of two parts: the core *zapovednik* and a hunting reserve.[41] The tsarist state then established a broader legal framework for the creation of nature reserves on 30 October 1916. This law granted the Minister of Agriculture and State Domains the right to create *zapovedniks* on lands owned exclusively by the treasury in order to both protect and expand the population size of economically important hunting animals and birds. Then, in the wake of the general *zapovednik* decree, the Senate approved the creation of the Barguzin *Zapovednik* in particular on 26 December 1916 (and the law was published in 20 January 1917). And, with that, the Barguzin *Zapovednik* came into existence.[42]

The early years of Barguzin were difficult to say the least. The tsarist state collapsed almost before the ink was dry on the law. World War One, revolutions and civil war ensured that there were no immediate resources to develop the expedition's grand plans. Only Svatosh remained on site during these years – suffering all sorts of deprivations as he tried to eke out an existence at Sosnovka. The guards disappeared, poaching of sable went on without restriction and the two sables that had been caught to serve as the foundation for the breeding farm were captured and killed. When an official sent by the Soviet government arrived to see where things stood in 1922, there was barely anything left (except for Svatosh standing his post).[43]

However, these grim early years did not last. In January 1926, the RFSFR Council of People's Commissars (Sovnarkom) breathed renewed life into the sable protection around Baikal when it issued a decree (re-)establishing the

---

40. Iankus, *Zenon Svatosh*, pp. 41–48.

41. Freidberg, *Baikal, Barguzinskii Zapovednik*, pp. 15–16.

42. Doppel'mair, pp. 10–11; 'Ob ustanovlenii pravil'; 'Ob uchrezhdenii Barguzinskogo zapovednika'.

43. At that point, the *zapovednik* also stood nominally outside of the Soviet state's jurisdiction in the short-lived, Japanese-controlled Far Eastern Republic. Turov, 'K voprosu', p. 3–20; Iankus, *Zenon Svatosh*, pp. 76–119; GARB f. R-562, op. 4, d. 10.

The Origins of the Barguzin Nature Reserve

Barguzin *Zapovednik*. Through much of the Soviet era, the Barguzin reserve continued to serve the functions initially set out for it by the tsarist-era scientists: to protect sable from localised extinction so that the species could remain a viable economic resource for the local peoples as well as for the state as a whole; and secondarily to protect the sable territory from other economic enterprises to make possible extensive scientific research in the ecology of the flora and fauna of the region. It is a measure of its success in meeting the goals of the founders that the population of the Barguzin sable increased significantly and have been used to repopulate several different locations in Siberia. The scientific research done in the reserve (on sable, and then on the other flora and fauna in the protected zone) has been extensive and influential. The land, water, air, flora and fauna remain today a testament to the vision of the *zapovednik*'s founders and the ongoing relationship between humans and nature at Barguzin.[44]

ACKNOWLEDGEMENTS

Research for this chapter was supported by funding from a Leverhulme Trust International Network Grant (for the project 'Exploring Russia's Environmental History and Natural Resources'), National Endowment for the Humanities, National Council for Eurasian and East European Research (NCEEER), under authority of a Title VIII grant from the US Department of State, American Philosophical Society, American Council of Learned Societies, Davis Center for Russian and Eurasian Studies, Kennan Institute for Advanced Russian Studies, Mershon Center for International Security Studies and The Ohio State University. Any views, findings, conclusions or recommendations expressed in this chapter do not necessarily reflect those of the National Endowment for the Humanities or any of the other funding agencies. Earlier versions of this chapter were presented at the National Convention of the American Association for the Advancement of Slavic Studies (2013), the World Congress of Environmental History conference (2014), and at the Leverhulme Trust seminar in Davsha, Barguzin *Zapovednik* (2015). I thank the panellists and the audience at these conferences for their comments and suggestions.

BIBLIOGRAPHY

Barguzin *Zapovednik* Museum, Davsha (visited 2015).

---

44. GARB f. R-562, op. 4, d. 10; GARB f. R-562, op. 4, d. 143; GARB f. R-562, op. 44, d. 113. See also the multiple publications in *Trudy Barguzinskogo gosudarstvennogo zapovednika*.

Nicholas B. Breyfogle

Baturin, A.D. 1926 'Sobol' i sobolinyi promysel: B. Sobolinyi promysel'. In G.G. Doppel'mair (ed.), *Sobolinyi promysel na severo-vostochnom poberezh'i Baikala. Materialy Barguzinskoi ekspeditsii G.G. Doppel'maira 1914–1915*, pp. 103–145. Verkhneudinsk-Leningrad, Izdanie Gosplana BMASSR.

Breyfogle, Nicholas. 2013. 'The Fate of Fishing in Tsarist Russia: The Human-Fish Nexus in Lake Baikal'. *Sibirica: Interdisciplinary Journal of Siberian Studies* 12 (2): 1–29.

Brown, B. 2004. 'Thing Theory'. In B. Brown (ed.), *Things*. Chicago: University of Chicago Press.

Doppel'mair, G.G. 1926. *Sobolinyi promysel na severo-vostochnom poberezh'i Baikala. Materialy Barguzinskoi ekspeditsii G.G. Doppel'maira 1914–1915*. Verkhneudinsk-Leningrad: Izdanie Gosplana BMASSR.

Doppel'mair, G.G. and K.A. Zabelin. 1926. 'Naselenie Barguzinskogo uezda, v ego otnoshenii k sobolinomu promyslu'. In G.G. Doppel'mair (ed.), *Sobolinyi promysel na severo-vostochnom poberezh'i Baikala. Materialy Barguzinskoi ekspeditsii G.G. Doppel'maira 1914–1915*, pp. 197–270. Verkhneudinsk-Leningrad: Izdanie Gosplana BMASSR.

Dowie, Mark. 2009. *Conservation Refugees: The Hundred-Year Conflict between Global Conservation and Native Peoples*. Cambridge, MA: MIT Press.

Egorov, O.A. 1990. *Anatolii Alekseevich Silant'ev*. Moscow: VO Agropromizdat.

Etkind, Alexander. 2011. 'Barrels of Fur: Natural Resources and the State in the Long History of Russia'. *Journal of Eurasian Studies* 2 (2): 164–71.

Fisher, H. R. 1943. *The Russian Fur Trade, 1550–1700*. Berkeley: University of California Press.

Freidberg, Aleksei. 1993. *Baikal, Barguzinskii Zapovednik*. Moscow: AO TsEPRUSS i MGP 'Severnye prostory'.

Gissibl, Bernhard, Sabine Höhler and Patrick Kupper (eds). 2012. *Civilizing Nature: National Parks in Global Historical Perspective*. New York: Berghahn Books.

Gosudarstvennyi Arkhiv Respubliki Buriatii (GARB, State Archive of the Republic of Buriatiia).

Grove, Richard. 1995. *Green Imperialism: Colonial Expansion, Tropical Island Edens and the Origins of Environmentalism, 1600–1860*. New York: Cambridge University Press.

Gusev, Oleg. 1979. 'Sobolinyi krai – Podlemor'e'. *Smena*. No. 5: 16–17. http://smena-online.ru/sites/default/files/05_-_1979.pdf

Gusev, Oleg. 1990. *Na ocharovannom beregu*. Moscow: Sovetskaia Rossiia.

Iankus, A.G. 2011. *Zenon Svatosh. Puteshestvennik, zoolog, director pervogo v Rossii zapovednika. Afrika, Arktika, Baikal*. Moscow: BiznesInform, ITs Postscriptum.

Iankus, G.A. 2006. 'Istoricheskii opyt sozdaniia i raboty Barguzinskogo zapovednika'. In *Istoriia i sovremennost' osobo okhraniaemykh prirodnykh territorii Baikal'skogo regiona (Mater. region. nauchno-praktich. konf., posviashch. 90-letiiu zapovednogogo dela Rossii).* Ulan-Ude: Izdatel'stvo BGSKhA.

Jones, Ryan Tucker. 2014. *Empire of Extinction: Russians and the North Pacific's Strange Beasts of the Sea, 1741–1867.* New York: Oxford University Press.

Kohn, Eduardo. 2013. *How Forests Think: Toward an Anthropology beyond the Human.* Berkeley and Los Angeles: University of California Press.

Kupper, Patrick. 2014. *Creating Wilderness: A Transnational History of the Swiss National Park.* New York: Berghahn Books.

Latour, Bruno. 2007. *Reassembling the Social: An Introduction to Actor-Network-Theory.* New York: Oxford University Press.

LeCain, Timothy J. 2017. *The Matter of History: How Things Create the Past.* New York: Cambridge University Press.

Mitchell, Timothy. 2002. *Rule of Experts: Egypt, Techno-Politics, Modernity.* Berkley and Los Angeles: University of California Press.

Moon, David. 2013. *The Plough that Broke the Steppes: Agriculture and Environment on Russia's Grasslands, 1700–1914.* New York: Oxford University Press.

Nasimovich, A.A. 1979. 'Dorevoliutsionnyi period v razvitii zapovednogo dela'. In A.A. Nasimovich and Iu.A. Isakov (eds), *Opyt raboty i zadachi zapovednikov SSSR,* pp. 7–19. Moscow: Nauka.

Nash, Linda. 2005. 'The Agency of Nature or the Nature of Agency?' *Environmental History* **10** (1): 67–69.

'Ob ustanovlenii pravil ob okhotnich'ikh zapovednikakh'. 1916. *Sobranii uzakonenii i rasporiazhenii pravitel'stva.* 30 October. No. 304, Article 2396. St. Peterburg: Senatskaia tipografiia.

'Ob uchrezhdenii Barguzinskogo zapovednika'. 1917. *Sobranie uzakonenii i rasporiazhenii pravitel'stva.* 20 January. No. 18, Article 107. St. Peterburg: Senatskaia tipografiia.

Odling-Smee, F. John, Kevin N. Laland and Marcus W. Feldman. 2003. *Niche Construction: The Neglected Process in Evolution.* Princeton: Princeton University Press.

Oliver-Smith, Anthony. 2009. 'Evicted from Eden: Conservation and the Displacement of Indigenous and Traditional Peoples'. In Anthony Oliver-Smith (ed.), *Development and Dispossession: The Crisis of Forced Displacement and Resettlement,* pp. 141–62. Santa Fe: School for Advanced Research Press.

Richards, John F. 2006. *The Unending Frontier: An Environmental History of the Early Modern World.* Berkeley and Los Angeles: University of California Press.

Roe, Alan. 2020. *Into Russian Nature: Tourism, Environmental Protection, and National Parks in the Twentieth Century.* New York: Oxford University Press.

Nicholas B. Breyfogle

Russell, Edmund. 2011. *Evolutionary History: Uniting History and Biology to Understand Life on Earth*. New York: Cambridge University Press.

Savenkova, T.P. 2002. *Atlas: okhraniaemye prirodnye territorii basseina ozera Baikal*. Irkutsk: Izdatel'stvo Ottisk.

Sheail, John. 2010. *Nature's Spectacle: The World's First National Parks and Protected Places*. London and Washington, DC: Earthscan.

Shillinger, F. 1914. 'Sovremennoe sostoiane okhotnich'iago khoziaistva v Vostochnoi Sibiri i sposoby uluchsheniia ego'. *Semiia okhotnikov* 7 (6): 142–143 and (7): 163–165.

Shtilmark, Feliks. 2003. *History of the Russian Zapovedniks*. Translated by G.H. Harper. Edinburgh: Russian Nature Press.

Shubin, A.S. 2001. *Evenki Pribaikal'ia*. Ulan-Ude: Izdatel'stvo Belig.

Solov'ev, D.K. 1921. 'Zapovedniki, ikh vydelenie, znachenie, organizatsiia i pr.' In D.K. Solov'ev (ed.), *Saianskii promyslovo-okhotnichii raion i sobolinyi promysel v nem*, pp. 267–309. Petrograd: Gosizdat.

Startsev, A.V. 2015. 'Gosudarstvennoe regulirovanie okkhotnich'ego promysla v Rossii v XVIII–nachale XX v'. *Vestnik Tomskogo gosudarstvennogo universiteta*. No. 400: 152–156. doi: 10.17223/15617793/400/25.

Trudy Barguzinskogo gosudarstvennogo zapovednika. 1960. Vol. 2. Ulan-Ude: Buriatskoe knizhnoe izdatel'stvo.

Tsivilev, Nikolai Ivanovich. 1998. 'Zametki o severobaikal'skikh tungusakh (1880–1916 gg.)'. *Taltsy: arkhitektura, etnografiia, etnicheskaia istoriia, toponimika, filologiia: nauchno-popularnyi illiustrirovannyi zhurnal*. No. 1: 8–12.

Turov, S. 1922. 'K voprosu o Barguzinskom sobolinom zapovednike'. *Izvestiia Vostochno-Sibirskogo otdela Imperatorskogo Russkogo geograficheskogo obshchestva*. 46 (2): 3–20.

UNESCO. 2019. 'Barguzinskyi Biosphere Reserve, Russian Federation'. https://en.unesco.org/biosphere/eu-na/barguzinskyi.

Ustinov, S. 1979. *Zapovednik na Baikale*. Irkutsk: Vostochno-Sibirskoe knizhnoe izdatel'stvo.

Weiner, Douglas. 2000 [1988]. *Models of Nature: Ecology, Conservation, and Cultural Revolution in Soviet Russia*. 2nd ed. Pittsburgh: University of Pittsburgh Press.

Weiner, Douglas. 2002. *A Little Corner of Freedom: Russian Nature Protection from Stalin to Gorbachev*. Berkeley and Los Angeles: University of California Press.

Zabelin, K. 1925. 'Promyslovye okhoty v Barguzinskom krae'. *Zhizn' Buriatii* 2 (5–6): 38–50.

13.

BAIKAL WATERS:
INDUSTRIAL DEVELOPMENT AND
INSTITUTIONAL DEBATES, 1950s–1970s

Elena Kochetkova

This chapter examines the differing opinions between industrial and scientific institutions over the use of the waters of Lake Baikal in the context of Soviet development policies in Siberia, beginning in the 1950s. It argues that institutions and people experienced Baikal as a place of contradiction, clearly illustrating that Soviet industry posed the risk of harm to the natural environment. In different professional layers of Soviet society, Baikal became an arena of conflict over water (and nature more broadly) and the lake's own, natural ability to purify chemical waste discharged into the waters. Employing new archival sources, such as institutional and individual correspondence and reports, this chapter discusses the role of Baikal in the interplay between industry and environment at the institutional level and contributes to the scholarship on Soviet postwar environmental history.

As the geographer Philip Pryde wrote in 1991, a highly industrialised society such as the Soviet Union could not be free from 'unwanted chemical intrusions', which were 'the dark side of 'progress'.[1] Beginning in the 1950s, the long-running debate over industrial construction near Lake Baikal became a vivid illustration of this statement. Industrial development in Siberia after World War Two led to diversion of chemical waste into a lake previously not heavily touched by pollutants. The intent to use Baikal waters in the interests of Soviet pulp making caused a division of views among industrial and research institutions. From the 1950s until the early 2010s, several waves of protest erupted in the area. Many scholarly works have examined the position of Soviet environmental scientists and journalists in their efforts to protect the lake and,

---

1.   Pryde, *Environmental Management in the Soviet Union*, p. 93.

Elena Kochetkova

more broadly, examine those who took part in environmental development.[2] This chapter is focused on the construction of two plants near Lake Baikal in the context of strains between various institutional actors involved. It illustrates the conflicts between various institutions, in particular between industry-oriented organisations, such as ministries and Gosstroi (the State Committee for Construction in the Soviet Union),[3] on the one hand, and research institutes such as the Siberian Branch of the Academy of Sciences, on the other. Both sides had voices for and against the construction, but in the end the industrial point of view was stronger. This chapter examines how, despite protests, Baikal changed from an industrially untouched lake into a lake that saw 'migrating zones of contamination'.[4]

The supporters of construction saw Baikal as an industrial resource, whilst the protesters decried its pollution. The large body of unexploited water was valuable to both groups, but for different reasons. To industrialists, it represented the promise of abundant resources easily tapped, whilst to protectors, it was a pristine work of nature untouched by humans and industrial changed represented risk. As Doreen Massey says, instead of 'thinking of places as areas with particular boundaries around, they should be imagined as articulated moments in networks of social relations and understandings'.[5] Because both place and space are socially constructed, the shaping of place results from struggles

---

2. Lubomudrov, 'Environmental Politics in the Soviet Union'; Gustafson, *Reform in Soviet Politics*; Josephson, *New Atlantis Revisited*; Weiner, *A Little Corner of Freedom*; Yanitsky, 'From Nature Protection to Politics'; Coumel and Elie, 'A Belated and Tragic Ecological Revolution'; and Breyfogle, 'At the Watershed', among others. See also the chapters in this volume by the Kalikhmans and Breyfogle on the role of scientists in protection of Lake Baikal and its natural surroundings.

3. Like many other Soviet institutes, Gosstroi was reorganised several times during its history. Thus, in 1962 it became the State Council on Construction of the Council of Ministers of the USSR; in 1963 it was reorganised into the State Committee for Construction Affairs; in 1978 it became the State Committee of the USSR on Construction. The responsibilities of the institute changed over time, but in general it remained responsible for technical politics and construction development in the USSR.

4. This chapter continues my previous research, which resulted in two earlier articles. The first is devoted to technology transfer between Svetogorsk/Leningrad and Baikal. The second is devoted to the activities of engineers in the Central Research Institute for Paper and Pulp who developed the water treatment facilities for Baikal. See Kochetkova, 'Between Water Pollution' and 'Ekologicheskaia kontroverza'.

5. Massey, 'The Practical Place of Locality Studies', p. 28. See also Hillier, 'Values, Images, Identities'.

between the images, aspirations and values of various actors.[6] Discussing these struggles, this story illustrates how different groups perceived and constructed Baikal. It also asks whether the way in which these actors approached Baikal demonstrates that the Soviet Union was a risk society, which, as the sociologist Ulrich Beck argues, 'begins where nature ends'.[7] In his view, industrial modernisation, and technology in particular, produce insecurities and risks whilst mastering nature; industrial societies create environmental risks and unintended consequences. Some institutions even lose control of the threats they produce.[8] Given these theoretical insights, did Soviet institutions involved in the construction on Baikal see the project as risky and why? Was it, indeed, a risk for nature? How did institutions experience and construct Baikal as industrial or untouchable space?

The first part of this chapter discusses Soviet industrial development policies and practices in Siberia. The following sections examine the transformation of views among various institutions involved in the question of industrial construction on Baikal from the 1950s through the 1970s. The last section gives an overview of the later history of the question.

Economic Exploration of Siberia and the Baikal Region

Intensive economic exploration of the Baikal region began with construction of the Trans-Baikal section of the Trans-Siberian Railway in the 1890s. The project included both mineral and land surveys and hydrographic expeditions to Lake Baikal headed by the famous hydrographer Fedor Drizhenko. These expeditions produced a number of influential publications, such as aquatic maps, atlases and physiographic descriptions of the lake.[9]

After World War Two, the economic significance of the territory increased, as the Soviet leadership considered Siberia and the Far East prospective territories for development. These areas opened up opportunities for the Soviet state to exploit various types of rich natural resources, such as fossil fuels, water energy, fish and others. The organisation that played a big role in exploring new areas

---

6. See Hillier, 'Imagined Value'.

7. Beck, *Risk Society*, p. 10. But at the same time 'risk' in the future is to a large extent something which starts before nature ends. Tvedt and Oestigaard, 'A History of the Ideas of Water', p. 7.

8. Beck, *Risk Society*.

9. See, for example, a fundamental work that summarised the results of the expeditions in 1896–1902, Drizhenko (ed.), *Lotsiia i fiziko-geograficheskii ocherk ozera Baikal*.

Elena Kochetkova

was the Council on the Exploration of Productive Forces (*Sovet po izucheniiu proizvoditel'nykh sil*, SOPS), founded in 1930 within the Soviet Academy of Sciences.[10] It played a significant role in organising scientific expeditions to Siberia and the Urals, Kazakhstan and other regions of the country. As a result, the postwar activities of the Council contributed to the 'explanation of economic rationality of exploring hydroenergetic resources of the Angara and Enisei rivers, the increase of excavation of coal in Kuzbass, the creation of a metal-working plant in Cherepovets, exploring oil resources in the shelf of Apsheronskii Peninsula, the enlargement of lands for irrigated agriculture in the basins of the Syr Daria and Amur Daria rivers, the use of iron stone in the Turgaiskii basin'.[11]

Some scientists supported this view about the need to advance industrial development into new regions. In 1947, an important point in the relations between nature and the economy in Siberia, the Academy of Sciences held a conference to examine the productive forces in the Irkutsk region.[12] The event gathered leading scientists, including the vice president of the Academy of Sciences, Academician Ivan Bardin, and another academician, Lev Sheviakov, who headed SOPS. Among other things, attendees concluded that it was important to create a general plan for economic development in eastern Siberia. In particular, they concluded that cheap hydropower and fuel resources of the Irkutsk region should be the main objective for economic expansion in the region.[13] Another result of this conference was the establishment of the East Siberian Branch of the Academy of Sciences in Irkutsk in February 1949. By the late 1950s, the branch had grown into a large scientific organisation which consisted of two institutes (geology and chemistry), three departments (biology, energy and economy and geography) and twelve laboratories. Its initial aim was to conduct and coordinate scientific research in the region as well as explore the region's natural resources through economic, geological, and other research. When the Baikal question arose, however, this organisation became a source of criticism and the main opponent to the constructors of the pulp making plants.

---

10. It was formed on the basis of the Commission for the Exploration of Natural Productive Forces (KEPS) that acted between 1915 and 1930. See more in Kol'tsov, *Sozdanie i deiatel'nost' Komissii po izucheniu estestvennykh proizvoditel'nykh sil Rossii*.

11. Granberg, 'Izuchenie proizvoditel'nykh sil Rossii', p. 581.

12. Conferences on the exploration of productive forces in other regions took place before. See also proceedings of 1947 conference in *Materialy Konferentsii po izucheniui proizvoditel'nykh sil Irkutskoi oblasti*.

13. Timoshenko, 'Strategiia sdviga proizvoditel'nykh sil SSSR na vostok', p. 305.

Nikita Khrushchev's epoch continued and even intensified industrial development in eastern regions. Although this time saw environmental initiatives, 'the environmental turn of Khrushchev's Russia was short-lived'.[14] It was a period of drive for a rapid industrial development to modernise Soviet industry, some branches of which already had been recognised as backward at the start of Khrushchev's governance.[15] There was a particularly strong belief in chemistry and its extensive possibilities for chemicals in a myriad of industrial production techniques and facilities, most threatening land, soil, air, trees and water. In addition, there was a desire to develop manufacturing of pulp and pulp-based products. The following years saw intensive construction and industrial development in different parts of Siberia. Thus, for example, in 1957, the construction of a large metal-working plant near Novokuznetsk was begun. In the Irkutsk region, the Korshunovskii mining and ore processing plant was established to excavate the copious iron stone deposits of eastern Siberia and a significant number of nonferrous-metal industrial facilities were constructed.[16]

The prevailing discourse on nature protection was clear in official documents and speeches. As Khrushchev told the 22nd Congress of the Communist Party of the Soviet Union in 1961, Soviet society needed to protect Soviet nature, rationally use its resources and increase the productivity of its natural resources. Even before the Baikal project in the 1950s, the Council of Ministers of the USSR published several resolutions on water protection. In the years to follow, similar resolutions were issued by the republics. The number of such decrees was quite high. They encouraged the building of water and wastewater treatment facilities in factories located near large rivers and prohibited the construction of enterprises which did not use such facilities.[17] A new law, 'On Nature Protection', introduced in the Russian Republic (RSFSR) in 1960, stressed the importance of nature as the basis of the Soviet economy and the need to protect nature, in part by building waste treatment facilities. Moreover, a special resolution of the Council of Ministers introduced 'responsibility' (not

---

14. Coumel, 'A Failed Environmental Turn?', p. 189.

15. The year of 1955 can be seen as a launch of Khruchshev's modernisation. This year the resolution 'On the Improvement of the Examination and Implementation of the Experience and Achievements of Advanced Domestic and Foreign Techniques into National Economy' was issued. See more in Kochetkova, 'Tekhnologicheskaia modernizatsiia v SSSR'.

16. Timoshenko, 'Strategiia sdviga proizvoditel'nykh sil SSSR na vostok', p. 308. See also Timoshenko, *Gosudarstvennaia politika formirovaniia i zakrepleniia naseleniia v raionakh promyshlennogo osvoeniia Sibiri v 1950–1980-e gody*.

17. Gosudarstvennyi arkhiv Rossiiskoi Federatsii (GARF) f. 5446, op. 1, d. 60, ll. 132–3.

Elena Kochetkova

precisely defined) for irrational use of water. Factories were prohibited from starting operations without equipment for water cleaning.[18] This resolution, however, did not propose how to deal with current problems, and did not create appropriate conditions for systematic programs for water cleaning.[19]

In general, as David Duke puts it, 'in the Soviet period, Siberia represented the new frontier: a vast, harsh, inhospitable region where the construction of Communism would be tested to its limits. It was the task of Soviet engineers and workers to bend nature, here at its most dangerous and difficult, to their will.'[20] Few scientists said that it was possible to use the rich resources of new areas rationally without significant damage to nature and ecosystems, though their true thoughts and motives are unclear. For instance, G. Iu. Vereshchagin, limnologist and expert on Baikal, wrote in the mid-1940s that Baikal was important in the Soviet economy for developing water transport, cheap energy and fisheries.[21] An influential zoologist, L.S. Berg, said in 1948 that Baikal and the area nearby had a lot of resources, such as fish, trees and fowl that should be exploited by growing Soviet industries.[22] Some Soviet scientists at that time combined 'faith in progress with a strong belief in the possibility to avoid its negative impact through technological solutions'.[23] If the European part of the USSR was already domesticated, as Soviet planners saw it, Siberia was a new frontier and challenge.

The development of the pulp and paper industry was one important direction for industrial growth in Siberia and the Far East.[24] The postwar leadership aimed to increase production of paper and pulp as well as introduce new types of these materials. Vast forest resources in Siberia and its waters were necessary conditions for building the pulp and paper industry. During the 1960s and 1970s, the Krasnoiarsk Pulp and Paper Plant, the Bratsk Forestry Industry Complex and the Amur Pulp and Cardboard Plant were constructed, among others. In addition, Lake Baikal seemed to be an appropriate place for

---

18. 'O merakh po uporiadocheniiu ispol'zovaniia i usileniiu okhrany vodnykh resursov SSSR', p. 49.

19. Douglas Weiner says that this law did not have a lot of effect. Weiner, *A Little Corner of Freedom*, p. 269.

20. Duke, 'Seizing Favours from Nature', p. 3.

21. Vereshchagin, *Baikal. Nauchno-populiarnyi ocherk*.

22. Berg, *Baikal, ego priroda i znachenie v narodnom khoziaistve*.

23. Josephson, *New Atlantis Revisited*, p. 182.

24. See more in the report issued by the Academy of Sciences in 1980. Velikhov, Gvishiani and Mikulinsky (eds), *Science, Technology and the Future*.

manufacturing a super-strong rayon cord, a new material produced on the basis of the technology transferred from the United States. Baikal's pure water allowed for making this strong material, required for aviation and other uses.[25] Due to this, two enterprises were launched near the lake: the Baikal'sk Pulp and Paper Plant on the south shore near the Solzan River and the pulp and cardboard plant in the delta of the Selenga River. As Peter Thompson says, 'Khrushchev is reputed to have said, "Baikal, too, must work".'[26] As in other regions globally at that time, the state, engineers and some scientists saw the lake as a possible resource for industrial purposes and use. However, each sector had its own view on how significant the pollution would be.

Discussions around the Baikal and Selenga Plants

Even though some scientists supported industrial expansion into Siberia and other new territories, the chosen locations of the two pulp-making enterprises near Baikal caused dissatisfaction among professionals. It became clear that Baikal would suffer significant industrial pollution from chemicals. In the late 1950s, several articles supporting this view were published in the newspaper *Literaturnaia Gazeta* by writers, journalists and scientists. Thus, in 1958 scientists G.I. Galazii, E.K. Grechishchev, M.M. Kozhov, writers G.F Kungurov and K.F. Sedykh and the builders of the Irkutsk hydroelectric station, among others, published an article titled 'In Defence of Baikal'. They said that Baikal belongs to the future generations, or 'people of communism', and should be treated carefully. They warned the proposals could lower the lake's water level, destroy fish spawning areas and endanger water supplies of nearby settlements.[27] In February 1962, N.G. Prozorovskii gave a paper entitled 'On the Protection and Use of Water Resources of Lake Baikal' at the All-Union Society for Nature Protection, which concluded that, even with water treatment facilities, the Baikal and Selenga plants could release 'relatively pure' waters that were still harmful to fish, fauna and flora. The technological scheme of wastewater treatment that was accepted by the builders, they said, had not been tested in the Soviet Union.[28] The same year, the expert commission of the Presidium of the East Siberian Branch of the Academy of Sciences, which included Galazii, M.M. Odintsov, N. Klimov and M. Shestakovskii concluded that the project

---

25. Josephson, *New Atlantis Revisited*, p. 163.

26. Thompson, *Sacred Sea*, p. 176.

27. Bochkin et al., 'V zachshitu Baikala', 2 Sept. 1958.

28. GARF f. 5446, op. 97, d. 833, ll. 48–9.

did not guarantee full treatment and protection of Baikal waters.[29] As the geographer I. Gerasimov wrote, the construction on Baikal would entail dangerous consequences 'that are not acceptable in the eye of science and further rational use of ultra-pure Baikal waters'.[30] Indeed, the method of water treatment proposed by engineers was new not only in the Soviet Union but internationally, and in fact was expected to be tested at Baikal.

In 1963 the East Siberian Branch of the Academy of Sciences, which was established a few years earlier, issued a statement on the construction near Baikal. It said the construction site had been chosen

> without any exploration of the question [industrial production and its impact on the lake -E.K.] and consequences of exploitation of the plants for the complex use of Baikal's natural resources. Professional scientists (*uchenye-spetsialisty*) who worked on Baikal had not been involved in choosing the location, whilst the geological services had not been involved in evaluating the engineering and geological conditions of the construction of industrial buildings and housing.[31]

They complained that engineering and geological research on the site was completed only in 1961 for the Baikal plant and in 1962 for the Selenga plant, long after construction had begun. In 1963, they wrote, there were no confirmed project specifications on water treatment facilities, even though the engineers promised water purity to legitimate the building of the Baikal plant. The statement agreed that Baikal's pure waters had specific chemical content and were the only option for making high quality pulp, and this is why the choice of Lake Baikal for building this kind of plant was understandable. However, the Selenga's waters were not as pure as Baikal's and making cardboard did not require water from this particular river. Thus, they noted that 'if the importance of the products manufactured by the Baikal plant justifies its location near Baikal because this manufacturing requires exclusively pure water, the Selenga plant does not depend on the quality of water and its location near Baikal is not justified'.[32] Even whilst being critical of the possible environmental impacts of construction, these scientists underscored that production could be prioritised if there was no other way. The geographer I. Gerasimov agreed, writing that if the Baikal plant is constructed for 'manufacturing of especially high quality,

29. GARF f. 5446, op. 101, d. 768, l.11.

30. Arkhiv Rossiiskoi Akademii Nauk (ARAN) f. 1850, op. 1, d. 24, l. 5. See more in Snytko, Sobisevich, 'Vklad akademika I.P. Gerasimova v problemu monitoringa prirodnoi sredy'.

31. GARF f. 5446, op. 97, d. 836, l. 5.

32. Ibid., l. 6.

which requires ultra-pure water, the Selenga plant does not require consuming such kind of water'.[33] Scientists saw the Selenga River as not critical to industrial production and could be spared.

In general, unlike Gosstroi, the East Siberian Branch of the Academy spoke against industrial construction on the Selenga River from the very beginning, and only later became increasingly critical of the building of the Baikal plant. They argued the project's high economic and environmental costs were unjustified given the fact the plant would only produce regular container cardboard (in 1959 it had been redesigned to produce cardboard instead of viscose pulp). They argued the engineer-specialists proposed a 'paradoxical solution' to choose to spend more to build the plant in a location of high seismic intensity and that would need a costly water purification system. The scientists recommended discontinuing construction on the Selenga and looking for another, geologically more stable, place, for example near Ulan-Ude.[34] At the same time, they suggested accelerating construction of water treatment facilities for the Baikal plant. The construction plans called for biological water treatment, using special micro-organisms, a new and promising kind of purification process the planners promised would return pure water from the plant to Baikal.[35]

The same year, Gosstroi held a meeting devoted to the construction of the plants. The participants agreed that, despite the criticism, construction should be continued. As they said, scientists of the Academy had already suggested cancelling the construction several times since 1959, stalling a project 'so important for the country'.[36] They referred to the commission organised by the government in March 1962, including specialists from different institutes, though all construction-oriented, like V. Dymshits from Gosplan (the State Planning Commission) of the USSR, A. Goregliada from the State Committee for the Economy (*Glavekonomsovet*), Grishmanova and Kucherenko from Gosstroi and Orlov from the State Committee for Forestry, Pulp and Paper and Wood Processing Industry and Silviculture. The commission had determined to continue with both enterprises whilst the Presidium of the Council of Ministers supported this decision.

In addition, Gosstroi made up a commission of scientists who did not work in the East Siberian Branch and who were, as its report said, 'highly qualified specialists' on engineering seismology, geology, water supply and

---

33. Gerasimov, *Preobrazovanie prirody i razvitie geograficheskoi nauki v SSSR*, p. 53.

34. GARF f. 5446, op. 97, d. 836, l. 20.

35. Kochetkova, 'Ekologicheskaia kontroverza'.

36. GARF f. 5446, op. 97, 836, l. 32.

wastewater treatment. The commission was headed by Aleksei Zhukov, a deputy chief engineer of the State Trust on the Planning of Water Supply and Sewage (*Vodokanalproekt*) and included applied scientists who worked in the technical sector. The commission decided to continue the construction of the Selenga plant, saying that the seismological activity in the region was less intensive than suggested by the Academy, and this decrease would be enough to make a decision in favour of the construction. In addition, the commission said that it was important to set up sand filters that could purify water. They also declined the suggestion of the Siberian Academy of Sciences to direct effluent discharge into the Irkut River instead of Lake Baikal. At the 1963 meeting of Gosstroi and the Committee on the Construction in the USSR 'all the participants in the meetings, except Professor Solonenko who was a representative of the Siberian Branch of the Academy of Sciences, unanimously approved the suggestion of the Gosstroi commission'.[37]

The argument of Gosstroi, like industry-oriented institutions in general, was that the country needed the Selenga cardboard plant and the planned water treatment techniques would work to keep Baikal pure. In the 1963 report, Gosstroi stated clearly that 'it is time now to stop the discussion on the construction of the Selenga plant, make orders for equipment and machinery for this plant ... and take all the required measures for an enforced construction of this enterprise that is so significant for the country'.[38] Later the report chided, 'It is time to stop useless discussions' and begin the manufacturing of products 'urgently required for our national economy'.[39]

Gosstroi found support from the highest levels of the state. Thus, the Presidium of the Council of Ministers considered a recommendation letter written by Georgii Orlov, who was a significant figure in the Soviet forestry industry for a few decades and at that time headed the State Committee for Timber, Pulp and Paper, Wood Processing and Silviculture. Orlov confirmed that the sites for 'both objects are chosen correctly'. The Presidium ordered the Committee and the Council of Ministers of the RSFSR to accept the analyses of both Gosstroi and the Siberian Academy of Sciences, and begin their planning from the principle that 'it was necessary to avoid the contamination of Lake Baikal by waste waters'.[40] Whilst this task was clear and Baikal-friendly, it was not apparent how to consider suggestions and opposing arguments, in

---

37.   Ibid., l. 39.
38.   Ibid., l. 43.
39.   Ibid., l. 47.
40.   Ibid., l. 51.

particular those concerning seismic risk. Even trying to balance viewpoints and conceding that nature should not be significantly polluted, the Council of Ministers was inclined to support the construction. In March 1962, based on the decision of the Presidium of the Council of Ministers, Gosstroi recommended continuing the construction of both enterprises.

Because the construction received support from leading industries, Academician Mikhail Lavrent'ev sent a letter to Nikita Khrushchev in May 1963. He insisted that the seismic activity in the region of the two plants was a source of danger and stressed that 'it makes the construction much more expensive and does not guarantee ... people's lives will be safe in the coming five years'. In addition, he pointed out that the wastewater outlet would contaminate the lake whilst deforestation of the mountains around Baikal would lead to the destruction of soils and cause natural disasters.[41] His fears were not unfounded: cutting trees in newly exploited areas, such as Baikal, had proven extensive and wasteful in many other regions of the USSR. In Siberia and the Far East, too much wood was left as waste. It had to be transported to waste deposits or left to litter enterprises.[42] G. Galazii, the head of the Limnological Institute of the Siberian Academy of Sciences, a famous figure in the movement to prevent industrial development on Baikal, published arguments against the plant's construction. In response to Galazii's publications, Nikolai Cherepanov, appointed head of the Baikal plant, published an article in the central newspaper *Leninskoe znamia* in February 1962 titled 'A Response of Many Thousands of Builders of the Baikal'sk Pulp Making Plant'. It deplored the 'unjustified and continuous revisions of the decrees of the party and government regarding the construction of the pulp-making plant on Lake Baikal because of "harmful pollutant emissions", "high seismic activities", "the absence of raw materials"'. He argued instead 'to focus scholars' attention towards assisting project and research institutes who solve problems connected to the construction and exploitation of the Baikal'sk pulp making plant'.[43] Like other industrial men, Cherepanov thus appealed to the need to construct an important enterprise, and proposed that scientists should not resist but assist the construction.

The resistance of Siberian scientists, such as Galazii, A. Trofimuk, M. Lavrent'ev and others, was significant. In April 1963, the Academy of Sciences appealed in a letter to the Party-State Control Committee (*Komitet partiino-gosudarstvennogo kontrolia*) and asked them to check on the construction

41.   Ibid., l. 53.

42.   GARF f. 5446, op. 97, d. 838, l. 9.

43.   GARF f. 5446, op. 97, d. 833, l. 27.

Elena Kochetkova

projects. After this address, local party authorities entered the debates. Thus, the secretary of the Buriat *obkom* (oblast'-level committee) of the Communist Party, A. Modogoev, 'asked about confirming the decision of Gosstroi of the USSR on the construction of the Selenga pulp and cardboard making plant'. Not entering the debates on the Baikal plant, they talked about the Selenga plant, which was located on the Buriat side of Baikal. Modogoev indicated that 'ongoing groundless declarations of some scientists of the Siberian Branch of the Academy of Sciences against the construction of the Selenga plant, which have taken place for several years, have, it seems, the sole aim of preventing the construction on Baikal of any enterprises that would release wastewater into the lake'. He argued that the argument about the enterprises being potential significant polluters were groundless because good water treatment equipment should have been installed there.[44] He thus stated clearly that the party organ was on the side of the builders, seeing the enterprise as an important step in the development of the national economy.

In April 1963, a group of specialists from Gosstroi travelled to the construction site of the Baikal plant and made their recommendations. The Siberian Branch of the Academy of Sciences criticised these recommendations. In particular, they did not agree with applying existing 'Rules for Surface Water Protection' (*Pravila okhrany poverkhnostnykh vod*) and argued that these rules were not acceptable for Baikal because of the unique chemical structure of its water, which made the lake crystal-clear and fertile with oxygen.[45] In addition, the Commission of Gosstroi had proposed erecting sedimentation basins – artificial cisterns that separated suspended impurities from wastewater and purified them with reagents. The Academy, however, said that it was not technically possible on Baikal: the lake was deep and previously, when these sorts of basins had been constructed at other lakes, the separation pools had been installed in shallow waters only. The Academy's scientists argued that South Baikal had a circulating current, so wastes would not leave the lake – a hydrological fact that meant that 'waste outlet must be prohibited'.[46] Later, the Siberian Academy conceded a point in the debate: in April 1963, it agreed with the suggestion to include sand filters in wastewater treatment facilities, although prior to this time they had not allowed any waste release at all and had suggested instead releasing wastewater into water basins other than Bai-

---

44. GARF f. 5446, op. 97, d. 836, l. 57.

45. GARF f. 5446, op. 97, d. 836, l. 8. See more on the specifics of Baikal waters, flora and fauna as explored in the 1960s in Kozhov, *Biologiia ozera Baikal,* among others.

46. Ibid., l. 9.

kal.[47] The main argument of these scientists was that existing methods of water treatment could not guarantee the protection of the lake. For this reason, they proposed treating wastewater but, due to insufficient technology, they recommended releasing wastes into the Irkut River.[48] At the same time, in 1963 the Siberian Academy of Sciences asked the Supreme Council of National Economy (VSNKh) to induce the State Committee for the Pulp and Paper Industry to enhance the construction of water treatment facilities.

Overall, this position was expressed by local scientists who worked in the Siberian Branch of the Academy. Most Moscow scientists supported the construction, making Siberian scientists, who saw a significant risk to nature, the main if not only vocal opponents of the factories.[49] In 1966, the Soviet government created another expert commission, led by Academicians N. Zhavoronkov and S. Vol'fkovich, who were expected to offer the last word and decide if the construction should take place or not. The commission concluded in particular that the Baikal plant would not be dangerous for the lake and, thus, the construction should be finished. Zhavoronkov, who headed the Department of General Non-Organic Chemistry in the Academy of Sciences, in particular, said that the lake could even withstand a few plants. A few influential Academicians – such as A. Vinogradov, A. Alexandrov, M. Keldysh and others – supported this view. The Baikal plant was finally opened in 1966, whilst the Selenga plant required more time for construction.

Contamination of the Lake and Later 'Struggles for Baikal'

From the winter of 1965, a Siberian Academy commission, chaired by A. Trofimuk and including N. Vorontsov, Odintsov, Galazii and others, worked on the problem of plant construction. The commission revealed a 'series of mistakes' ranging from the site selection to surveys to 'the consequences for Baikal'. 'Eliminating all the mistakes', the commission concluded, was 'already impossible, but the danger of pollution may be averted'.[50]

Indeed, despite promises, the building of water treatment systems was slow. In December 1967, the Council of Ministers of the RSFSR ordered the Ministry of Melioration and Water Economy and the Ministry of Health of the RSFSR, local hydro-meteorological services, the project institute 'Sibgipro-

---

47. Ibid., l. 20.

48. Ibid., l. 9.

49. Korytnyi, *Ekho ekologo-ekonomicheskikh skandalov*.

50. Josephson, *New Atlantis Revisited*, p. 178.

Elena Kochetkova

bum' and others to control the work of water treatment facilities at the Baikal plant. They found that the 'projected regime of wastewater treatment of the enterprise was infringed systematically'.[51] Thus, the released wastewater was much more polluted and contained five to ten times more suspended materials than the norms prescribed. They also revealed that between January and June of 1967 there were 162 cases when the wastewater did not correspond to the project norms. One of the reasons, they argued, was that the plant had been launched without the waste treatment facilities operational, although VSNKh and the Presidium of the Council of Ministers forbade this in 1965 and 1966 respectively.[52] At that moment, they said, there was not a single organisation studying the impact of the Baikal plant on the biological life in Baikal.[53]

In December 1967, the volume of chemicals released into the lake was almost twice the legal limit. The reason for this breach was a lack of chlorine used for water treatment and the release of sulphides, which were 'the most dangerous polluters for Baikal waters'. Because of this, it was decided in 1967 to establish an office of the Institute for Pulp and Paper in the Baikal region. This institute, the only one of its kind in the USSR, was located in Leningrad but led the building of water treatment facilities installed at the Baikal plant. Its engineers conducted experiments far away, and contacts were infrequent and control generally absent over the facilities at the plant. The plant itself was responsible for controlling water treatment, but within just a couple of years after the launch it became clear that it could not cope with the task. In 1967 the Council of Ministers of the RSFSR also decreed that the Siberian Branch of the Academy of Sciences needed to be involved in researching the lake because of water contamination.[54]

This situation caused concern at the highest levels. In March 1968, the vice chairman of the Council of Ministers, N. Tikhonov, held a meeting concerning Baikal. The meeting included a few specialists, such as V. Korzun from the Meteorological Services, N. Timofeev from the Ministry of the Forestry and Paper Industry, Ts. Georgievskii from the Ministry of Medium Machine-Building Industry of the USSR and N. Zhavoronkov from the Academy of Sciences. They decided to send the vice chairman of the ministry N. Chistiakov to Baikal 'in order to take all the possible measures in the location

51. GARF f. 5446, op. 102, d. 750, l.1.

52. Ibid., l. 2.

53. Ibid., l. 4.

54. Ibid., l. 7.

and organise a normal regime of plant work and to not allow pollution of Lake Baikal with wastewater from the plant'.[55]

On 28 March 1968, just a week after this decision was made, Chistiakov and the commission of specialists from various industrial research organisations and ministries came to the plant in order to check the water treatment equipment. They concluded that the plant leadership had taken measures and water treatment had now improved significantly.[56] I do not have more details on what this commission saw at the plant and what improvements were made, but I assume that it was rather a pro forma, predetermined decision. To illustrate, for example, in December 1968, Semenov, the head of the People's Control Organization of the Buriat Autonomous Republic, a low-level volunteer organisation, published an article in *Pravda* titled 'Unhurried Projectors'. He said that recently it had been revealed that the construction of water treatment facilities was delayed because the Ministry and Gosstroi had not provided the required technical documentation. This caused delays and problems in implementing technologies on time.[57] Interestingly, the Ministry of the Timber, Pulp and Paper and Wood Processing Industry responded to the article immediately, explaining that the delay had been caused by fishery and water control organs that had not approved the project designs of the facilities.[58] In fact, nature control organs did not agree with the technical solutions proposed by industrial organisation and saw them as insufficient for cleaning Baikal.

The plants, especially the Baikal enterprise, were launched even though the water treatment facilities were not ready and had a lot of unfinished parts (*nedodelki,* as archival documents put it).[59] The ministry accepted the plan of work of the Baikal plant despite 55 uncompleted components, including fourteen unfinished parts of the water treatment facilities.[60] As a result, beginning in 1967, if not earlier, the expressions 'zones of contamination' and 'pollution bubbles' appeared in the reports of institutions that examined the impact of liquid wastes on Baikal's waters. This meant that there were migrating bubbles of contaminants and a 'contamination zone' of ten to twelve square kilometres near the Baikal plant.

---

55.   GARF f. 5446, op. 102, d. 750, l. 24.

56.   GARF f. 5446, op. 102, d. 750, l. 28.

57.   GARF f. 5446, op. 101, d. 748, l. 20.

58.   GARF, f.5446, op. 101, d. 747, l. 19.

59.   GARF f. 5446, op. 102, d. 750, l.1.

60.   GARF f. 5446, op. 101, d. 768, l. 14.

Elena Kochetkova

Yet the division of opinion on the destiny of Lake Baikal was still significant. The ministries in charge of the plants said that the lake would not be damaged significantly and it was possible to solve technical problems that the water treatment facilities revealed. Some organisations, like the Hydrological and Hydrochemical Institutes, said that these zones were localised and would disappear quickly due to the natural purification processes of Baikal's waters.[61] In contrast, the Academy of Sciences of the USSR stated that the danger of Baikal becoming contaminated had increased, and that the lake was 'on the verge of irreversible changes'.[62] In the following years, the Academy of Sciences cautioned that Baikal 'was facing irreversible degradation'.[63] Some other institutes, such as the Hydrometeorological Services, were concerned with the situation, saying that if wastes continued to be released to the same extent, and with the same failures in the functioning of the facility, the zone of contamination would expand to 200 to 250 square kilometres.[64] In addition, ecological activists from the 1960s to the 1990s described numerous consequences and damage to Baikal. As early as 1961, Galazii, who became one the most famous activists fighting contamination of the lake, predicted significant pollution of Baikal, asking, 'Why cut one's own throat?'[65] In 1968 he wrote that fish catches had dropped significantly, whilst the populations of omul, a locally renowned endemic fish species, were endangered. The water purification systems could only handle between forty and sixty per cent of the industrial wastes.[66]

The environmentally-threatening situation on Baikal was apparent for all to see and caused concern at higher government levels, but production continued. For example, in June 1971, the Central Committee of the CPSU and Council of Ministers of the USSR passed a resolution, 'On Supplementary Measures to Guarantee the Rational Use and Conservation of the Natural Wealth of Baikal'. According to this document, 'pollution control equipment was to be upgraded and operated properly, the maximum levels of pollutants to be determined'.[67] Six years later, in 1977, they passed another resolution 'On Measures for the further Development and Rational Use of Natural Resources in the Basin of Lake Baikal', which decreed a cessation to the release of wastewater into Baikal

61. GARF f. 5446, op. 101, d. 768, l. 21.

62. Pryde, *Environmental Management in the Soviet Union*, p. 86.

63. Weiner, *A Little Corner of Freedom*, p. 373.

64. GARF f. 5446, op. 101, d. 768, l. 43.

65. GARF f. 5446, op. 97, d. 833, l. 3.

66. Galazii, *Baikal i problema chistoi vody v Sibiri*, p. 7.

67. Josephson, *New Atlantis Revisited*, p. 184

by 1985. Despite it, the situation did not change radically and the authorities continued issuing resolutions admitting to significant pollution and calling to stop it. The plant itself was not capable of solving the problem, and transition to ecological production would require large investments, both financial and intellectual. In the 1990s, the concentration of sulphates and chlorine in Baikal was increasing without interruption.[68]

During the Perestroika years (1986–91) and after the demise of the USSR in 1991, scientists who spoke against industrial development in the Baikal region said that the activist movement in the Soviet Union failed because it was weak. Thus, in the preface of a 2001 book by O. Gusev, a specialist on Baikal, the publisher V. Boreiko, the head of the Kiev ecological and cultural centre, said that Baikal was a sacred space, the subject of love and care and special religious respect. He also said that Baikal was a specific 'ecological Stalingrad' where the 'forces of evil' and a 'thin bodyguard of Soviet nature protectionists-writers, scientists, and journalists' crossed their swords.[69]

The protectors of Baikal also talked about deception. As Galazii said in 1995, 'the majority let things slide on Baikal, as if there was no tomorrow', leaving environmentalists 'just absolutely helpless. We do not have anyone to address. If we go on strike, who will note it? ... No one cares about scientists today. If you behave badly, you will be dismissed at one stroke'.[70] Galazii negatively appraised those Academicians who supported the construction much earlier. In general, local scientists believed they failed in the struggle because they had no support from others.

Conclusions

This chapter has examined the debates involving various Soviet industrial and scientific institutions around construction projects on Lake Baikal. An industrialised Baikal promised to fulfill Soviet aspirations for technological modernisation and industrial progress. For these reasons, the builders often claimed that scientists hampered the construction of a very important industrial project. From their point of view, two components seemed to be enough to avoid the risk of pollution: the natural ability of the lake to purify itself and technology. However, when the scale of industrial development in the Baikal area turned

---

68. Kimtach, Meybeck and Baroudy (eds), *A Water Quality Assessment of the Former Soviet Union*, p. 506.

69. Gusev, *Nash vek ot goria ogradi*.

70. Galazii, 'Baikal "spasaiut" litsemery', 2 Sept. 1995.

Elena Kochetkova

grander, it became clear that rational exploitation turned into over-exploitation and inevitable pollution. For scientists who worked in the East Siberian Branch of the Academy of Sciences, the factories were a risk to nature and the lake, which had been seen as an untouched and untouchable place. For them, risk was closely connected with the consequences of technological production and the inability of technology to provide water purification. Although at the outset of the story they were inclined to agree that it was better to release wastewater into other water basins (such as the Irkut River) instead of Baikal, later they opposed releasing wastes at all. For some, however, the promise of technological improvements was convincing enough to accept building the factories. Some also underscored that the Baikal plant and its production were important for the state, admitting that economic aims prevailed. Later, however, it was revealed that the production at Baikal was not irreplaceable. The industrial plans and their impact on nature turned out to be in vain.

These events reveal tensions between local and central levels of decision-making and authority, in particular between scientists who lived in the region and those who worked in Moscow, Leningrad and other centres. The East Siberian Branch of the Academy of Sciences was established as an institute for exploring new regions, but due to the Baikal question it became the opposing force. The state, which initiated the plant's construction and saw it as an important possibility for national economic development and modernisation, took a two-fold position. On the one hand, the highest state organs said that it was important to consider the position of the scientists. On the other hand, led by the plan and its economic aims, they promoted further construction. In fact, even 'zones of contamination' that appeared a few years after the construction did not change the power dynamics. The builders insisted that technical problems were temporary and could be easily corrected. In this situation, the scientists felt betrayed, in particular a few decades after construction ended.

The Selenga plant stopped releasing wastewater into the Selenga River in 1990.[71] Conversely, the Baikal plant remained an ongoing and serious polluter despite the promises of the private owners, who took over the plant after the demise of the USSR, to develop and improve the facilities. In 2008, the Baikal plant was temporarily closed until the producer was allowed by the government to continue manufacturing and releasing waste into the waters in 2010. Finally, the story ended in 2013 with the permanent closure of the plant after protests by environmentalists, journalists, scientists and others.

---

71.   See more in Tulokhonov (ed.), *Baikal*.

BIBLIOGRAPHY

Arkhiv Rossiiskoi Akademii Nauk (ARAN, Archive of the Russian Academy of Sciences)

Beck, Ulrich. 1998. *Risk Society: Towards a New Modernity*. London: SAGE.

Berg, L.S. 1948. *Baikal, ego priroda i znachenie v narodnom khoziaistve*. Moscow: Pravda.

Breyfogle, Nicholas. 2015. 'At the Watershed: 1958 and the Beginnings of Lake Baikal Environmentalism'. *The Slavonic and East European Review* **93** (1): 147–80.

Bochkin, Andrei, Grigorii Galazii, Aleksandr Gaidai, Evgenii Grechishchev, Iakov Grushko, Mikhail Kozhov, Gavriil Kungurov, Sergei Moiseev, Piotr Moskovskikh, Konstantin Sedykh, Pavel Silinskii, Frants Taurin and Vladimir Shotskii. 1958. 'V zachshitu Baikala'. *Literaturnaia gazeta*. 21 October. http://www.magicbaikal.ru/ecology/in-defence-of-baikal.htm.

Coumel, Laurent. 2013. 'A Failed Environmental Turn? Khrushchev's Thaw and Nature Protection in Soviet Russia'. *The Soviet and Post-Soviet Review* **40** (2): 167–89.

Coumel, Laurent and Marc Elie. 2013. 'A Belated and Tragic Ecological Revolution: Nature, Disasters, and Green Activists in the Soviet Union and the Post-Soviet States, 1960s–2010s'. *The Soviet and Post-Soviet Review* **40** (2): 157–65.

Drizhenko, Fedor (ed.). 1908. *Lotsiia i fiziko-geograficheskii ocherk ozera Baikal*. St. Peterburg: Izdanie Glavnogo gidrograficheskogo upravleniia.

Duke, David. 2006. 'Seizing Favours from Nature: The Rise and Fall of Siberian River Diversion'. In Terje Tvedt and Eva Jakobsson (eds), *A History of Water*. Series I, Vol. 1, *Water Control and River Biographies*, pp. 3–34. London: I.B. Tauris.

Galazii, Grigorii. 1968. *Baikal i problema chistoi vody v Sibiri*. Irkutsk.

Galazii, Grigorii. 1995. 'Baikal "spasaiut" litsemery'. *Sovetskaia molodezh'*. 2 September. http://84.237.19.2:8081/baikal/sm/publ/95-9-2.htm.

Gosudarstvennyi arkhiv Rossiiskoi Federatsii (GARF, State Archive of the Russian Federation).

Gerasimov, Innokentii. 1967. *Preobrazovanie prirody i razvitie geograficheskoi nauki v SSSR (Ocherki po konstruktivnoi geografii)*. Moscow: Izdatel'stvo 'Znanie'.

Granberg, Aleksandr. 1996. 'Izuchenie proizvoditel'nykh sil Rossii'. *Vestnik Rossiiskoi Akademii nauk* 7: 579–84.

Gusev, Oleg. 2001. *Nash vek ot goriia ogradi (Golos v zashchitu Baikala)*. Kiev: Kievskii ekologo-kul'turnyi tsentr.

Gustafson, Thane. 1981. *Reform in Soviet Politics. The Lessons of Recent Policies on Land and Water*. Cambridge: Cambridge University Press.

Hillier, Jean. 2001. 'Imagined Value: The Poetics and Politics of Place'. In A. Madanipour, P. Haley and A. Hull (eds), *The Governance of Place: Space and Planning Processes*, pp. 73–106. Aldershot: Ashgate.

Elena Kochetkova

Hillier, Jean. 1997. 'Values, Images, Identities: Cultural Influences in Public Participation'. *Geography Research Forum* 17: 18–36.

Josephson, Paul. 1997. *New Atlantis Revisited: Akademgorodok, the Siberian City of Science*. Princeton: Princeton University Press.

Kimstach, Vitaly, Michel Meybeck and Ellysar Baroudy (eds). 1998. *A Water Quality Assessment of the Former Soviet Union*. London and New York: E. & F.N. Spon.

Kochetkova, Elena. 2018. 'Between Water Pollution and Protection in the Soviet Union, Mid-1950s–1960s: Lake Baikal and River Vuoksi'. *Water History* 10 (2–3): 223–241.

Kochetkova, Elena. 2019. 'Ekologicheskaia kontroverza: sovetskie inzhenery i biologicheskii metod ochistki promyshlennykh vod, 1950-60-e gg.' *Ab Imperio* 2019 (1): 153–180.

Kochetkova, Elena. 2014. 'Tekhnologicheskaia modernizatsiia v SSSR v 1950-e – 1960-e gg. (na primere Svetogorskogo tselliulozno-bumazhnogo kombinata'. *Vestnik Permskogo universiteta. Istoriia i politologiia*. No. 1: 194–205.

Kol'tsov, Anatolii. 1999. *Sozdanie i deiatel'nost' Komissii po izucheniu estestvennykh proizvoditel'nykh sil Rossii*. St Petersburg: Nauka.

Korytnyi, Leonid. 2011. *Ekho ekologo-ekonomicheskikh skandalov*. Novosibirsk: Izdatel'stvo SO RAN.

Kozhov, Mikhail. 1962. *Biologiia ozera Baikal*. Moscow: Izdatel'stvo Akademii nauk SSSR.

Lubomudrov, Slava. 1978. 'Environmental Politics in the Soviet Union: The Baikal Controversy'. *Canadian Slavonic Papers* 20 (4): 529–43.

Massey, Doreen. 1991. 'The Practical Place of Locality Studies'. *Environment and Planning* 23: 267–82.

Materialy Konferentsii po izucheniiu proizvoditel'nykh sil Irkutskoi oblasti. 1947. Irkutsk: Irkutskoe oblastnoe izdatel'stvo.

'O merakh po uporiadocheniiu ispol'zovaniia i usileniiu okhrany vodnykh resursov SSSR'. 1961. In O. Kolbasov (ed.), *Okhrana prirody: Sbornik zakonodatel'nykh aktov*. Moscow.

Pryde, Philip. 1991. *Environmental Management in the Soviet Union*. Cambridge: Cambridge University Press.

Snytko, Valerian and Aleksei Sobisevich. 2017. 'Vklad akademika I.P. Gerasimova v problemu monitoringa prirodnoi sredy'. *Problemy ekologicheskogo monitoringa i modelirovaniia ekosistem*. No. 28: 9–17.

Thomson, Peter. 2007. *Sacred Sea: A Journey to Lake Baikal*. Oxford: Oxford University Press.

Timoshenko, Al'bina. 2009. *Gosudarstvennaia politika formirovaniia i zakrepleniia naseleniia v raionakh promyshlennogo osvoeniia Sibiri v 1950-1980-e gody: Plany i real'nost'*. Novosibirsk: Sibirskoe nauchnoe izdatel'stvo.

Baikal Waters

Timoshenko, Al'bina. 2015. 'Strategiia sdviga proizvoditel'nykh sil SSSR na Vostok v gody poslevoennykh piatiletok (1946–1965)'. *Irkutskii istoriko-ekonomicheskii ezhegodnik*: 304–13.

Tvedt, Terje and Terje Oestigaard. 2010. 'A History of the Ideas of Water: Deconstructing Nature and Constructing Society'. In T. Tvedt and T. Oestigaard (eds). *A History of Water*. Series II, Vol. 1, *The Ideas of Water from Antiquity to Modern Times*, pp. 1–36. London: I.B. Tauris.

Tulokhonov, Arnold. 2009. *Baikal: Priroda i liudi: entsiklopedicheskii spravochnik*. Ulan-Ude: EKOS.

Velikhov, Evgenii, Jermen Gvishiani and Semen Mikiulinsky. 1980. *Science, Technology and the Future: Soviet Scientists' Analysis of the Problems of and Prospects for the Development of Science and Technology and Their Role in Society*. Oxford: Pergamon Press.

Vereshchagin, G.Iu. 1949. *Baikal. Nauchno-populiarnyi ocherk*. Moscow: Geografgiz.

Weiner, Douglas. 1999. *A Little Corner of Freedom: Russian Nature Protection from Stalin to Gorbachev*. Berkeley: University of California Press.

Yanitsky, Oleg Nikolaevich. 'From Nature Protection to Politics: The Russian Environmental Movement, 1960–2010'. *Environmental Politics* 21 (6): 922–940.

14.

HUNTING, CIVIL SOCIETY AND WILDLIFE CONSERVATION IN THE RUSSIAN FAR EAST

Mark Sokolsky

Russia's Pacific province of Primor'e (formally known as Primorskii Krai, the Maritime Territory), situated at the south-eastern corner of the Russian Far East, is probably best known as the home of the Amur (Siberian) tiger. A tiger graces Primor'e's official crest, and tigers feature prominently in foreign and domestic media coverage of the region. Most of the existing population of Amur tigers lives in the province, and their survival is rightly regarded as one of the signal successes of Soviet conservation in general and, in particular, of the *zapovedniks* (nature reserves), the inviolable state reserves earmarked for scientific study. The experience of neighbouring Chinese Manchuria, where the animal was almost extirpated during the twentieth century, underscores the achievement.[1]

Yet wildlife conservation in Primor'e began neither as an effort to protect tigers, nor as a high-minded exercise in ecological science. Rather, conservation emerged from the leisure activities and voluntary societies of Primor'e's imperial elite, who sought to protect less charismatic fauna – particularly the spotted (sika) deer – in order to pursue 'gentlemanly' hunting.[2] Scholarship on Russian and Soviet nature protection efforts has tended to focus on science and the state,[3] and while both institutions played important roles in Primor'e's story,

---

1. Pikunov, 'Population and Habitat of the Amur Tiger in the Russian Far East', pp. 145–9; Josephson et al., *An Environmental History of Russia*, pp. 110–11.

2. Here I refer to conservationism as the belief natural resources should be conserved *for* future human use, as opposed to preservationism, the protection of nature *from* human use for aesthetic, moral and/or spiritual reasons. On the distinction between the two, see especially Worster, *Nature's Economy*, pp. 150–54; Brain, *Song of the Forest*, p. 2.

3. As in Shtilmark, *History of the Russian Zapovedniks*; Weiner, *Models of Nature*; Weiner, *A Little Corner of Freedom*.

314

the territory's experience underscores the importance of recreation, voluntary organisations and local initiative in the development of conservation.[4]

Primor'e, acquired from Qing China in 1858–60, has long been known for its natural beauty – its rolling mountains, dramatic seashore, lush forests and tremendous variety of flora and fauna. It was also the centre of late-tsarist colonisation efforts in the Far East. Migration to Primor'e from Russia, Ukraine, China and Korea put significant pressure on animal populations by the end of the nineteenth century. In response, a group of merchants, landowners, naturalists and officials came together, beginning in 1887, to protect mammalian species, especially spotted deer (*Cervus Dubowksi nippon*), Manchurian elk (*Cervus elaphus xanthopygus*) and goral, a wild goat (*Naemorhedus caudatus*) in order to preserve one of their favourite pastimes – hunting. They created game reserves and breeding farms, supported the introduction of hunting restrictions and advocated for 'proper' (*pravil'nye*) hunting methods. As with members of the Russian Geographical Society (RGO) or Agricultural Society, Primor'e's hunting clubs sought to work alongside the state in the pursuit of progress and improvement, and they proved to be an influential force in public life. Their goals were fairly narrow and their achievements modest, but their efforts provided a space in which more comprehensive forms of nature protection could grow during the twentieth century.

Primor'e's hunting societies, however, reflected the region's ethnic and class divisions, as did state conservation efforts. Tensions between imperial elites, peasants and Cossacks overlapped with regionally-specific fault lines that ran between and among Slavonic and East Asian migrants. Wildlife conservation efforts embodied the paternalism that marked discussions of the 'peasant question', as well as the ethnocentrism that was increasingly widespread among the late tsarist elite. Much like their counterparts in other colonial contexts, Primor'e's elites lamented what they viewed as the cruel and irrational destruction of wildlife by foreigners – especially Chinese commercial hunters – and by peasant and Cossack settlers. In this regard, the views and approaches of Primor'e's conservationists were strikingly similar to those of their contemporaries in the United States and the British Empire, where conservation went hand-in-hand with classism and ethnic exclusion.[5]

---

4. On the role of voluntary organisations in late-tsarist society, see especially Bradley, 'Subjects into Citizens'; Bradley, *Voluntary Associations in Tsarist Russia.*

5. See, for example, Jacoby, *Crimes against Nature*; MacKenzie, *The Empire of Nature*, pp. 167–224; Cartmill, *A View to a Death in the Morning*, pp. 133–156.

Mark Sokolsky

Despite the narrow focus and elite orientation of such game conservation efforts, Primor'e's hunting societies ultimately played an important role in the development of nature protection in the territory. Hunting society members advocated for hunting regulations before World War One and, in 1916, combined with state officials to create the region's first nature reserve, or *zapovednik*. During the Russian Civil War, private game reserves and deer farms were among the few protected spaces in the region, preserving animal stocks (particularly of spotted deer) that might otherwise have been destroyed. With the advent of Soviet power in the Russian Far East in 1922, conservation retained its focus on protecting deer, elk and sable, but over time broadened to include a wider range of species. In this way, the roots of Soviet nature protection in Primor'e lay in the region's history of elite – and very un-proletarian – organisations. And while Soviet-era nature protection in Primor'e expanded far beyond its nineteenth-century roots, the attitudes and prejudices that marked the territory's hunting societies reverberated in the social and economic changes of the following century.

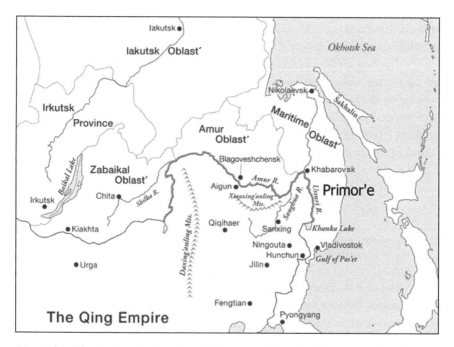

Map 14.1. The Russian Far East in 1860. Source: Kimitaka Matsuzato, 'The Creation of the Priamur Governor-Generalship in 1884 and the Reconfiguration of Asiatic Russia', p. 367. Adapted with permission from the author.

Colonisation and Hunting

Primor'e, the area south of the Amur River and east of the Ussuri (see Map 14.1),[6] was one of tsarist Russia's last acquisitions, seized from the Qing Dynasty of China between 1858 and 1860. The tsarist government prioritised settlement of the new, strategically sensitive territory, and from the 1880s on, Primor'e's population of migrants from European Russia boomed, reaching roughly 500,000 by 1917. At the same time, tens of thousands of Chinese and Koreans settled in the territory and the adjacent Amur Oblast', while others sojourned in Russian territory on a seasonal basis to hunt, forage, fish and work.[7]

Primor'e's natural environment attracted immediate attention. Naturalists travelling in the region in the 1850s and 1860s discovered an astonishing range of species living together, including dozens hitherto unknown to European science.[8] As explorers travelled up the Ussuri River and through the foothills of the Sikhote-Alin Mountains, they found familiar boreal plants along with a wide range of temperate species. Animals common to much of Russia, such as sable, brown bear and lynx, lived alongside raccoon dogs, tigers, leopards and other unfamiliar species. Marvelling at the profusion of wildlife, one visitor opined that Primor'e's collection of flora and fauna was so strange it was either a 'riddle or a joke of nature'.[9]

The jungle-like forests and unusual wildlife gave descriptions of Primor'e an exotic and colonial flavour. Stories of tigers were particularly common in writing on the region, with accounts of the animals rampaging through peasant settlements, plucking Chinese residents from their beds and stalking Russian soldiers.[10] For some commentators, their main point of reference was India. The 'terror of this place,' wrote Nikolai Aliab'ev, 'is the Bengal tiger'.[11] Similarly, the

---

6. The current borders of Primorskii krai do not reach to the Amur, but historically 'Primor'e' often referred to the entire area south of the Amur.

7. Kabuzan, *Dal'nevostochnyi krai v XVII–nachale XX vv.*; Stephan, *The Russian Far East*; Vashchuk et al., *Etnomigratsionnye protsessi v Primor'e v XX veke*, pp. 10–21.

8. Komarov, *Izbrannye Sochineniia*, pp. 24–6.

9. Ossendowski, *Man and Mystery in Asia*, p. 93.

10. See, for instance, Atkinson, *Travels in the Regions of the Upper and Lower Amoor*, pp. 375–6; Przheval'skii, *Puteshestvie v Ussuriiskom krae, 1867–1869 g.*, 42–43; Aliab'ev, *Dalekaia Rossiia*, 69–70, 73–74.

11. Aliab'ev, *Dalekaia Rossiia*, p. 69.

Mark Sokolsky

Polish-Russian 'conquistador', Nikolai Przheval'skii insisted that Amur tigers were 'no less powerful than a Bengal'.[12]

As Mark Bassin has observed, many Russians imagined that they were 'civilizing a savage realm' in the Far East. [13] One way of doing so, at least symbolically, was to subdue the region's most exotic and dangerous animal – the tiger. Przheval'skii, for instance, enthused that whereas once the indigenous Nanai had fallen to their knees in prayer when they saw a tiger, they had begun to 'doubt in the omnipotence of this god' with the coming of Russians.[14] A later Russian commentator wrote that the tiger had been 'tsar of the country' before the arrival of the Russians. But with the coming of the tsarist empire, all this changed: 'the tiger has learned to respect man and beware entering into conflict with a European, who differs greatly from a Chinese or Korean'.[15]

While tigers had strong cultural valence, they were not the primary targets of Primor'e's hunters. Tigers' pelts, bones and other organs were valuable, but there were less hazardous animals about that had equal or greater commercial value.[16] Also, tigers, being intelligent, stealthy and even vengeful, were dangerous to hunt.[17] They rarely attacked humans unprovoked, but were known to turn the tables on hunters, circling around them in order to strike from behind. '[Tiger] hunting it is extremely dangerous', wrote one hunter, 'and therefore every year there is no rarity of human victims.'[18] Primor'e's inhabitants certainly killed tigers – which were nearly extirpated from the region by the 1930s – but the pursuit of other animals was a less chancy and hazardous undertaking.

It was Primor'e's more docile creatures – spotted and musk deer, elk, goral and sable – that attracted the most interest, primarily because of their commercial value. Spotted deer and Manchurian elk were especially important, both for Primor'e's hunting economy and for the history of conservation in the region. As with other animals (musk deer, bears and others), these ungu-

---

12. Przheval'skii, *Puteshestvie v Ussuriiskom krae*, p. 42. On Przheval'skii as a 'conquistador', see Schimmelpenninck van der Oye, *Toward the Rising Sun*, pp. 37–41.

13. Bassin, *Imperial Visions*, pp. 174–82.

14. Przheval'skii, *Puteshestvie v Ussuriiskom krae*, p. 92.

15. Iuzhakov, 'Po Ussuriiskomu Kraiu', pp. 545–6.

16. Aliab'ev, *Dalekaia Rossiia*, pp. 64, 70; James, *The Long White Mountain*, p. 350; Arsen'ev, *Kratkii voenno-geograficheskii i voenno-statisticheskii ocherk Ussuriiskogo kraia 1901–1911 gg.*, p. 185; Shreider, *Nash Dal'nii Vostok (Tri goda v Ussuriiskom krae)*, pp. 315–22.

17. For a colourful recent account of Amur tigers' intelligence and proclivity for vengeance, see Vaillant, *The Tiger*.

18. RGIA DV f. 702, op. 2, d. 299, l. 104.

lates were desirable because of their value in the Chinese medical tradition. Practitioners believed substances derived from the velvet coating the animals' spring antlers could be used to treat a variety of medical conditions.[19] Chinese merchants played a key role in the deer hunting economy, because only they knew how to convert antler velvet into the prized medicinal substance.[20] Deer and elk were also a source of food and clothing for indigenous peoples and settlers, but it was their medicinal value that made them particularly important to commercial hunting, cross-border trade and local economic life.

The monetary value of antler velvet was extraordinary. In 1879, one official found that that antlers could fetch between 150 and 400 roubles – more than the price of a horse at the time – while another account suggested that a price of 200 roubles was common.[21] Prices rose yet further as the animals became increasingly scarce. By the 1890s, hunters regularly sold antlers for 250 roubles or more, and sometimes for as much as 800. In 1906, according to the famous explorer-scholar Vladimir Arsen'ev, the most valuable antlers could garner as much as 1,200 roubles for a single pair. The naturalist Nikolai Baikov, Arsen'ev's counterpart in Manchuria, found even higher prices there for deer antlers during the 1920s.[22]

In the context of strong commercial demand, thousands took to hunting and trapping deer and elk. Many Chinese, Korean and indigenous hunter-foragers sojourned in Russian territory on a seasonal basis, and permanent residents (Chinese, Koreans, Russian settlers, Cossacks and indigenous peoples) also hunted to varying degrees.[23] For instance, one family of Old Believers, the Khudiakovs, hunted boar and deer for their own consumption, supplied workers at a lumber mill with ducks and pheasants and sold deer antlers to local

19. Ellis, *Tiger Bone & Rhino Horn*, pp. 68–70; Aramilev, 'Sika Deer in Russia', p. 479. The tendons, foetuses, and tails of deer and elk were also highly valued for their medicinal qualities.

20. Skal'kovskii, *Russkaia torgovlia v Tikhom okeane...*, p. 42.

21. Nadarov, *Ocherk sovremennago sostaianiia Severno-Ussuriiskago kraia*, p. 26; Shreider, *Nash Dal'nii Vostok*, p. 302.; Shestakov, 'Opisanie s"emki r. Bikina, proizvedennoi sotnikom A.M. Shestakovym', pp. 34, 39–42; RGA VMF f. 410, op. 2, d. 4046, l. 43ob. The rouble was worth between US$0.45 and US$0.50 during the period under consideration here. See Lindert and Mironov, 'Russia_Ag_content_ruble_1535-1913'; National Mining Association', 'Historical Gold Prices'; Carroll Davidson Wright, *The New Century Book of Facts*, p. 568.

22. N.A. Kriukov, *Ocherk sel'skago khoziaistva v Primorskoi oblasti*, p. 315; James, *The Long White Mountain*, p. 13; Arsen'ev, 'Polevye dnevniki ekspeditsii V.K. Arsen'eva 1906 goda (prodolzhenie)', p. 48; N.A. Baikov, *Iziubr i iziubrevodstvo*, p. 10.

23. Coquin, *La Sibérie: peuplement et immigration paysanne au XIXe siècle*, p. 672–3.

Mark Sokolsky

Chinese.[24] Arsen'ev found that, for peasants in the coastal Ol'ga Bay area, hunting and fishing, not agriculture, 'comprise[d] almost their main occupation'.[25] Even a small number of hunters could have a significant impact. In 1895, a forest guard arrested four Chinese hunters who had, in two weeks killed sixty goral and deer.[26] Similarly, Arsen'ev encountered a group of Chinese hunters who had amassed over 450 kilograms of dried deer tendons, suggesting they had caught scores of the animals.[27]

Russian settlers usually hunted with firearms, but Chinese and Korean hunters generally employed traps, foremost among them those known as *lu-deva* (Russian: *zaseka*). These consisted of palisades that channelled game into a narrow corridor and led them to deep pits studded with spikes. The trapper left gaps in the fence with pit traps just beyond the gaps, which captured animals trying to escape. *Lu-deva* could be hundreds of metres long, employing up to forty pit traps, and they worked with deadly efficiency. They also killed animals indiscriminately. Tigers and bears could escape if not injured by their fall, but for most large mammals the traps were fatal.[28]

Not surprisingly, populations of elk, deer, goral, sable and other mammals quickly diminished, prompting widespread concern from Russian observers. A correspondent for the journal *Morskoi Sbornik* (*Naval Digest*), Vsevolod Krestovskii, warned in 1883 that Chinese hunting threatened to exhaust animal stocks throughout the Far East, particularly of deer.[29] In 1886, Baron A.N. Korf, the governor-general of the Priamur,[30] expressed concern about declining animal populations and advocated the institution of hunting seasons for sable, goral and deer and the destruction of the *lu-deva* traps.[31] By the turn of the century, the publicist Dmitrii Shreider warned that 'the determined hunt for [spotted deer] has in no small part contributed to its disappearance from

---

24. Khudiakov, 'Avtobiografiia', pp. 36–44.

25. Arsen'ev, 'Polevye dnevniki ekspeditsii V.K. Arsen'eva 1906 goda', p. 36.

26. Sil'nitskii, *Kulturnoe vlianie ussuriiskoi zheleznoi dorogi na iuzhno-ussuriiskii krai*, p. 107.

27. Arsen'ev, 'Polevye dnevniki ekspeditsii V.K. Arsen'eva 1906 goda', pp. 14–16, 22–23.

28. Skal'kovskii, *Russkaia torgovlia v Tikhom okeane*, p. 46; Arsen'ev, *Kratkii voenno-geograficheskii i voenno-statisticheskii ocherk Ussuriiskogo kraia 1901–1911 gg.*, pp. 124–5; Baikov, *Iziubr i iziubrevodstvo*, p. 8.

29. RGA VMF f. 410, op. 2, d. 4046, ll. 241–2ob.

30. Established in 1884, the Priamur Governor-Generalship encompassed present-day Primorskii krai as well as much of Khabarovskii krai, the Amur Oblast', and the Jewish Autonomous District.

31. RGIA DV f. 1, op. 5, d. 502, ll. 1–4.

the surroundings of inhabited places'.[32] A decade later, local landowner I.M. Iankovskii observed that 'remorseless and thoughtless slaughter' had all but emptied the territory of wild deer.[33]

Primor′e′s Hunting Societies

While the decline of Primor′e′s fauna was a matter of public concern by the late nineteenth century, it was private hunting societies, catering to Far Eastern elites, which took the first concrete steps toward wildlife conservation. Though hunting societies existed elsewhere in the empire, in Primor′e they proved particularly influential to wildlife conservation. The understanding of 'proper' resource use espoused by these groups and their exclusionary methods presaged and contributed to the approaches adopted by both tsarist and Soviet states.

A year after Governor-General Korf had raised the question of regulating hunting, a small group of sportsmen acquired hunting rights on Askol′d and Rikord islands, situated just off the coast near Vladivostok, in Peter the Great Bay (see Map 14.2). Together with a handful of others, they soon founded the Vladivostok Society for Amateur Hunters, VOLO, which included 25 permanent and eight seasonal members. Hunters in Nikol′sk-Ussuriisk (present-day Ussuriisk) created a similar organisation, the South Ussuri Society for Proper Amateur Hunting, in 1899.

VOLO was an organisation of and for imperial elites, bringing together some of the city's most prominent public officials and scholars, including Arsen′ev, who joined the organisation in 1901 and eventually served as its director. Russian and foreign merchants were also well represented in the group. From the outset, the Hunting Society had friends in high places: Grand Duke Alexander Mikhailovich, grandson of Nicholas I, was the organisation's official patron and sponsor, and Major-General Unterberger, who served as military governor of Primor′e (1888–1897) and later as Priamur governor-general (1906–1910), was an honourable member. The Society also received recognition and a large donation from Governor-General Korf.[34]

---

32. Shreider, *Nash Dal′nii Vostok*, p. 302.

33. Iankovskii, 'Olenovodstvo v Iuzhno-Ussuriiskom krae', p. 292. See also Arsen′ev, *Kratkii voenno-geograficheskii i voenno-statisticheskii ocherk Ussuriiskogo kraia 1901–1911 gg.*, p. 121.

34. Obshchestvo liubitelei okhoty, *Otchety 1888–1896 g.g.*, pp. 12–13.; Khisamutdinov, *The Russian Far East*, p. 2, 53, 83–4.

Mark Sokolsky

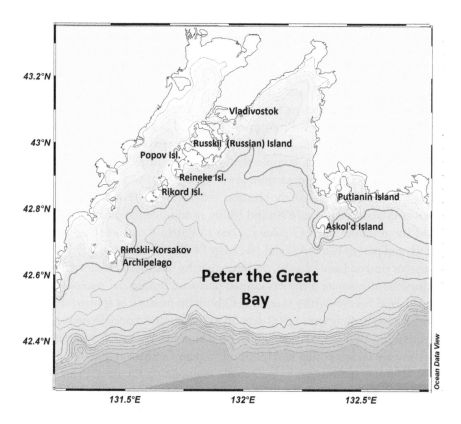

Map 14.2. *Islands in and around Peter the Great Bay. Source: TOI DVO RAN, 'Fiziko-geograficheskie kharakteristika'. Created using Ocean Data View (https://odv.awi.de/). Adapted with permission from TOI DVO RAN.*

Primor'e's hunting societies were committed to conserving key game species, particularly spotted deer and goral, if only to be able to kill them at their leisure. A combination of elitism and utilitarian conservationism is evident in members' writings and in their approach to game management. VOLO's founders cited a decline in game species at the hands of settlers and trappers as their motivation for forming the society. They argued that, with settlement of the territory, spotted deer and goral, decimated by commercial hunters and local peasants, had fled to remote areas where they were inaccessible to the 'cultured' part of the population.[35] Club members emphasised a 'proper' approach to hunting, which is to say hunting in a manner that was

---

35.   Obshchestvo liubitelei okhoty, *Otchety, 1888–1896 gg.*, pp. 51–2.

sporting – i.e., using firearms, not traps – and sustainable, with members implored to avoid killing does or fawns, for instance, to observe hunting seasons, and to protect game birds' nesting sites. Both organisations contrasted their own activities with those of commercial and subsistence hunters, particularly the Ussuri Cossacks and local Chinese. Thus, VOLO members complained of 'year-round, merciless destruction' of wildlife near Lake Khanka, primarily by Cossacks. 'One can imagine how many wounded birds are lost,' one member wrote, as Cossacks 'smashed up birds', destroyed nests and eggs and generally conducted their hunt in a 'completely rapacious manner'.[36]

To protect game species from lower-class groups and Chinese migrants, VOLO focused its efforts on the creation and maintenance of a system of game reserves, established in the 1880s and 1890s. In addition to holdings on Askol'd and Rikord islands, VOLO gained access to Putianin and Rimskii-Korsakov islands and part of Russian Island (see Map 14.2). In 1895, the society secured a lease for land on Lake Khanka, the large, marshy lake that straddles the Russo-Chinese border, where members hunted pheasant, grouse and waterfowl.[37] By filling island reserves with game, VOLO built up its stock of spotted deer and goral. By 1898, there were 1,300 deer on Askol'd Island alone. To finance their organisation, VOLO sold deer antlers, goral horns and pelts – thereby enlisting the commercial forces that had killed off so many animals in the first place.[38]

Natural and human hazards made maintaining the reserves and game stocks challenging. Disease and inclement winter weather could kill dozens or even hundreds of animals suddenly. Losses were especially bad in years of heavy snowfall, when the animals had difficulty grazing.[39] In areas on or close to the mainland, predation by tigers and eagles also occurred. Poaching, however, was VOLO's main problem. The society employed up to twelve guards to enforce the limits of the reserves, but illegal hunting remained common. The legal fine for poaching (25 roubles) was insufficient to dissuade would-be hunters, given the value of even low-quality antlers. In the spring of 1889, two guards on Askol'd Island were found dead, probably killed by poachers. In the Lake Khanka reserve, local Cossacks continued to cut forests and hunt waterfowl, and some guards even took to killing animals for their own consumption. During the Russo-Japanese War (1904–1905), peasants travelled to Askol'd and other islands with firearms, ostensibly to protect themselves, then proceeded to hunt.

36. RGIA DV f. 702, op. 2, d. 299, ll. 53, 89–90.

37. RGIA DV f. 1, op. 4, d. 1889, ll. 1, 13.

38. Obshchestvo liubitelei okhoty, *Otchety, 1888–1896 gg.*, pp. 8–10.

39. Bromlei and Kucherenko, *Kopytnye iuga Dal'nego Vostoka SSSR*, p. 135.

'The Island presents a sad picture,' one VOLO member reported, 'here there are headless carcasses, since the heads with their antlers the poachers take with them, and a strong, putrid smell fills the air.' Soldiers stationed on Russian Island during the war poached on VOLO's reserves; in one case, the crew of a Russian submarine opened fire on animals grazing along the shore of Askol'd Island. By the end of the war, all of the deer on Rikord and Rimskii-Korsakov islands had died or been killed. Reflecting upon the destruction, a VOLO member lamented that Russians were squandering the 'wealth of nature conferred upon us', and were simply 'malicious predators, destroying everything'.[40]

In the face of such difficulties, VOLO members turned to supporting private deer farms, where spotted deer were kept in captivity and their antlers harvested. Deer farms were oriented toward private interests, but they proved important for the survival of spotted deer into the Soviet period. Russian settlers had begun keeping spotted deer as early as the 1860s, possibly having learned the practice from the Chinese.[41] Michael Iankovskii, one of VOLO's more prominent members, established a deer farm after a herd wandered onto his land during the winter of 1888. Though the animals were difficult to manage, the farm was very lucrative.[42] Several other families also began to keep and raise deer, with perhaps 6,000 on a farm or preserve by the time of the Russo-Japanese War. After the war, VOLO began transporting many of its remaining deer to private farms, where the animals weathered the upheavals of the following decade.[43]

While the goals of Primor'e's hunting societies were narrow, some members also saw themselves as advocates for nature protection more generally. VOLO representatives proposed legal protection for some birds and mammals, for instance, and sought to educate the populace about proper hunting practices. The hunting societies, as one member put it, had a 'moral duty to appeal to Russian society, to stop poaching and exploitative (*razboinicheskie*) relations with nature'.[44] VOLO's annual report for 1904 – possibly written by Arsen'ev

40. Aramilev, 'Sika Deer in Russia', p. 479; RGIA DV f. 702, op. 2, d. 299, ll. 91–3.

41. Aramilev, 'Sika Deer in Russia', p. 479; Abramov and Kuchurenko, p. 156. According to Baikov, elk-raising appeared in the Transbaikal in 1843. By the 1880s, some 300 households harvested the antlers of 800 captive elk in the Transbaikal. Similar practices were also common in the Altai Mountains region. See Baikov, pp. 11–12.

42. Iankovskii, 'Olenovodstvo v Iuzhno-Ussuriiskom krae', pp. 292–297.

43. Baikov, *Iziubr i iziubrevodstvo*, p. 12; Aramilev, 'Sika Deer in Russia', pp. 479–480.

44. RGIA DV f. 702, op. 2, d. 299, ll. 53, 89–90.

– contained a rather pessimistic plea for better wildlife conservation, situating Primor'e's experience in global context:

> In the nineteenth century, man has destroyed sixteen species of various animals. Unmistakably, we can say that in the twentieth century the following will be destroyed: whale, elephant, lion, ostrich, and here in the Far East: tiger, snow leopard, moose, elk, spotted deer, goral, sable, beaver, sea otter, pheasant, hazelhen, grouse, bustard, wood grouse and others. In Japan almost all beasts and birds have been destroyed, in France for about 25 years they have hunted only for larks and rabbits. And, indeed, our region, with its rich fauna, awaits the same fate! Indeed, here as well, with guns in arms, we will have to be satisfied with only sparrows!

The report concluded with a plea for a comprehensive hunting law that would encompass all of Siberia and the Far East, along with further support for the Far Eastern hunting societies.[45]

Several VOLO members were also involved in the Society for the Study of the Amur Region (OIAK, also known as the Amur Society), an organisation that also helped draw attention to ecological problems. Founded in April 1884, the Amur Society's purpose was to promote the study of the Amur basin and Russia's Pacific shores and to organise a library on the region. It soon became the preeminent scholarly organisation in Vladivostok, and, like VOLO, its members represented the cream of Far Eastern society.[46] Prominent members included Arsen'ev, Fridol'f Heeck (who donated items from his arctic explorations), Julius Bryner (a shipping magnate and grandfather of actor Yul Brynner) and the wealthy merchant Iakov Semenov, among others. Luminaries such as Nikolai Przheval'skii, Lev Shternberg and Anton Chekhov donated books and artefacts. The Amur Society also enjoyed the patronage of the Grand Duke Alexander Mikhailovich, and received choice bits of land in Vladivostok, along with money and construction materials, to build a library-museum that still stands in the city centre.[47]

The research and advocacy of the Amur Society and VOLO members – particularly Arsen'ev – contributed to the development of state conservation measures during the early twentieth century. Drawing on Arsen'ev's studies of

45. Obshchestvo liubitelei okhoty, *Otchety, 1888–1896 g.g.*, p. 114. Although anonymous, this report's survey of animal species is very similar to that included in Arsen'ev's *Kratkii voenno-geograficheskii i voenno-statisticheskii ocherk.*

46. Khisamutdinov, *The Russian Far East*, pp. 39–41.

47. Khisamutdinov, *The Russian Far East*, pp. 42–5; Stephan, *The Russian Far East*, pp. 93–4; Shadrin (ed.), *Obshchestvo izucheniia Amurskogo kraia, 1884–2004*, pp. 1–5.

Far Eastern wildlife, Priamur Governor-General Gondatti instituted a temporary ban on sable trading in 1910, and then promulgated the first comprehensive hunting regulations for the territory (1911).[48] The latter emphasised the conservation of commercially valuable species (including sable, deer and others), while offering no protection to predators. Though the rules instituted hunting seasons and banned the killing of females and young of certain species (including spotted deer, elk, musk deer and moose), they specifically permitted year-round hunting of tigers, leopards, lynx, wolves, bears and birds of prey by any means except poison. Such an approach was entirely consistent with the 'proper' hunting methods promoted by Primor'e's hunting societies, and – especially in their disregard for predators – with hunting laws introduced shortly before in European Russia.[49]

State conservation efforts, like those of VOLO, were inseparable from the Far East's social and ethnic tensions. Forestry laws, which had been introduced beginning in the 1880s, targeted trapping methods favoured by Chinese, Korean and indigenous hunters and the (supposedly) irrational land use practices of Russian settlers.[50] Similarly, the hunting regulations promulgated in 1911 specifically outlawed the traps favoured by the Chinese, Koreans and indigenous peoples. While meant to target the sources of wildlife destruction, such measures also privileged the priorities of VOLO and other elements of the imperial elite. Without cooperation from the territory's population, moreover, enforcement of conservation laws was extremely difficult.[51]

Prosecution of hunters dovetailed with the tsarist state's increasingly harsh measures against the region's Chinese and Korean populations. Beginning in the 1890s, Russian authorities conducted periodic sweeps through the taiga to catch foreign hunters and smugglers. In 1907–08, military detachments evicted 'hunters and vagrant elements' from the Ol'ga Bay region, as they had 'illegally occupied Russian land'.[52] Similarly, in 1914, Gondatti requested financial assistance from the Forest Department of the Main Administration of Land Use

---

48. GAPK f. 1351, op. 1, d. 1, l. 2ob.

49. Pravilova, *A Public Empire*, pp. 70–1.

50. Man'ko, *Lesnoe delo na rossiiskom Dal'nem Vostoke*, pp. 85–93; Anuchin, ed., *Mery, prinimaemye k uporiadocheniiu ustroistva lesov Priamurskogo kraia*, pp. 82–4; RGIA DV f. 1, op. 4, d. 169, ll. 1–2; RGIA DV f. 1, op. 4, d. 1975, ll. 4–11; RGIA DV f. 94, op. 1, d. 97, ll. 1–8.

51. On enforcement problems, see especially Man'ko, *Lesnoe delo na rossiiskom Dal'nem Vostoke*, pp. 79–80.

52. RGIA DV, f. 1, op. 4, d. 1910, ll. 1–10, 59–60, 102–103, 159ob.

and Agriculture (GUZZ) to drive foreign hunter-foragers from the taiga and to confiscate the pelts, ginseng and antlers they had illegally acquired. Chinese and Koreans, he argued, were engaged in the destruction of the 'natural riches of the territory'.[53] Not surprisingly, resident Chinese resented Russian rule in part because tsarist authorities 'prosecute[d] them for plundering the taiga, for illegal logging of the forest'.[54]

The state's interest in conservation eventually combined with the concerns of naturalists and voluntary societies to produce Primor'e's first *zapovednik*. Calls for protected (*zapovednye*) zones to safeguard forests around salmon spawning areas and keep 'barbaric' hunters at bay had arisen during the early 1900s.[55] When Gondatti (unsuccessfully) requested assistance from St Petersburg to flush out foreign hunters, the director of the Forest Department suggested forming *zapovedniks* instead. Since there was no way to police the entire territory, he argued, it would be best to protect forests and animals in bounded areas.[56] Soon afterward, Gondatti supported an effort championed by the Amur Society, Primor'e's newly-formed Forest Society and a group of forestry officers to create a reserve in the Kedrovaia River valley, in southwestern Primor'e, which contained stands of Korean pine and some of the last wild spotted deer. Thus, in 1916, Primor'e's first *zapovednik*, Kedrovaia Pad' (Pine Valley) came into existence.[57]

From Deer to Tigers

The revolutions of 1917 and the Civil War brought chaos to the Far East, along with intervention by Japanese, American and other foreign forces. Bolshevik commentators later remembered this as a time of foreign destruction of forests and wildlife.[58] After Primor'e became part of the Soviet Union in 1922, wildlife conservation picked up where it had left off in 1916. As before 1917, the protection of commercially valuable species was the priority. Although such an emphasis was consistent with the instrumentalist view of nature protection

---

53. GARF f. 387, op. 19, d. 67789, 1–3ob, l.19

54. Arsen'ev, 'Polevye dnevniki ekspeditsii V.K. Arsen'eva 1906 goda', 29.

55. GAPK f. 1351, op. 1, d. 1, ll. 1–4.

56. GARF, f. 387, op. 19, d. 67789, ll. 19, 29.

57. *Arsen'evskie chteniia*, p. 21; Shtilmark, *History of the Russian Zapovedniks*, pp. 92–94.

58. See, for instance, G.F. Bromlei's recollections, 'Letopis prirody', in GARF, f. A-358, op. 2, d. 437.

that prevailed among Communist Party officials, particularly in the Stalin era, it was by no means a departure from pre-revolutionary patterns.

Spotted deer and sable remained central to conservation efforts in the 1920s and 1930s. Few wild deer remained after the war; according to Baikov, all of what was now called Primorskaia Guberniia (Province), which encompassed most of the former Priamur, yielded only 100 pairs of antlers from wild deer during the early 1920s. About 2,000 survived on farms, including in a state farm that had been the Iankovskiis' estate.[59] In 1923, at the suggestion of local specialists, administrators approved the creation of a new reserve, the Suputinskii (now Ussuriiskii) *Zapovednik*, and later expanded Kedrovaia Pad'.[60] Advocates argued that the *zapovedniks* would provide laboratories for the study of plants and animals and serve as reserves for spotted deer. In 1925, the zoologist Arnol'd Mol'trekht, one of the founders of the Forest Society, led an expedition to south-eastern Primor'e, where he found spotted deer, elk and goral in abundance. Warning that without immediate protection these populations would be decimated, Mol'trekht recommended the creation of a reserve that ultimately formed the core of the Sudzukhinskii (now Lazovskii) *Zapovednik*.[61]

Finally, following studies by the zoologist Iurii Salmin and Konstantin Abramov – an avid hunter and long-time Bolshevik – the Committee on *Zapovedniks*, the state fur company (Soiuzpushnina) and senior Party officials agreed to the creation of the Sikhote-Alin *Zapovednik* in June 1935. The Sikhote-Alin *Zapovednik* encompassed a million hectares upon its formation in 1935, including 150,000 hectares allocated to the Sudzukhinskii reserve, which became separate in 1940. It also included an offshore island, Petrov Island, which contained deer, goral and rare vegetation.[62]

The origins of Primor'e's *zapovedniks* thus began primarily as efforts to protect ungulates and sable, much like pre-revolutionary initiatives, and in this sense but were consistent with pre-revolutionary approaches.[63] The protection of spotted deer, elk, goral and sable justified the formation of *zapovedniks*, and it was only later that the reserves expanded their role to include tigers and

59. *Sovetskoe Primor'e*, 131.
60. GAPK f. 1506, op. 1, d. 35, ll. 15–16ob; Korkeshko and Miroliubov, 'Gosudarstvennyi zapovednik "Kedrovaia Pad'"', 1936, p. 33.
61. GAPK f. 1506, op. 1, d. 36, ll. 1–1ob.
62. GARF f. A-358, o., 2, d. 437, ll. 19–23.
63. This supports Weiner's contention that regional officials were, at least in the case of Primorskii krai, more supportive of the creation and expansion of *zapovedniks* than their counterparts in Moscow. Weiner, *A Little Corner of Freedom*, pp. 69–70.

leopards, animals that were initially outside the realm of protection. Indeed, *zapovednik* staff hunted down predators, such as wolves, leopards and martens, which they considered a threat to the commercially valuable species.[64] Similarly, hunting rules promulgated in 1939 once again allowed for the killing of predators, including bears, wolves and birds of prey, year-round – but, for the first time, not tigers or leopards. [65]

It was only after the establishment of the Far Eastern *zapovedniks* that scientists realised just how rare the big cats had become. Biologists working in the Sikhote-Alin Mountains in 1934 had found that populations of 'elk, sable and especially moose, tiger and raccoon dog' had fallen 'catastrophically' by 1934.[66] Similarly, the biologist Lev Kaplanov added further evidence to this claim in his work, *Tiger, Deer, Elk and Moose*, published posthumously in 1948 (he was killed, probably by poachers, in 1943).[67] Kaplanov argued that tigers were 'on the edge of total extinction,' and recommended a complete ban on tiger hunting throughout the Far East. Such a ban came into effect in 1947. [68]

Poaching and Power

While Soviet-era nature protection in Primor'e built upon tsarist-era developments, a key point of discontinuity was a sharp reduction in poaching that occurred after World War Two. Throughout the 1920s and 1930s, locals turned to the taiga for subsistence and income, and the cross-border trade in antlers and other items continued.[69] Despite official protection, poachers killed nearly all of the spotted deer in Kedrovaia Pad' and Ussuriiskii *zapovedniks* by the mid-1920s. *Zapovednik* staff restored wild populations using captive stocks, but these populations were also subject to poaching during the war, when food shortages led peasants and soldiers to pursue game for subsistence.[70]

64.   Shtilmark, *History of the Russian Zapovedniks*, pp. 92–94.

65.   GARF f. A-358, op. 2, d. 34, l. 17; GAPK f. 1351, op. 1, d. 2, l. 1, 16ob.

66.   GARF f. A-358, op. 2, d. 437, ll. 16–17; GARF f. A-358, op. 2, d. 23, l. 31.

67.   Some scholars have argued that soldiers stationed in the *zapovednik* shot Kaplanov after he tried to stop their poaching, and even that their commanding officer covered up the murder. See Shtilmark, *History of the Russian Zapovedniks*, pp. 95–6, 281; Suvorov, *Zapovednoe Primor'e*, pp. 19–25.

68.   Kaplanov, *Tigr, Olen', Iziubr', Los'*, pp. 54–55.

69.   Gaponov, *Istoriia taezhnogo prirodopol'zovaniia Iuzhno-Ussuriiskogo regiona*, p. 184.

70.   Aramilev, 'Sika Deer in Russia', p. 483.

Mark Sokolsky

However, by the post-war period, changes in the political and economic context – stricter border controls, a more robust state presence and the transformation of the countryside – made the enforcement of anti-poaching measures more effective. First, collectivisation had destroyed or relocated hundreds of homesteads that had previously been scattered through the taiga. Old Believer and Cossack families, who had been prominent in the hunting economy, were especially hard hit, as were indigenous communities, many of which were forcefully relocated. Collective farm workers hunted, but they were subject to more stringent state oversight. Second, with the coming of war with Germany in 1941, many skilled hunters were sent to the front, and some never returned. Third, Primor'e's Chinese and Korean populations were almost entirely deported or exiled internally to Central Asia by the end of 1938. Finally, in the geopolitical context of the Cold War and Sino-Soviet split, Primor'e's international borders became highly militarised and better guarded than in the past.[71]

Such changes, together with state protections and the efforts of *zapovednik* staff, enabled several species to recover their numbers. The reduction in poaching, combined with further reintroduction of farm-raised deer, finally allowed wild deer populations to recover and thrive.[72] The 1947 ban on tiger hunting was followed by a prohibition, beginning in 1956, of the capture of cubs. These two measures contributed greatly to tigers' recovery, as did the greater availability of ungulates and other prey.[73] Some animals, such as goral and Amur leopards, remained relatively rare – today, the leopards are critically endangered – but wildlife protection made significant headway after years of difficulties.

We are thus left with a rather disturbing picture: the dislocations of the 1930s and 1940s, which were terrible for much of Primor'e's human population, facilitated the successes of post-war conservation. The fates of Primor'e's human and non-human populations were also closely connected. Soviet policies were more extreme than what had come before, but they drew on the same paternalism and ethnocentrism that had marked pre-revolutionary conservation. Conservationists, including VOLO members, had advocated for greater control over peasants' and East Asians' use of land and wildlife, and state conservation

---

71. Gaponov, *Istoriia taezhnogo prirodopol'zovaniia Iuzhno-Ussuriiskogo regiona*, pp. 177–82.

72. Baikov, *Iziubr i iziubrevodstvo*, 11–12; Bromlei and Kucherenko, *Kopytnye iuga Dal'nego Vostoka SSSR*, p. 156; Aramilev, 'Sika Deer in Russia', p. 479; RGIA DV f. 702, op. 2, d. 299, l. 111.

73. Smirnov and Miquelle, 'Population Dynamics of the Amur Tiger in Sikhote-Alin Zapovednik, Russia', pp. 62–9; Matiushkin, *Amurskii tigr v Rossii*.

efforts reflected similar views. Peasant settlers, Cossacks, Koreans, Chinese and indigenous groups had all contributed to the decline of Primor'e's game populations; their subjugation or removal could not but have an effect on the exploitation of wildlife. But the violent transformation of Primor'e's hinterland went far beyond anything tsarist-era elites had envisioned,[74] and any benefits to wildlife were ancillary to the goals of defence and the construction of socialism.

Conclusions

On the surface, nature protection in late twentieth century Primor'e was very different from pre-revolutionary conservation, but Soviet-era initiatives were deeply rooted in the tsarist past. Changes in Primor'e's wildlife populations, primarily a result of colonisation and commercial hunting, prompted wide-spread concern among late tsarist elites. Representatives of the region's civil society established protected spaces for a select range of game species, primarily so they could continue to engage in 'gentlemanly' hunting. While modest and narrowly-focused, their efforts combined with those of other voluntary organisations and state officials to produce broader forms of nature protection by 1917. During the early Soviet period, the methods and priorities that had prevailed during the pre-revolutionary era – especially the protection of commercial species, like spotted deer – continued and expanded into a more comprehensive system of *zapovedniks* and hunting controls. What had begun as a very limited conception of conservation among an elite part of Far Eastern society eventually provided the institutional basis for many Soviet-era successes.

Voluntary societies and local initiative were thus critical to the development of conservation in Primor'e. The territory's experience, in this sense, supports Joseph Bradley's view that late tsarist civil society was a cohesive and influential force, even if it tended to work with (or for) the state, rather serving as an independent counterweight to it.[75] The region's hunting societies and affiliated organisations, whose ranks included educated state servitors and commercial elites, shared the state's commitment to the Enlightenment ideals of improvement and progress, and collaborated with the state in the pursuit of wildlife conservation. In contrast to the over-hunting in the North Pacific during the eighteenth century, as examined by Ryan Jones, ecological decline in

---

74. With the possible exception of the Chinese and Korean deportations, which had been discussed before 1917.

75. Bradley, 'Subjects into Citizens'; Bradley, *Voluntary Associations in Tsarist Russia*, pp. 2–6.

Mark Sokolsky

Primor'e did not lead to a general critique of empire. Rather, citizens concerned with conservation – and leisure activities – looked to imperial authorities for financial and legal support.[76]

The history of Primor'e's hunting societies, and tsarist-era conservationism more generally, also illustrates the similarity between the Russian experience and that of other colonial powers, particularly Britain and the United States. The conservation movement that emerged in Primor'e reflected deep social and ethnic tensions, with VOLO members and state officials associating over-hunting with Chinese migrants and 'uncultured' settlers. Indeed, their views would not have been out of place in Theodore Roosevelt's Boone and Crockett Club, for instance, or on safari in British Africa. There, too, concern for nature combined with ethnic biases and classism, leading authorities to prescribe 'proper' usage of natural spaces – and exclude long-time users.[77] In the Russian, British and American contexts, conservationists required and received state backing. In Soviet Primor'e, state nature protection became more inclusive and robust. State power, however, cut in several directions. Most troublingly, collectivisation, the deportation of East Asians and other policies entailed tremendous violence, even as they contributed to the survival and proliferation of several mammal species. They also drew on paternalistic attitudes and ethnocentric fears that had long characterised Far Eastern governance and pre-revolutionary conservationism, though without the relative moderation of the tsarist era.[78]

BIBLIOGRAPHY

Aliab'ev, N. 1872. *Dalekaia Rossiia: Ussuriiskii krai*. St Petersburg: Obshchestvennaia pol'za.

Anuchin, D.G. (ed.). 1883. *Mery, prinimaemye k uporiadocheniiu ustroistva lesov Priamurskogo kraia*. Vol. 5, *Lesa Priamurskago kraia*. Sbornik glavneishikh offitsial'nykh dokumentov po upravleniiu Vostochnoiu Sibir'iu. Irkutsk: Tipografiia shtaba Vostochnago Sibirskago voennago okruga.

---

76. As described in Jones, *Empire of Extinction*. Arsen'ev, who espoused more sentimental, preservationist views late in life, could be considered a partial exception, though he was certainly an ally of the tsarist regime while it existed. For an in-depth discussion of his views, see Beu, 'A Journey towards Environmental Wisdom'.

77. Spence, *Dispossessing the Wilderness*, pp. 55–70; Jacoby, *Crimes against Nature*; MacKenzie, *The Empire of Nature*, pp. 167–224.

78. On continuities in such attitudes between tsarist and Soviet eras, see especially Beer, *Renovating Russia;* Holquist, 'To Count, to Extract, and to Exterminate'; Kotsonis, *Making Peasants Backward*.

Hunting, Civil Society and Wildlife Conservation in the Russian Far East

Aramilev, Vladimir V. 2008. 'Sika Deer in Russia'. In Dale R. McCullough, Seiki Takatsuki, and Kōichi Kaji (eds), *Sika Deer Biology and Management of Native and Introduced Populations*, pp. 475–99. Tokyo; New York: Springer.

Arsen'ev, V.K. 1912. *Kratkii voenno-geograficheskii i voenno-statisticheskii ocherk Us- suriiskogo kraia 1901–1911 gg.* Khabarovsk.

Arsen'ev, V.K. 2002. 'Polevye dnevniki ekspeditsii V.K. Arsen'eva 1906 goda'. *Zapiski Obshchestva izucheniia Amurskogo kraia* 36 (1): 11-66.

Arsen'ev, V.K. 2004. 'Polevye dnevniki ekspeditsii V.K. Arsen'eva 1906 goda (prodolz- henie)'. *Zapiski Obshchestva izucheniia Amurskogo kraia* 37 (1): 10–69.

Arsen'evskie chteniia: Materialy regional'noi nauchno-prakticheskoi konferentsii posvi- ashchennoi 130-letiiu so dnia rozhdeniia V.K. Arsen'eva, 28–29 avgusta 2002 goda. 2002. Vladivostok: Izdatel'stvo Dal'nevostochnogo Universiteta.

Atkinson, Thomas. 1860. *Travels in the Regions of the Upper and Lower Amoor, and the Russian Acquisitions on the Confines of India and China.* London: Hurst and Blackett.

Baikov, N.A. 1925. *Iziubr i iziubrevodstvo.* Kharbin: Obshchestvo izucheniia man'chzhurskogo kraia.

Bassin, Mark. 1999. *Imperial Visions: Nationalist Imagination and Geographical Expan- sion in the Russian Far East, 1840–1865.* New York: Cambridge University Press.

Beer, Daniel. 2008. *Renovating Russia: The Human Sciences and the Fate of Liberal Modernity, 1880–1930.* Ithaca: Cornell University Press.

Beu, I., 1998. 'A Journey towards Environmental Wisdom: Environmental Themes in V.K. Arsenyev's Thought and Writing with Special Reference to his books Devoted to Dersu Uzala'. Ph.D. diss., Victoria University.

Bradley, J., 2009. *Voluntary Associations in Tsarist Russia: Science, Patriotism, and Civil Society.* Cambridge, MA: Harvard University Press.

Bradley, J., 2002. 'Subjects into Citizens: Societies, Civil Society, and Autocracy in Tsarist Russia'. *American Historical Review* 107 (4): 1094–1123.

Brain, Stephen. 2011. *Song of the Forest: Russian Forestry and Stalinist Environmentalism, 1905–1953.* Pittsburgh, PA.: University of Pittsburgh Press.

Bromlei, G.F. and S.P. Kucherenko. 1983. *Kopytnye iuga Dal'nego Vostoka SSSR.* Mos- cow: Nauka.

Cartmill, Matt. 1993. *A View to a Death in the Morning.* Cambridge, MA: Harvard University Press.

Coquin, François-Xavier. 1969. *La Sibérie: peuplement et immigration paysanne au XIXe siècle.* Paris: Institut d'études slaves.

Ellis, Richard. 2005. *Tiger Bone & Rhino Horn: The Destruction of Wildlife for Tradi- tional Chinese Medicine.* Washington: Island Press.

Gaponov, V.V. 2005. *Istoriia taezhnogo prirodopol'zovaniia Iuzhno-Ussuriiskogo regiona.* Vladivostok: WWF Russia.

Mark Sokolsky

Goodrich, John M., Dale G. Miquelle, Evgeny N. Smirnov, Linda L. Kerley, Howard B. Quigley and Maurice G. Hornocker. 2010. 'Spatial Structure of Amur (Siberian) Tigers (Panthera Tigris Altaica) on Sikhote-Alin Biosphere Zapovednik, Russia'. *Journal of Mammalogy* **91** (3): 737–48.

Gosudarstvennyi arkhiv Primorskogo Kraia (GAPK, State Archive of Primorskii krai).

Gosudarstvennyi arkhiv Rossiiskoi Federatsii (GARF, State Archive of the Russian Federation).

Holquist, Peter. 2001. 'To Count, to Extract, and to Exterminate: Population Statistics and Population Politics in Late Imperial and Soviet Russia'. In Ronald Grigor Suny and Terry Martin (eds), *A State of Nations: Empire and Nation-Making in the Age of Lenin and Stalin*, pp. 111–44. New York: Oxford University Press.

Iankovskii, Iu.M. 1913. 'Olenovodstvo v Iuzhno-Ussuriiskom krae'. In Ia. Eggenberg and D.I. Zolotov (eds), *Otchet o s"zde sel'skikh khoziaiev Primorskoi oblasti, 11–14 noiabria 1912 goda v g. Nikol'ske-Ussuriiskom*, 292–98. Khabarovsk: Tipografiia Kantseliarii Priamurskago General-Gubernatora.

Iuzhakov, Sergei Nikolaevich. 1903. 'Po Ussuriiskomu kraiu'. In A. Kruber, S. Grigor'ev, A. Barkov and S. Chefranov (eds), *Aziatskaia Rossiia: Illiustrirovannyi geograficheskii sbornik*, 543–46. Moscow: Tipografiia I.N. Kushnerev i ko.

Jacoby, Karl. 2003. *Crimes against Nature: Squatters, Poachers, Thieves, and the Hidden History of American Conservation*. Berkeley and Los Angeles: University of California Press.

James, H.E.M. 1888. *The Long White Mountain, or A Journey in Manchuria*. London and New York: Longmans, Green, and Co.

Jones, Ryan Tucker. 2014. *Empire of Extinction: Russians and the North Pacific's Strange Beasts of the Sea, 1741–1867*. Oxford: Oxford University Press.

Josephson, Paul, Nicolai Dronin, Ruben Mnatsakanian, Aleh Cherp, Dmitry Efremenko and Vladislav Larin. 2013. *An Environmental History of Russia*. New York: Cambridge University Press.

Kabuzan, V. M. 1985. *Dal'nevostochnyi krai v XVII–nachale XX vv.: istoriko-demograficheskii ocherk*. Moscow: Nauka.

Kaplanov, L.G. 1948. *Tigr, olen', iziubr', los'*. Moscow: Izdatel'stvo Moskovskogo obshchestva ispitatelei prirody.

Khisamutdinov, A.A. 1993. *The Russian Far East: Historical Essays*. Honolulu: A.A. Khisamutdinov.

Khudiakov, Sergei Afanas'evich. 1989. 'Avtobiografiia'. University of Hawai'i at Manoa.

Komarov, V.L. 1949. *Izbrannye Sochineniia*. Vol. 3, *Flora man'chzhurii*. Moscow: Izdatel'stvo Akademii nauk SSSR.

Kotsonis, Yanni. 1999. *Making Peasants Backward: Agricultural Cooperatives and the Agrarian Question in Russia, 1861–1914*. New York: St. Martin's Press.

Kriukov, N.A. 1894. *Nekotorye dannye o polozhenii rybolovstva v Priamurskom krae*. St Petersburg: Tipografiia Imperatorskoi akademii nauk.

Lindert, Peter and Boris Mironov. 2006. 'Russia_Ag_content_ruble_1535-1913'. *Global Price and Income History Group*. http://gpih.ucdavis.edu/files/Russia_Ag_content_ruble_1535-1913.xls.

MacKenzie, John M. 1988. *The Empire of Nature: Hunting, Conservation and British Imperialism*. Manchester and New York: Manchester University Press.

Man'ko, Iu.I. 2011. *Lesnoe delo na rossiiskom Dal'nem Vostoke*. Vladivostok: Dal'nauka.

Matsuzato, K., 2012. 'The Creation of the Priamur Governor-Generalship in 1884 and the Reconfiguration of Asiatic Russia'. *Russian Review* 71 (3): 365–390.

Matiushkin, E.N. 1998. *Amurskii tigr v Rossii*. Moscow: World Wildlife Foundation.

Nadarov, Ivan P. 1883. *Ocherk sovremennago sostaianiia Severno-Ussuriiskago kraia: po rezul'tatam puteshestviia general'nago shtaba podpolkov, Nadarova: 1882–83 gg.*

National Mining Association. 2008. 'Historical Gold Prices – 1833 to Present'. http://www.nma.org/pdf/gold/his_gold_prices.pdf.

Obshchestvo liubitelei okhoty. 1897. *Otchety sostoiashchago pod pokrovitel'stvom ego imperatorskago vysochestva velikago kniazia Aleksandra Mikhailovicha Obshchestva liubitelei okhoty, 1888–1896 gg.* Vladivostok: Tipografiia gazety *Dal'nii Vostok*.

Organ Primorskogo gubernskogo ekonomicheskogo soveshchaniia. 1925. *Sovetskoe Primor'e*. No. 5. Vladivostok: OPGES.

Ossendowski, Ferdinand. 1924. *Man and Mystery in Asia*. Edited by Lewis Stanton Palen. New York: E.P. Dutton & Co.

Pikunov, D.G., I.V. Seryodkin, and V.A. Solkin. 2010. *The Amur Tiger: History, Distribution, Population Dynamics, Ecology, and Conservation Strategies*. Vladivostok: Dal'nauka.

Pikunov, Dmitry G. 2014. 'Population and Habitat of the Amur Tiger in the Russian Far East'. *Achievements in the Life Sciences* 8 (2): 145–49.

Pravilova, Ekaterina. 2014. *A Public Empire: Property and the Quest for the Common Good in Imperial Russia*. Princeton: Princeton University Press.

Przheval'skii, N.M. 1947. *Puteshestvie v Ussuriiskom krae, 1867–1869 g.* Moscow: Gosudarstvennoe izdatel'stvo geograficheskoi literatury.

Rossiiskii gosudarstvennyi arkhiv Voenno-Morskogo Flota (RGA VMF, Russian State Naval Archive)

Rossiiskii gosudarstvennyi istoricheskii arkhiv Dal'nego Vostoka (RGIA DV, Russian State Historical Archive of the Far East).

Schimmelpenninck van der Oye, David. 2001. *Toward the Rising Sun: Russian Ideologies of Empire and the Path to War with Japan*. DeKalb, IL.: Northern Illinois University Press.

Mark Sokolsky

Shadrin, B.D. and Primorskaia Kraevaia Publichnaia Biblioteka im. A.M. Gor'kogo (eds). 2004. *Obshchestvo izucheniia Amurskogo kraia, 1884–2004*. Vladivostok: Tipografiia OOO 'Reia'.

Shestakov, A.M. 2010. 'Opisanie s"emki r. Bikina, proizvedennoi sotnikom A. M. Shestakovym'. In A.A. Gorchakov, E.M. Goncharova and N.A. Troitskaia (eds), *Iz istorii zaselenii Pozharskogo raiona: Dokumenty i materialy*. Vladivostok: RGIA DV, pp. 25–43.

Shreider, D.I. 1897. *Nash Dal'nii Vostok. (Tri goda v Ussuriiskom krae)*. St Petersburg: A.F. Devrien.

Shtilmark, Feliks. 2003. *History of the Russian Zapovedniks*. Translated by G.H. Harper. Edinburgh: Russian Nature Press.

Skal'kovskii, K. 1883. *Russkaia torgovlia v Tikhom okeane: Ekonomicheskoe issliedovanie russkoi torgovli i morekhodstva v Primorskoi oblasti Vostochnoi Sibiri, Koreie, Kitaie, Iaponii i Kalifornii*. St Petersburg: Tipografiia A.S. Suvorina.

Smirnov, Evgeny N. and Dale G. Miquelle. 1999. 'Population Dynamics of the Amur Tiger in Sikhote-Alin Zapovednik, Russia'. In *Riding the Tiger: Tiger Conservation in Human-Dominated Landscapes*, pp. 61–70. Cambridge: Cambridge University Press.

Stephan, John J. 1994. *The Russian Far East: A History*. Stanford: Stanford University Press.

Tikhookeanskii okeanologicheskii institut im. V.I. Il'icheva Dal'nevostochnogo otdeleniia Rossiiskoi akademii nauk (TOI DVO RAN, V.I. Il'ichev Pacific Oceanological Institute of the Far Eastern Branch of the Russian Academy of Sciences). 2020. 'Fiziko-geograficheskie kharakteristika / Zaliv Petra Velikogo'. http://portal.esimo. ferhri.ru/portal/portal/poi/main/pacificKISWindow;jsessionid=3AD9BA0383A6 04CE08A66641B9F803F6?action=2&uri=/japan/physi-geo/?4

Vaillant, John. 2010. *The Tiger: A True Story of Vengeance and Survival*. New York: Vintage.

Vashchuk, A.S., E.N. Chernolutskaia, V.A. Koroleva, G.B. Dudchenko, and L.A Gerasimova. 2002. *Etnomigratsionnye protsessi v Primor'e v XX veke*. Vladivostok: DVO RAN.

Weiner, Douglas R. 1988. *Models of Nature: Ecology, Conservation, and Cultural Revolution in Soviet Russia*. Bloomington: Indiana University Press.

Weiner, Douglas R. 1999. *A Little Corner of Freedom: Russian Nature Protection from Stalin to Gorbachev*. Berkeley: University of California Press.

Worster, Donald. 1977. *Nature's Economy: The Roots of Ecology*. San Francisco: Sierra Club Books.

Wright, Carroll Davidson. 1910. *The New Century Book of Facts: A Handbook of Ready Reference*. Springfield, MA: King-Richardson Company.

GLOSSARY

altyn – Imperial Russian monetary unit equal to 0.06 roubles

arshin – Measurement of length equal to 0.71 metres

artel' – A cooperative group of peasants, craftsmen, or workers; a work cooperative

ataman – Cossack leader

de-kulakisation – Refers to the campaign of political repression against *kulaks* (see below) during Stalin-era collectivisation of agriculture, primarily between 1929 and 1932

desiatina – A measurement of area equal to 1.09 hectares

iasak – Tribute or tax in kind, typically paid by Siberian indigenous peoples to Russian authorities in the form of furs.

inorodets (plural: *inorodtsy*) – Term for non-Russian ethnicities in the Russian Empire, and the official categorization of Siberian indigenous peoples after the reforms of M. Speranskii (1822)

kontor – Self-government office in the Buriat lands of the Russian Empire

krai – Administrative division or territory; can also refer to an 'edge' or a borderland region

kulak – Literally 'fist', refers to a rich peasant; in the Soviet Union, often applied to any rural dwellers designated as anti-Soviet

obkom – Oblast'-level Communist Party committee

oblast' – Province

obrok – Quitrent; rent paid in cash or kind by peasants in pre-revolutionary Russia.

raion – District (esp. in the Soviet Union and post-Soviet Russia)

sazhen' - Unit of linear measurement equal to about 2.1 metres

ulus – A term from the Mongol and Turkic languages that can refer to settlements, states, nations, or empires. In this volume, it refers to Buriat villages.

versta – Unit of length equal to 1.06 kilometres

volost' - District (or canton); the smallest administrative unit in the tsarist empire

zakaznik – A protected natural area, sometimes established on a temporary basis, in which some economic activity (such as hunting) may be permitted

zapovednik – Inviolable state nature reserves earmarked primarily for scientific study and conservation

INDEX

Index

Index

Lightning Source UK Ltd.
Milton Keynes UK
UKHW021149140221
378694UK00001B/6